# REAL WORLD

# MACRO

## THIRTY-THIRD EDITION

EDITED BY ALEJANDRO REUSS, LUIS ROSERO, BRYAN SNYDER, CHRIS STURR,

AND THE *DOLLARS & SENSE* COLLECTIVE

# REAL WORLD MACRO, THIRTY-THIRD EDITION

Published by:
Economic Affairs Bureau, Inc. d/b/a *Dollars & Sense*
89 South Street, Suite LL02, Boston, MA 02111
617-447-2177; dollars@dollarsandsense.org.
For order information, contact Economic Affairs Bureau or visit: www.dollarsandsense.org.

*Real World Macro* is edited by the *Dollars & Sense* Collective, which also publishes *Dollars & Sense* magazine and the classroom books *Microeconomics: Individual Choice in Communities*, *Real World Micro*, *Current Economic Issues*, *Real World Globalization*, *The Economic Crisis Reader*, *America Beyond Capitalism*, *Labor and the Global Economy*, *Real World Latin America*, *Real World Labor*, *Real World Banking and Finance*, *The Wealth Inequality Reader*, *The Economics of the Environment*, *Introduction to Political Economy*, *Unlevel Playing Fields: Understanding Wage Inequality and Discrimination*, *Striking a Balance: Work, Family, Life*, and *Grassroots Journalism*.

The 2016 *Dollars & Sense* Collective:
Betsy Aron, Nancy Banks, Nina Eichacker, Peter Kolozi, John Miller, Jawied Nawabi, Kevin O'Connell, Alejandro Reuss, Dan Schneider, Zoe Sherman, Bryan Snyder, Chris Sturr, De'En Tarkpor, William Whitham, Jeanne Winner

Co-editors of this volume: Alejandro Reuss, Luis Rosero, Bryan Snyder, and Chris Sturr
Editorial assistant: Sarah Cannon

Design and layout: Alejandro Reuss
Cover photo: Alexandre Vialle, "Rouages," Musée des Arts et Métiers, 24 July 2010, Creative Commons Attribution 2.0 Generic license.

Printed in U.S.A.

# CONTENTS

## CHAPTER 5 • WEALTH, INEQUALITY, AND POVERTY

## CHAPTER 6 • FISCAL POLICY, DEFICITS, AND AUSTERITY

## CHAPTER 7 • MONEY AND MONETARY POLICY

## CHAPTER 8 • SAVINGS, INVESTMENT, AND FINANCE

# THE TWO ECONOMIES

**I**t sometimes seems that the United States has not one, but two economies. The first exists in economics textbooks and in the minds of many government policy-makers. It is an economy in which no one is unemployed for long, families are rewarded with an ever-improving standard of living, and anyone who works hard can live the American Dream. In this economy, people are free and roughly equal, and each individual carefully looks after him- or herself, making voluntary choices to advance his or her own economic interests. Government has some limited roles in this world, but it is increasingly marginal, since the macroeconomy is a self-regulating system of wealth generation.

The second features vast disparities of income, wealth, and power. It is an economy where economic instability and downward mobility are facts of life. Jobs disappear, workers suffer long spells of unemployment, and new jobs seldom afford the same standard of living as those lost. And, periodically, market economies unravel, much like today. As for the government, it sometimes adopts policies that ameliorate the abuses of capitalism, and other times does just the opposite, but it is always an active and essential participant in economic life.

If you are reading this introduction, you are probably a student in an introductory college course in macroeconomics. Your textbook will introduce you to the first economy, the harmonious world of self-regulating stability. *Real World Macro* will introduce you to the second.

## Why "Real World" Macro?

A standard economics textbook is full of powerful concepts. It is also, by its nature, a limited window on the economy. What is taught in most introductory macroeconomics courses today is a relatively narrow set of concepts. Inspired by classical economic theory, most textbooks depict an inherently stable economy in little need of government intervention. Fifty years ago, textbooks were very different. Keynesian economic theory, which holds that government action can and must stabilize modern monetized economies, occupied a central place in introductory textbooks. Even Marxist economics, with its piercing analysis of class structure and instability in capitalism, appeared regularly on the pages of those textbooks. The contraction of economics education has turned some introductory courses into little more than celebrations of today's economy as "the best of all possible worlds."

1

*Real World Macro*, designed as a supplement to standard macroeconomics textbooks, is dedicated to widening the scope of economic inquiry. Its articles confront mainstream theory with a more complex reality—providing vivid, real-world illustrations of economic concepts. And where most texts uncritically present the key assumptions and propositions of traditional macroeconomic theory, *Real World Macro* asks provocative questions: What are alternative propositions about how the economy operates and who it serves? What difference do such propositions make? If this is not the best of all possible macroeconomic worlds, what might make the actual world better?

For instance, *Real World Macro*'s authors question the conventional wisdom that economic growth "lifts all boats," or benefits all of us. While mainstream textbooks readily allow that economic growth has not benefited us all to the same degree, we go further and ask: Who benefits from economic growth and how much? Who has been left behind by the economic growth of the last few decades? The answers are quite disturbing. Today, economic growth, when it occurs, benefits far fewer of us than it did just a few decades ago. Economic growth during the last business-cycle expansion did more to boost profits and less to lift wages than during any economic upswing since World War II. This pattern has continued during the current slow recovery following the Great Recession. Spreading the benefits of economic growth more widely, through public policies intended to improve the lot of most people in the work-a-day world, would not only make our economy more equitable, but would also start to resolve today's economic crisis.

Today's economy is emerging from what is widely recognized to be the worst crisis since the Great Depression. But you might not know that the day-to-day operation of the market economy—unregulated financial markets, the increasing concentration of power in the hands of business, and burgeoning inequality—caused the accumulation of debt that set the stage for the crisis. Explaining how and why that happened and what to do about it is every responsible economist's job.

Today, employment growth remains stubbornly sluggish and the decline in the unemployment rate has been driven not just by people moving from unemployment into jobs, but in large measure by people dropping out of the labor force altogether. That supports the argument that government needs to step in to ensure full employment. Similarly, with the financial system having been shaken to the core, the government needs to properly regulate financial markets and institutions. Those two steps would go a long way toward improving the lot of those who have fallen on hard times and would reduce the likelihood of future crises. Finally, genuine and sustained full employment, with unemployment rates as low as 2%, would lead to "a major reduction in the incidence of poverty, homelessness, sickness, and crime," as William Vickery, the Nobel Prize-winning economist, once argued. We think that policies like these, and the alternative perspectives that lie behind them, are worth debating—and that requires hearing a range of views.

## What's in This Book

*Real World Macro* is organized to follow the outline of a standard economics text. Each chapter leads off with a brief introduction, including study questions for the chapter, and then provides several articles, mostly drawn from *Dollars & Sense* magazine, that illustrate the chapter's key concepts. Here is a quick walk through the contents.

**Chapter 1, Perspectives on Macroeconomic Theory**, introduces alternatives to classical-inspired macroeconomic theory. The chapter explains in everyday language the roots of the economic crisis—the extreme inequality, elite power, and unregulated financial markets of today's economy. It looks at what's wrong with neoliberal policies that would turn the operation of the domestic and international economy over to unregulated markets. Finally, the chapter moves beyond Keynesianism, to develop Marxist and environmentalist perspectives on the macroeconomy.

**Chapter 2, Macroeconomic Measurement**, takes a critical look at the standard measures of economic activity, such as GDP, the unemployment rate, and the Consumer Price Index. What do those measures actually tell us about the quality of life in today's economy, and what crucial aspects of economic life do they leave uncounted? This chapter underscores that economic measurement issues are not just dry, technical questions for economists to answer—they play a critical role in defining the economic problems that face us and the economic goals we aspire to reach.

**Chapter 3, Economic Growth and Business Cycles**, covers two of the most important issues in macroeconomics: the causes of cyclical fluctuations in economic activity—the boom-and-bust patterns of capitalist economies—and the factors determining long-term economic growth and development. This chapter includes articles analyzing the causes of the global "Great Recession," the stagnation that has set in since then, and the experiences of particular countries. It also addresses the challenges facing the developing world, such as transitioning away from dependence on resource extraction and commodities booms, developing domestic demand-driven approaches to growth and development, and avoiding debt traps.

**Chapter 4, Unemployment and Inflation**, looks at the relationships between these two macroeconomic variables and addresses the causes of unemployment today. It begins with a discussion of the "natural rate of unemployment," offering an alternative interpretation very different from that intended by its originators. It considers alternate views of the causes of mass unemployment during the Great Recession and the weak recovery of the present day. It examines the impacts of unemployment on different groups in society. And it looks at the precipice on which many economies have teetered in recent years: the danger of deflation.

**Chapter 5, Wealth, Inequality, and Poverty**, examines these three outcomes of economic activity and growth. *Dollars & Sense* authors show who is accumulating wealth and who isn't, both in the United States and worldwide. They examine the reasons for increasing inequality in the United States over the last several decades and argue that inequality is not a prerequisite for economic growth, but rather a major contributor to today's economic problems.

**Chapter 6, Fiscal Policy, Deficits, and Austerity**, assesses government spending and tax policy. The chapter's authors examine the arguments made against fiscal stimulus in the face of the Great Recession and argue that the government could and should have done more. Current deficit and debt levels, they argue, do not constitute a crisis and should not be an impediment to government action. They look at current tax policy, explaining the realities of taxes on both rich and poor and their relation to investment and growth. The chapter concludes with a look at the current economic crisis in Greece and the impact of austerity policies.

**Chapter 7, Money and Monetary Policy**, looks at how money is created and how the Federal Reserve (aka "the Fed") conducts monetary policy. It details the Fed's efforts to bail out financial institutions brought down in the crisis and explains how those institutions have become yet larger and more powerful. And it examines Fed attempts at stimulating lending during the crisis and why these have had limited effect.

**Chapter 8, Savings, Investment, and Finance**, peers inside the world of finance and comes up with some probing questions. What factors affect the pace of investment? What role did financial deregulation and exotic new financial instruments play in the economic crisis? And what alternative public policies can promote stable investment and functional financial markets?

**Chapter 9, The Global Economy**, assesses the prevailing neoliberal policy prescriptions for the global economy. The articles criticize globalization based on "free trade" and financial liberalization, looking closely at its effects on economic growth and development, as well as inequality, poverty, and labor conditions. They consider the changing place of the United States in the global economy, the role of the dollar, the promotion of new "trade and investment" agreements, and the impacts on U.S. businesses and households. The chapter also includes a discussion of alternative institutions for dealing with international financial imbalances.

**Chapter 10, Resistance and Alternatives**, returns to many of the issues covered in the course of the previous nine chapters, but with a special focus on challenges to prevailing economic policies and institutions. Among the issues addressed are employment, the environment, health care, financial regulation, international investment, labor conditions, and economic development. ❑

# Chapter 1

# PERSPECTIVES ON MACROECONOMIC THEORY

## INTRODUCTION

Years ago, political economist Bob Sutcliffe developed a sure-fire economic indi-cator that he called the Marx/Keynes ratio—the ratio of references to Karl Marx to references to John Maynard Keynes in Paul Samuelson's *Economics*, the best-selling introductory economics textbook in the decades following World War II. During a recession or period of sluggish economic growth, the Marx/Keynes ratio would climb, as social commentators and even economists fretted over the future of capitalism. During economic booms, however, Marx's predictions of the collapse of capitalism disappeared from the pages of Samuelson's textbook, while the paeans to Keynesian demand-management policies multiplied.

Today, Sutcliffe's ratio wouldn't work very well. Marx has been pushed off the pages of most introductory macroeconomics textbooks altogether, and even Keynes has been left with only a minor role. Our authors disagree. In this chapter, they criti-cally assess the classical-inspired mainstream models and reintroduce the dissident schools of thought that have been purged from economics textbooks in recent de-cades. And they offer a serious look at the forces that brought on the economic crisis and what to do about them.

David M. Kotz examines the current crisis of capitalism in "A Great Fall: The Ori-gins and Crisis of Neoliberalism" (Article 1.1). He traces today's problems to the "neo-liberal capitalism"—"free market" or "liberalized" capitalism—forged a generation ago. Kotz explains the origins of neoliberal capitalism in the 1970s crisis of post-World War II "regulated capitalism." Neoliberal capitalism, he argues, restored capitalist profitability, but its main effects—stagnant wages, rising income inequality, increasing "financializa-tion" of the economy, and repeated asset bubbles in stocks and real estate—set the stage for the current crisis.

Next, economist Robert Pollin (Article 1.2) tackles the underpinnings of neoliberal policy prescriptions for the global economy. As he sees it, unfettered globalization will be unable to resolve three basic problems: an ever-larger "reserve army of the unemployed" that reduces the bargaining power of workers in all countries (the "Marx problem"); the inherent instability and volatility of investment and financial markets (the "Keynes problem"); and the erosion of the protections of the welfare state (the "Polanyi problem").

Economist Alejandro Reuss contributes a primer on Marxist economics (Article 1.3). Marx rejected the idea of a self-equilibrating economy, and argued that capitalism was inherently dynamic and unstable. Reuss describes some of Marx's key ideas, including the nature of capitalist exploitation, and what Marx saw as two ingredients of an eventual crisis of capitalism: overproduction and the falling rate of profit.

In "Sharing the Wealth of the Commons" (Article 1.4), Peter Barnes focuses our attention on the oft-ignored forms of wealth that we do not own privately, but are held in "commons." He challenges the way that conventional economists view the environment and other goods that are shared by many people.

Finally, environmentalist Jonathan Rowe offers a green perspective on the economy. He is critical of economists' worship of economic growth, and their use of measures (like GDP) that count environmental destruction, worsening health, and ruinous over-consumption as contributions to economic growth. These, he argues, have misled economists, policymakers, and the public about the goals we should be pursuing (Article 1.5).

## Discussion Questions

1. (Article 1.1) Kotz argues that both "regulated" capitalism and "neoliberal" capitalism had inherent tendencies that made them go into crisis. Can we imagine a way of structuring capitalism that would not be crisis-prone?

2. (Article 1.2) Summarize the Marx, Keynes, and Polanyi problems. Why does Pollin think that neoliberal globalization policies will be unable to resolve them?

3. (Article 1.3) What roles do a "falling rate of profit," a "reserve army of the un-employed," and "overproduction" play in Marx's theory of capitalist crisis? Do you think today's macroeconomy displays any of those tendencies?

4. (Article 1.4) What is a "commons"? According to Barnes, how has our common wealth been "given away"? What do you think of his plans on how to take it back?

5. (Article 1.5) Why does Rowe argue that more economic growth and rising GDP are not necessarily desirable? How would he change the ground rules of the economy to produce more genuine economic growth?

*Article 1.1*

# A GREAT FALL
*The Origins and Crisis of Neoliberalism*

## BY DAVID M. KOTZ
*November/December 2015*

In the fall of 2008, a massive financial and economic crisis struck the United States and much of the world. The biggest American banks were suddenly insolvent and survived only thanks to government bailouts. A deep recession spread around the globe. The unemployment rate in the United States jumped up to 10%. Over the following five years, more than four million U.S. homeowners were tossed out of their homes due to foreclosure, as home values plummeted below the mortgage debt owed and unemployment cut household incomes. The economies of the United States, Europe, and much of the rest of the world have been stuck in stagnation or worse since 2008.

This condition is not something new in the history of capitalism. Capitalist economic systems—in which a small percentage of the population owns the enterprises, hires wage workers, and sells the products aiming for a profit—have brought economic growth but also periodic severe economic crises. To understand these recurring crises, we need to take account of the quite different forms of capitalism over time. While always having the key features noted above, capitalism has nevertheless not looked the same at all times. For several decades following World War II, the United States had a "regulated capitalism" in which government, trade unions, and other non-market institutions played major roles in regulating the economy. Since 1980, we have lived under "neoliberal capitalism," in which the government retreated from regulation of business and markets, and trade unions were marginalized. In the past, each form of capitalism has worked well on its own terms—fostering investment and economic growth—for a few decades, after which snowballing problems gave rise to severe economic crises such as today's.

The crisis of neoliberal capitalism has made it vulnerable to replacement by something else. Every past economic crisis of this severity has been followed by major changes in economic and political institutions. Earlier so-called "free-market" forms of capitalism have produced economic crises before in U.S. history—in the 1890s and the end of the 1920s. In each case, the crisis was followed by the construction of some kind of regulated capitalism, in response to the forces that had brought on the crisis. After 1900, Progressive Era reforms together with the rise of powerful Wall Street banks led to a corporate-dominated form of regulated capitalism. This lasted until the end of World War I, when another shift brought a decade of relatively unhindered pursuit of profit—the Roaring Twenties—that culminated in the 1929 crash. Eventually, a more thoroughly regulated capitalism, this time based on capital-labor compromise, emerged in the late 1940s. While history does not always repeat itself, there is good reason to expect that, if U.S. capitalism is to surmount the stagnation that has followed the crash of 2008, it will do so through another version of regulated capitalism, which can potentially address the problems that led to the current crisis.

## FIGURE 1: RATE OF PROFIT OF U.S. NONFINANCIAL CORPORATE BUSINESS SECTOR, 1948-2007

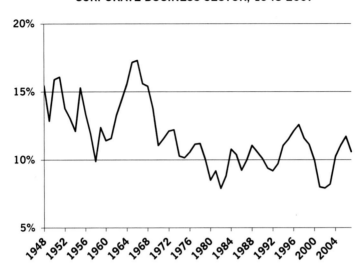

*Source:* U.S. Bureau of Economic Analysis (2013), NIPA Table 1.14, Fixed Assets Table 4.1.

Several big questions cry out for answers. Why did the last sea change, from regulated to neoliberal capitalism, take place—not just in the United States but in much of the world—around 1980? Why did a radically different form of capitalism emerge after decades of active state regulation and strong trade unions? Why did the post-1980 "neoliberal capitalism" eventually produce such a big economic crisis after 25 years of seemingly stable, if lackluster and unequally distributed, economic growth? And most immediately, what kind(s) of economic change are possible and likely today? The relative strength and determination of key economic classes has decided the direction of economic change in past crisis periods, and the current one is not likely to be an exception.

## Big Business and the Origins of Regulated Capitalism

The post-World War II "regulated capitalism" emerged in the United States in the late 1940s, following a decade of labor militancy, the formation of strong industrial unions, and militant strikes and factory occupations in the 1930s. After the wartime no-strike pledge ended in 1945, labor militancy resumed. At that point, a decisive section of big business concluded that its long-standing effort to crush unions had failed and decided to strike a deal with the labor movement.

A threatening world pushed big business in that direction. Labor, Social Democratic, Socialist, and Communist parties were in power or contending for power in the UK, France, Italy, and Japan. Even in the United States there was a relatively strong Communist party. A suddenly enlarged and empowered bloc of states—encompassing some 35% of the world's population—was ruled by Communist parties. Despite the unsavory features of those regimes, which limited their appeal to workers in the West, big business feared that they lent credence to the possibility of a viable alternative to capitalism.

Not least, big business leaders (like many others) feared that, with the end of the huge public spending of World War II, the Great Depression would return. The Committee for Economic Development (CED), the leading big-business policy organization of that period, warned that another big depression might give rise to a "growing receptivity to futile or dangerous ideas that appear to promise relief from all ills"—that is, they feared a growing receptivity to socialism.

CED policy statements endorsed collective bargaining with unions, expansion of Social Security, and a Keynesian program of government spending and tax cuts to fend off another depression and keep the unemployment rate relatively low. Big business formed an informal coalition with organized labor that completed the construction of regulated capitalism, which had begun with the New Deal reforms of the 1930s.

Some analysts refer to a "capital-labor accord" after World War II, but that term suggests a more cordial relationship than the uneasy compromise actually hammered out. Big business leaders held their noses as they agreed to arrangements that legitimized unions and reduced management power in certain ways (employers accepted collective bargaining over wages, benefits, and conditions, contract grievance procedures, and so on). In return, unions accepted "management rights" clauses in collective bargaining agreements—leaving decisions over the production process, technology, product design, pricing, etc. as the employers' exclusive domain—and accepted responsibility to crack down against worker job actions like slowdowns or wildcat strikes outside of contract-negotiation periods. While this deal did deliver labor relations that were more stable in some ways, it did not eliminate class conflict at the workplace, as major strikes still occurred frequently during the 1950s and 1960s. The capital-labor accord, along with the other features of regulated capitalism, delivered relatively robust economic growth, with rising profits for business alongside increasing wages for workers—what some observers came to call the "Golden Age of Capitalism."

## FIGURE 2: AVERAGE ANNUAL UNEMPLOYMENT RATE

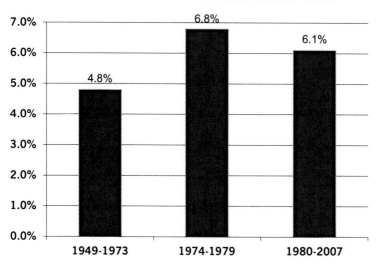

*Source:* U.S. Bureau of Labor Statistics (2013).

## The Crisis of the Postwar System and the Big Business Response

No form of capitalism, however, works smoothly forever. In the late 1960s, the average rate of profit began to fall in the United States, the UK, and France. In the United States, it declined by more than half from 1966 to 1982 (see Figure 1), a development that big business spokespeople blamed on excessive wage gains. The aim of business is profit, and when profit falls for an extended period of time this tends to destabilize the economy. In the 1970s, the economy became increasingly unstable, with rising inflation and unemployment. The Bretton Woods international monetary system dating back to 1944—with fixed currency exchange rates based on the U.S. dollar—tottered and then collapsed in 1973.

For a decade, big business sought to solve its growing problems within the system of regulated capitalism. However, modest reform efforts failed to resolve the crisis, and by the late 1970s it had changed its position. The main big-business lobbying group of that period, the Business Roundtable, began to blame a strong labor movement for the decline in profits. Big business was also agitated by the victories, in alliance with organized labor, of the environmental, occupational-health, and consumer-product-safety movements, and the resulting expansion of government regulation of industry in the 1970s. Groups like the Business Roundtable grabbed onto neoliberal ideas and policies as the way to resolve the problems facing big business.

As big business deserted its previous coalition with organized labor, and allied with small business organizations that had never supported regulated capitalism, it was able to rapidly sweep away the institutions and dominant ideas of regulated capitalism. While organized labor was relatively strong at that time, it could not

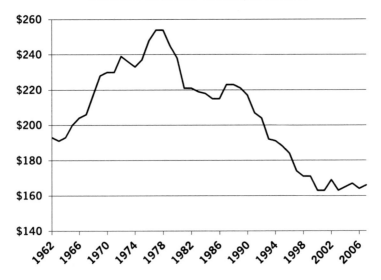

FIGURE 3: MONTHLY BENEFIT PER RECIPIENT UNDER AID TO FAMILIES WITH DEPENDENT CHILDREN OR TEMPORARY ASSISTANCE FOR NEEDY FAMILIES IN 2009 DOLLARS, 1962-2007

*Source:* U.S. Department of Health and Human Services (2013).

**FIGURE 4: AVERAGE HOURLY EARNINGS OF NON-SUPERVISORY WORKERS IN 2011 DOLLARS, 1948-2007**

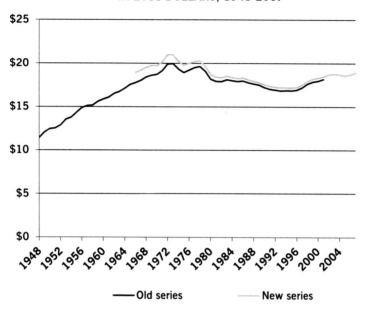

*Source:* Economic Report of the President (1990, 2003, 2010).

*Note:* The Bureau of Labor Statistics revised the methodology for the series for average hourly earnings in 2004, adn so there is no single series available from 1948 to 2007.

stop a determined push by a united business class to carry out economic restructuring at the expense of labor and the majority of the population. By the early 1980s, a new form of capitalism had emerged—the neoliberal capitalism that we still live under to the present day.

The end of regulated capitalism and the rise of neoliberalism brought with it a new orthodoxy in economics. Gone were the days when professors at America's leading universities taught that capitalist economies required close regulation by the government to avoid big depressions and high unemployment, and that trade unions played a positive role in reducing inequality. In its place arose a new worship of "free markets," rejecting any role for government or trade unions in improving economic outcomes.

Starting in the early 1980s the declining profit rate reversed and trended upward thereafter:

The neoliberal mantra of privatization, liberalization, and deregulation, as put into practice, served to crush organized labor and put employers in control. Liberalizing foreign trade and removing barriers to capital flight put American workers in more direct competition with low-wage labor in poor countries. Stopping Keynesian policies aimed at a low unemployment rate gave rise to a higher unemployment rate after 1980 than from the late 1940s to early 1970s:

This weakened labor's bargaining power. Privatizing and cutting back social welfare programs, too, weakened workers' fallback position in bargaining with employers:

Lax enforcement of labor law facilitated the corporate agenda of driving out unions and extracting huge wage concessions. Deregulation of basic industries resulted in cutthroat competition replacing the stable environment of government regulation—and relatively high-wage jobs won by unions gave way to rapidly declining pay and worsening working conditions.

Big business could not have effectively argued that wages must fall so that profits could rise, that welfare recipients were too rich while CEOs were too poor, that the unemployment rate should be driven up so that wages could be driven down, or that American workers should be forced into a "race to the bottom" with the poorest workers in the world. However, neoliberal restructuring of American and global capitalism achieved all those aims by promising great economic benefits for all citizens once the magic of the "free market" was unleashed.

## Economic Foundations of Neoliberal Capitalism

For some 25 years, neoliberal capitalism in the United States produced long, if tepid, economic expansions with low inflation. Former Federal Reserve Chairman Ben Bernanke coined the term "The Great Moderation" to describe what neoliberal economists believed was a newly stabilized capitalism, a result of lifting the heavy hand of government from the back of big business, and the "grasping" hand of unions from its pockets. While the rich got richer at an astonishing and accelerating rate, the majority did not fare well. As long as neoliberal capitalism was delivering

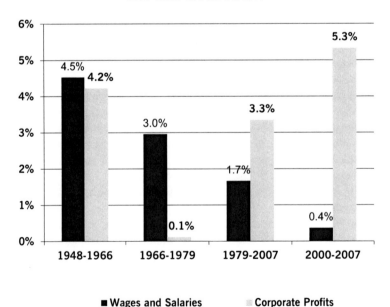

**FIGURE 5: ANNUAL GROWTH RATES OF WAGES AND SALARIES AND CORPORATE PROFIT**

■ Wages and Salaries    Corporate Profits

*Source:* U.S. Bureau of Economic Analysis (2013), NIPA Table 1.14, 1.1.4; U.S. Bureau of Labor Statistics (2013).

**FIGURE 6: PROFITS OF FINANCIAL CORPORATIONS AS A PERCENTAGE OF THE PROFITS OF ALL CORPORATIONS IN THE U.S., 1948-2012**

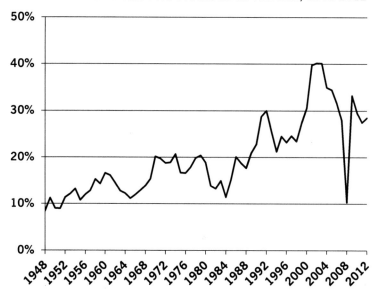

*Source:* U.S. Bureau of Economic Analysis (2013), NIPA Table 1.14.

rising profits and growing riches for those at the top, however, it was difficult for critics to make much headway against it.

Beneath the surface, though, long-run trends guaranteed an unhappy ending down the road. Neoliberal capitalism brought three key developments that led to the crash of 2008.

The first was rapidly growing inequality. As neoliberal restructuring undermined labor's bargaining power, real wages stagnated:

This allowed profits to recover from their long decline. The big gap emerging, after 1979, between profit growth and wage and salary growth jumped sharply upward after 2000:

The second key development was the transformation of financial institutions and their role in the economy. Bank deregulation began in 1980-1982, and soon financial institutions began to create a raft of so-called "financial innovations"—new types of financial assets such as subprime mortgage-backed securities, collateralized debt obligations, and credit default swaps. The high profitability of such maneuvers pushed the profits of the financial sector from about 20% of all corporate profit to a remarkable 40% in the early 2000s:

The term "financialization" arose to describe the expanding and changing role of the financial sector in contemporary capitalism.

The third development was a series of large asset bubbles—that is, the continuing rise in the prices of assets like real estate or corporate stocks, driven by speculative expectations of further price increases. The 1980s saw a bubble in southwestern commercial real estate, whose collapse sank a large part of the savings-and-loan industry. In the second half of the 1990s, a giant stock market bubble arose. And in the 2000s, a still larger bubble engulfed the U.S. real estate market. The preceding period of regulated capitalism had no large asset bubbles. The rapidly rising flow of income into corporate profit and rich households exceeded the available productive investment opportunities, and some of that flow found its way into investment in assets. The eagerness of the deregulated financial institutions to lend for speculative purposes enabled incipient asset bubbles to grow larger and larger.

## Neoliberal Capitalism and the Crisis of 2008

Growing inequality, the speculative financial sector, and the series of large asset bubbles all contributed to the long economic expansions in the U.S. economy during the neoliberal era—1982–1990, 1991–2000, and 2001–2007.

These trends, however, were unsustainable in the long run. From 1980 to 2007, household debt doubled relative to household income. Financial institutions, finding limitless profit opportunities in the wild financial markets of the period, borrowed heavily to pursue those opportunities. As a result, financial-sector debt increased from 21% of GDP in 1980 to 117% of GDP in 2007. At the same time, financial institutions' holdings of the new high-risk securities grew rapidly. In addition, unused resources in the industrial sector gradually crept upward over the period from 1979 to 2007, as consumer demand increasingly lagged behind the total productive capacity of the economy.

As long as a big asset bubble continued to inflate, people remained willing to borrow more and more, and financial institutions remained willing to lend to them. But every asset bubble eventually must burst. When the biggest one—the real estate bubble—started to deflate in 2007, the crash followed. As households lost the ability to borrow against their no-longer-inflating home values, consumer spending dropped at the beginning 2008, driving the economy into recession. Falling consumer demand meant more excess productive capacity, leading business to reduce its investment in plant and equipment. The deflating housing bubble also worsened investor expectations, further depressing investment. Finally, in the fall of 2008, the plummeting market values of the new-fangled financial securities, which had been dependent on real-estate prices, suddenly drove the highly indebted major commercial banks and investment banks into insolvency, bringing a financial meltdown.

Thus, the big financial and broader economic crisis that began in 2008 is explained by the way neoliberal capitalism worked. The very same mechanisms that brought 25 years of long expansions under neoliberal capitalism were bound to eventually give rise to this sort of "big bang" crisis. ❑

*Article 1.2*

# WHAT'S WRONG WITH NEOLIBERALISM?
*The Marx, Keynes, and Polanyi Problems*

**BY ROBERT POLLIN**
*May/June 2004*

During the years of the Clinton administration, the term "Washington Consensus" began circulating to designate the common policy positions of the U.S. administration along with the International Monetary Fund (IMF) and World Bank. These positions, implemented in the United States and abroad, included free trade, a smaller government share of the economy, and the deregulation of financial markets. This policy approach has also become widely known as *neoliberalism*, a term which draws upon the classical meaning of the word *liberalism*.

Classical liberalism is the political philosophy that embraces the virtues of free-market capitalism and the corresponding minimal role for government interventions, especially as regards measures to promote economic equality within capitalist societies. Thus, a classical liberal would favor minimal levels of government spending and taxation, and minimal levels of government regulation over the economy, including financial and labor markets. According to the classical liberal view, businesses should be free to operate as they wish, and to succeed or fail as such in a competitive marketplace. Meanwhile, consumers rather than government should be responsible for deciding which businesses produce goods and services that are of sufficient quality as well as reasonably priced. Businesses that provide overexpensive or low-quality products will then be out-competed in the marketplace regardless of the regulatory standards established by governments. Similarly, if businesses offer workers a wage below what the worker is worth, then a competitor firm will offer this worker a higher wage. The firm unwilling to offer fair wages would not survive over time in the competitive marketplace.

This same reasoning also carries over to the international level. Classical liberals favor free trade between countries rather than countries operating with tariffs or other barriers to the free flow of goods and services between countries. They argue that restrictions on the free movement of products and money between countries only protects uncompetitive firms from market competition, and thus holds back the economic development of countries that choose to erect such barriers.

Neoliberalism and the Washington Consensus are contemporary variants of this longstanding political and economic philosophy. The major difference between classical liberalism as a philosophy and contemporary neoliberalism as a set of policy measures is with implementation. Washington Consensus policy makers are committed to free-market policies when they support the interests of big business, as, for example, with lowering regulations at the workplace. But these same policy makers become far less insistent on free-market principles when invoking such principles might damage big business interests. Federal Reserve and IMF interventions to bail out wealthy asset holders during the frequent global financial crises in the 1990s are obvious violations of free-market precepts.

Broadly speaking, the effects of neoliberalism in the less developed countries over the 1990s reflected the experience of the Clinton years in the United States. A high proportion of less developed countries were successful, just in the manner of the United States under Clinton, in reducing inflation and government budget deficits, and creating a more welcoming climate for foreign trade, multinational corporations, and financial market investors. At the same time, most of Latin America, Africa, and Asia—with China being the one major exception—experienced deepening problems of poverty and inequality in the 1990s, along with slower growth and frequent financial market crises, which in turn produced still more poverty and inequality.

If free-market capitalism is a powerful mechanism for creating wealth, why does a neoliberal policy approach, whether pursued by Clinton, Bush, or the IMF, produce severe difficulties in terms of inequality and financial instability, which in turn diminish the market mechanism's ability to even promote economic growth? It will be helpful to consider this in terms of three fundamental problems that result from a free-market system, which I term "the Marx Problem," "the Keynes problem," and "the Polanyi problem." Let us take these up in turn.

## The Marx Problem

Does someone in your family have a job and, if so, how much does it pay? For the majority of the world's population, how one answers these two questions determines, more than anything else, what one's standard of living will be. But how is it decided whether a person has a job and what their pay will be? Getting down to the most immediate level of decision-making, this occurs through various types of bargaining in labor markets between workers and employers. Karl Marx argued that, in a free-market economy generally, workers have less power than employers in this bargaining process because workers cannot fall back on other means of staying alive if they fail to get hired into a job. Capitalists gain higher profits through having this relatively stronger bargaining position. But Marx also stressed that workers' bargaining power diminishes further when unemployment and underemployment are high, since that means that employed workers can be more readily replaced by what Marx called "the reserve army" of the unemployed outside the office, mine, or factory gates.

Neoliberalism has brought increasing integration of the world's labor markets through reducing barriers to international trade and investment by multinationals. For workers in high-wage countries such as the United States, this effectively means that the reserve army of workers willing to accept jobs at lower pay than U.S. workers expands to include workers in less developed countries. It isn't the case that businesses will always move to less developed countries or that domestically produced goods will necessarily be supplanted by imports from low-wage countries. The point is that U.S. workers face an increased *credible* threat that they can be supplanted. If everything else were to remain the same in the U.S. labor market, this would then mean that global integration would erode the bargaining power of U.S. workers and thus tend to bring lower wages.

But even if this is true for workers in the United States and other rich countries, shouldn't it also mean that workers in poor countries have greater job opportunities and better bargaining positions? In fact, there are areas where workers in poor countries are gaining enhanced job opportunities through international trade and multinational investments. But these gains are generally quite limited. This is because a long-term transition out of agriculture in poor countries continues to expand the reserve army of unemployed and underemployed workers in these countries as well. Moreover, when neoliberal governments in poor countries reduce their support for agriculture—through cuts in both tariffs on imported food products and subsidies for domestic farmers—this makes it more difficult for poor farmers to compete with multinational agribusiness firms. This is especially so when the rich countries maintain or increase their own agricultural supports, as has been done in the United States under Bush. In addition, much of the growth in the recently developed export-oriented manufacturing sectors of poor countries has failed to significantly increase jobs even in this sector. This is because the new export-oriented production sites frequently do not represent net additions to the country's total supply of manufacturing firms. They rather replace older firms that were focused on supplying goods to domestic markets. The net result is that the number of people looking for jobs in the developing countries grows faster than the employers seeking new workers. Here again, workers' bargaining power diminishes.

This does not mean that global integration of labor markets must necessarily bring weakened bargaining power and lower wages for workers. But it does mean that unless some non-market forces in the economy, such as government regulations or effective labor unions, are able to counteract these market processes, workers will indeed continue to experience weakened bargaining strength and eroding living standards.

## The Keynes Problem

In a free-market economy, investment spending by businesses is the main driving force that produces economic growth, innovation, and jobs. But as John Maynard Keynes stressed, private investment decisions are also unavoidably risky ventures. Businesses have to put up money without knowing whether they will produce any profits in the future. As such, investment spending by business is likely to fluctuate far more than, say, decisions by households as to how much they will spend per week on groceries.

But investment fluctuations will also affect overall spending in the economy, including that of households. When investment spending declines, this means that businesses will hire fewer workers. Unemployment rises as a result, and this in turn will lead to cuts in household spending. Declines in business investment spending can therefore set off a vicious cycle: the investment decline leads to employment declines, then to cuts in household spending and corresponding increases in household financial problems, which then brings still more cuts in business investment and financial difficulties for the business sector. This is how capitalist economies produce mass unemployment, financial crises, and recessions.

Keynes also described a second major source of instability associated with private investment activity. Precisely because private investments are highly risky propositions, financial markets have evolved to make this risk more manageable for any given investor. Through financial markets, investors can sell off their investments if they need or want to, converting their office buildings, factories, and stock of machinery into cash much more readily than they could if they always had to find buyers on their own. But Keynes warned that when financial markets convert long-term assets into short-term commitments for investors, this also fosters a speculative mentality in the markets. What becomes central for investors is not whether a company's products will produce profits over a long term, but rather whether the short-term financial market investors *think* a company's fortunes will be strong enough in the present and immediate future to drive the stock price up. Or, to be more precise, what really matters for a speculative investor is not what they think about a given company's prospects per se, but rather what they think *other investors are thinking*, since that will be what determines where the stock price goes in the short term.

Because of this, the financial markets are highly susceptible to rumors, fads, and all sorts of deceptive accounting practices, since all of these can help drive the stock price up in the present, regardless of what they accomplish in the longer term. Thus, if U.S. stock traders are convinced that Alan Greenspan is a *maestro*, and if there is news that he is about to intervene with some kind of policy shift, then the rumor of Greenspan's policy shift can itself drive prices up, as the more nimble speculators try to keep one step ahead of the herd of Greenspan-philes.

Still, as with the Marx problem, it does not follow that the inherent instability of private investment and speculation in financial markets are uncontrollable, leading inevitably to persistent problems of mass unemployment and recession. But these social pathologies will become increasingly common through a neoliberal policy approach committed to minimizing government interventions to stabilize investment.

## The Polanyi Problem

Karl Polanyi wrote his classic book *The Great Transformation* in the context of the 1930s depression, World War II, and the developing worldwide competition with Communist governments. He was also reflecting on the 1920s, dominated, as with our current epoch, by a free-market ethos. Polanyi wrote of the 1920s that "economic liberalism made a supreme bid to restore the self-regulation of the system by eliminating all interventionist policies which interfered with the freedom of markets."

Considering all of these experiences, Polanyi argued that for market economies to function with some modicum of fairness, they must be embedded in social norms and institutions that effectively promote broadly accepted notions of the common good. Otherwise, acquisitiveness and competition—the two driving forces of market economies—achieve overwhelming dominance as cultural forces, rendering life under capitalism a Hobbesian "war of all against all." This same idea is also central for Adam Smith. Smith showed how the invisible hand of self-interest and competition will yield higher levels of individual effort that increases the wealth of nations, but that it will also produce the corruption of our moral sentiments unless the market is itself governed at a fundamental level by norms of solidarity.

In the post-World War II period, various social democratic movements within the advanced capitalist economies adapted to the Polanyi perspective. They argued in favor of government interventions to achieve three basic ends: stabilizing overall demand in the economy at a level that will provide for full employment; creating a financial market environment that is stable and conducive to the effective allocation of investment funds; and distributing equitably the rewards from high employment and a stable investment process. There were two basic means of achieving equitable distribution: relatively rapid wage growth, promoted by labor laws that were supportive of unions, minimum wage standards, and similar interventions in labor markets; and welfare state policies, including progressive taxation and redistributive programs such as Social Security. The political ascendancy of these ideas was the basis for a dramatic increase in the role of government in the post-World War II capitalist economies. As one indicator of this, total government expenditures in the United States rose from 8% of GDP in 1913, to 21% in 1950, then to 38% by 1992. The International Monetary Fund and World Bank were also formed in the mid-1940s to advance such policy ideas throughout the world—that is, to implement policies virtually the opposite of those they presently favor. John Maynard Keynes himself was a leading intellectual force contributing to the initial design of the International Monetary Fund and World Bank.

## From Social Democracy to Neoliberalism

But the implementation of a social democratic capitalism, guided by a commitment to full employment and the welfare state, did also face serious and persistent difficulties, and we need to recognize them as part of a consideration of the Marx, Keynes, and Polanyi problems. In particular, many sectors of business opposed efforts to sustain full employment because, following the logic of the Marx problem, full employment provides greater bargaining power for workers in labor markets, even if it also increases the economy's total production of goods and services. Greater worker bargaining power can also create inflationary pressures because businesses will try to absorb their higher wage costs by raising prices. In addition, market-inhibiting financial regulations limit the capacity of financial market players to diversify their risk and speculate.

Corporations in the United States and Western Europe were experiencing some combination of these problems associated with social democratic capitalism. In particular, they were faced with rising labor costs associated with low unemployment rates, which then led to either inflation, when corporations had the ability to pass on their higher labor costs to consumers, or to a squeeze on profits, when competitive pressures prevented corporations from raising their prices in response to the rising labor costs. These pressures were compounded by the two oil price "shocks" initiated by the Oil Producing Exporting Countries (OPEC)—an initial fourfold increase in the world price of oil in 1973, then a second four-fold price spike in 1979.

These were the conditions that by the end of the 1970s led to the decline of social democratic approaches to policymaking and the ascendancy of neoliberalism. The two leading signposts of this historic transition were the election in 1979 of Margaret Thatcher as prime minister of the United Kingdom and in 1980 of Ronald Reagan as the president of the United States. Indeed, it was at this point that Mrs. Thatcher made her famous pronouncement that "there is no alternative" to neoliberalism.

This brings us to the contemporary era of smaller government, fiscal stringency and deregulation, i.e., to neoliberalism under Clinton, Bush, and throughout the less-developed world. The issue is not a simple juxtaposition between either regulating or deregulating markets. Rather it is that markets have become deregulated to support the interests of business and financial markets, even as these same groups still benefit greatly from many forms of government support, including investment subsidies, tax concessions, and rescue operations when financial crises get out of hand. At the same time, the deregulation of markets that favors business and finance is correspondingly the most powerful regulatory mechanism limiting the demands of workers, in that deregulation has been congruent with the worldwide expansion of the reserve army of labor and the declining capacity of national governments to implement full-employment and macroeconomic policies. In other words, deregulation has exacerbated both the Marx and Keynes problems.

Given the ways in which neoliberalism worsens the Marx, Keynes, and Polanyi problems, we should not be surprised by the wreckage that it has wrought since the late 1970s, when it became the ascendant policy model. Over the past generation, with neoliberals in the saddle almost everywhere in the world, the results have been straightforward: worsening inequality and poverty, along with slower economic growth and far more unstable financial markets. While Margaret Thatcher famously declared that "there is no alternative" to neoliberalism, there are in fact alternatives. The experience over the past generation demonstrates how important it is to develop them in the most workable and coherent ways possible. ❑

*Article 1.3*

# OPENING PANDORA'S BOX
*The Basics of Marxist Economics*

**BY ALEJANDRO REUSS**
*February 2000*

In most universities, what is taught as "economics" is a particular brand of ortho-dox economic theory. The hallmark of this school is a belief in the optimal effi-ciency (and, it goes without saying, the equity) of "free markets."

The orthodox macroeconomists—who had denied the possibility of general economic slumps—were thrown for a loop by the Great Depression of the 1930s, and by the challenge to their system of thought by John Maynard Keynes and oth-ers. Even so, the orthodox system retains at its heart a view of capitalist society in which individuals, each roughly equal to all others, undertake mutually beneficial transactions tending to a socially optimal equilibrium. There is no power and no conflict. The model is a perfectly bloodless abstraction, without all the clash and clamor of real life.

## Karl Marx and the Critique of Capitalist Society

One way to pry open and criticize the orthodox model of economics is by returning to the idiosyncrasies of the real world. That's the approach of most of the articles in this book, which describe real-world phenomena that the orthodox model ignores or excludes. These efforts may explain particular facts better than the orthodoxy, while not necessarily offering an alternative general system of analysis. They punch holes in the orthodox lines but, ultimately, leave the orthodox model in possession of the field.

This suggests the need for a different conceptual system that can supplant or-thodox economics as a whole. Starting in the 1850s and continuing until his death in 1883, the German philosopher and revolutionary Karl Marx dedicated himself to developing a conceptual system for explaining the workings of capitalism. The system which Marx developed and which bears his name emerged from his criticism of the classical political economy developed by Adam Smith and David Ricardo. While Marx admired Smith and Ricardo, and borrowed many of their concepts, he approached economics (or "political economy") from a very different standpoint. He had developed a powerful criticism of capitalist society before undertaking his study of the economy. This criticism was inspired by French socialist ideas and focused on the oppression of the working class. Marx argued that wage workers—those work-ing for a paycheck—were "free" only in the sense that they were not beholden to a single lord or master, as serfs had been under feudalism. But they did not own prop-erty, nor were they craftspeople working for themselves, so they were compelled to sell themselves for a wage to one capitalist or another. Having surrendered their freedom to the employer's authority, they were forced to work in the way the em-ployer told them while the latter pocketed the profit produced by their labor.

Marx believed, however, that by creating this oppressed and exploited class of workers, capitalism was creating the seeds of its own destruction. Conflict between the workers and the owners was an essential part of capitalism. But in Marx's view of history, the workers could eventually overthrow the capitalist class, just as the capitalist class, or "bourgeoisie," had grown strong under feudalism, only to supplant the feudal aristocracy. The workers, however, would not simply substitute a new form of private property and class exploitation, as the bourgeoisie had done. Rather, they would bring about the organization of production on a cooperative basis, and an end to the domination of one class over another.

This line of thinking was strongly influenced by the ideas of the day in German philosophy, which held that any new order grows in the womb of the old, and eventually bursts forth to replace it. Marx believed that the creation of the working class, or "proletariat," in the heart of capitalism was one of the system's main contradictions. Marx studied capitalist economics in order to explain the conditions under which it would be possible for the proletariat to overthrow capitalism and create a classless society. The orthodox view depicts capitalism as tending towards equilibrium (without dynamism or crises), serving everyone's best interests, and lasting forever. Marx saw capitalism as crisis-ridden, full of conflict, operating to the advantage of some and detriment of others, and far from eternal.

## Class and Exploitation

Marx studied history closely. Looking at economic systems historically, he saw capitalism as only the latest in a succession of societies based on exploitation. When people are only able to produce the bare minimum needed to live, he wrote, there is no room for a class of people to take a portion of society's production without contributing to it. But as soon as productivity exceeds this subsistence level, it becomes possible for a class of people who do not contribute to production to live by appropriating the surplus for themselves. These are the masters in slave societies, the lords in feudal societies, and the property owners in capitalist society.

Marx believed that the owners of businesses and property—the capitalists—take part of the wealth produced by the workers, but that this appropriation is hidden by the appearance of an equal exchange, or "a fair day's work for a fair day's pay."

Those who live from the ownership of property—businesses, stocks, land, etc—were then a small minority and now are less than 5% of the population in countries like the United States. (Marx wrote before the rise of massive corporations and bureaucracies, and did not classify managers and administrators who don't own their own businesses as part of the bourgeoisie.) The exploited class, meanwhile, is the vast majority who live by earning a wage or salary—not just "blue collar" or industrial workers but other workers as well.

Marx's view of how exploitation happened in capitalist society depended on an idea, which he borrowed from Smith and Ricardo, called the labor theory of value. The premise of this theory, which is neither easily proved nor easily rejected, is that labor alone creates the value which is embodied in commodities and which creates profit for owners who sell the goods. The workers do not receive the full value created by their labor and so they are exploited.

Students are likely to hear in economics classes that profits are a reward for the "abstinence" or "risk" of a businessperson—implying that profits are their just deserts. Marx would argue that profits are a reward obtained through the exercise of power—the power owners have over those who own little but their ability to work and so must sell this ability for a wage. That power, and the tribute it allows owners of capital to extract from workers, is no more legitimate in Marx's analysis than the power of a slaveowner over a slave. A slaveowner may exhibit thrift and take risks, after all, but is the wealth of the slaveowner the just reward for these virtues, or a pure and simple theft from the slave?

As Joan Robinson, an important 20th-century critic and admirer of Marx, argues, "What is important is that owning capital is not a productive activity. The academic economists, by treating capital as productive, used to insinuate the suggestion that capitalists deserve well by society and are fully justified in drawing income from their property."

## The Falling Rate of Profit

Marx believed that his theory had major implications for the crises that engulf capitalist economies. In Marx's system, the raw materials and machinery used in the manufacture of a product do not create the extra value that allows the business owner to profit from its production. That additional value is created by labor alone.

Marx recognized that owners could directly extract more value out of workers in three ways: cutting their wages, lengthening their working day, or increasing the intensity of their labor. This need not be done by a direct assault on the workers. Capitalists can achieve the same goal by employing more easily exploited groups or by moving their operations where labor is not as powerful. Both of these trends can be seen in capitalism today, and can be understood as part of capital's intrinsic thirst for more value and increased exploitation.

With the mechanization of large-scale production under capitalism, machines and other inanimate elements of production form a larger and larger share of the inputs to production. Marx believed this would result in a long-term trend of the rate of profit to fall, as the enriching contribution of human labor declined (relative to the inert contribution of these other inputs). This, he believed, would make capitalism increasingly vulnerable to economic crises.

This chain of reasoning, of course, depends on the labor theory of value (seeing workers as the source of the surplus value created in the production process) and can be avoided by rejecting this theory outright. Orthodox economics has not only rejected the labor theory of value, but abandoned the issue of "value" altogether. After lying fallow for many years, value analysis was revived during the 1960s by a number of unorthodox economists including the Italian economist Piero Sraffa. Marx did not get the last word on the subject.

## Unemployment, Part I: The "Reserve Army of the Unemployed"

Marx is often raked over the coals for arguing that workers, under capitalism, were destined to be ground into ever-more-desperate poverty. That living standards improved in rich capitalist countries is offered as proof that his system is fatally flawed. While Marx was not optimistic about the prospect of workers raising their standard of living very far under capitalism, he was critical of proponents of the "iron law of wages," such as Malthus, who held that any increase in wages above the minimum necessary for survival would simply provoke population growth and a decline in wages back to subsistence level.

Marx emphasized that political and historical factors influencing the relative power of the major social classes, rather than simple demographics, determined the distribution of income.

One economic factor to which Marx attributed great importance in the class struggle was the size of the "reserve army of the unemployed." Marx identified unemployment as the major factor pushing wages down—the larger the "reserve" of unemployed workers clamoring for jobs, the greater the downward pressure on wages. This was an influence, Marx believed, that the workers would never be able to fully escape under capitalism. If the workers' bargaining power rose enough to raise wages and eat into profits, he argued, capitalists would merely substitute labor-saving technology for living labor, recreating the "reserve army" and reasserting the downward pressure on wages.

Though this has not, perhaps, retarded long-term wage growth to the degree that Marx expected, his basic analysis was visionary at a time when the Malthusian (population) theory of wages was the prevailing view. Anyone reading the business press these days—which is constantly worrying that workers might gain some bargaining power in a "tight" (low unemployment) labor market, and that their wage demands will provoke inflation—will recognize its basic insight.

## Unemployment, Part II: The Crisis of Overproduction

Marx never developed one definitive version of his theory of economic crises (recessions) under capitalism. Nonetheless, his thinking on this issue is some of his most visionary. Marx was the first major economic thinker to break with the orthodoxy of "Say's Law." Named after the French philosopher Jean-Baptiste Say, this theory held that each industry generated income equal to the output it created. In other words, "supply creates its own demand." Say's conclusion, in which he was followed by Smith, Ricardo, and orthodox economists up through the Great Depression, was that while a particular industry such as the car industry could overproduce, no generalized overproduction was possible. In this respect, orthodox economics flew in the face of all the evidence. In his analysis of overproduction, Marx focused on what he considered the basic contradiction of capitalism—and, in microcosm, of the commodity itself—the contradiction between "use value" and "exchange value." The idea is that a commodity both satisfies a specific need (it has "use value") and can be exchanged for other articles (it has "exchange value"). This distinction was not invented by Marx; it can be found in the work of Smith. Unlike Smith, however, Marx emphasized the way exchange value—what something is worth in the market—overwhelms the use value of a commodity. Unless a commodity can be sold, the portion of society's useful labor embodied in it is wasted (and the product is useless to those in need). Vast real needs remain unsatisfied for the majority of people, doubly so when—during crises of overproduction—vast quantities of goods remain unsold because there is not enough "effective demand."

It is during these crises that capitalism's unlimited drive to develop society's productive capacity clashes most sharply with the constraints it places on the real incomes of the majority to buy the goods they need. Marx developed this notion of a demand crisis over 75 years before the so-called "Keynesian revolution" in economic thought (whose key insights were actually developed before Keynes by the Polish economist Michal Kalecki on the foundations of Marx's analysis).

Marx expected that these crises of overproduction and demand would worsen as capitalism developed, and that the crises would slow the development of society's productive capacities (what Marx called the "forces of production"). Ultimately, he believed, these crises would be capitalism's undoing. He also pointed to them as evidence of the basic depravity of capitalism. "In these crises," Marx writes in the *Communist Manifesto*,

> there breaks out an epidemic that, in all earlier epochs would have seemed an absurdity, the epidemic of overproduction. Society suddenly finds itself put back into a state of momentary barbarism; it appears as if a famine, a universal war of devastation had cut off the supply of every means of subsistence; industry and commerce seem to be destroyed; and why? Because there is too much civilization, too much means of subsistence, too much industry, too much commerce …

> And how does the bourgeoisie get over these crises? On the one hand by destruction of productive resources; on the other hand, by the conquest of new markets, and by the more thorough exploitation of old ones.

This kind of crisis came so close to bringing down capitalism during the Great Depression that preventing them became a central aim of government policy. While government intervention has managed to smooth out the business cycle, especially in the wealthiest countries, capitalism has hardly become crisis-free.

While the reigning complacency about a new, crisis-free capitalism is much easier to sustain here than in, say, East Asia, capitalism clearly has not yet run up against any absolute barrier to its development. In fact, Marx's discussions (in the *Communist Manifesto* and elsewhere) of capitalism's irresistible expansive impulse— capital breaking down all barriers, expanding into every crevice, always "thirsting for surplus value" and new fields of exploitation—seem as apt today as they did 150 years ago.

## Marx as Prophet

Marx got a great deal about capitalism just right—its incessant, shark-like forward movement; its internal chaos, bursting forth periodically in crisis; its concentration of economic power in ever fewer hands. Judged on these core insights, the Marxist system can easily stand toe-to-toe with the orthodox model. Which comes closer to reality? The capitalism that incessantly bursts forth over new horizons, or the one that constantly gravitates towards comfortable equilibrium? The one where crisis is impossible, or the one that lurches from boom to bust to boom again? The one where perfect competition reigns, or the one where a handful of giants tower over every industry?

In all these respects, Marx's system captures the thundering dynamics of capitalism much better than the orthodox system does. As aesthetically appealing as the clockwork harmony of the orthodox model may be, this is precisely its failing. Capitalism is anything but harmonious.

There was also a lot that Marx, like any other complex thinker, predicted incorrectly, or did not foresee. In this respect, he was not a prophet. His work should be read critically, and not, as it has been by some, as divine revelation. Marx, rather, was the prophet of a radical approach to reality. In an age when the "free market" rides high, and its apologists claim smugly that "there is no alternative," Joan Robinson's praise of Marx is apt: "[T]he nightmare quality of Marx's thought gives it ... an air of greater reality than the gentle complacency of the orthodox academics. Yet he, at the same time, is more encouraging than they, for he releases hope as well as terror from Pandora's box, while they preach only the gloomy doctrine that all is for the best in the best of all *possible* worlds." ❑

*Sources*: Joan Robinson, *An Essay on Marxian Economics* (Macmillan, 1952); "Manifesto of the Community Party," and "Crisis Theory (from Theories of Surplus Value)," in Robert C. Tucker, ed., *The Marx-Engels Reader* (W.W. Norton, 1978); Roman Rosdolsky, *The Making of Marx's 'Capital'* (Pluto Press, 1989); Ernest Mandel, "Karl Heinrich Marx"; Luigi L. Pasinetti, "Joan Violet Robinson"; and John Eatwell and Carlo Panico, "Piero Sraffa"; in John Eatwell, Murray Milgate, and Peter Newman, eds., *The New Palgrave: A Dictionary of Economics* (Macmillan, 1987).

*Article 1.4*

# SHARING THE WEALTH OF THE COMMONS

## BY PETER BARNES
*November/December 2004*

W e're all familiar with private wealth, even if we don't have much. Economists and the media celebrate it every day. But there's another trove of wealth we barely notice: our common wealth.

Each of us is the beneficiary of a vast inheritance. This common wealth includes our air and water, habitats and ecosystems, languages and cultures, science and technologies, political and monetary systems, and quite a bit more. To say we share this inheritance doesn't mean we can call a broker and sell our shares tomorrow. It does mean we're responsible for the commons and entitled to any income it generates. Both the responsibility and the entitlement are ours by birth. They're part of the obligation each generation owes to the next, and each living human owes to other beings.

At present, however, our economic system scarcely recognizes the commons. This omission causes two major tragedies: ceaseless destruction of nature and widening inequality among humans. Nature gets destroyed because no one's unequivocally responsible for protecting it. Inequality widens because private wealth concentrates while common wealth shrinks.

The great challenges for the 21st century are, first of all, to make the commons visible; second, to give it proper reverence; and third, to translate that reverence into property rights and legal institutions that are on a par with those supporting private property. If we do this, we can avert the twin tragedies currently built into our market-driven system.

## Defining the Commons

What exactly is the commons? Here is a workable definition: The commons includes all the assets we inherit together and are morally obligated to pass on, undiminished, to future generations.

This definition is a practical one. It designates a set of assets that have three specific characteristics: they're (1) inherited, (2) shared, and (3) worthy of long-term preservation. Usually it's obvious whether an asset has these characteristics or not.

At the same time, the definition is broad. It encompasses assets that are natural as well as social, intangible as well as tangible, small as well as large. It also introduces a moral factor that is absent from other economic definitions: it requires us to consider whether an asset is worthy of long-term preservation. At present, capitalism has no interest in this question. If an asset is likely to yield a competitive return to capital, it's kept alive; if not, it's destroyed or allowed to run down. Assets in the commons, by contrast, are meant to be preserved regardless of their return.

This definition sorts all economic assets into two baskets, the market and the commons. In the market basket are those assets we want to own privately and manage for profit. In the commons basket are the assets we want to hold in common and manage for long-term preservation. These baskets then are, or ought to be, the yin and yang of economic activity; each should enhance and contain the other. The role of the state should be to maintain a healthy balance between them.

## The Value of the Commons

For most of human existence, the commons supplied everyone's food, water, fuel, and medicines. People hunted, fished, gathered fruits and herbs, collected firewood and building materials, and grazed their animals in common lands and waters. In other words, the commons was the source of basic sustenance. This is still true today in many parts of the world, and even in San Francisco, where I live, cash-poor people fish in the bay not for sport, but for food.

Though sustenance in the industrialized world now flows mostly through markets, the commons remains hugely valuable. It's the source of all natural resources and nature's many replenishing services. Water, air, DNA, seeds, topsoil, minerals, the protective ozone layer, the atmosphere's climate regulation, and much more, are gifts of nature to us all.

Just as crucially, the commons is our ultimate waste sink. It recycles water, oxygen, carbon, and everything else we excrete, exhale, or throw away. It's the place we store, or try to store, the residues of our industrial system.

The commons also holds humanity's vast accumulation of knowledge, art, and thought. As Isaac Newton said, "If I have seen further it is by standing on the shoulders of giants." So, too, the legal, political, and economic institutions we inherit—even the market itself—were built by the efforts of millions. Without these gifts we'd be hugely poorer than we are today.

To be sure, thinking of these natural and social inheritances primarily as economic assets is a limited way of viewing them. I deeply believe they are much more than that. But if treating portions of the commons as economic assets can help us conserve them, it's surely worth doing so.

How much might the commons be worth in monetary terms? It's relatively easy to put a dollar value on private assets. Accountants and appraisers do it every day, aided by the fact that private assets are regularly traded for money.

This isn't the case with most shared assets. How much is clean air, an intact wetlands,

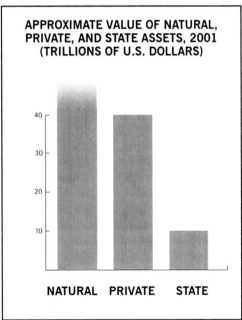

APPROXIMATE VALUE OF NATURAL, PRIVATE, AND STATE ASSETS, 2001 (TRILLIONS OF U.S. DOLLARS)

NATURAL   PRIVATE   STATE

or Darwin's theory of evolution worth in dollar terms? Clearly, many shared inheritances are simply priceless. Others are potentially quantifiable, but there's no current market for them. Fortunately, economists have developed methods to quantify the value of things that aren't traded, so it's possible to estimate the value of the "priceable" part of the commons within an order of magnitude. The surprising conclusion that emerges from numerous studies is that the wealth we share is worth more than the wealth we own privately.

This fact bears repeating. Even though much of the commons can't be valued in monetary terms, the parts that can be valued are worth more than all private assets combined.

It's worth noting that these estimates understate the gap between common and private assets because a significant portion of the value attributed to private wealth is in fact an appropriation of common wealth. If this mislabeled portion was subtracted from private wealth and added to common wealth, the gap between the two would widen further.

Two examples will make this point clear. Suppose you buy a house for $200,000 and, without improving it, sell it a few years later for $300,000. You pay off the mortgage and walk away with a pile of cash. But what caused the house to rise in value? It wasn't anything you did. Rather, it was the fact that your neighborhood became more popular, likely a result of the efforts of community members, improvements in public services, and similar factors.

Or consider another fount of private wealth, the social invention and public expansion of the stock market. Suppose you start a business that goes "public" through an offering of stock. Within a few years, you're able to sell your stock for a spectacular capital gain.

Much of this gain is a social creation, the result of centuries of monetary-system evolution, laws and regulations, and whole industries devoted to accounting, sharing information, and trading stocks. What's more, there's a direct correlation between the scale and quality of the stock market as an institution and the size of the private gain. You'll fetch a higher price if you sell into a market of millions than into a market of two. Similarly, you'll gain more if transaction costs are low and trust in public information is high. Thus, stock that's traded on a regulated exchange sells for a higher multiple of earnings than unlisted stock. This socially created premium can account for 30% of the stock's value. If you're the lucky seller, you'll reap that extra cash—in no way thanks to anything you did as an individual.

Real estate gains and the stock market's social premium are just two instances of common assets contributing to private gain. Still, most rich people would like us to think it's their extraordinary talent, hard work, and risk-taking that create their well-deserved wealth. That's like saying a flower's beauty is due solely to its own efforts, owing nothing to nutrients in the soil, energy from the sun, water from the aquifer, or the activity of bees.

## The Great Commons Giveaway

That we inherit a trove of common wealth is the good news. The bad news, alas, is that our inheritance is being grossly mismanaged. As a recent report by the advocacy group Friends of the Commons concludes, "Maintenance of the commons is terrible, theft is rampant, and rents often aren't collected. To put it bluntly, our common wealth—and our children's—is being squandered. We are all poorer as a result."

Examples of commons mismanagement include the handout of broadcast spectrum to media conglomerates, the giveaway of pollution rights to polluters, the extension of copyrights to entertainment companies, the patenting of seeds and genes, the privatization of water, and the relentless destruction of habitat, wildlife, and ecosystems.

This mismanagement, though currently extreme, is not new. For over 200 years, the market has been devouring the commons in two ways. With one hand, the market takes valuable stuff from the commons and privatizes it. This is called "enclosure." With the other hand, the market dumps bad stuff into the commons and says, "It's your problem." This is called "externalizing." Much that is called economic growth today is actually a form of cannibalization in which the market diminishes the commons that ultimately sustains it.

Enclosure—the taking of good stuff from the commons—at first meant privatization of land by the gentry. Today it means privatization of many common assets by corporations. Either way, it means that what once belonged to everyone now belongs to a few.

Enclosure is usually justified in the name of efficiency. And sometimes, though not always, it does result in efficiency gains. But what also results from enclosure is the impoverishment of those who lose access to the commons, and the enrichment of those who take title to it. In other words, enclosure widens the gap between those with income-producing property and those without.

Externalizing—the dumping of bad stuff into the commons—is an automatic behavior pattern of profit-maximizing corporations: if they can avoid any out-of-pocket costs, they will. If workers, taxpayers, anyone downwind, future generations, or nature have to absorb added costs, so be it.

For decades, economists have agreed we'd be better served if businesses "internalized" their externalities—that is, paid in real time the costs they now shift to the commons. The reason this doesn't happen is that there's no one to set prices and collect them. Unlike private wealth, the commons lacks property rights and institutions to represent it in the marketplace.

The seeds of such institutions, however, are starting to emerge. Consider one of the environmental protection tools the U.S. currently uses, pollution trading. So-called cap-and-trade programs put a cap on total pollution, then grant portions of the total, via permits, to each polluting firm. Companies may buy other firms' permits if they want to pollute more than their allotment allows, or sell unused permits if they manage to pollute less. Such programs are generally supported by business because they allow polluters to find the cheapest ways to reduce pollution.

Public discussion of cap-and-trade programs has focused exclusively on their trading features. What's been overlooked is how they give away common wealth to polluters.

To date, all cap-and-trade programs have begun by giving pollution rights to existing polluters for free. This treats polluters as if they own our sky and rivers. It means that future polluters will have to pay old polluters for the scarce—hence valuable—right to dump wastes into nature. Imagine that: because a corporation polluted in the past, it gets free income forever! And, because ultimately we'll all pay for limited pollution via higher prices, this amounts to an enormous transfer of wealth—trillions of dollars—to shareholders of historically polluting corporations.

In theory, though, there is no reason that the initial pollution rights should not reside with the public. Clean air and the atmosphere's capacity to absorb pollutants are "wealth" that belongs to everyone. Hence, when polluters use up these parts of the commons, they should pay the public—not the other way around.

## Taking the Commons Back

How can we correct the system omission that permits, and indeed promotes, destruction of nature and ever-widening inequality among humans? The answer lies in building a new sector of the economy whose clear legal mission is to preserve shared inheritances for everyone. Just as the market is populated by profit-maximizing corporations, so this new sector would be populated by asset-preserving trusts.

Here a brief description of trusts may be helpful. The trust is a private institution that's even older than the corporation. The essence of a trust is a fiduciary relationship. A trust holds and manages property for another person or for many other people. A simple example is a trust set up by a grandparent to pay for a grandchild's education. Other trusts include pension funds, charitable foundations, and university endowments. There are also hundreds of trusts in America, like the Nature Conservancy and the Trust for Public Land, that own land or conservation easements in perpetuity.

If we were to design an institution to protect pieces of the commons, we couldn't do much better than a trust. The goal of commons management, after all, is to preserve assets and deliver benefits to broad classes of beneficiaries. That's what trusts do, and it's not rocket science.

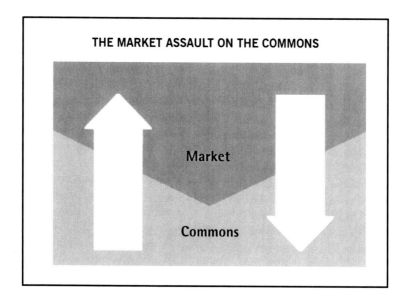

Over centuries, several principles of trust management have evolved. These include:

- Trustees have a fiduciary responsibility to beneficiaries. If a trustee fails in this obligation, he or she can be removed and penalized.
- Trustees must preserve the original asset. It's okay to spend income, but don't invade the principal.
- Trustees must assure transparency. Information about money flows should be readily available to beneficiaries.

Trusts in the new commons sector would be endowed with rights comparable to those of corporations. Their trustees would take binding oaths of office and, like judges, serve long terms. Though protecting common assets would be their primary job, they would also distribute income from those assets to beneficiaries. These beneficiaries would include all citizens within a jurisdiction, large classes of citizens (children, the elderly), and/or agencies serving common purposes such as public transit or ecological restoration. When distributing income to individuals, the allocation formula would be one person, one share. The right to receive commons income would be a nontransferable birthright, not a property right that could be traded.

Fortuitously, a working model of such a trust already exists: the Alaska Permanent Fund. When oil drilling on the North Slope began in the 1970s, Gov. Jay Hammond, a Republican, proposed that 25% of the state's royalties be placed in a mutual fund to be invested on behalf of Alaska's citizens. Voters approved in a referendum. Since then, the Alaska Permanent Fund has grown to over $28 billion, and Alaskans have received roughly $22,000 apiece in dividends. In 2003 the per capita dividend was $1,107; a family of four received $4,428.

What Alaska did with its oil can be replicated for other gifts of nature. For example, we could create a nationwide Sky Trust to stabilize the climate for future generations. The trust would restrict emissions of heat-trapping gases and sell a declining number of emission permits to polluters. The income would be returned to U.S. residents in equal yearly dividends, thus reversing the wealth transfer built into current cap-and-trade programs. Instead of everyone paying historic polluters, polluters would pay all of us.

Just as a Sky Trust could represent our equity in the natural commons, a Public Stock Trust could embody our equity in the social commons. Such a trust would capture some of the socially created stock-market premium that currently flows only to shareholders and their investment bankers. As noted earlier, this premium is sizeable—roughly 30% of the value of publicly traded stock. A simple way to share it would be to create a giant mutual fund—call it the American Permanent Fund—that would hold, say, 10% of the shares of publicly traded companies. This mutual fund, in turn, would be owned by all Americans on a one share per person basis (perhaps linked to their Social Security accounts).

To build up the fund without precipitating a fall in share prices, companies would contribute shares at the rate of, say, 1% per year. The contributions would be the price companies pay for the benefits they derive from a commons asset, the large, trusted market for stock—a small price, indeed, for the hefty benefits. Over time, the mutual fund would assure that when the economy grows, everyone benefits. The top 5% would still own more than the bottom 90%, but at least every American would have some property income, and a slightly larger slice of our economic pie.

## Sharing the Wealth

The perpetuation of inequality is built into the current design of capitalism. Because of the skewed distribution of private wealth, a small self-perpetuating minority receives a disproportionate share of America's nonlabor income.

Tom Paine had something to say about this. In his essay "Agrarian Justice," written in 1790, he argued that, because enclosure of the commons had separated so many people from their primary source of sustenance, it was necessary to create a functional equivalent of the commons in the form of a National Fund. Here is how he put it:

> There are two kinds of property. Firstly, natural property, or that which comes to us from the Creator of the universe—such as the earth, air, water. Secondly, artificial or acquired property—the invention of men. In the latter, equality is impossible; for to distribute it equally, it would be necessary that all should have contributed in the same proportion, which can never be the case .... Equality of natural property is different. Every individual in the world is born with legitimate claims on this property, or its equivalent.

Enclosure of the commons, he went on, was necessary to improve the efficiency of cultivation. But:

> The landed monopoly that began with [enclosure] has produced the greatest evil. It has dispossessed more than half the inhabitants of every nation of their natural inheritance, without providing for them, as ought to have been done, an indemnification for that loss, and has thereby created a species of poverty and wretchedness that did not exist before.

The appropriate compensation for loss of the commons, Paine said, was a national fund financed by rents paid by land owners. Out of this fund, every person reaching age 21 would get 15 pounds a year, and every person over 50 would receive an additional 10 pounds. (Think of Social Security, financed by commons rents instead of payroll taxes.)

## A Progressive Offensive

Paine's vision, allowing for inflation and new forms of enclosure, could not be more timely today. Surely from our vast common inheritance—not just the land, but the atmosphere, the broadcast spectrum, our mineral resources, our threatened habitats and water supplies—enough rent can be collected to pay every American over age 21 a modest annual dividend, and every person reaching 21 a small start-up inheritance.

Such a proposal may seem utopian. In today's political climate, perhaps it is. But consider this. About 20 years ago, right-wing think tanks laid out a bold agenda. They called for lowering taxes on private wealth, privatizing much of government, and deregulating industry. Amazingly, this radical agenda has largely been achieved.

It's time for progressives to mount an equally bold offensive. The old shibboleths—let's gin up the economy, create jobs, and expand government programs—no longer excite. We need to talk about fixing the economy, not just growing it; about income for everyone, not just jobs; about nurturing ecosystems, cultures, and communities, not just our individual selves. More broadly, we need to celebrate the commons as an essential counterpoise to the market.

Unfortunately, many progressives have viewed the state as the only possible counterpoise to the market. The trouble is, the state has been captured by corporations. This capture isn't accidental or temporary; it's structural and long-term.

This doesn't mean progressives can't occasionally recapture the state. We've done so before and will do so again. It does mean that progressive control of the state is the exception, not the norm; in due course, corporate capture will resume. It follows that if we want lasting fixes to capitalism's tragic flaws, we must use our brief moments of political ascendancy to build institutions that endure.

Programs that rely on taxes, appropriations, or regulations are inherently transitory; they get weakened or repealed when political power shifts. By contrast, institutions that are self-perpetuating and have broad constituencies are likely to last. (It also helps if they mail out checks periodically.) This was the genius of Social Security, which has survived—indeed grown—through numerous Republican administrations.

If progressives are smart, we'll use our next New Deal to create common property trusts that include all Americans as beneficiaries. These trusts will then be to the 21st century what social insurance was to the 20th: sturdy pillars of shared responsibility and entitlement. Through them, the commons will be a source of sustenance for all, as it was before enclosure. Life-long income will be linked to generations-long ecological health. Isn't that a future most Americans would welcome? ❑

Article 1.5

# THE GROWTH CONSENSUS UNRAVELS

## BY JONATHAN ROWE
July/August 1999

Economics has been called the dismal science, but beneath its gray exterior is a system of belief worthy of Pollyanna. Yes, economists manage to see a dark cloud in every silver lining. Downturn follows uptick, and inflation rears its ugly head. But there's a story within that story—a gauzy romance, a lyric ode to Stuff. It's built into the language. A thing produced is called a "good," for example, no questions asked. The word is more than just a term of art. It suggests the automatic benediction which economics bestows upon commodities of any kind.

By the same token, an activity for sale is called a "service." In conventional economics there are no "dis-services," no actions that might be better left undone. The bank that gouges you with ATM fees, the lawyer who runs up the bill—such things are "services" so long as someone pays. If a friend or neighbor fixes your plumbing for free, it's not a "service" and so it doesn't count.

The sum total of these products and activities is called the Gross Domestic Product, or GDP. If the GDP is greater this year than last, then the result is called "growth." There is no bad GDP and no bad growth; economics does not even have a word for such a thing. It does have a word for less growth. In such a case, economists say growth is "sluggish" and the economy is in "recession." No matter what is growing—more payments to doctors because of worsening health, more toxic clean-up—so long as there is more of it, then the economic mind declares it good.

This purports to be "objective science." In reality it is a rhetorical construct with the value judgments built in, and this rhetoric has been the basis of economic debate in the United States for the last half century at least. True, people have disagreed over how best to promote a rising GDP. Liberals generally wanted to use government more, conservatives less. But regarding the beneficence of a rising GDP, there has been little debate at all.

If anything, the Left traditionally has believed in growth with even greater fervor than the Right. It was John Maynard Keynes, after all, who devised the growth-boosting mechanisms of macroeconomic policy to combat the Depression of the 1930s; it was Keynesians who embraced these strategies after the War and turned the GDP into a totem. There's no point in seeking a bigger pie to redistribute to the poor, if you don't believe the expanding pie is desirable in the first place.

Today, however, the growth consensus is starting to unravel across the political spectrum and in ways that are both obvious and subtle. The issue is no longer just the impact of growth upon the environment—the toxic impacts of industry and the like. It now goes deeper, to what growth actually consists of and what it means in people's lives. The things economists call "goods" and "services" increasingly don't strike people as such. There is a growing disconnect between the way people experience growth and the way the policy establishment talks about it, and this gap is becoming an unspoken subtext to much of American political life.

The group most commonly associated with an antigrowth stance is environmentalists, of course. To be sure, one faction, the environmental economists, is trying to put green new wine into the old bottles of economic thought. If we would just make people pay the "true" cost of, say, the gasoline they burn, through the tax system for example, then the market would do the rest. We'd have benign, less-polluting growth, they say, perhaps even more than now. But the core of the environmental movement remains deeply suspicious of the growth ethos, and probably would be even if the environmental impacts somehow could be lessened.

In the middle are suburbanites who applaud growth in the abstract, but oppose the particular manifestations they see around them—the traffic, sprawl and crowded schools. On the Right, meanwhile, an anti-growth politics is arising practically unnoticed. When social conservatives denounce gambling, pornography, or sex and violence in the media, they are talking about specific instances of the growth that their political leaders rhapsodize on other days.

Environmentalists have been like social conservatives in one key respect. They have been moralistic regarding growth, often scolding people for enjoying themselves at the expense of future generations and the earth. Their concern is valid, up to a point—the consumer culture does promote the time horizon of a five year old. But politically it is not the most promising line of attack, and conceptually it concedes too much ground. To moralize about consumption as they do is to accept the conventional premise that it really is something chosen—an enjoyable form of self-indulgence that has unfortunate consequences for the earth.

That's "consumption" in the common parlance—the sport utility vehicle loading up at Wal-Mart, the stuff piling up in the basement and garage. But increasingly that's not what people actually experience, nor is it what the term really means. In economics, consumption means everything people spend money on, pleasurable or not. Wal-Mart is just one dimension of a much larger and increasingly unpleasant whole. The lawyers' fees for the house settlement or divorce; the repair work on the car after it was rear-ended; the cancer treatments for the uncle who was a three-pack-a-day smoker; the stress medications and weight loss regimens—all these and more are "consumption." They all go into the GDP.

Cancer treatments and lawyer's fees are not what come to mind when environmentalists lament the nation's excess consumption, or for that matter when economists applaud America's "consumers" for keeping the world economy afloat. Yet increasingly such things are what consumption actually consists of in the economy today. More and more, it consists not of pleasurable things that people choose, but rather of things that most people would gladly do without.

Much consumption today is addictive, for example. Millions of Americans are engaged in a grim daily struggle with themselves to do less of it. They want to eat less, drink less, smoke less, gamble less, talk less on the telephone—do less buying, period. Yet economic reasoning declares as growth and progress that which people themselves regard as a tyrannical affliction.

Economists resist this reality of a divided self, because it would complicate their models beyond repair. They cling instead to an 18th century model of human psychology—the "rational" and self-interested man—which assumes those complexities away. As David McClelland, the Harvard psychologist, once put it, economists "haven't even discovered Freud, let alone Abraham Maslow." (They also haven't discovered the Apostle Paul, who lamented that "the good that I would I do not, but the evil that I would not, that I do.")

Then too there's the mounting expenditure that sellers foist upon people through machination and deceit. People don't choose to pay for the corrupt campaign finance system or for bloated executive pay packages. The cost of these is hidden in the prices that we pay at the store. The *Washington Post* recently reported that Microsoft hired Ralph Reed, former head of the Christian Coalition, and Grover Norquist, a right-wing polemicist, as lobbyists in Washington. When I bought this computer with Windows 95, Bill Gates never asked me whether I wanted to help support a bunch of Beltway operators like these.

This is compulsory consumption, not choice, and the economy is rife with it today. People don't choose to pay some $40 billion a year in telemarketing fraud. They don't choose to pay 32% more for prescription drugs than do people in Canada. ("Free trade" means that corporations are free to buy their labor and materials in other countries, but ordinary Americans aren't equally free to do their shopping there.) For that matter, people don't choose to spend $25 and up for inkjet printer cartridges. The manufacturers design the printers to make money on the cartridges because, as the *Wall Street Journal* put it, that's "where the big profit margins are."

Yet another category of consumption that most people would gladly do without arises from the need to deal with the offshoots and implications of growth. Bottled water has become a multibillion dollar business in the United States because people don't trust what comes from the tap. There's a growing market for sound insulation and double-pane windows because the economy produces so much noise. A wide array of physical and social stresses arise from the activities that get lumped into the euphemistic term "growth."

The economy in such cases doesn't solve problems so much as create new problems that require more expenditure to solve. Food is supposed to sustain people, for example. But today the dis-economies of eating sustain the GDP instead. The food industry spends some $21 billion a year on advertising to entice people to eat food they don't need. Not coincidentally there's now a $32 billion diet and weight loss industry to help people take off the pounds that inevitably result. When that doesn't work, which is often, there is always the vacuum pump or knife. There were some 110,000 liposuctions in the United States last year; at five pounds each that's some 275 tons of flab up the tube.

It is a grueling cycle of indulgence and repentance, binge and purge. Yet each stage of this miserable experience, viewed through the pollyanic lens of economics, becomes growth and therefore good. The problem here goes far beyond the old critique of how the consumer culture cultivates feelings of inadequacy, lack and need so people will buy and buy again. Now this culture actually makes life worse, in order to sell solutions that purport to make it better.

Traffic shows this syndrome in a finely developed form. First we build sprawling suburbs so people need a car to go almost anywhere. The resulting long commutes are daily torture but help build up the GDP. Americans spend some $5 billion a year in gasoline alone while they sit in traffic and go nowhere. As the price of gas increases this growth sector will expand.

Commerce deplores a vacuum, and the exasperating hours in the car have spawned a booming subeconomy of relaxation tapes, cell phones, even special bibs. Billboards have 1-800 numbers so commuters can shop while they stew. Talk radio thrives on traffic-bound commuters, which accounts for some of the contentious, get-out-of-my-face tone. The traffic also helps sustain a $130 billion a year car wreck industry; and if Gates succeeds in getting computers into cars, that sector should get a major boost.

The health implications also are good for growth. Los Angeles, which has the worst traffic in the nation, also leads—if that's the word—in hospital admissions due to respiratory ailments. The resulting medical bills go into the GDP. And while Americans sit in traffic they aren't walking or getting exercise. More likely they are entertaining themselves orally with a glazed donut or a Big Mac, which helps explain why the portion of middle-aged Americans who are clinically obese has doubled since the 1960s.

C. Everett Koop, the former Surgeon General, estimates that some 70% of the nation's medical expenses are lifestyle induced. Yet the same lifestyle that promotes disease also produces a rising GDP. (Keynes observed that traditional virtues like thrift are bad for growth; now it appears that health is bad for growth too.) We literally are growing ourselves sick, and this puts a grim new twist on the economic doctrine of "complementary goods," which describes the way new products tend to spawn a host of others. The automobile gave rise to car wash franchises, drive-in restaurants, fuzz busters, tire dumps, and so forth. Television produced an antenna industry, VCRs, soap magazines, ad infinitum. The texts present this phenomenon as the wondrous perpetual motion machine of the market— goods beget more goods. But now the machine is producing complementary ills and collateral damages instead.

Suggestive of this new dynamic is a pesticide plant in Richmond, California, which is owned by a transnational corporation that also makes the breast cancer drug tamoxifen. Many researchers believe that pesticides, and the toxins created in the production of them, play a role in breast cancer. "It's a pretty good deal," a local physician told the East Bay Express, a Bay Area weekly. "First you cause the cancer, then you profit from curing it." Both the alleged cause and cure make the GDP go up, and this syndrome has become a central dynamic of growth in the U.S. today.

Mainstream economists would argue that this is all beside the point. If people didn't have to spend money on such things as commuting or medical costs, they'd simply spend it on something else, they say. Growth would be the same or even greater, so the actual content of growth should be of little concern to those who promote it. That view holds sway in the nation's policy councils; as a result we try continually to grow our way out of problems, when increasingly we are growing our way in.

To the extent conventional economics has raised an eyebrow at growth, it has done so mainly through the concept of "externalities." These are negative side effects suffered by those not party to a transaction between a buyer and a seller. Man buys car, car pollutes air, others suffer that "externality." As the language implies, anything outside the original transaction is deemed secondary, a subordinate reality, and therefore easily overlooked. More, the effects upon buyer and seller—the "internalities" one might say—are assumed to be good.

Today however that mental schema is collapsing. Externalities are starting to overwhelm internalities. A single jet ski can cause more misery for the people who reside by a lake, than it gives pleasure to the person riding it.

More importantly, and as just discussed, internalities themselves are coming into question, and with them the assumption of choice, which is the moral linchpin of market thought.

If people choose what they buy, as market theory posits, then—externalities aside—the sum total of all their buying must be the greatest good of all. That's the ideology behind the GDP. But if people don't always choose, then the model starts to fall apart, which is what is happening today. The practical implications are obvious. If growth consists increasingly of problems rather than solutions, then scolding people for consuming too much is barking up the wrong tree. It is possible to talk instead about ridding our lives of what we don't want as well as forsaking what we do want—or think we want.

Politically this is a more promising path. But to where? The economy may be turning into a kind of round robin of difficulty and affliction, but we are all tied to the game. The sickness industry employs a lot of people, as do ad agencies and trash haulers. The fastest-growing occupations in the country include debt collectors and prison guards. What would we do without our problems and dysfunctions?

The problem is especially acute for those at the bottom of the income scale who have not shared much in the apparent prosperity. For them, a bigger piece of a bad pie might be better than none.

This is the economic conundrum of our age. No one has more than pieces of an answer, but it helps to see that much growth today is really an optical illusion created by accounting tricks. The official tally ignores totally the cost side of the growth ledger—the toll of traffic upon our time and health for example. In fact, it actually counts such costs as growth and gain. By the same token, the official tally ignores the economic contributions of the natural environment and the social structure; so that the more the economy destroys these, and puts commoditized substitutes in their places, the more the experts say the economy has "grown." Pollute the lakes and oceans so that people have to join private swim clubs and the economy grows. Erode the social infrastructure of community so people have to buy services from the market instead of getting help from their neighbors, and it grows some more. The real economy—the one that sustains us—has diminished. All that has grown is the need to buy commoditized substitutes for things we used to have for free.

So one might rephrase the question thus: how do we achieve real growth, as opposed to the statistical illusion that passes for growth today? Four decades ago, John Kenneth Galbraith argued in *The Affluent Society* that conventional economic reasoning is rapidly becoming obsolete. An economics based upon scarcity simply doesn't work in an economy of hyper-abundance, he said. If it takes a $200 billion (today) advertising industry to maintain what economists quaintly call "demand," then perhaps that demand isn't as urgent as conventional theory posits. Perhaps it's not even demand in any sane meaning of the word.

Galbraith argued that genuine economy called for shifting some resources from consumption that needs to be prodded, to needs which are indisputably great:

schools, parks, older people, the inner cities and the like. For this he was skewered as a proto-socialist. Yet today the case is even stronger, as advertisers worm into virtually every waking moment in a desperate effort to keep the growth machine on track.

Galbraith was arguing for a larger public sector. But that brings dysfunctions of its own, such as bureaucracy; and it depends upon an enlarging private sector as a fiscal base to begin with. Today we need to go further, and establish new ground rules for the economy, so that it produces more genuine growth on its own. We also need to find ways to revive the nonmarket economy of informal community exchange, so that people do not need money to meet every single life need.

In the first category, environmental fiscal policy can help. While the corporate world has flogged workers to be more productive, resources such as petroleum have been in effect loafing on the job. If we used these more efficiently the result could be jobs and growth, even in conventional terms, with less environmental pollution. If we used land more efficiently—that is, reduced urban sprawl—the social and environmental gains would be great.

Another ground rule is the corporate charter laws. We need to restore these to their original purpose: to keep large business organizations within the compass of the common good. But such shifts can do only so much. More efficient cars might simply encourage more traffic, for example. Cheap renewable power for electronic devices could encourage more noise. In other words, the answer won't just be a more efficient version of what we do now. Sooner or later we'll need different ways of thinking about work and growth and how we allocate the means of life.

This is where the social economy comes in, the informal exchange between neighbors and friends. There are some promising trends. One is the return to the traditional village model in housing. Structure does affect content. When houses are close together, and people can walk to stores and work, it encourages the spontaneous social interaction that nurtures real community. New local currencies, such as Time Dollars, provide a kind of lattice work upon which informal nonmarket exchange can take root and grow.

Changes like these are off the grid of economics as conventionally defined. It took centuries for the market to emerge from the stagnation of feudalism. The next organizing principle, whatever it is, most likely will emerge slowly as well. This much we can say with certainty. As the market hurtles towards multiple implosions, social and environmental as well as financial, it is just possible that the economics profession is going to have to do what it constantly lectures the rest of us to do: adjust to new realities and show a willingness to change. ❑

# Chapter 2

# MACROECONOMIC MEASUREMENT

## INTRODUCTION

**M**ost macroeconomics textbooks begin with a snapshot of today's economy as seen through the standard measures of economic performance. This chapter provides a different view of today's economy, one far more critical of current economic policy and performance, one that asks what the standard measures of economic performance really tell us and what they might be missing.

Zoe Sherman (Article 2.1) turns Ronald Reagan's famous 1980 presidential debate question—"Are you better off than you were four years ago?"— into a look at the changes in the quality of life in the United States in recent decades. She asks whether we're better off as a society than we were forty years ago. Certainly, per capita income is higher (as mainstream economists would define being "better off"), but we also have rising inequality, increased burdens of work, greater insecurity, and serious problems of environmental sustainability.

Increases in real gross domestic product (GDP) define economic growth and, for most economists, rising real GDP per capita shows that a nation's standard of living is improving. But our authors are not convinced. The next two articles focus on critiques of GDP. Feminist economist Nancy Folbre zeroes in on the exclusion of household labor and production from official government economic accounts, and how this distorts both our understanding of the economy and the policies governing it (Article 2.2). Alejandro Reuss summarizes the three main lines of criticism, focusing on the failure of GDP to take into account income distribution, environmental quality, and non-market production (Article 2.3).

The next article focuses on an alternative way to measure economic performance, by considering the economy a means of achieving social goals rather than treating economic activity as an end in itself. Reuss (Article 2.4) describes the ins and outs of the Human Development Index (HDI), the United Nations Development Programme's alternative to GDP as a single-number measure of economic well-being.

John Miller shows how the official (or "headline") unemployment rate understates the extent of unemployment. Correcting the headline rate for underemployed workers and discouraged job-seekers, unemployment has remained unusually high even years after the beginning of the current "recovery" (Article 2.5).

Miller then pivots from unemployment to recent controversies about how to measure inflation (Article 2.6). When government benefits are adjusted to keep pace with the rising cost of living, the version of the Consumer Price Index (CPI) used has a big impact on real people. Miller argues that using the "chained CPI" for benefits like Social Security would hurt seniors, and would make less sense than using new price indices geared specifically to seniors' spending patterns.

## Discussion Questions

1. (Article 2.1) What aspects of well-being does Sherman think are not very well captured by looking at economic growth alone?

2. (Article 2.2) In Folbre's view, how has the failure to count household labor and production in official economic data had negative consequences, both on our economic understanding and economic policies?

3. (Article 2.3) How is GDP measured, and what does it represent? What are the three main criticisms of GDP described by Reuss? Do you find them convincing?

4. (Articles 2.4) How does the HDI differ from GDP per capita? What problems of GDP as a measure of well-being does the HDI attempt to overcome? How successful do you think the HDI is in overcoming these problems?

5. (Article 2.5) Is the overall unemployment rate a deceptive measure of economic hardship? What would be a better measure?

6. (Article 2.6) Miller acknowledges that, when the price of a product goes up, people tend to buy less of it, often substituting another product. Why, then, does he disagree with the proposal to use the "chained CPI" (which takes this into account) to index government benefits like Social Security?

*Article 2.1*

# WHAT DOES IT MEAN TO BE "BETTER OFF"?

*Taking stock of how U.S. society has progressed or faltered over the last forty years.*

## BY ZOE SHERMAN
*November/December 2014*

In 1980, Ronald Reagan, trying to defeat Jimmy Carter's bid for a second term as president, asked, "Are you better off than you were four years ago?" A conservative turn in American politics was already underway and, campaigning on that question, Reagan rode the wave into the presidency. Forty years into the political epoch he symbolizes, and forty years into this magazine's history, we might well echo Reagan's question: Are you better off than you were forty years ago?

It is a deceptively simple question. What would it mean to be better off? Probably a lot of good things and a lot of bad things have happened to you in forty years (or however many of those years you've been alive) and to decide whether you are better off you would have to do some weighing. For many of us the final answer would be, "well, yes and no…" For any one person many of the then-vs.-now differences are largely a matter of the life cycle—maybe you were a child decades ago and an adult now. It really makes more sense to ask whether we as a society are better off that we were forty years ago.

The well-being of a society cannot be measured in a single dimension any more than a single person's well-being can. Assessments of our national well-being often begin—and too often end—with gross domestic product (GDP). Per capita GDP basically answers the question, "Are we collectively, on average, richer, as measured by the dollar value of the things we produce and sell to one another?" (This includes the government's provision of goods and services, even if they are not really "sold.")

Not only is GDP limited to measuring just one dimension of well-being—it doesn't even measure that dimension all that well. It fails to count the work we do for one another at home or in other non-monetized ways. It gives us only an aggregate with no information about how access to all those goods and services is distributed. And goods and bads get added together so long as they cost money and therefore generate income for someone—that is, a thousand dollars spent on cigarettes and treatments for emphysema add just as much to GDP as a thousand dollars spent on healthy foods and preventive medicine.

We'll certainly want to go beyond just GDP per capita, as we take a tour through various dimensions of well-being and take stock of how we have progressed or faltered over the last forty years.

## Income and Stuff

Though we know from the outset that we will not stop here, we may as well start in the traditional starting place: Changes in our national income, taking into account population growth and inflation. Real per capita GDP was $25,427 in 1974 (in 2009 U.S. dollars) and now it is almost double that at $49,810. A lot of that GDP growth represents more of the good stuff we already had in 1974 or cool, well-being-enhancing new stuff that we have now but didn't have then. I really like having a dishwasher and enough dishes that we don't have to wash the plates and forks after every meal (more of the already-invented good stuff). I am also awfully fond of my computer, Internet service, DVDs, and streaming video (cool new stuff).

But some of the higher production/higher income measured by GDP represents not-so-great things. Longer car commutes, for example, are costly and contribute to GDP through spending on gasoline, car repairs and replacement, and purchases of more cars per household. But long car commutes add nothing and likely subtract from the commuters' well-being. They also add pollutants to the air that affect us all.

Even if we subtract out the bads, the goods themselves can get to be too much of a good thing. Plenty of people know the experience of feeling that they are choking on stuff, crowded out of their living spaces by their belongings. Self storage ranks as the fastest growing segment of the commercial real estate industry since 1975. Self storage businesses brought in revenues of $24 billion dollars in 2013. Now, consider that the average size of a new single family home increased 57% from 1970 to the early 2000s. That means we spent $24 billion to store the things that we can't fit in our homes, even though many of our homes are bigger than ever! (See the interview with Juliet Schor in the September/October 2014 issue for a discussion of how we get trapped in this self-destructive overconsumption cycle.)

## Economic and Social Inequality

If the distribution of income had remained roughly the same over the last forty years, then the fact that per capita GDP nearly doubled would mean that everyone's income had nearly doubled. That's not what happened. Instead, those at the top of the income distribution have vastly more income than 40 years ago while those at the bottom have less. The real income of a household at the 20th percentile (above 20% of all households in the income ranking) has scarcely budged since 1974—it was $20,000 and change then and is $20,000 and change now. For those below the 20th percentile, real income has fallen. The entire bottom 80% of households ranked by income now gets only 49% of the national pie, down from 57% in 1974. That means that the top 20% has gone from 43% to 51% of total income. Even within the top 20%, the distribution skews upward. Most of the income gains of the top 20% are concentrated in the top 5%; most of the gains of the top 5% are concentrated in the top 1%; most of the gains in the top 1% are concentrated in the top 0.1%.

By 1974, labor force participation rates were in the midst of a marked upward trend, driven largely by the entry of women into the paid labor force. Starting from a low of 59% in the early 1960s, the labor force participation rate passed 61% in 1974 and peaked at 67% in the late 1990s. Labor force participation has drifted back downward somewhat since then through a combination of baby boomer retirement and discouraged workers giving up on the labor force since the crisis that began in 2007, but it remains at 63%, still higher than in 1974. That means that even while more of us are participating in market work, the market is concentrating its rewards in a shrinking cabal of increasingly powerful hands.

More of us are working, but the share of national income that goes to ordinary workers is smaller. National income can be sorted into categories based on the route it takes to a person's pocket. One category of income—wages and salaries earned in return for work—is labor income. The other categories—profit, dividends, rent, interest—are all forms of income that result from owning. For many decades, the labor share of national income held fairly steady, but beginning in the mid-1970s it started falling. Economist James Heintz found that the share of the national income earned as private-business-sector wages (excluding executive compensation) fell from 58% in 1970 to 50% in 2010; the share that went to non-supervisory workers fell from 45% to 31%.

Even as hourly pay for a broad swath of people in the middle—between the 20th and 80th percentiles—has just about kept pace with inflation, the traditional tickets to the middle class have become more of a reach. Rising costs of higher education and housing have consigned many to a near-permanent state of debt peonage to maintain a tenuous grasp on middle-class social status, while others are blocked from access entirely.

While more employers now require a college degree before letting a job applicant set foot on the bottom rung of the career ladder, college tuitions have risen more than three times as fast as inflation since 1974. The total volume of outstanding student debt has passed $1 trillion—greater than even the volume of outstanding credit card debt.

Housing, too, has become more unaffordable. For white people who bought houses in the mid 20th century with the benefits of supportive government policies, a home was a secure form of both savings and shelter. (Discriminatory neighborhood redlining prevented most nonwhites from enjoying these benefits.) Within recent decades, however, home prices have risen faster than median incomes and deceptive lending practices trapped many home-buyers in unaffordable mortgages. For those who were lucky, and bought and sold at the right times, the housing bubble was a windfall. For many more, the home has become a millstone of debt and the threat of foreclose has rendered shelter uncertain.

The division of the national income pie may be more skewed, but do we all have an equal shot at finding our way into the charmed circle of plenty? The probability that a person who starts out in the bottom income quintile will make it into the top quintile has stayed remarkably constant since the mid twentieth century. A child born in the bottom quintile in 1971 had an 8.4% chance of making it to the top quintile; for a child born in 1986, the probability is 9.0%. Our national mythology notwithstanding, mobility is lower in the United States than in other comparably developed economies.

Now for some good news: although wealth and income disparities have worsened, we have made real strides in reducing disparities based on race and gender. Long-standing identity-based hierarchies have weakened, though they certainly have not disappeared. The narrowing of race and gender gaps in economic well-being owes everything to the social movements of the twentieth century. The gaps' persistence can be attributed both to differential impacts of ostensibly race- or gender-neutral policies and to our low levels of social mobility. The war on drugs and other "get tough on crime" polices really mean the mass incarceration of black men. "Welfare reform" withdrew much of whatever limited support there was for the intense labor—mostly women's—of raising children with minimal cash resources. Even as bigotry, in several forms, has lost explicit government sanction, the lack of social mobility casts the shadow of the more explicit inequities of the past longer and deeper.

Not only is income unequally distributed, it is also, for many, insecure. Having income is a good thing and helps to meet present needs. If there's some left over, present income might even help meet future needs. But confidence in future income

## Narrowing Race and Gender Gaps

The Civil Rights Movement, which achieved many of its judicial and legislative successes between 1954 (Brown v. Board of Education) and 1965 (Voting Rights Act), and the Women's Movement, whose judicial and legislative successes followed soon after (Title IX in 1972; Roe v. Wade in 1973) have reduced the role of outright, explicit discrimination. This is no small matter. Yet there are still wide gaps between white and nonwhite, especially black Americans in measures of economic well-being, and also gaps between men and women of all races.

|  | White Men | White Women | Black Men | Black Women |
|---|---|---|---|---|
| 1974 Median Income (in 2013 dollars) | 38,517 | 13,944 | 23,372 | 11,988 |
| 2013 Median Income (in 2013 dollars) | 40,122 | 23,780 | 24,855 | 20,044 |
| 1974 Unemployment rate | 3.5% | 5.1% | 7.4% | 8.8% |
| 2013 Unemployment rate | 6.2% | 5.7% | 12.9% | 11.3% |

*Sources:* Median income: Census Bureau, Current Population Survey, Table P02 (census.gov); Unemployment: Bureau of Labor Statistics (bls.gov).

The resources that would close the racial income gap are hard for individuals and families to come by. There is a strong correlation between educational attainment and future earnings, but black children on average get less from their public schools than white children get. The racial income gap has narrowed slightly between

matters to us a lot. We worry about whether we will be able to meet our needs tomorrow—and we have more reasons to worry now than ever.

Employment is a sometime thing: Workers on short-term contracts—like the majority of undergraduate college instructors who work on an adjunct basis—and the self-employed, whose income is also unpredictable, add up to 30% of the U.S. workforce with uncertain, episodic income. (See Gerald Friedman, "The Gig Economy," *D&S*, March/April 2014.) It is difficult to know exactly how the current level of job insecurity compares to 1974 because the Census Bureau only began systematic data collection on contingent labor in 1995. Median job tenure (years with one's current employer) has fallen for men over the past generation, though it has risen for women. Perhaps the feeling of greater insecurity is a result of men's paid work coming to resemble the precariousness of women's paid work, even while many families still think of a man's income as the mainstay.

The constant churn of a short-term-employment labor system means that for most who fall into poverty, poverty is not a permanent condition. By the mid-1970s, a decade into the War on Poverty, the poverty rate had fallen to 11%, but the reduction was not sustained. Since then, the poverty rate has fluctuated between 11% and 15% with no consistent long-term trend. Today, we are in a high poverty phase: somewhere in the neighborhood of 15% of the population is living in poverty during

1974 and now, but the median white household still has more than six times the wealth of the median nonwhite or Hispanic household. Low wealth reduces nonwhite families' ability to buy housing in better-funded public school districts or invest in college education—or in private K-12 substitutes if the public schools available to them are sub-par.

People with criminal convictions, once released, face enormous barriers to employment. For the more than one-in-six black men who have been incarcerated (a rate six times that for white men), a criminal record consigns them to the margins of the labor market. In some states, moreover, a felony conviction results in a permanent loss of voting rights and therefore the loss of one of the most powerful tools for political change.

The story for the gender gap in economic well-being is mixed. Women earn lower average incomes and suffer higher poverty rates than men (despite now graduating from college in greater numbers than men). But the female unemployment rate is, on average, lower than for men, and it has become less volatile; in the last few business-cycle downturns men have been more at risk of job loss than women.

|  | White Individuals | Black Individuals | White Households, no adult male present | Black Households, no adult male present |
|---|---|---|---|---|
| 1974 Poverty Rate | 7.7% | 30.3% | 24.6% | 55.7% |
| 2013 Poverty Rate | 9.6% | 27.2% | 22.9% | 42.4% |

**Source:** Census Bureau, Historical Poverty Data, Table 2 (census.gov).

any given month. While most spells of poverty last well under a year (6.6 months is the median), a large minority of the population cycles in and out of poverty. From January 2009 to December 2011, 31.6% of the population spent at least two consecutive months below the poverty line.

Families can fall into poverty for a number of reasons. Loss of employment, certainly, is a major cause. Another common precipitating event is the birth of a child—without guaranteed paid family leave, childbirth often means a simultaneous increase in household size (and expenses) and decrease in income. Health problems are another trigger for economic distress. Medical bills are the number-one cause of personal bankruptcy; even those who have health insurance may be unable to pay for their medical care. Insecurity is our constant companion.

## What Money Can't Buy

Many measures of our well-being cannot be viewed through the lens of income and the consumer spending it enables. A full life is not just made of purchased goods. Some of the most important gains in well-being are about the political and social gains achieved by social movements countering sexism and racism. The Civil Rights and Women's Liberation movements helped achieve an increase in economic well-being, sure, but also an increase in dignity and political power.

In the mid-1970s, marriage was still a strikingly unequal contract that subordinated wives to husbands. (Same-sex marriage was not permitted anywhere in the United States. Though there were already legal cases on the issue in the early 1970s, the courts upheld same-sex marriage bans.) The criminal laws did not grant married women a right to sexual autonomy and did little to protect their physical or emotional safety; rape laws contained exemptions in the case of husbands, and domestic violence was largely hidden from view. But change was beginning. The Women's Movement brought attention to gender-based violence and built a network of support for survivors; the earliest rape crisis centers and emergency shelters are now marking their fortieth anniversaries, taking stock of the considerable progress we've made, and pressing on with the work that still needs to be done. By 1993, all states had changed their rape laws, withdrawing a husband's unlimited sexual access to his wife's body. In 1994, President Clinton signed into law the Violence Against Women Act, which devotes federal resources to the investigation and prosecution of violent crimes targeting women. Indeed, marriage contracts are now legally symmetrical (even if marriage is not yet symmetrical in practice)—and 33 states license marriages between any two unrelated adults, regardless of sex.

Not only are women safer at home than we were forty years ago, we have also claimed larger roles outside the home. Amendments made in 1972 to the Civil Rights Act expanded legal prohibitions on sex discrimination, including the Title IX provision prohibiting educational institutions receiving federal financial assistance from discriminating on the basis of sex. Protections against workplace discrimination are also stronger—the term "sexual harassment," unknown in 1974, is now recognized as describing a form of discrimination that can carry serious legal consequences. In the political arena, the number of women in Congress has more than tripled since the mid-seventies. Prior to 1974, only four women had ever served as state governors. Since then, 32 more women have held that office.

Important work combating racial discrimination was also underway forty years ago. The Equal Employment Opportunity Commission, responsible for enforcing the Civil Rights Act in the workplace, was not yet a decade old in 1974, still early in the process of setting legal precedent for documenting and opposing workplace discrimination, including the disguised discrimination of disparate impact (when a seemingly neutral rule disproportionately affects members of a protected group). The battle to make banks' mortgage lending data public was won in the mid-1970s, which then allowed organized (and ongoing) opposition to the "redlining" that the publicized data revealed. Twenty years after *Brown v. Board of Education* prohibited explicit, legally mandated school segregation, education activists in the mid-1970s pushed governments to take a more proactive role in school integration, albeit with mixed and in many places only temporary results.

## A Time for Every Matter

The good life for most of us means not just money to buy the stuff we need, but also plenty of time off the job to participate in social and civic life and to rest. The inequities of the labor market have divided us into two categories—the overworked and the underemployed. For those with consistent employment, the work is often too much work. Even as output per worker hour rises—meaning that, as a society we could increase our material standard of living while holding leisure time steady, or hold our material standard of living steady while increasing leisure time, we have instead increased average work hours per year. Hours of paid labor per employee were about the same in 2000 as in 1973, but since more people were in the paid labor force, the average number of hours per working age person rose from 1,217 to 1,396, equivalent to a full extra month of forty-hour workweeks.

One consequence is that we have a leisure shortage. Chronic sleep deprivation has become the norm. According to a study by the National Academy of Sciences, Americans' average amount of sleep fell by 20% over the course of the 20th century. Meanwhile, the unemployed and underemployed have hours on their hands that they either spend job hunting, in the endless sequence of bureaucratic tasks necessary to access the meager benefits available through the threadbare social safety net, or idle, their unclaimed hours more a burden than a gift. The supposed benefit of unemployment—leisure time to mitigate the loss of income—is not in evidence in the subjective well-being of the unemployed, who are more likely to suffer depression and family stress.

The time crunch resulting from more hours of paid work also squeezes our ability to keep up with the necessary unpaid work at home. Sociologist Arlie Hochschild was already noting in her research during the 1980s that dual-income households were giving up leisure or letting the standards of housework and at-home caregiving slip—often a mix of both. When a stay-at-home mother goes out to work for pay and reduces her hours of home production, the household's increase in cash income gets added to GDP but the household's loss of unpaid labor time is not subtracted. Or, if she hires a housecleaning service and a babysitter, the wages earned by the mother, the housecleaner, and the babysitter all get added to GDP, but the work done by the housecleaner and babysitter are substituting for unpaid work that was already being done. Correcting for the loss of home production that has accompanied the rise in female participation in the paid labor force requires us to revise downward the increase in output over the period 1959–2004—the largest hit came between 1959 and 1972 with the withdrawal of about 500 hours of household labor per year, a reduction of almost 20%.

## Common Resources and Public Goods

Just as mothers' labor is treated by official measures as a freely available resource, so are the gifts of nature. Nature is the source of the resources our lives depend on—trace back any production process and the earth's resources are there at the origin. Nature is also the sink into which all the refuse and byproducts of our production get dumped. Environmental concerns were at the core of another one of the 1970s' mass social movements. The first Earth Day was celebrated in 1970, and the Environmental Protection Agency (EPA) was created that same year. Concerns and activism around air pollution, water pollution, and the loss of biodiversity led, over the course of the 1970s, to the Clean Air, Clean Water, and Endangered Species Acts. Since the 1970s, the harms of an automotive culture have been lessened with emissions standards, fuel-efficiency standards, and the ban on leaded gasoline. Municipal recycling programs now divert tons of materials back into the human production cycle, reducing the strains on the planet as both a source of materials and as a sink for waste products.

---

### Private Wealth, Public Squalor

Just as we are depleting the gifts of nature, we are depleting or withdrawing many of the gifts we have collectively bestowed on ourselves, our publicly provided goods. We are consuming our public infrastructure—as seen dramatically in the 2004 failure of the levies in New Orleans during Hurricane Katrina and in the 2007 collapse of a bridge in Minneapolis.

Public goods can only be sustained if we each contribute. If we don't trust one another to contribute, we each feel the need to hoard our resources privately. When we hoard our resources privately, we discourage others from contributing, and our public goods wither.

The hoarding is especially extreme at the top of the income distribution. The top marginal tax rate has fallen from 70% in the 1970s to less than 40% today. The money not put into the common kitty instead pays for private substitutes—private schools (instead of public), private clubs (instead of public parks), gated communities (instead of neighborhoods that welcome visitors), and private security to defend these private goods against the claims of those who are excluded.

---

Over the past 40 years, we have made some important gains in how we make use of the gifts of nature, but our gains are nowhere near enough. Probably the most disastrous shortcoming of all is our collective failure to maintain the atmospheric balance. Since the middle of the twentieth century, we have known that an increased concentration of carbon dioxide ($CO_2$) in the atmosphere will cause dangerous climate change. Despite that, we have continued to emit $CO_2$ at a staggering rate. Even if we were to stop tomorrow, the effects on the global climate would play out at an accelerating rate for centuries. Several of the destabilizing shifts—melting of the polar ice caps, thawing of the arctic permafrost—are only in the early stages of "positive feedback loops," in which the result of some warming triggers more warming. Rising sea levels threaten coastal cities around the world. Severe storms will continue to increase in frequency. Wider year-to-year variations in temperature and rainfall will disrupt food production.

## Looking Backward, Looking Forward

When Reagan asked, "Are you better off than you were four years ago?" he predicted that many people would say "no" and that those who answered "no" would vote for change (not necessarily the kinds of change, as it turns out, that would solve their problems). We are still in the era that Reagan helped to usher in. How is it working for us? Are we better off now, or is it time for a change?

We have seen average income rise, though not as fast as it had in the post-World War II era. Many of the most important gains we have made, moreover, are not dependent on rising average income. The achievements of the Civil Rights and Women's Movements were about dismantling barriers to full participation in a society wealthy enough that it already could provide for all. Now rising income inequality is throwing up new barriers to inclusion.

There are enough ways in which we have lost ground that it must be time for a change. Not a change back—I would not trade the real gains we've made for a return to the so-called "Golden Age" of the 1940s-1970s—but a change that can carry us forward to a world we will still want to live in forty years from now.

The environmental crisis means that continuing with business as usual would sink us soon. Salvation can only come with a turn away from the fetish of GDP growth. About 40 years ago, research began systematically documenting the failure of rising average income to keep delivering rising levels of happiness (a phenomenon known as the "Easterlin paradox," for researcher Richard Easterlin). Unorthodox economists rethought the growth imperative: E.F. Schumacher wrote *Small is Beautiful* and Herman Daly penned *Steady-State Economics*. The kingdom of Bhutan famously rejected GDP and instituted instead the measurement of Gross National Happiness. All urged a turn away from defining well-being according to money incomes.

Once a society reaches a level of income that overcomes deprivation—when nobody need go hungry or homeless, nor suffer or die from preventable disease—more income has little affect on the dimensions of well-being that have intrinsic value.

Instead we must turn toward maximizing equality. In their book *The Spirit Level*, Richard Wilkinson and Kate Pickett demonstrate how consistently the empirical evidence shows that more equal societies have better social outcomes in many dimensions: including longer life expectancy, better educational outcomes, stronger environmental protection, lower rates of incarceration, obesity, and teen pregnancy. Perhaps—after forty more years of trying and failing to find our way to well-being through more and more market activity, in a quest for more and more income, which has been distributed more and more unequally—we are finally ready to set our priorities straight. It is equality and environmental sustainability that will allow for human flourishing. ❑

*Sources:* Self Storage Association (selfstorage.org); Margot Adler, "Behind the Ever-Expanding American Dream House," National Public Radio (npr.org); U.S. Census Bureau, Current Population Survey, Tables H-1 and H-2 (census.gov); Bureau of Labor Statistics, CPI Detailed Report, Data for August 2014 (bls.gov); Case-Shiller Home Price Index (us.spindices.com); Census Bureau, Table H-8 (census.gov); Jim Tankersley, "Economic mobility hasn't changed in a half-century in America, economists declare," *Washington Post*, Jan. 23, 2014 (washingtonpost. com); The Equality of Opportunity Project (equality-of-opportunity.org); U.S. Census 2012 Statistical Abstract, Table 721 (census.gov); NAACP, Criminal Justice Fact Sheet (naacp.org); Ibby Caputo, "Paying the Bills One Gig at a Time," WGBH, Feb. 1, 2012 (wgbh.org); Bureau of Labor Statistics, "Employee Tenure in 2014" (bls.gov); Ashley N. Edwards, "Dynamics of Economic Well-Being: Poverty, 2009-2011," Report Number: P70-137, January 2014 (census.gov); Moms Rising, Maternity/Paternity Leave (momsrising.org); Dan Mangan, "Medical Bills Are the Biggest Cause of US Bankruptcies: Study," CNBC, June 25, 2013 (cnbc.com); Christina LaMontagne, "NerdWallet Health finds Medical Bankruptcy accounts for majority of personal bankruptcies," March 26, 2014 (nerdwallet.com); Juliet Schor, "Sustainable Consumption and Worktime Reduction," *Journal of Industrial Ecology*, 2005; Edward Wolff, Ajit Zacharias, and Thomas Masterson, "Long-Term Trends in the Levy Institute Measure of Economic Well-Being (LIMEW), United States, 1959-2004," Levy Economics Institute of Bard College (levyinstitute.org); Nancy Folbre, *The Invisible Heart*, Chapter 3: "Measuring Success" (New Press, 2001); Environmental Protection Agency, "Earth Day and EPA History" (epa.gov); Environmental Protection Agency, Laws and Executive Orders (epa.gov).

*Article 2.2*

# HOUSEHOLD LABOR, CARING LABOR, UNPAID LABOR

## AN INTERVIEW WITH NANCY FOLBRE
*September/October 2015*

**N**ancy Folbre is a professor emerita of economics at the University of Massachusetts-Amherst. She is the author of numerous books, including Who Pays for the Kids? Gender and the Structures of Constraint *(1994),* The Invisible Heart: Economics and Family Values *(2001), and* Valuing Children: Rethinking the Economics of the Family *(2008), related to household and caring labor.*

**Dollars & Sense**: You've written about the tendency in economics to view household labor (and especially women's labor) as "unproductive." Can you explain how this is reflected in conventional macroeconomic measures?

**Nancy Folbre:** Non-market household services such as meal preparation and childcare are not considered part of what we call "the economy." This means they literally don't count as part of Gross Domestic Product, household income, or household consumption.

This is pretty crazy, since we know that these services contribute to our living standards and also to the development of human capabilities. They are all at least partially fungible: time and money may not be perfect substitutes, but there is clearly a trade-off. You can, in principle, pay someone to prepare your meals (as you do in a restaurant), or to look after your kids.

If you or someone else in your household provides these services for no charge (even if they expect something in return, such as a share of household earnings) that leaves more earnings available to buy other things. In fact, you could think of household income after taxes and after needs for domestic services have been met as a more meaningful definition of "disposable income" than the conventional definition, which is simply market income after taxes.

**D&S:** What is the practical consequence of not measuring household labor and production? Are economic policies and institutions different, especially in their impact on women, than what they would be if household labor were fully reflected in statistics on total employment or output?

**NF:** One macroeconomic consequence is a tendency to overstate economic growth when activities shift from an arena in which they are unpaid to one in which they are paid (all else equal). When mothers of young children enter paid employment, for instance, they reduce the amount of time they engage in unpaid work, but that reduction goes unmeasured. All that is counted is the increase in earnings that results, along with the increase in expenditures on services such as paid childcare.

As a result, rapid increases in women's labor force participation, such as those typical in the United States between about 1960 and the mid-1990s, tend to boost the rate of growth of GDP. When women's labor force participation levels out, as it has in the United States since the mid 1990s, the rate of growth of GDP slows down. At least some part of the difference in growth rates over these two periods simply reflects the increased "countability" of women's work.

Consideration of the microeconomic consequences helps explain this phenomenon. When households collectively supply more labor hours to the market, their market incomes go up. But they have to use a substantial portion of those incomes to purchase substitutes for services they once provided on their own—spending more money on meals away from home (or pre-prepared foods), and child care. So, the increase in their money incomes overstates the improvement in their genuinely disposable income.

A disturbing example of policy relevance emerges from consideration of the changes in public assistance to single mothers implemented in the United States in 1996, which put increased pressure on these mothers to engage in paid employment. Many studies proclaimed the success because market income in many of these families went up. But much of that market income had to be spent paying for services such as child care, because public provision and subsidies fell short.

**D&S:** You've also written extensively about "caring labor"? What is caring labor? To what extent is this labor (and the output of services associated with it) directly or indirectly captured by conventional measures like GDP?

**NF:** Everything I've discussed above is about quantity. But quality is also important. I define caring labor as labor where the quality of the services provided is likely to be affected by concern for the well-being of the care recipient. Love, affection, and commitment almost always enhance the care of dependents, and this is a big reason why market-provided services are not always perfect substitutes for those provided by family members and friends.

On the other hand, many people—especially women—work in occupations like child care, elder care, education, medicine, or social services where they genuinely care about their clients or "consumers." The market value of this work is counted as part of Gross Domestic Product and household income. But in many cases, the wage paid is considerably less than the value of the services provided. Workers in these jobs often give more in the way of quality than they are actually paid for.

**D&S:** As a practical matter, how could one go about measuring the value of services currently provided by unpaid household labor? In your estimation, how would our picture of economic life change if we did?

**NF:** It is pretty easy to estimate a lower-bound for the value of unpaid work by counting the number of hours that people spend engaging in it (which in the United States adds up to almost exactly the same total as hours of market work), and multiplying those hours times the hourly wage one would pay for a replacement.

Measures of hours worked in different activities such as meal preparation, child care, cleaning, shopping, and so on are typically based on a nationally representative survey of individuals who report all of their activities on the preceding day. The American Time Use Survey, administered since 2003 on an annual basis as a supplement to the Current Population Survey, provides reliable, high-quality data on time use.

Several studies have used these data to assign a dollar value to non-market work in what is called a "satellite" national income account (because it revolves around, rather than replacing the conventional account). Obviously, including this value in a measure of "extended GDP" makes the economy look bigger. More importantly, it revises estimates of how the economy has grown over time—in the downward direction.

Counting the value of non-market work has an equalizing effect on measures of household income, not because low-income households do a lot more of it, but because most households of similar size and composition do about the same amount. Here again, the trends are more interesting than the levels: since the relative importance of non-market work has declined over time, its equalizing effect has probably also declined. ❑

*Article 2.3*

# GDP AND ITS DISCONTENTS

## BY ALEJANDRO REUSS
*April 2013*

Economists have been thinking for a long time about what it means for a country or its people to be rich or poor. That was one of the main questions Adam Smith, the British philosopher often described as the "father of modern economics," took on in his most famous book *The Wealth of Nations* (1776). At the very outset, Smith made a point of defining the "real wealth" of a country as consisting in the "annual produce of the land and labour of the society." (Note that Smith was using the word "wealth" in a way that is closer to the colloquial meaning of the word than to its current technical meaning in economics. He was actually defining a country's income rather than its wealth.) That definition might seem uncontroversial now. Many economists would certainly respond that *of course* it's the production of goods and services that makes a country wealthy. But Smith had an important axe to grind. He was arguing against the view, widespread in his day, that a country's wealth consisted in the accumulation of gold and silver—an aim that led to a set of policies (especially promoting exports and suppressing imports) known as "mercantilism." In his own time, Smith was a maverick.

The kind of approach that Smith advocated, of counting up the total quantities of goods and services produced in a country in a year, is now a central part of macroeconomic measurement. When economists tabulate a country's gross domestic product (GDP), they're trying to measure the "annual produce ... of the society" more or less as Smith proposed. GDP attempts to add up the total value, counted in money units, of the goods and services produced within a country in the course of a year. This approach, while a big advance over the view that a country's wealth consisted primarily of its hoards of precious metals, however, is more problematic and controversial than it might appear at first glance. Economists and other social scientists have, in various ways, criticized the ways that GDP is counted and used as a measure of a country's "wealth" or "development." Here, we'll focus on three key critiques: 1) the distributional critique, 2) the feminist critique, and 3) the environmental critique. The first is really a criticism of the approach of looking at the total (or average) production of goods and services for a society as a whole, and ignoring the distribution of access among its members. The other two argue that GDP is misleading because it fails to count all goods and services (focusing narrowly on those that are easiest to put prices on).

## What is GDP Per Capita?

Gross domestic product (GDP) per capita is the standard measure of average income used by mainstream economists, and it has become widely used as a measure of economic well-being. Gross domestic product is a measure of the total value of all the goods and services produced in a country in a year, which we can also think of as the total incomes of all the people in that country. A country's total GDP is a very poor measure of how "rich" or "poor" its people are. A country can have a very high total income, even if the average income is low, just because it has a very high population. China, for example, now has the highest total income of any country in the world, even the United States. Its average income, however, is about one-sixth that of the United States, in terms of real purchasing power. China ranks so high in total income because it is the largest country (by population) in the world. By the same token, a country can have a very large average income, but have a low total income, because it has small population. Developed countries have relatively high levels of income per capita. The top twenty countries, by this measure, include thirteen European countries, the United States and two other British offshoots (Australia and Canada), and Japan. Two of the remaining three members of this exclusive list, Qatar and United Arab Emirates, are small, oil-rich countries.

This problem, unlike those spotlighted in the three critiques we'll discuss below, is easy to solve. Instead of stopping at total GDP, we can calculate a country's GDP per capita. The phrase "per capita" simply means per person. ("Capita" comes from the Latin word meaning "head," so "per capita" means "per head.") To get GDP per capita, we just divide a country's GDP by its population. This gives us the average GDP for that country, or a measure of the average income. (Other measures of a country's total income, such as Gross National Product or Gross National Income are similar to GDP, so GNP per capita or GNI per capita are similar to GDP per capita.) Income per capita gives us a better picture of the standards of living in a country than total income.

## What's Wrong with GDP Per Capita?

Mainstream economists and policymakers have treated increasing GDP per capita as virtually synonymous with development, so it's important to discuss GDP in more detail. Here, we will focus on three major criticisms of GDP per capita as a measure of well-being or "development":

### *The Distributional Critique*

Average income can be misleading. Average (mean) income is one estimate of the "middle" of the distribution of income in a country. Most people, however, do not get the average income. Most get less than the average, some get more (and a few get much, much more). A relatively small number of people with very high incomes can pull the average up by a great deal, making the average less representative of most people's standard of living.

Figure 1, for example, shows the income distribution for Brazil in 2007. The population has been ranked by income, and then divided into five equal parts (or quintiles). Each bar represents the difference between the average income for one of these quintiles and the average income for the country as a whole. The bar furthest to the left represents the difference between the average income of the lowest-income quintile and the overall average. The next bar represents this difference for the next-lowest-income quintile, and so on, all the way up to the bar at the far right, which represents this difference for the highest-income quintile. (The lowest-income quintile is called the "first" quintile, the next-to-lowest is called the "second" quintile, and so on, up to the highest-income, or "fifth," quintile.) The GDP per capita for Brazil in 2007 was about $9800. Notice that

**INCOME DISTRIBUTION, BRAZIL, 2007 (DIFFERENCE BETWEEN EACH
QUINTILE'S AVERAGE INCOME AND OVERALL AVERAGE INCOME)**

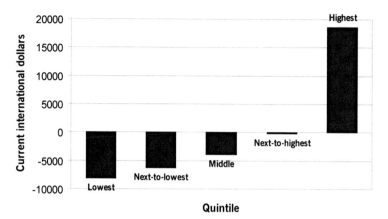

*Source:* World Bank, World Development Indicators: Income share held by lowest 20%, second 20%, third 20%, fourth 20%, highest 20%; GDP per capita, PPP (constant 2005 international $); GDP, PPP (constant 2005 international $) (data.worldbank.org/indicator).

the average income for each of the bottom four quintiles is less than the GDP per capita (or average income) for the society as a whole, as indicated by the bars extending down. The average income for Brazil as a whole is more than six times as much as the average income for the first (lowest-income) quintile, almost three times as much as the average income for the second quintile, and more than one-and-a-half times as much as the average income for the third quintile. Even the average income for the fourth quintile is a little less than the average income for the whole country (so many people in the fourth quintile have incomes below the national average, though some have incomes above it.)

More than two-thirds of Brazil's population, then, have incomes below the country's per capita income—many of them, far below it. The reason GDP per capita for Brazil is so much higher than the incomes of most Brazilians is that the income distribution is so unequal. The average income for the fifth (highest-income) quintile is almost three times the average income for Brazil as a whole.

## *The Feminist Critique*

GDP only counts part of the goods and services produced in a country. Earlier, we said that GDP was "a measure of the total value of goods and services" produced in a country. This is true, but it is a very flawed measure. GDP only includes the value of goods that are produced for sale in markets, ignoring goods and services that people produce for their own consumption, for the consumption of family members, and so on. In developed economies, most individuals or households have money incomes that allow them to buy most of the things they need to live. They also, however, produce goods and services for themselves, family members, and others. For example, people care for and educate their children, cook meals for themselves and other members of their family, clean their own homes, drive themselves and family members to work, school, and errands, and so on. These kinds of goods and services count as part of GDP when someone is paid to do them (for example, when we pay tuition to a school, the bill at a restaurant, the fee to a professional cleaning crew, or the fare to a taxi driver), but not when people do it for themselves, family members, or others free of charge. One could add many other examples, but the first lesson here is that GDP undercounts the total output of goods and services. Since so much of the labor that produces these uncounted goods and services is done by women, feminist economists have been in the forefront of this critique of GDP as a measure of economic development or well-being. (See Marilyn Waring, *If Women Counted: A New Feminist Economics* (Harper & Row, 1988).)

In some developing economies, the uncounted goods and services may form a larger part of the overall economy than in developed countries. Many people may have small farms and grow their own food. Some people weave their own cloth and make their own clothes. Some people build their own shelters. As economies "develop" economically, they may become more "monetized." This means that people produce fewer goods for their own consumption, for their families, or to trade for other goods (barter), relative to the total amount of goods and services. Instead, they start selling either goods they produce or selling their own labor for money, and buying the things they need. An increase in GDP over time may, in part, reflect an increasing output of goods and services. But it may also reflect, in part, that some goods went uncounted before (because they were not produced for sale in markets) and are now being counted. This means that GDP (or GDP per capita) may exaggerate the growth of economies over time.

### The Environmental Critique

GDP does not account for changes in the natural environment. We can think of parts of the natural environment as providing people with valuable "natural services." Until recently, economic measurement has almost completely ignored natural services. Once we start thinking about the environment serieous, it becomes obvious how critical they are for our well-being. A forest, for example, absorbs carbon dioxide from and provides oxygen to the atmosphere, provides flood control, reduces soil erosion, provides habitat for wildlife, offers natural beauty and outdoor recreation, provides some people with sources of food and fuel (especially in lower-income countries), and so on.

If GDP only counts human-produced goods and services, then, it is undercounting the total goods and services. If a forest is cut down for timber, and the wood is sold in a market, this adds to GDP. However, the value of the services the forest provided are not deducted from GDP as conventionally measured, since these are not sold in markets and do not have prices. Cutting down a forest may both add something (harvested wood, which can be used, for example, to build houses or make furniture) and subtract something (natural services) from the well-being of society. There is no way to say, in general, whether what it gained is greater or less than what is lost. However, as long as we think that the services the forest provided were worth *something*, we can say for certain that what GDP measures as being gained is greater than what it is really gained—since GDP only counts what is gained and ignores what is lost.

## If Not GDP, then What?

Part of the power of GDP per capita is that it boils everything down to one easy-to-digest number. It is easy to create a table comparing the GDPs of many countries.

(Obviously, it would be harder to compare many countries in more complex ways, including a bunch of descriptive numbers for each.) This is also at the core of the weaknesses of GDP per capita. When we calculate a total or average of anything, we are, in effect, throwing out the information we have about variation between different individuals. This problem is at the heart of the first critique: Calculating total GDP or GDP per capita means excluding information about income distribution. In addition, calculating the total output of goods and services, when a modern economy includes thousands and thousands of different kinds of goods, requires some unit in which we can measure these output of each one. (We can't add together pounds of potatoes and pounds of steel, much less goods and services that can't be measured in pounds at all, like electricity or haircuts.) GDP has accomplished this by measuring everything in terms of monetary units. This leads to the second and third critiques. Monetary measurement has led to a blind spot for goods and services that do not have market prices (household production, environmental services) and are not easy to measure in money terms.

There are three major possibilities. One is to go on calculating GDP per capita, but to do a better job at capturing what GDP misses. For example, some scholars have tried to put a dollar values on non-market production (like subsistence farming or household production) and add these to GDP to get a more accurate estimate.

Another is to come up with an alternative one-number measure to compete with GDP. Two important ones are the genuine progress indicator (GPI) and the human development index (HDI). The GPI incorporates, in addition to market production, measures of both nonmarket production and environmental destruction into a single summary figure (in money terms). It does not address the distributional critique. Calculated by the United Nations Development Programme (UNDP), the HDI combines GDP per capita, average educational attainment, and average life expectancy into a single numerical index. It addresses neither the feminist nor the environmental critique, and it does not explicitly address the distributional critique. However, more equal societies tend to rank better on HDI than on GDP per capita, because they tend to achieve higher average education and life expectancy. (The UNDP also calculates an inequality-adjusted HDI, which explicitly penalizes inequality.)

Finally, a third approach is to abandon the quest for a single summary measurement. Some environmental economists oppose attempts to incorporate environmental changes into GDP or other monetary measures, which requires reducing environmental services to money values. This implies, they argue, that some quantity of produced goods can substitute for any environmental good, which is not true. They propose instead "satellite accounts" that measure environmental changes alongside GDP. Widely used measures of income inequality also exist, and can enhance our picture of an economy. Measurements of median income, access to basic goods (like health and education), economic inequality, nonmarket production, environmental quality, and other factors all should figure, in some way, into our understanding of economic life. We may just have to accept that we need to take into account multiple measures, and that no single-number "bottom line" will do. ❑

Article 2.4

# MEASURING ECONOMIC DEVELOPMENT
## The "Human Development" Approach

**BY ALEJANDRO REUSS**
April 2012

Some development economists have proposed abandoning GDP per capita, the dominant single-number measure of economic development, in favor of the "human development" approach—which focuses less on changes in average income and more on widespread access to basic goods.

Advocates of this approach to the measurement of development, notably Nobel Prize-winning economist Amartya Sen, aim to focus attention directly on the *ends* (goals) of economic development. Higher incomes, Sen notes, are *means* people use to get the things that they want. The human development approach shifts the focus away from the means and toward ends like a long life, good health, freedom from hunger, the opportunity to get an education, and the ability to take part in community and civic life. Sen has argued that these basic "capabilities" or "freedoms"—the kinds of things almost everyone wants no matter what their goals in life may be— are the highest development priorities and should, therefore, be the primary focus of our development measures.

If a rising average income guaranteed that everyone, or almost everyone, in a society would be better able to reach these goals, we might as well use average income (GDP per capita) to measure development. Increases in GDP per capita, however, do not always deliver longer life, better health, more education, or other basic capabilities to most people In particular, if these income increases go primarily to those who are already better-off (and already enjoy a long life-expectancy, good health, access to education, and so on), they probably will not have much effect on people's access to basic capabilities.

Sen and others have shown that, in "developing" countries, increased average income by itself is not associated with higher life expectancy or better health. In countries where average income was increasing, but public spending on food security, health care, education, and similar programs did not increase along with it, they have found, the increase in average income did not appear to improve access to basic capabilities. If spending on these "public supports" increased, on the other hand, access to basic capabilities tended to improve, whether average income was increasing or not. Sen emphasizes two main lessons based on these observations: 1) A country cannot count on economic growth alone to improve access to basic capabilities. Increased average income appears to deliver "human development" largely by *increasing the wealth a society has available for public supports*, and not in other ways. 2) A country does not have to prioritize economic growth—*does not have to "wait" until it grows richer*—to make basic capabilities like long life, good health, and a decent education available to all.

# The Human Development Index (HDI)

The "human development" approach has led to a series of annual reports from the United Nations Development Programme (UNDP) ranking countries according to a "human development index" (HDI). The HDI includes measures of three things: 1) health, measured by average life expectancy, 2) education, measured by average years of schooling and expected years of schooling, and 3) income, measured by GDP per capita. The three categories are then combined, each counting equally, into a single index. The HDI has become the most influential alternative to GDP per capita as a single-number development measure.

Looking at the HDI rankings, many of the results are not surprising. The HDI top 20 is dominated by very high-income countries, including thirteen Western European countries, four "offshoots" of Great Britain (Australia, Canada, New Zealand, and the United States), and two high-income East Asian countries (Japan and South Korea). Most of the next 20 or so are Western or Eastern European, plus a few small oil-rich states in the Middle East. The next 50 or so include most of Latin America and the Caribbean, much of the Middle East, and a good deal of Eastern Europe (including Russia and several former Soviet republics). The next 50 or so are a mix of Latin American, Middle Eastern, South and Southeast Asian, and African countries. The world's poorest continent, Africa, accounts for almost all of the last 30, including the bottom 24.

## TABLE 1: HDI RANKS COMPARED TO INCOME PER CAPITA RANKS (2010)

| Highest HDI ranks compared to income per capita ranks (difference in parentheses)* | Lowest HDI ranks compared to income per capita ranks (difference in parentheses) |
| --- | --- |
| New Zealand (+30) | Equatorial Guinea (-78) |
| Georgia (+26) | Angola (-47) |
| Tonga (+23) | Kuwait (-42) |
| Tajikistan (+22) | Botswana (-38) |
| Madagascar (+22) | South Africa (-37) |
| Togo (+22) | Qatar (-35) |
| Fiji (+22) | Brunei (-30) |
| Ireland (+20) | Gabon (-29) |
| Iceland (+20) | United Arab Emirates (-28) |
| Ukraine (+20) | Turkey (-26) |

* The numbers in parentheses represent a country's GDP-per-capita rank minus its HDI rank. Remember that in a ranking system, a "higher" (better) rank is indicated by a lower number. If a country is ranked, say, 50th in GDP per capita and 20th in HDI, its number would be 50 – 20 = +30. The positive number indicates that the country had a "higher" HDI rank than GDP per capita rank. If a country is ranked, say, 10th in GDP per capita and 35th in HDI, its number would be 10 – 35 = -25. The negative number indicates that the country had a "lower" HDI rank than GDP per capita rank.

Source: United Nations Development Programme, Indices, Getting and using data, 2010 Report—Table 1: Human Development Index and its components (hdr.undp.org/en/statistics/data/).

It is not surprising that higher GDP per capita is associated with a higher HDI score. After all, GDP per capita counts for one third of the HDI score itself. The relationship between the two, however, is not perfect. Some countries have a higher HDI rank than GDP per capita rank. These countries are "over-performing," getting more human development from their incomes, compared to other countries. Meanwhile, some countries have a lower HDI rank than GDP per capita rank. These countries are "under-performing," not getting as much human development from their incomes, compared to other countries. The list of top "over-performing" countries includes three very high-income countries that had still higher HDI ranks (Iceland, Ireland, and New Zealand), three former Soviet republics (Georgia, Tajikistan, and Ukraine), two small South Pacific island nations (Fiji, Togo), and two African countries (Madagascar, Tonga). The list of top "under-performing" countries includes four small oil-rich countries (Brunei, Kuwait, Qatar, and United Arab Emirates) and five African countries (Angola, Botswana, Equatorial Guinea, Gabon, and South Africa).

The UNDP also calculates an inequality-adjusted HDI. Note that, for all the measures included in the HDI, there is inequality within countries. The inequality-adjusted HDI is calculated so that, the greater the inequality for any measure included in the HDI (for health, education, or income), the lower the country's score. Since all countries have some inequality, the inequality-adjusted HDI for any country is always lower than the regular HDI. However, the scores for countries with greater inequality drop more than for those with less inequality. That pushes some countries up in the rankings, when inequality is penalized, and others down. Among the thirteen countries moving up the most, five are former So-

## TABLE 1: INEQUALITY-ADJUSTED HDI RANKS
## COMPARED UNADJUSTED HDI RANKS

| Highest inequality-adjusted hdi ranks compared unadjusted hdi ranks (difference in parentheses) | Lowest inequality-adjusted hdi ranks compared unadjusted hdi ranks (difference in parentheses) |
|---|---|
| Uzbekistan (+17) | Peru (-26) |
| Mongolia (+16) | Panama (-20) |
| Moldova (+16) | Colombia (-18) |
| Kyrgystan (+15) | South Korea (-18) |
| Maldives (+14) | Bolivia (-17) |
| Ukraine (+14) | Belize (-16) |
| Philippines (+11) | Brazil (-15) |
| Sri Lanka (+11) | Namibia (-15) |
| Tanzania, Viet Nam, Indonesia, Jamaica, Belarus (+9) | El Salvador (-14) |
| | Turkmenistan (-12) |

*Source:* United Nations Development Programme, 2010 Report, Table 3: Inequality-adjusted Human Development Index (hdr. undp.org/en/media/HDR_2010_EN_Table3_reprint.pdf).

viet republics. Among the ten moving down the most, seven are Latin American countries. The United States narrowly misses the list of those moving down the most, with its rank dropping by nine places when inequality is taken into account.

## GDP Per Capita and HDI

The relationship between income per capita and the HDI is shown in the "scatterplot" graph below. (Instead of GDP per capita, the graph uses a closely related measure called Gross National Income (GNI) per capita.) Each point represents a country, with its income per capita represented on the horizontal scale and its HDI score represented on the vertical scale. The further to the right a point is, the higher the country's per capita income. The higher up a point is, the higher the country's HDI score. As we can see, the cloud of points forms a curve, rising up as income per capita increases from a very low level, and then flattening out. This means that a change in GDP per capita from a very low level to a moderate level of around $8000 per year is associated with large gains in human development. Above that, we see,

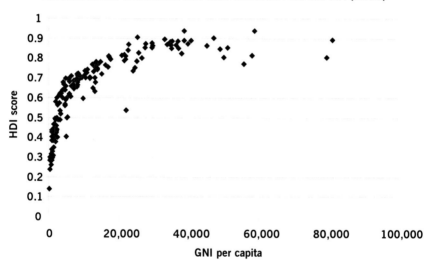

**RELATIONSHIP BETWEEN HDI AND INCOME PER CAPITA (2010)**

*Source:* United Nations Development Programme, Indices, 2010 Report - Table 1 Human Development Index and its components (hdr.undp.org/en/statistics/data/).

the curve flattens out dramatically. A change in income per capita from this moderate level to a high level of around $25,000 is associated with smaller gains in human development. Further increases in income per capita are associated with little or no gain in human development.

This relationship suggests two major conclusions, both related to greater economic equality.

First, achieving greater equality in incomes between countries, including by redistributing income from high-income countries to low-income countries, could result in increased human development. Over the highest per capita income range, from about $25,000 on up, increases in income are not associated with higher human development. Decreases in income above this threshold, by the same token, need not mean lower human development. On the other hand, over the lowest income range, below $8000, increases in income are associated with dramatic gains in HDI (largely due to increased public supports). Therefore, the redistribution of incomes from high-income countries to low-income countries could increase human development in the latter a great deal, while not diminishing human development in the former by very much (if at all)—resulting in a net gain in human development.

Second, high-income countries might make greater gains in HDI, as their incomes continued to increase, if a larger share of income went to low-income people or to public supports. Part of the reason that the relationship between per capita income and HDI flattens out at high income levels may be that there are inherent limits to variables like life expectancy (perhaps 90-100 years) or educational attainment (perhaps 20 years). These "saturation" levels, however, have clearly not been reached by all individuals, even in very high-income countries. In the United States, as of 2008, the infant mortality rate for African-Americans was more than double that for whites. The life expectancy at birth for white females was more than three years greater than that of African-American females; for white males, more than five years greater than for African-American males. As of 2010, over 40% of individuals over 25 years old have no education above high school. Over 60% have no degree from a two- or four-year college. It is little wonder that higher income would not bring about greatly increased human development, considering that, over the last 30 years, many public supports have faced sustained attack and most income growth has gone to people already at the top. ❑

*Sources:* Amartya Sen, *Development as Freedom* (New York: Oxford University Press, 1999); United Nations Development Programme, Indices, Getting and using data, *2010 Report*, Table 1 Human Development Index and its components (hdr.undp.org/en/statistics/data/); United Nations Development Programme, *2010 Report*, Table 3: Inequality-adjusted Human Development Index (hdr.undp.org/en/media/HDR_2010_EN_Table3_reprint.pdf); U.S. Census Bureau, The 2012 Statistical Abstract, Births, Deaths, Marriages, & Divorces: Life Expectancy, Table 107: Expectation of Life and Expected Deaths by Race, Sex, and Age: 2008; Educational Attainment, Population 25 Years and Over, U.S. Census Bureau, Selected Social Characteristics in the United States, 2010 American Community Survey, 1-Year Estimates.

Article 2.5

# THE *REAL* UNEMPLOYMENT RATE

## BY JOHN MILLER

*July/August 2009; last updated March 2014*

In February 2014, after nearly five years of economic recovery, the official unemployment rate stood at 6.7%, down from its October 2009 peak of 10.1% during the Great Recession. But even at that, the unemployment rate was still well above the 4.4% unemployment rate at the onset of the Great Recession, and higher than the unemployment rate five years into any of the last three economic recoveries. Even the recovery from the 1982 recession, which was the most severe economic slump between the Great Depression of the 1930s and the recent Great Recession, was followed by a faster reduction in unemployment. (See figure 2.)

Some groups of workers faced even higher official unemployment rates. As of February 2014, unemployment rates for black, Hispanic, and teenage workers were 12.0%, 8.7% and 21.4%, respectively. Workers without a high-school diploma confronted a 9.8% unemployment rate. Some 13.1% of construction workers were still unemployed. In Rhode Island, the hardest hit state, unemployment was at 9.3% (in December, 2013). Unemployment rates in four other states were above 8.0% as well.

Other telltale signs suggested that the unemployment picture was yet worse than those official rates indicate. More than one in three of the officially unemployed have gone without work for more than one half a year. The long term unemployed never exceeded one quarter of the unemployed in the sixty years prior to the Great Recession. The proportion of workers employed part time who would prefer to work full-time remained at historically high levels as well. "Those observations," Janet Yellen, the new head of the Federal Reserve Board, told Congress, "underscore the importance of considering more than the unemployment rate when evaluating the condition of the U.S. labor market."

She is right. As bad as they are, the official figures dramatically understate the true extent of unemployment. First, they exclude anyone without a job who is ready to work but has not actively looked for a job in the previous four weeks. The Bureau of Labor Statistics (BLS) classifies such workers as "marginally attached

| THE FEBRUARY 2014 UNEMPLOYMENT PICTURE (DATA IN THOUSANDS, NOT SEASONALLY ADJUSTED) | |
|---|---:|
| Civilian Labor Force | 155,027 |
| Employed | 144,134 |
| Unemployed | 10,893 |
| Marginally Attached Workers | 2,303 |
| Discouraged workers | 755 |
| Reasons other than discouragement | 1,548 |
| Part-time for Economic Reasons | 7,397 |
| Slack work or business conditions | 4,506 |
| Could only find part-time work | 2,598 |

*Sources:* Bureau of Labor Statistics, Tables A-1, A-8. A-15, A-16. Data are not seasonally adjusted because seasonally adjusted data for marginally attached workers are not available.

## RISE IN THE OFFICIAL UNEMPLOYMENT RATE IN SIX RECESSIONS (MONTHLY RATES, SEASONALLY ADJUSTED)

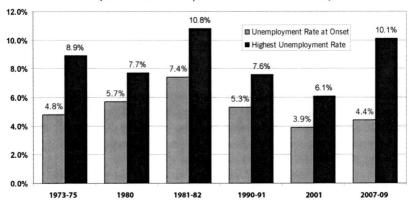

*Source:* Table A-1, Bureau of Labor Statistics, U.S. Labor Department, at *www.bls.gov.*

to the labor force" so long as they have looked for work within the last year. Marginally attached workers include so-called discouraged workers who have given up looking because repeated job searches were unsuccessful, plus others who have given up for reasons such as school and family responsibilities, ill health, or transportation problems.

Second, the official unemployment rate leaves out part-time workers looking for full-time work: part-time workers are "employed" even if they work as little as one hour a week. The vast majority of people working part-time involuntarily have had their hours cut due to slack or unfavorable business conditions. The rest are working part-time because they could only find part-time work.

To its credit, the BLS has developed alternative unemployment measures that go a long way toward correcting the shortcomings of the official rate. The broadest alternative measure, called U-6, counts as unemployed "marginally attached workers" as well as those employed "part time for economic reasons." And even the business press, including *The Wall Street Journal*, has taken to reporting this more comprehensive measure of unemployment along with the official unemployment rate.

In February 2014, the broader measure of the unemployment rate was 12.6%, just about double the official, or U-3 rate. While considerably below its peak of 17.4% back in October 2009, the February 2014 adjusted unemployment rate was still higher than any time between 1994, when the BLS introduced the U-6 measure, and the onset of the Great Recession in 2008.

Why is the real unemployment rate so much higher than the official, or U-3, rate? First, since the Great Recession forced part-time work has reached higher levels than anytime since 1956. In February 2014, 7.4 million workers were forced to work part time for economic reasons. Forced part-timers are concentrated in wholesale and retail trade, leisure and hospitality, and education and health service; they are nearly equally men and women but disproportinately younger workers (20 to 24 years old) and older workers (over 55 years old). The number of discouraged workers is also quite high today. In February 2014, the BLS counted 2.3 million "marginally

### Calculating the Real Unemployment Rate

The BLS calculates the official unemployment rate, U-3, as the number of unemployed as a percentage of the civilian labor force. The civilian labor force consists of employed workers plus the officially unemployed, those without jobs who are available to work and have looked for a job in the last 4 weeks. Applying the data found in Table 2 yields an official unemployment rate of 7.0%, or a seasonally adjusted rate of 6.7% for February 2014.

The comprehensive U-6 unemployment rate adjusts the official rate by adding marginally attached workers and workers forced to work part time for economic reasons to the officially unemployed. To find the U-6 rate the BLS takes that higher unemployment count and divides it by the official civilian labor force plus the number of marginally attached workers. (No adjustment is necessary for forced part-time workers since they are already counted in the official labor force as employed workers.)

Accounting for the large number of marginally attached workers and those working part-time for economic reasons raises the count of unemployed from 10.9 million to 20.6 million workers for February 2014. Those numbers push up the U-6 unemployment rate to 13.1% or a seasonally adjusted rate of 12.6%.

attached" workers. That figure exceeds the number of marginally attached workers in any month prior the Great Recession going back to 1994, when the agency introduced the measure.

In February 2014, nearly five years into an economic recovery, U.S. labor markets continued to impose devastating costs on society and much of the burden goes unaccounted for by a traditional unemployment rate. Of those who are counted as unemployed by the traditional measure, 37% had gone more 27 weeks without work. The persistence of such high levels of long term unemployment are sure to sever further the connection of those without work to the labor force. After many months of looking for work, some of the long-term unemployed are likely to give up the search, falling into the category of marginally attached and disappearing from the official measure of unemployment. And even more of the victims of the malfunctioning U.S. labor market will go uncounted by the traditional unemployment rate in the month and years ahead. ❏

*Sources:* U.S. Dept. of Labor, "The Unemployment Rate and Beyond: Alternative Measures of Labor Underutilization," *Issues in Labor Statistics*, June 2008; John E. Bregger and Steven E. Haugen, "BLS introduces new range of alternative unemployment measures," *Monthly Labor Review*, October 1995. "Fed's Yellen Sets Course for Steady Bond-Buy Cuts," by Hilsenrath and McGrane, *Wall Street Journal*, Feb. 11, 2014; and, "Don't Sweat the Rise in the Unemployment Rate," by Izzo, *Wall Street Journal*, March 7, 2014.

*Article 2.6*

# THE CHAINED CPI IS BAD FOR
# SENIORS AND FOR ACCURACY

## BY JOHN MILLER
*MAY/JUNE 2013*

> The word "thuggish" comes to mind. "I'm not a number," says the
> older man in a television ad funded by the seniors' lobby AARP. ... "But
> I am a voter. So Washington, before you even think about cutting my
> Medicare and Social Security benefits, here's a number you should re-
> member: 50 million."
>
> This unyielding position, undergirded by a multimillion-dollar ad
> campaign, is as wrongheaded as the equivalent line-drawing of Grover
> Norquist and the no-new-taxes crowd. ...
>
> [T]he brutal fact is that Social Security cannot pay all promised
> benefits, and a debt discussion is a useful place to make reasonable
> tradeoffs.
>
> —*Washington Post*, "Congress should reject AARP's self-centered
> appeals on Social Security," Nov. 4, 2011.

That AARP television ad sure raised the hackles of the *Washington Post* editors
back in 2011. The editors called AARP's threat—to vote out any politician who
supported a reduction in the cost-of-living adjustment (COLA) for Social Security
benefits—"thuggish," "self-centered," in denial about the crisis of Social Security,
and as "wrongheaded" as conservative power-broker Grover Norquist. That last one
had to hurt.

Back then, the proposal to reduce the Social Security COLA by switching to
the "chained" Consumer Price Index (CPI) didn't come to pass. But now it's back,
this time as part of the 2014 Obama budget proposal and going by its technical economic name—the "superlative CPI." Make no mistake, though. It's the same idea
now as then, and would reduce the COLAs for Social Security and veterans' benefits, as well as the inflation adjustment for income-tax brackets.

What's all the fuss about? The Social Security Administration currently uses
the CPI-W, a measure of the price of a basket of goods and services typically purchased by urban wage-earners and clerical workers, to calculate COLAs for Social
Security recipients. The "chained CPI-U," as it is officially designated by the Bureau
of Labor Statistics (BLS), grows at a slower rate than the CPI-W. Therefore, calculating the COLAs using the chained CPI will reduce future Social Security benefits by
more and more each year. If that sounds to you like a roundabout way to hold down
spending on Social Security, you've got it right.

The proposal is meant to establish Obama's deficit-reduction bona fides and to
lure Republicans and conservative Democrats into a "grand bargain" boosting tax
revenues and cutting entitlements spending. For good measure, the Obama admin-

istration is selling the superlative CPI as just that—"a more accurate measure of the average change in the cost of living than the standard CPI." And the *Washington Post* is once again on board, endorsing the Obama proposal for "Social Security spending restraint" as part of the "worthy end" of entitlement reform.

Using the chained CPI to reduce future Social Security spending, however, is far from the even-handed proposal the *Post* editors suggest. In truth, it is neither fair nor accurate. Worse yet, it would fall most heavily on some of the most vulnerable in our society—older women, veterans, and the disabled.

## The CPI in Chains

To understand why, we need to look at just how the COLA for Social Security benefits is calculated. In 2013, the COLA was 1.7%, equal to the increase in the CPI-W from the third quarter of 2011 to the third quarter of 2012. For the typical Social Security retiree, this translated into about $250, boosting the average retirement benefit to just over $15,000 a year in 2013.

The CPI-W is what economists call a "fixed-weight" index. It measures the price of a fixed "basket" of 211 different items. (The basket of goods is updated every two years to keep up with changes in consumers' buying patterns.)

According to the persistent complaints of conservative politicians and economists, however, that fixed basket results in the CPI-W overstating the rate of inflation. They argue that consumers typically purchase less of those goods whose prices are rising compared to those of other goods. Take the example provided by BLS: If the price of pork rises while the price of beef falls, consumers are likely to purchase less pork and more beef.

That's the supposed problem the chained CPI is intended to correct. The "U" in "CPI-U," by the way, stands for all urban consumers, a broader group than urban workers. The basket used for the chained CPI, therefore, differs from that for the CPI-W. More importantly, however, the chained CPI uses a flexible basket of goods that captures how consumers adjust their purchases in reaction to rising prices. The basket used for the final chained CPI is updated monthly. In the example of rising pork prices and declining beef prices, then, declining pork consumption means that pork prices will have less weight in the calculation of the index. By the same token, rising beef consumption means that beef will have greater weight inthe index.

The long and the short of it is that the chained CPI reports a lower rate of inflation than the fixed-basket CPI-W. The Social Security Administration estimates that using the chained CPI instead of the CPI-W would reduce annual Social Security COLAs by about 0.3 percentage points per year. If the chained CPI had been used to calculate the Social Security COLA, the average retiree would have gotten $45 less in benefits this year.

Perhaps it is these small figures that have the *Post* editors convinced that AARP is "wrongheaded" about the switch. The loss of benefits, however, gets larger each year, and the cumulative effect is substantial. The average 65-year-old is now expected to live about 19 additional years. According to AARP projections, a chained-CPI COLA would cost the average Social Security retiree more than $5,000 over the first 15 years of retirement and more than $9,000 over the first 20.

Nor is the chained CPI an accurate measure of the cost of living for most seniors. The typical senior spends a larger share of her income on medical care and housing than other consumers. The cost of both items has risen more quickly than other costs and it is hard to substitute for either item with other purchases. In addition, because seniors are less mobile than other consumers, it is harder for them to change their consumption patterns. This makes the chained CPI, whether or not it is valid for other individuals, inappropriate for calculating COLAs affecting seniors' retirement incomes.

## Double and Triple Whammies

The reduction of the COLA would hit hardest on some of the most vulnerable in our society.

Older women would suffer, as the National Women's Law Center puts it, a "triple-whammy." First, the effects of the change would increase over time, and women tend to live longer than men. (A 65-year-old woman is more than 1.5 times as likely to live into her 90s as a 65-year-old man.) By age 90, a typical single woman who retired at age 65 would have lost $15,000 of benefits from the switch to a chained-CPI COLA.

Second, women rely more heavily on their Social Security benefits than men do. Among beneficiaries 80 or older, Social Security accounts for two-thirds of women's income, compared to three-fifths of men's. So any reduction in benefits will cost women a larger share of their total income than it will men.

Third, older women are more economically vulnerable than older men. Among women receiving Social Security benefits, almost 10% remain in poverty, nearly twice the rate as for men. Shifting to the chained CPI would heighten the risk of poverty for these women.

Veterans would also be hit by the switch to the chained CPI. Because veterans with twenty years of service are eligible for their pensions as early as age 50, the cumulative effect of a reduced COLA would be particularly large. Disabled veterans would face a double whammy. With a chained-CPI COLA, they would collect lower Social Security benefits and lower veterans' benefits.

The story is similar for those receiving disability benefits. The disabled typically start receiving Social Security benefits before retirement age, so their cumulative loss of future income will be much greater than retirees'. For instance, someone who began collecting disability benefits at age 30 would collect nearly 10% less in benefits at age 65 under the chained CPI, and the annual loss would get larger each year after that.

The switch to the chained CPI would also lower the inflation adjustment for income-tax brackets. While income taxes would go up across the board, more than three-quarters of the additional taxes would be paid by those with adjusted gross incomes under $200,000.Those with incomes between $30,000 and $40,000 would suffer the largest declines in their after-tax incomes, according to the Tax Policy Center.

## Fair and Accurate

If accuracy were the goal of reforming the COLA, it would be far better to adopt the BLS's new CPI-E (for "elderly"). This fixed-weight experimental index is derived specifically from seniors' spending patterns, placing higher weights on housing and medical care than other indices, including the CPI-W. The BLS reports that between December 1982 and December 2011, the CPI-E added 0.2 percentage points to the annual inflation rate, compared to the CPI-W. (The difference between the two rates has shrunk recently as the rise in health-care costs has slowed.) Using the CPI-E would make it clear that the honest way to lower the COLA for seniors would be to rein in health costs and therefore slow the growth in their actual cost of living.

Finally, reducing benefits is neither right nor necessary to avoid the projected shortfall in Social Security payments starting in 2033. Currently, wage income above $113,700 is not subject to the payroll tax. Lifting this cap would eliminate the entire projected shortfall in one easy step. And unlike a reduction in the COLA, which would hurt the most vulnerable, lifting the cap would put the burden on some of those who benefited most from the lopsided economic growth of the last three decades. ❑

***Sources:*** "Obama's 2014 budget is an offer to negotiate," *Washington Post*, April 10, 2013; Joan Entmacher and Katherine Gallagher Robbins, "Cutting the Social Security COLA by Changing the Way Inflation Is Calculated Would Especially Hurt Women," National Women's Law Center, June 2011 (nwlc.org); Tax Policy Center, "Distributional Effects of Using Chained CPI" (taxpolicycenter.org); Clark Burdick and Lynn Fisher, "Social Security Cost-of-Living Adjustments and the Consumer Price Index," *Social Security Bulletin*, Vol. 67, No. 3, 2007 (socialsecurity.gov); Alison Shelton, "Inflation Indexation in Major Federal Benefit Programs: Impact of the Chained CPI," AARP Public Policy Institute, March 2013.

# Chapter 3

# ECONOMIC GROWTH AND BUSINESS CYCLES

## INTRODUCTION

Economic growth and business cycles could hardly be a more pertinent topic than they are today—with the world having just gone through the deepest economic crisis since the Great Depression, and experiencing sluggish growth and persistent economic fragility since then.

Heading up the chapter, economist Rick Wolff explains that the conventional wisdom about the causes of the recent Great Recession is wrong (Article 3.1). The problems, Wolff argues, did not begin in the financial sector. Rather, stagnating wages and the resulting tilt in the income distribution from workers to owners of capital—decades in the making—created a fragile house of cards. It resulted in the increased reliance on credit by workers to maintain their standards of living, and in increased financial game-playing and risk-taking by banks and other financial institutions.

John Miller (Article 3.2) addresses the debate among economists on the causes of "secular stagnation"—the long-term trend of sluggish growth—in the U.S. economy since the Great Recession. Miller argues that it is possible to achieve robust, sustainable growth with policies aimed at increased public investment and reduced income inequality. The key stumbling blocks to achieving this, he concludes, are not economic, but political.

In the next article, Miller argues that Germany, once known for "high road" labor relations, has turned sharply in recent years toward wage repression (Article 3.3). This meant not just stagnant incomes for German workers, but also inadequate domestic demand and sluggish growth for the country as a whole. Furthermore, it has reduced the costs of German goods compared to those of its neighbors, bolstering Germany's trade surplus and contributing to huge trade deficits for countries like Greece.

Junji Tokunaga (Article 3.4) describes the interventions by the Japanese government to address the country's decades-long economic stagnation. Policies that make perfect sense to boost demand—expansionary monetary and fiscal policies—have gone along with others that are likely to impede the country's economic recovery, such as tax cuts for corporations coupled with tax hikes on ordinary people.

The last two articles in the chapter turn our attention toward developing economies.

Alejandro Reuss examines the role of debt in economic development—considering both international borrowing as a means of financing development projects and the burdens of debt service as impediments to development (Article 3.5). He argues that developing countries could achieve major development objectives without resorting to debt. But the global economy must be reformed to reverse mechanisms that extract wealth from developing countries and concentrate it in a few rich countries.

Finally, Jayati Ghosh offers an overview of the linkages between the high-income countries, "emerging" manufacturing economies like China, and raw-material and intermediate input producers (Article 3.6). She argues that slow economic growth in high-income countries has caused a slowdown in the emerging economies and an end to the commodity boom that fueled growth for raw-materials exporters. In her view, however, economic growth should not be the goal, and developing countries can do much better at improving the standards of living of the majority if they cast off the focus on maximizing GDP growth.

## Discussion Questions

1. (Article 3.1) The dominant narrative from the mainstream media has been that the recent U.S. economic crisis was, at its root, a "financial crisis." Why does Wolff think that is incorrect?

2. (Article 3.2) If "secular stagnation" (long-term, not just cyclical, slow economic growth) is an economic problem, why does Miller say the real roots of the problem are *political*?

3. (Article 3.3) Policies that have led to stagnant wages in Germany sound like a negative for German workers. Why do some see them as the source of recent German economic success? Rising German exports sound like a good thing. Why do some argue that they have been bad for Europe in general and even Germany in particular?

4. (Article 3.4) Why, in Tokunaga's view, have the Japanese government's policies been ineffective in overcoming economic stagnation? What do you think about the policies he proposes to create sustainable growth?

5. (Article 3.5) If a country has gotten deeply into debt, doesn't it make sense for it to cut back dramatically on its spending to bring the debt burden down as fast as possible? Why does Reuss argue that this is misguided?

6. (Article 3.5) Is a system of global wealth redistribution desirable? Is it realistic?

7. (Article 3.6) Are rising wages a good thing or a bad thing for developing economies? Why have policymakers seen them as a bad thing? Why does Ghosh see them as a good thing?

*Article 3.1*

# CAPITALISM HITS THE FAN
*The crisis did not start or edn with finance.*

**BY RICK WOLFF**
*November/December 2008*

Let me begin by saying what I think this crisis is not. It is not a financial crisis. It is a systemic crisis whose first serious symptom happened to be finance. But this crisis has its economic roots and its effects in manufacturing, services, and, to be sure, finance. It grows out of the relation of wages to profits across the economy. It has profound social roots in America's households and families and political roots in government policies. The current crisis did not start with finance, and it won't end with finance.

## Rising Productivity, Wages, and Consumption

From 1820 to around 1970, 150 years, the average productivity of American workers went up each year. The average workers produced more stuff every year than they did the year before. They were trained better, they had more machines, and they had better machines. So productivity went up every year. And, over this period of time, the wages of American workers rose every decade. Every decade, real wages—the amount of money you get in relation to the prices you pay for the things you use your money for—were higher than the decade before. Profits also went up.

The American working class enjoyed 150 years of rising consumption, so it's not surprising that it would choose to define its own self-worth, measure its own success in life, according to the standard of consumption. Americans began to think of themselves as successful if they lived in the right neighborhood, drove the right car, wore the right outfit, went on the right vacation.

## Wages and Productivity Diverge

But in the 1970s, the world changed for the American working class in ways that it hasn't come to terms with—at all. Real wages stopped going up. As U.S. corporations moved operations abroad to take advantage of lower wages and higher profits and as they replaced workers with machines (and especially computers), those who lost their jobs were soon willing to work even if their wages stopped rising. So real wages trended down a little bit. The real hourly wage of a worker in the 1970s was higher than what it is today. What you get for an hour of work, in goods and services, is less now that what your parents got.

Meanwhile, productivity kept going up. If what the employer gets from each worker keeps going up, but what you give to each worker does not, then the difference becomes bigger, and bigger, and bigger. Employers' profits have gone wild, and all the people who get their fingers on employers profits—the professionals who sing the songs they like to hear, the shareholders who get a piece of the action on each company's profits—have enjoyed a bonanza over the last thirty years.

The only thing more profitable than simply making the money off the worker is handling this exploding bundle of profits—packaging and repackaging it, lending it and borrowing it, and inventing new mechanisms for doing all that. That's called the finance industry, and they have stumbled all over themselves to get a hold of a piece of this immense pot of profit.

## The Working-Class Borrowing Binge

What did the working class do? What happens to a population committed to measuring people's success by the amount of consumption they could afford when the means they had always had to achieve it, rising wages, stop? They can go through a trauma right then and there: "We can't anymore—it's over." Most people didn't do that. They found other ways.

Americans undertook more work. People took a second or third job. The number of hours per year worked by the average American worker has risen by about 20 percent since the 1970s. By comparison, in Germany, France, and Italy, the number of hours worked per year per worker has dropped 20 percent. American workers began to work to a level of exhaustion. They sent more family members—and especially women—out to work. This enlarged supply of workers meant that employers could find plenty of employees without having to offer higher pay. Yet, with more family members out working, new kinds of costs and problems hit American families. The woman who goes out to work needs new outfits. In our society, she probably needs another car. With women exhausted from jobs outside and continued work demands inside households, with families stressed by exhaustion and mounting bills, interpersonal tensions mounted and brought new costs: daycare, psychotherapy, drugs. Such extra costs neutralized the extra income, so it did not solve the problem.

The American working class had to do a second thing to keep its consumption levels rising. It went on the greatest binge of borrowing in the history of any working class in any country at any time. Members of the business community began to realize that they had a fantastic double opportunity. They could get the profits from flat wages and rising productivity, and then they could turn to the working class traumatized by the inability to have rising consumption, and give them the means to consume more. So instead of paying your workers a wage, you're going to lend them the money—so they have to pay it back to you! With interest!

That solved the problem. For a while, employers could pay the workers the same or less, and instead of creating the usual problems for capitalism—workers without enough income to buy all the output their increased productivity yields—rising worker debt seemed magical. Workers could consume ever more; profits exploding in every category. Underneath the magic, however, there were workers who were completely exhausted, whose families were falling apart, and who were now ridden with anxiety because their rising debts were unsustainable. This was a system built to fail, to reach its end when the combination of physical exhaustion and emotional anxiety from the debt made people unable to continue. Those people are, by the millions, walking away from those obligations, and the house of cards comes down.

If you put together (a) the desperation of the American working class and (b) the efforts of the finance industry to scrounge out every conceivable borrower, the idea that the banks would end up lending money to people who couldn't pay it back is not a tough call. The system, however, was premised on the idea that that would not happen, and when it happened nobody was prepared.

## Two Responses to the Crisis: Conservative and Liberal

The conservatives these days are in a tough spot. The story about how markets and private enterprise interact to produce wonderful outcomes is, even for them these days, a cause for gagging. Of course, ever resourceful, there are conservatives who will rise to the occasion, sort of like dead fish. They rattle off twenty things the government did over the last twenty years, which indeed it did, and draw a line from those things the government did and this disaster now, to reach the conclusion that the reason we have this problem now is too much government intervention. These days they get nowhere. Even the mainstream press has a hard time with this stuff.

What about the liberals and many leftists too? They seem to favor regulation. They think the problem was that the banks weren't regulated, that credit-rating companies weren't regulated, that the Federal Reserve didn't regulate better, or differently, or more, or something. Salaries should be regulated to not be so high. Greed should be regulated. I find this astonishing and depressing.

In the 1930s, the last time we had capitalism hitting the fan in this way, we produced a lot of regulation. Social Security didn't exist before then. Unemployment insurance didn't exist before then. Banks were told: you can do this, but you can't do that. Insurance companies were told: you can do that, but you can't do this. They limited what the board of directors of a corporation could do ten ways to Sunday. They taxed them. They did all sorts of things that annoyed, bothered, and troubled boards of directors because the regulations impeded the boards' efforts to grow their companies and make money for the shareholders who elected them.

## The Self-Destruct Button on Liberal Regulation

You don't need to be a great genius to understand that the boards of directors encumbered by all these regulations would have a very strong incentive to evade them, to undermine them, and, if possible, to get rid of them. Indeed, the boards went to work on that project as soon as the regulations were passed. The crucial fact about the regulations imposed on business in the 1930s is that they did not take away from the boards of directors the freedom or the incentives or the opportunities to undo all the regulations and reforms. The regulations left in place an institution devoted to their undoing. But that wasn't the worst of it. They also left in place boards of directors who, as the first appropriators of all the profits, had the resources to undo the regulations. This peculiar system of regulation had a built-in self-destruct button.

Over the last thirty years, the boards of directors of the United States' larger corporations have used their profits to buy the President and the Congress, to buy the public media, and to wage a systematic campaign, from 1945 to 1975, to evade the regulations, and, after 1975, to get rid of them. And it worked. That's why we're here now. And if you impose another set of regulations along the lines liberals propose, not only are you going to have the same history, but you're going to have the same history faster. The right wing in America, the business community, has spent the last fifty years perfecting every technique that is known to turn the population against regulation. And they're going to go right to work to do it again, and they'll do it better, and they'll do it faster.

## A Socialist Alternative

So what do we do? Let's regulate, by all means. Let's try to make a reasonable economic system that doesn't allow the grotesque abuses we've seen in recent decades. But let's not reproduce the self-destruct button. This time the change has to include the following: The people in every enterprise who do the work of that enterprise, will become collectively their own board of directors. For the first time in American history, the people who depend on the survival of those regulations will be in the position of receiving the profits of their own work and using them to make the regulations succeed rather than sabotaging them.

This proposal for workers to collectively become their own board of directors also democratizes the enterprise. The people who work in an enterprise, the front line of those who have to live with what it does, where it goes, how it uses its wealth, they should be the people who have influence over the decisions it makes. That's democracy.

Maybe we could even extend this argument to democracy in our political life, which leaves a little to be desired—some people call it a "formal" democracy, that isn't real. Maybe the problem all along has been that you can't have a real democracy politically if you don't have a real democracy underpinning it economically. If the workers are not in charge of their work situations, five days a week, 9 to 5, the major time of their adult lives, then how much aptitude and how much appetite are they going to have to control their political life? Maybe we need the democracy of economics, not just to prevent the regulations from being undone, but also to realize the political objectives of democracy. ❏

*Artilce 3.2*

# THE SPECTER OF SECULAR STAGNATION
*Will economists face up to the crummy, unequal economy?*

**BY JOHN MILLER**
May/June 2015

> "The secular stagnation challenge then is not just to achieve reasonable growth, but to do so in a financially sustainable way."
> — Lawrence Summers, *"What to do About Secular Stagnation," World Economic Forum, Oct. 31, 2014.*

> "Does the U.S. economy face secular stagnation? I am skeptical, and the sources of my skepticism go beyond the fact that the U.S. economy looks to be well on the way to full employment today."
> — Ben Bernanke, *"Why are interest rates so low, part 2: Secular stagnation," Ben Bernanke's Blog, Brookings Institution, March 31, 2015.*

Hyman Minsky, one of the 20th century's leading theorists of financial fragility, used to say that there was nothing wrong with the discipline of macroeconomics that another Great Depression wouldn't cure. Today, almost six years since the official end of the Great Recession, such an effect might finally be taking hold.

Economist (and former treasury secretary and World Bank chief economist) Lawrence Summers is championing what he calls the "secular stagnation" hypothesis: the United States and other industrialized economies have been suffering for nearly two decades from a chronic lack of demand—a shortfall of both private and public spending not just inducing a temporary recession, but causing long-term (or "secular") economic growth to slow. Summers maintains that underlying economic growth has declined to the point that "it may be impossible to achieve full employment, satisfactory growth and financial stability simultaneously simply through the operation of conventional monetary policy [that lowers interest rates]."

It's certainly ironic that Larry Summers is today's chief proponent of the secular stagnation hypothesis, since he played a key role in enacting policies that contributed to stagnation. As treasury secretary under Clinton, Summers led the charge to deregulate derivatives trading, which would contribute mightily to the financial crisis. And as chief economic advisor in the Obama administration, Summers quashed proposals to enlarge the size of the fiscal stimulus, which would have gone a long way toward boosting growth.

Nonetheless, should the secular stagnation hypothesis take hold, it could help open up space for policies that could improve many people's lives.

## The Secular Stagnation Debate

Nearly five years into the economic recovery, the U.S. economy expanded by just 2.4% in 2104, a far cry from the 4.1% average for all other economic recoveries since

1960. Even more importantly, secular stagnation is not just the "new mediocre" since the Great Recession. The U.S. economy has produced just two periods of rapid growth in the last twenty years—in the late 1990s and in the mid 2000s. Both were supported by low interest rates, massive debt, and speculative bubbles. Summers concludes that the U.S. economy has been unable to achieve adequate growth for a long time, but that this has been "masked by unsustainable finances."

The signs of stagnation are even clearer around the world. The IMF has repeatedly lowered its growth forecast for Japan, which is mired in decades of stagnation, and has done the same for the eurozone since 2007. It estimates growth in both Japan and the eurozone at little more than 1% a year through 2020.

The mediocre growth persists despite very low interest rates, embraced by governments to encourage borrowing and boost spending. As far back as the early 1990s, the Bank of Japan cut short-term interest rates by dramatically expanding the money supply. With the onset of the Great Recession in 2008, the European Central Bank and the U.S. Federal Reserve Board did the same, with the Fed also buying long-term corporate and government bonds (engaging in "quantitative easing") in an attempt to bring down long-term interest rates. "Interest rates have been, and remain, very low," Federal Reserve Chair Janet Yellen rightly cautions, "and if underlying conditions had truly returned to normal, the economy should be booming."

Today, central bank-controlled short-term interest rates remain barely above zero: 0.25% in the United States, 0.1% in Japan, and 0.05% in the eurozone. Such low interest rates leave central banks with practically no room to cut interest rates further to boost economic growth.

Real (inflation-adjusted) long-term interest rates are down as well. Real interest rates on ten-year government bonds in the Group of Seven (G7) industrialized countries (Canada, France, Germany, Italy, Japan, the UK, and the United States) have fallen from just under 5% in the early 1990s to 0.6% at the end of 2013.

What explains this decline in interest rates? Expansionary monetary policy, initiated by central banks to lower rates and counteract slowing economic growth, is part of the answer. For Summers, however, the chief explanation for the drop in the real interest rate (the price of savings), is the chronic excess of savings (the supply of savings) over investment (the demand for savings). He calls this the "essence of secular stagnation." Private savings (largely retained earnings held by corporations) have exceeded private investment in the eurozone since 2001, in Japan since well before 2000, and in the United States since 2008 (after the housing bubble burst).

## Demand-Side or Supply-Side?

Summers attributes the excess of savings to too little private investment. A shortfall of overall spending (or "aggregate demand") is holding investment below the levels necessary for full employment. In the middle of last year (second quarter 2014) business investment in the G-7 countries stood at 12.4% of GDP, well below the 13.3% level in 2008 and further behind the 13.8% peak in 2001.

That's not the way former Fed Chair Ben Bernanke sees it. Yes, economic growth is slow, interest rates are low, and private investment has fallen short of private savings. But Bernanke attributes that shortfall to a "savings glut," an over-supply of savings, rather than a paucity of investment. What held back economic growth (outside of the housing sector) from 2002 to 2006, he argues, was that China and other countries with large trade surpluses saved more than they invested and used their excess savings to buy U.S. securities. That helped to finance the housing boom, but also drove up the value of the dollar, making Chinese exports cheaper for U.S. buyers, and causing domestic production to suffer.

Does it really matter if the problem is a glut of savings or a dearth of investment opportunities? In fact, it does. The policy implications are quite different. If what's plaguing the global economy is Bernanke's savings glut, the appropriate policy is to get emerging economies "to reduce interventions in foreign exchange markets for the purpose of gaining trade advantage." But chalking up excess savings entirely to developing-world trade policies, as Bernanke does—not acknowledging the role of ever-rising domestic inequality and massive debt burdens—is literally one-sided. Moreover, changing exchange rates, as Summer points out, merely transfers spending from one country to another, instead of adding to it.

On the other hand, if Summers is right and the main problem is a persistent shortfall in private-sector demand (in particular, due to lack of investment demand), then the public sector needs to boost spending. For economist Paul Krugman, who has long maintained that today's economy suffers from a chronic lack of demand, that makes the secular stagnation hypothesis "a very radical manifesto."

## A Radical Manifesto?

The secular stagnation hypothesis does have radical implications, some more radical than others.

Summers, for instance, favors a program of enlarged and sustained public investment, "a natural instrument to promote growth." Public investment is, indeed, much needed. Net public investment (subtracting out depreciation) in the United States fell from 1.5% of GDP in 2008 to just 0.5% of GDP in 2012, and had actually turned negative in the eurozone. And he has an answer for those concerned that increasing public spending would push government debt to unsustainable levels: In a world with near-zero real interest rates for government debt, public investment projects would generate enough revenue to service the associated debt as long as those projects yielded any positive return. For those in the United States still concerned about the buildup of public debt, Summers has proposed that the U.S. government enact a carbon and gas tax to pay for infrastructure investments.

There are yet more radical implications of the stagnation hypothesis that get us closer to the roots of the ongoing economic crisis. Among the factors that Summers lists as contributing to a shortfall of investment is income inequality. Stagnant wages and booming profits have reduced consumer spending and added to corporate retained earnings. Worsening inequality—which Summers says threaten to turn the United States into a "Downton Abbey economy"—does not only diminish demand. It also empowers moneyed interests to resist public spending that would bring about continuous full employment.

In the last analysis, the secular stagnation problem is a political problem rather than an economic one. With sufficient political will—and political might—we could enact a program of large-scale public investment that would put an end to secular stagnation. Investments in clean energy (retro-fitting homes, upgrading the electrical system, building mass-transit) and education (reducing class size, improving school buildings, and boosting financial aid for students) are both worthwhile for their own sake and have been shown to effectively create jobs.

Surely that would be far better than an economy that depends financial bubbles and unsustainable household debt to keep it from stagnating—and that rewards the elites who stand in the way of needed reforms. ❏

*Sources:* Lawrence Summers, "What to do About Secular Stagnation," World Economic Forum, Oct. 31, 2014; Ben Bernanke, "Why are interest rates so low," part1, part 2, : Secular stagnation," Ben Bernanke's Blog, Brookings Institution, March, 30, 2015 and March 31, 2015: Lawrence Summers, "America risks becoming a Downton Abbey economy," *Financial Times*, Feb. 16, 2014; Lawrence Summers, "U.S. Economic Prospects," Business Economics, Vol. 49, Issue 2,, 2014 John Cassidy, "Is The Economy Still Threatened by Secular Stagnation," *The New Yorker*, Jan. 28, 2015; Matias Vernengo, "Bernanke and Summers on global savings glut and secular stagnation," Naked Keyneisianism, April 4, 2015; Lawrence Summers, "On Secular Stagnation: Larry Summers responds to Ben Bernanke," Ben Bernanke's Blog, Brookings Institution, April 1, 2015; Secular Stagnation, Facts, Causes, and Cures edited by Coen Teulings and Richard Baldwin, VoxEU.org eBook, 2014; Janet Yellen, "The New Normal Monetary Policy," Federal Reserve Bank of San Francisco, San Francisco, March 27, 2015; Paul Krugman, "What Secular Stagnation Isn't," *New York Times*, Oct. 27, 2014; Paul Krugman, "Secular Stagnation, Coalmines, Bubbles, and Larry Summers," *New York Times*, Nov. 16, 2013.

*Article 3.3*

# GERMAN WAGE REPRESSION
*Getting to the Roots of the Eurozone Crisis*

BY JOHN MILLER
*September/October 2015*

> Germany has been insistent that the so-called peripheral countries increase their competitiveness through slower wages rises or even wage cuts. Wage increases in Germany are an equally important, and symmetrical, part of this necessary adjustment process.
>
> The wage increases are steps in the right direction, but relatively small steps. More gains for German workers in the future would be both warranted and a win-win proposition for Germany and its trade partners.
>
> — *Ben Bernanke, "German wages hikes: A small step in the right direction," Brookings Institution, April 13, 2015.*

**B**en Bernanke not only supports recent German wage increases, he also thinks further wage increases for German workers are "warranted and a win-win proposition for Germany and its trade partners"?

Now that's a jaw-dropper. Has the former head of the Federal Reserve Board—the guardian of "price stability" that makes policy designed to keep U.S. wages in check—switched sides in the class war, now that he is retired?

Hardly. Rather, it's that catering to the demands of German high finance and other elites has been so disastrous that even the former chair of the Fed cannot deny the undeniable: unless Germany changes course and boosts workers' wages, the euro crisis will only worsen.

Let's look more closely at just how German wage repression and currency manipulation pushed the eurozone into crisis, ignited a conflict between northern and southern eurozone countries (with Germany as the enforcer of austerity), and left Greece teetering on the edge of collapse.

## From "Sick Man" to Export Bully

In the year 2000, Germany was widely considered "the sick man of Europe." Through much of the previous decade, the German economy grew more slowly than the European Union average, its manufacturing base shrunk, and its unemployment rate rose to near double-digits levels. Nor was Germany an export powerhouse, with its current account (the mostly widely used and most comprehensive measure of a nation's financial balance with the rest of the world) showing a modest deficit in 2000.

Adopting the euro as its sole currency, in January 2002, was no panacea. For the next two years, Germany's economy continued to stagnate. But converting to the euro—whose value was more or less an average of that of the stronger and weaker former currencies of the member countries—soon did improve Germany's competitive position internationally. German exports, no longer valued in strong deutschmarks, but in weaker euros, became cheaper to buyers in other countries. At the same time, the exports of countries that used to have weaker currencies, such as the Greek drachma and the Spanish peseta, became more expensive. That alone transformed Germany's current account deficit into a surplus.

China is widely accused of "currency manipulation," keeping the renminbi weak to boost its exports. But few see that the eurozone—the now 19-country bloc sharing the euro as its common currency—has functioned for Germany as a built-in currency manipulation system. And much like China, Germany used a lethal combination of wage repression and an undervalued currency to boost its exports and output at the expense of its trading partners.

Following the adoption of the euro, Germany instituted a set of "labor-market flexibility" policies intended to further improve its international competitiveness. Known as the Agenda 2010 Reforms, the new policies reduced pensions, cut medical benefits, and slashed the duration of unemployment benefits from nearly three years to just one. They also made it easier to fire workers, while encouraging the creation of part-time and short-term jobs. Employers increasingly divided formerly full-time jobs into state-subsidized, low-paying, insecure "mini-jobs." A decade later, one in five German jobs was a mini-job.

Germany's repressive labor policies kept a lid on wage growth. In every year from 2000 through the onset of the financial crisis in 2009, German compensation per employee increased more slowly than the eurozone average, and less even than in the United States.

During the 1990s, German workers' real (inflation-adjusted) wages rose along with productivity gains, meaning that employers could pay the higher wages without facing higher labor costs per unit of output. After 1999, wage gains no longer kept pace with productivity, and the gap between the two widened. As wages stagnated, inequality worsened, and poverty rates rose. Total labor compensation (wages and benefits) fell from 61% of GDP in 2001 to just 55% of GDP in 2007, its lowest level in five decades.

German wage repression went even further than necessary to meet the 2% inflation target mandated by the eurozone agreement, and insisted upon by German policymakers. Unit labor costs (workers' compensation per unit of output) is perhaps the most important determinant of prices and competitiveness. Unit labor costs rise with wage increases but fall with gains in productivity. From 1999 to 2013, German unit labor costs increased by just 0.4% a year. The reason was not German productivity growth, which was no greater than the eurozone average over the period; rather, it was that German labor market policies kept wage growth in check.

This combination of a built-in system of currency manipulation afforded by the euro and labor-market policies holding labor costs in check turned Germany into the world's preeminent trade-surplus country. As its competitive advantage grew, its exports soared. Germany's current account surplus became the largest in the world relative to the size of its economy, reaching 7.6% of the country's GDP, more than twice the size of China's surplus compared to its GDP.

## Beggar Thy Neighborhood

Germany's transformation into an export powerhouse came at the expense of the southern eurozone economies. Despite posting productivity gains that were equal or almost equal to Germany's, Greece, Portugal, Spain, and Italy saw their labor costs per unit of output and prices rise considerably faster than Germany's. Wage growth in these countries exceeded productivity growth, and the resulting higher unit labor costs pushed prices up by more than the eurozone's low 2% annual inflation target (by a small margin).

The widening gap in unit labor costs gave Germany a tremendous competitive advantage and left the southern eurozone economies at a tremendous disadvantage. Germany amassed its ever-larger current account surplus, while the southern eurozone economies were saddled with worsening deficits. Later in the decade, the Greek, Portuguese, and Spanish current account deficits approached or even reached alarming double-digit levels, relative to the sizes of their economies.

In this way, German wage repression is an essential component of the euro crisis. Heiner Flassbeck, the German economist and longtime critic of wage repression, and Costas Lapavitsas, the Greek economist best known for his work on financialization, put it best in their recent book *Against the Troika: Crisis and Austerity in the Eurozone*: "Germany has operated a policy of 'beggar-thy-neighbor' but only after 'beggaring its own people' by essentially freezing wages. This is the secret of German success during the last fifteen years."

While Germany's huge exports across Europe and elsewhere created German jobs and lowered the country's unemployment rate, the German economy never grew robustly. Wage repression subsidized exports, but it sapped domestic spending. And, held back by this chronic lack of domestic demand, Germany's economic growth was far-from-impressive, before or after the Great Recession. From 2002 to 2008, the German economy grew more slowly than the eurozone average, and over the last five years has failed to match even the sluggish growth rates posted by the U.S. economic recovery. With low wage growth, consumption stagnated. German corporations hoarded their profits and private investment relative to GDP fell almost continuously from 2000 on. The same was true for German public investment, held back by the eurozone budgetary constraints.

At the same time, Germany spread instability. Germany's reliance on foreign demand for its exports drained spending from elsewhere in the eurozone and slowed growth in those countries. That, in turn, made it less likely that German banks and elites would recover their loans and investments in southern Europe.

## Wage Repression and the Crisis

No wonder Bernanke now describes higher German wages as an important step toward reducing Europe's trade imbalances. More spending by German workers on domestic goods and imports would help Germany and its trading partners grow, and improve the lot of working people throughout the eurozone.

Of course, much more needs to be done. Putting an end to the austerity measures imposed on Greece and the other struggling eurozone economies would boost their demand as well. In fact, it would also better serve the interests of Germany and the profitmaking class, by helping to stabilize a system from which they have benefited so greatly at the expense of much of the region's population.

Still, raising the wages of German workers to match productivity gains is, as Bernanke recognizes, surely a step in the right direction. Raising U.S. wages to match productivity gains would help defuse U.S. wage repression and boost economic growth here as well. If Bernanke throws his weight behind that proposition, we'll truly wonder which side is he on. ❏

*Article 3.4*

# CAN "ABENOMICS" REVIVE JAPAN'S ECONOMY?

*Why we need a progressive alternative embracing greater income equality and alternative energy investment.*

## BY JUNJI TOKUNAGA
May/June 2015

Japan's conservative Liberal Democratic Party (LDP)—led by Prime Minister Shinzo Abe (pronounced "AH-bay")—won a landslide victory in the December 2014 snap election for the House of Representatives, the lower house of the national parliament. The Liberal Democrats and their partner party in the ruling coalition, the Komeito, won 326 of 475 seats, giving them a two-thirds supermajority in the House of Representatives.

Why did Abe win so handily? Since the end of 2012, the Abe government has carried out an economic revitalization program called "Abenomics"—its response to Japan's ongoing economic stagnation, the "lost decades" of the 1990s and 2000s. Abenomics consists of three "arrows": aggressive monetary "quantitative easing," massive fiscal stimulus, and "structural reforms" to the economy. The main reason for Abe's resounding victory is that he succeeded in persuading the electorate to stay the course, with slogans like "Abenomics is progressing" and "There is no other way to economic recovery." Meanwhile, he shifted voters' attention away from more controversial matters, such as his plans to restart Japan's nuclear power plants (which were shuttered after the March 2011 Fukushima nuclear disaster) and to bolster the country's military forces.

Rather than leading to a rebound of domestic consumption and investment spending, which could lift the economy as a whole, however, Abe's neoliberal reforms would lead to rising inequality and continued stagnation. We certainly need significant public spending. The Abe government, however, has carried out porkbarrel public projects that will not revive the Japanese economy in the long term, while averting another recession. Rather, we must explore programs to facilitate the development of new industries, such as renewable energy (RE), instead of the defense and nuclear power industries that the Abe cabinet favors.

## What is Abenomics?

Abenomics has been mainly about more aggressive monetary "quantitative easing"—central bank purchases of various kinds of bonds (other than short-term government bonds, purchases of which are considered "conventional" expansionary monetary policy) from banks and other private owners of financial assets. The Bank of Japan, the country's central bank, has been engaging in "Quantitative and Qualitative Monetary Easing" (QQE) since April 2013, with the goal of raising the inflation rate to 2% within two years.

According to advocates of Abenomics, inflationary expectations driven by aggressive monetary easing would reduce real interest rates (that is, interest rates adjusted for inflation, which are calculated by subtracting the inflation rate from the nominal interest rate). In turn, lower real interest rates will make corporations willing to borrow more, raising investment spending and generating domestic employment. The increase in investment would lead to strong corporate profits, eventually translating into higher wages, which would in turn increase consumption spending by households. This is basically a form of "trickle-down economics," in the sense that, according to its advocates, strong corporate profits would trickle down to everyone else in the economy.

Under the QQE program, the Bank of Japan (BOJ) pledged to double the size of the monetary base (currency in circulation plus banks' reserves on deposit at the central bank). By the end of October 2014, unsatisfied with the results of the program, it decided to accelerate this enlargement of the monetary base. With the BOJ being twice as aggressive as the U.S. Federal Reserve in its bond-buying, its balance sheet has gone above 50% of GDP.

Economist Paul Krugman has strongly supported Abenomics—"the sharp turn toward monetary and fiscal stimulus adopted by the government of Prime Minster Shinzo Abe"—and hailed it as a model for other countries to emulate. In a 2013 column in the *New York Times*, he stressed that Japan could be the first major country to climb out of the kind of recession and stagnation in which has also befallen Western countries since the global financial crisis in 2008.

## What Have the Effects of Abenomics Been So Far?

The effects of aggressive monetary easing have, mainly, been limited to higher stock prices on the Tokyo Stock Exchange and the drastic depreciation of the Japanese yen in foreign exchange markets. The Nikkei 225, the index for the Tokyo stock market (analogous to the S&P 500 for the New York Stock Exchange and NASDAQ), has soared. The yen, meanwhile, has depreciated by more than 42% relative to the dollar in the last two years. Some have pointed to these developments as proof that Abenomics is working.

In fact, these effects will not contribute to the trickle-down economics which advocates of Abe's policy expect, for two reasons. First, aggressive monetary easing will not stimulate overall household consumption spending. The dramatic stock market rally has sparked a "wealth effect," which might lead those who own a lot of financial assets—feeling flush with their new riches—to spend more. Meanwhile, however, workers' wages have not kept pace with inflation. In addition, the Abe government introduced a sales tax hike, from 5% to 8%, in April 2014. Such conditions tend to make ordinary people reduce their consumption spending. The benefits of trickle-down Abenomics clearly have not reached everyone.

Second, corporations, particularly big multinationals, are hoarding their profits. Corporate profits have been rising significantly, underpinned by the drastic depreciation of the yen. This has boosted the competitiveness of Japanese industry in global markets. But corporations have held onto most of these profits as internal reserves, rather than engaging in investment spending that would lift the economy. According to Japan's Finance Ministry, the reserves of Japanese nonfinancial companies reached a record 304 trillion yen (nearly $3 trillion) by of the end of fiscal year 2013. As a consequence, Japan's GDP shrunk for two consecutive quarters, a common definition for recession, after the second quarter of 2014. (Figures for the first quarter of 2015 were not available at this writing.)

## What Kinds of Policies Will Abe Push Now?

Abe's landslide victory in the snap election could not only enable him to stay in office until late 2018, making him longest-serving prime minister in Japan since World War II, but also give him abundant political capital for further pursuing his economic agenda.

On what kind of policies will Abe spend this political capital? First of all, he will likely purse the "third arrow" of Abenomics: structural reforms of the economy. The Abe cabinet announced a "Revision of Japan Revitalization Strategy: 10 Key Reforms" in June 2014. Parts of the strategy, such as enhancing women's labor-force participation and advancement could be epoch-making in Japan, if they worked well. But most of structural reform plans are based on a neoliberal approach of low corporate taxation, deregulation, reduction of fiscal deficits, and free trade.

Broadly, Abe would likely push four neoliberal policies:

First, lowering corporate taxes, while planning the second stage of the sales tax hike from 8% to 10% in April 2017. The Abe government has agreed on the basic outline of fiscal year 2015 tax reforms, including a 2.51 percentage-point reduction in the effective corporate tax rate. The tax cut could be a further boost for big corporations that have already received the windfall from the depreciation of the yen.

Second, accelerating the push for labor market "flexibility." Labor market deregulation would make it easier for big corporations to fire full-time employees, lowering incomes for wage earners even further.

Third, radically reducing social welfare spending in the fiscal year 2015 budget, in order to reduce the massive fiscal deficit.

Finally, completing the final stage of negotiations over a free-trade agreement, the Trans-Pacific Partnership (TPP), with the United States. The TPP would open the agricultural market in Japan to an unprecedented level of imports, which would inflict big damage on many Japanese farmers.

## Do We Have a Progressive Alternative for Reviving the Economy?

Many voters understood the problems with Abenomics before the December snap election. An November opinion poll by Nikkei, Japan's leading economics and business news company, reported that 51% of the public opposed Abenomics, compared with 33% who favored it. Disappointingly, a lack of strongly progressive alternatives from the opposition parties helped Abe win his landslide victory.

What kind of policy should we implement to avert a return to recession? As economist Richard Koo argues in his recent book *The Escape from Balance Sheet Recession and the QE Trap*, we have to carry out not austerity policies but fiscal stimulus, which can stabilize the economy. Reasonably, the Abe government announced expenditures totaling 3.5 trillion yen (US$29 billion) in 2015. But fiscal stimulus and monetary easing can only buy time to sow the seeds of economic revival in Japan. Now is the time to explore an alternative program for long-term recovery.

First, we need to increase real wages, which could lead to a rise in consumption spending. Abe and Haruhiko Kuroda, governor of the Bank of Japan, are trying to encourage big companies to raise wages in 2015, which is part of their program to achieve 2% inflation. To spread the benefits of economic recovery through the economy as a whole, however, we have to extend higher wages not only to workers at big corporations, but also to those at small- and medium-sized enterprises (SMEs), which are the main engines of the Japanese economy.

Second, we need a new set of public investment projects that could foster basic industry for the next generation. Japan is a global leader in renewable energy technology. In fact, the country accounts for the majority of renewable-energy patent applications worldwide. (Japan's share is 55%; the United States', 20%; Europe's, 9%.) The Japanese government should drastically redirect the energy research and development (R&D) budget away from nuclear power generation—which reached 69% of total energy R&D spending in 2010—and toward renewables.

The financial system in Japan has the potential to serve as a bridge between lenders and financial investors who want to finance RE projects, and borrowers who plan to start renewable energy businesses. On the lending side, Japanese individual investors have been among those most interested, worldwide, in "World Bank Green Bonds," which are designed to raise funds for green economy projects in developing countries. On the borrowing side, many firms and entrepreneurs, some supported by local governments, have applied to start businesses including solar, wind, geothermal, and biomass power generation.

A "feed-in-tariff" (FIT) law, passed in July 2012, allows private providers to sell renewable energy to big electricity companies at prices to be fixed by the central government. This has fostered a boom in RE business, particularly in solar power generation. According to Japan's Agency for Natural Resources and Energy, renewable-energy generating capacity has increased from about 567,000 kilowatts in July 2012 to nearly 72 million kilowatts in October 2014. These developments imply that Japan has both extraordinary financial resources that could provide funds to RE businesses and numerous firms and entrepreneurs eager to make use of them, if given a chance.

As Koo explains, Japan's "lost decades" and its deflation are attributable to insufficient private investment demand. It could take a significant amount of time for these alternative programs to create new investment opportunities and lift the economy as a whole. But Japan has to learn the lessons of the Fukushima nuclear disaster and start to develop renewable energy. This could end deflation and move the country onto a path of sustainable economic growth. ❑

*Sources:* Paul Krugman, "Japan the model," *New York Times,* May 23, 2013; "Without reforms, Japan's leader remains vulnerable," *Wall Street Journal,* Dec. 15, 2014; "Acquisitions, financing worries behind Japan Inc.'s bulging reserves," *Nikkei Asian Review,* June 23, 2014; Richard Koo, *The Escape from Balance Sheet Recession and the QE Trap* (Wiley, 2015); "Japan cabinet approves Y3.5tn stimulus spending," *Financial Times,* Dec. 27, 2014; "Patent-based Technology Analysis Report-Alternative Energy Technology," World Intellectual Property Organization, 2009; "Japan and nuclear power," *Mainichi,* Jan. 22, 2012.

*Article 3.5*

# DEBT AND DEVELOPMENT: FREQUENTLY ASKED QUESTIONS

## BY ALEJANDRO REUSS
*November 2015*

**W**e used to hear all the time about the "Third World" debt crisis—and how it was keeping Latin America and Africa poor. But now I hear that those economies have actually been growing pretty fast. Was all that talk about debt overblown?

For both regions, the return to economic growth was far removed from the severe debt crises in the 1980s and 1990s. In Latin America, the entire 1980s came to be known as the "lost decade." Per capita gross domestic product (GDP) for the region as a whole was actually lower in 1990 than it was in 1980. For sub-Saharan Africa, the story was even worse. In 1974, the region's per capita GDP was just over $950, according to World Bank data. Over the next two decades, it would plunge by more than 20%, and would not regain its 1974 level until 2008.

Per capita GDP has indeed grown again in Latin America since the 1990s (and more rapidly since the early 2000s). In sub-Saharan Africa, per capita GDP bottomed out in the early 1990s, and growth through the rest of the decade was so modest as to be practically nonexistent. GDP growth for the region, as for Latin America, has been faster in the 2000s. Economies in both regions have grown, in part, due to the boom in agricultural and mineral commodities prices. In Latin America, center-left governments in several countries have adopted policies to reduce income inequality, which has also boosted economic growth. In both regions, too, burdens of external debt have declined in recent years—in Africa, partially due to debt-cancellation campaigns—and this has also played a role.

None of this is to say that external debt—that is, debt owed to foreign financial institutions or governments—was the sole cause for economic crisis and stagnation in either region. However, debt has certainly played a large negative role, in the recent history of much of the "developing world," by thwarting economic development.

*If debt is bad for economic development, shouldn't developing countries just avoid getting into debt in the first place?*

Well, debt isn't always bad from the standpoint of economic growth or development. A developing country may borrow to finance an infrastructural or industrial project—for example, to pay for imports of machinery, materials, energy, or other needed inputs that are not produced domestically—expecting that it will more than pay for itself. That is, the resulting revenues will be large enough that the loan can be paid back with interest, plus leave some revenue left over.

We don't usually think of the United States as a "developing country," but in the mid-to-late 19th century, it was going through a period of rapid industrialization, financed in large measure by external debt. As economist Jayati Ghosh put it in a recent interview: "If you think about it, the United States would not be a developed economy if throughout the 19th century it had not been able to borrow vast sums, mostly from England. ... So in fact the United States ran current account deficits between 5-7% of GDP for nearly 70 years. And this is what really enabled it to become the industrial power that we saw before the First World War."

Note that the experience of the United States was unusual, especially in that it enjoyed such large and steady flows of credit for so long. Other countries were not so fortunate. Ghosh has pointed out that other countries in Britain's informal commercial empire during the mid-to-late 19th century—like Argentina—also received very large credit flows, but these were subject to sudden interruptions. A sudden interruption of credit can be very damaging—forcing the borrower to suddenly come up with payment for the full principal, causing the discontinuation of long-term projects for want of further credit, and so on. In the 1890s, for example, a major British bank went bankrupt after many of its loans in Argentina went bad, triggering a much broader shut-off of credit to Argentina and playing a major role in the "reversal" of the country's economic development.

*In a way, that suggests a loss of access to credit can be a big problem. Are there ways that debt itself can impede economic development?*

One way is that the burden of debt repayment (or "debt service") is so great that it leaves little left over for high-priority domestic spending, including basics like nutrition, health housing, and education, as well as investments on infrasctructure or industy to promote economic growth.

Economists James K. Boyce and Léonce Ndikumana estimated, in their recent book *Africa's Odious Debts*, that each dollar in external debt service is associated with a decrease of about $0.29 in public health spending. Just one consequence of this reduction, in turn, is increased infant mortality—seven more infant deaths per year for every $290,000 reduction in health spending. In other words, every additional $1 million in debt service results in seven more infant deaths. Boyce and Ndikumana estimate that there are 77,000 more infant deaths per year, for Africa as a whole, from just the portion of debt service (about 60% of the total) that has fueled capital flight.

High debt service on past loans can also impede domestic "capital formation"— new investment in assets like machinery, factories, infrastructure, etc.—and therefore economic growth. Slow growth, in turn, can make it difficult to repay even the principal on past debts, so the country could go on making interest payments indefinitely. There are many cases where countries have, in effect, repaid international debts many times over for exactly this reason.

Sub-Saharan Africa in the 1980s and 1990s illustrates this vicious circle. In 1981, the region's debt service (payments of principal and interest) was less than 4% of GDP. It would drop again below that threshold in 2010. In the 28 years between, it would average over 7% of GDP, twice hitting a full 10% of GDP. Another common way to look at the debt service burden is as a percent of the region's exports. Exports mean a flow of goods out of the country, and a flow of payments back in. These payments can be used to pay back principal and interest on previous debt, so this ratio is sometimes used as a measure of a country's ability to pay its debt. Here, we're more interested in it as showing the diversion to debt repayment of resources that could otherwise have been used for domestic development. Again, we find much the same story. For sub-Saharan Africa, debt service goes from about 15% of exports in the early 1980s to an average of over 30% for the 20 years between 1982 and 2001. In other words, the region's debt crisis meant that it was paying up to one-tenth of its total income, or nearly one-third of its revenue from exports, just to service its debts. Domestic capital formation, meanwhile, was substantially lower than it had been since the late 1960s.

*So how do countries actually get into debt trouble? It seems that what we usually hear about is a country having big trade deficits—or "living beyond their means"—and having to borrow heavily to finance them.*

That's a misleading story, for several reasons. First, the phrase "living beyond their means" suggests that the borrowing is being done to finance consumption beyond the country's own capacity for production. Developing countries, however, often run trade deficits (or the slightly broader concept of current account deficits) because they import large quantities of production goods, rather than consumption goods. The "import substitution industrialization" policies adopted by many Latin America countries in the 1950s and 1960s, for example, were designed to reduce reliance on imports of manufactured consumer goods. Tariffs and other "barriers" were put in place to protect budding domestic industries from import competition. And yet trade deficits increased, largely due to rising imports of machinery and other production goods needed for domestic industrialization.

Second, there are other factors in trade balances besides the physical quantities of imports and exports. Changes in the relative prices of a country's imports and exports may have a big effect on its trade balance. This is especially true for countries that are exporters of "primary" goods—raw materials like agricultural products and minerals—whose prices tend to be highly volatile. A petroleum-exporting country, for example, might run large trade surpluses when oil prices are high, but trade deficits when oil prices are low. (By the same token, the reverse might be true for a petroleum importing country.) A country might not start running trade deficits because it is importing larger quantities of goods—or because its people are enjoying higher consumption—but because its exports are suddenly worth less, or its imports suddenly cost more.

Third, the actual cause-effect relationship often runs not from trade deficits to debt, but the other way around. The story can start with large capital flows into a country—when individuals, companies, or governments of other countries buy tangible assets, buy stocks or other securities, or make loans in that country. This can cause the currency of the country experiencing the financial inflows to increase in value relative to other currencies. A "stronger" (higher valued) currency makes the country's imports cheaper and its exports more expensive. Rising imports and declining exports, in turn, push the trade balance in a negative direction (from surplus towards deficit).

Finally, a country's debt burden depends not just on the amount borrowed, but also on the interest rates the country faces. Those rates depend on the risk that lenders assign to different borrowers. As a country becomes heavily indebted, lenders are likely to see it as a bigger credit risk, and it may have to pay higher interest rates to get further loans—if it can get them at all. The yield on long-term Greek government bonds (the IOUs that a government or other borrower issues for the money it borrows), for example, went from less than 6% as late as 2009 to as high as 36% in 2012. Lenders' calculations of how risky it is to lend to a particular country, however, may not be based solely on economic conditions within that country. During the Latin American debt crisis of the 1980s, for example, some countries' default on debt led to a tightening of credit throughout the region. (In effect, lenders were treating the entire region as a single unit, for the purpose of evaluating risk.)

The interest rates that one borrower faces, meanwhile, also depend on the interest rates that lenders can get elsewhere. This, too, was a big factor in the 1980s debt crisis. In the late 1970s, the United States government adopted policies to deliberately drive up interest rates, mainly to rein in domestic demand and reduce upward pressure on wages. Lenders prefer to make loans to borrowers who will pay higher interest rates, keeping in mind differences in risk. With interest rates on the rise in the United States, the country became a more attractive place for lenders to make loans. Borrowers in developing countries, therefore, suddenly had to pay higher rates to keep attracting credit.

*Are countries better off, if they start getting into debt trouble, tightening their belts to repay it as soon as they can, rather than getting deeper and deeper into the hole?*

A country's external debt may be public (owed by the government) or private (owed by private individuals and companies), but for now let's think about a large public debt. The pro-austerity reasoning is that the best way to bring down the debt fast is to cut spending and/or raise taxes. The resulting "primary surplus" (current revenues minus current expenditures, excluding payments on past debts) will then make it possible to pay down debt and bring down the country's debt-to-GDP ratio.

This argument for austerity seems to make sense if we're thinking about a single household—if it gets too deep in debt, it can cut back on its spending and maybe find more paid work or other income opportunities, and over time whittle down what it owes. Reasoning by analogy with an individual household, however, is not a good way to approach public policy. When we think about a household "tightening its belt" and cutting back on spending, we usually don't think of this as getting in the way of its income opportunities. The austerity policies described above, however, may have the effect of reducing demand, output, and incomes for the society as a whole.

Think about it this way: Governments often adopt fiscal "stimulus" programs when the economy goes into a downturn. By increasing spending and reducing taxes, they increase demand for goods and services. That causes businesses to increase their planned output, to increase their orders for inputs, and to hire more workers. The workers and suppliers, in turn, spend their new incomes, further boosting demand. Austerity programs, however, do just the opposite—reducing demand in the economy. If the idea is to bring down debt relative to GDP, this kind of policy can backfire—since it may bring down GDP. (It may also fail to bring about the sought-after primary surpluses, since recession conditions will usually reduce tax revenue and may actually increase some kinds of spending, such as unemployment insurance and other government social-welfare payments.) A big reason that Latin America's debt crisis turned into a "lost decade" was not the loss of access to credit itself, but that austerity policies—pushed, in many countries, by the International Monetary Fund—depressed these economies.

Austerity policies can also be aimed at pushing a country's trade balance in a positive direction (from deficit toward surplus). The reduction of demand reduces output and employment. The resulting unemployment, in turn, puts downward pressure on wages. Lower wages tend to make the country's goods cheaper relative to those of other countries, and therefore reduce its imports and increase its exports. Of all ways to accomplish this change in relative prices, however, austerity is just about the worst—coming at a high cost in lost output of goods and services and an even higher human cost, especially in the form of mass unemployment. An alternative way to accomplish this is through "devaluation"—making the country's currency weaker, and so its exports cheaper and imports more expensive. There may be impediments to such a policy for countries, however, that are in a fixed exchange-rate system or that share a currency with other countries.

Finally, no matter what policy is used to pay back debt—including devaluation or other policies that reduce imports and boost exports—we have to ask whose belts it is that are getting tightened. The burdens of debt are never borne equally by all—and are not necessarily even borne by those who took out the debt in the first place, or who benefited from taking it out. In many developing countries, external debt has not been used to develop infrastructure, promote industrialization, or reduce poverty—but to enrich the already rich and powerful. Economists Boyce and Ndikumana have shown that external debt is strongly associated with "capital flight." In some cases, autocratic rulers have stolen billions of dollars in loans, transferring the money to their own bank accounts overseas. Why should the people of these countries be responsible for repaying loans they neither took out nor benefited from? If the banks knew—or should have known—that the loans might be stolen, why should they not bear the cost if the loans are not paid back?

More generally, austerity policies tend to fall hardest on workers and poor people. This was certainly the case, for example, in the Latin American debt crisis of the 1980s. Austerity policies included cuts to public subsidies on basic goods like food and fuel, reductions in social welfare spending, reductions or elimination of minimum wages, cutbacks in public employment, and so on—all of which quite transparently targeted lower-income people. These policies transferred income not from the debtor countries to the creditor countries in general, but specifically from workers and the poor in the debtor countries to the wealthy bondholders in the creditor countries.

*OK, so if austerity policies aren't the solution, how are poor countries that get into debt trouble supposed to get out?*

If one is determined to make sure highly indebted low-income countries be able to repay their debts, then austerity is surely not the solution, because it is a recipe for "lost decades." An alternative would be policies that 1) include debt restructuring—that is, reduction or postponement of debt repayment—and 2) promote growth—so that debt can be repaid out of growing income. Many of today's high-income countries have benefited from debt restructuring in the past, or from "growing their way out of debt" over time, without demands for immediate payment when they could ill-afford it.

If one is not determined that debtor countries repay their debts—put another way, if one is not determined that, above all else, the banks should be repaid—then debt repudiation is an option. Many countries have repudiated (refused to pay) past debts. One argument in favor of repudiation is that of "odious debt"—sovereign debt that did not benefit the people of a country. This idea has been frequently invoked, in recent years, in regard to debt incurred by dictators—and largely used to enrich the dictators, their families, and their cronies. Advocates of repudiation argue that the people have no moral obligation to pay such debts.

With the possible move of debt repudiation up their sleeve, indebted countries need not knuckle under to creditors' demands for payment in full (whatever the suffering this may mean for their people). Rather, they can negotiate more favorable terms. One recent example is Argentina, which defaulted on its external debt in 2001, and then managed to negotiate a restructuring of its debts with the vast majority of its creditors. Getting some relief from debt repayments and avoiding austerity policies that would have undermined growth, Argentina enjoyed a surprising economic rebound. (Since then, the debt-restructuring deal has been endangered by the so-called "vulture funds." These are speculators who did not lend to Argentina at all, but bought Argentinean bonds after the default for a fraction of their face value. Now they're fighting in the courts to be paid the full value of the bonds, and standing in the way of the restructuring deal that most creditors had already accepted.)

One reason people give for thinking a country shouldn't default on its debts—that the country will cut itself off from future credit—turns out not to be generally true. This raises the question of why heavily indebted countries do not do this more often. There's no one simple answer, but the example of the Latin American debt crisis of the 1980s is instructive. As multiple Latin American countries had become heavily indebted, serious discussion emerged about forming a "debtors' cartel." If they all threatened to default, many argued, they would be able to get better terms from the banks. In the end, however, the proposed debtors' cartel did not materialize, and the various countries ended up accepting quite onerous debt-repayment conditions. One reason was that there were significant divisions between more-indebted and less-indebted countries, with policymakers in the latter thinking that they could negotiate better terms going it alone than if they threw in their lot with the worse-off. More importantly, elites in debtor countries faced a choice—either confront a creditors' alliance including the giant international banks, the U.S. government, and international institutions or push the burdens of repayment onto the workers and poor of their own societies. Not surprisingly, they chose not to confront the high and mighty, but the poor and downtrodden.

*Is there no way for lower-income countries to increase standards of living for their people without recourse to external debt?*

Raising future consumption requires that some current resources not be used to produce goods for consumption today, but rather goods that will make it possible to produce and consume more tomorrow. For example, rather than consumer goods like food, clothing, televisions, and houses, some resources are used instead to produce industrial machinery, factory buildings, and so on. If the alternative is to ferociously restrict consumption now, in order to finance such investments domestically, external debt may seem like the lesser evil.

There are ways, however, that countries that countries can promote economic development without having to "bite the bullet" and choose one of these two options. First, many developing countries could greatly reduce their need for credit or other inflows of capital, in order to finance investments in future production, if they did not suffer from enormous financial outflows. As economists Boyce and Ndikumana have documented, as of 2010, capital flight from the 33 countries of sub-Saharan Africa had resulted in total ownership, by citizens of those countries, of over $1 trillion in assets abroad. Basically, this is what the region is lending to the rest of the world. At the same time, the region's total external liabilities—basically, what is owes to the rest of the world—added up to less than $200 billion. In effect, Boyce and Ndikumana conclude, "making the region a net creditor to the rest of the world." Think about that. Heavily indebted sub-Saharan Africa—and the debt burdens are, indeed, large relative to average incomes—is not actually borrowing from the rest of the world, on balance, but lending! Capital flight is draining many countries of resources that could be used for domestic development. International credit is not only failing to fill the resulting void, but as Boyce and Ndikumana argue, is actually fueling much of this capital flight (as the wealthy and powerful divert loans, including public loans, into their own pockets).

Second, economic development and economic growth are not the same thing. If we define economic development, following economist and philosopher Amartya Sen, as the expansion of substantive human freedoms (or "capabilities"), then we can ask whether economic growth is either necessary or sufficient to achieve development. Sen emphasizes universal access to basic capabilities, like long life, good health, education, and the ability to participate in community life. Many countries have achieved substantial economic growth without achieving economic development in this sense. If the fruits of growth are mainly appropriated by the already well-off (and well-housed, well-fed, well-clothed, and well-educated), it's not surprising that growth would not bring about much improvement in the general level of these "capabilities." So economic growth is not sufficient for economic development. Neither, however, is substantial economic growth (raising per capita incomes) necessary for dramatic progress in "human development." High levels of human development can be (and have been) achieved, even at very low per capita incomes, in countries or sub-national regions where income is distributed quite equally and there is a strong public commitment to universal provision of basic goods (e.g., adequate nutrition, public health, elementary education, etc.).

On some level, we can imagine "unilateral" changes in the political and economic institutions of a lower-income country dramatically altering these two factors. More democratic and egalitarian societies are likely to be more successful both in avoiding the theft of resources by elites and in deploying the available resources to meet fundamental human needs. However, individual countries are also embedded in the capitalist world economy. The basic way capitalist economies operate is no different on the world scale than it is at the level of the individual enterprise—those who own resources only make them available to those who don't if the owners expect to profit by doing so. That is why so much discussion of development policy is about how lower-income countries can make themselves attractive for foreign investment. The only apparent way to get access to needed resources—by means of credit, foreign direct investment, etc.—is to convince the global banks or other global corporations that they will profit from it.

An alternative would be a world system in which there were large transfers from high- to low-income countries, without expectation of repayment or profit. These resources could be deployed, given sufficiently democratic and egalitarian institutions in the recipient countries, to spur development—including investments to increase future productive capacity and standards of living, but especially focusing on universal achievement of the basic capabilities that define "human development." Global mechanisms for wealth redistribution may seem like an unrealizable and utopian fantasy. In fact, they have existed in recent history—only operating in the reverse direction.

Colonialism, among other things, was a giant engine for transferring wealth from the "periphery" of the capitalist world economy (Africa, Asia, and Latin America) to the "core" (Western Europe and North America). Indeed, that system helped to create the division of the capitalist world into its "developed" and "underdeveloped" regions, producing development at one pole along with underdevelopment (subordinate, dependent development) at the other. In short, it created the world we know—not only one in which there are rich and poor countries, but in which the peripheral-ubordinate-poor are used for the further enrichment of the core-dominant-rich.

A system that did the opposite is not unimaginable, but it does require that we imagine a very different world. ❑

*Sources:* Jayati Ghosh, "Who Benefits from Sovereign Debt Crises?" The Real News Network, Oct. 26, 2015; World Bank, Data, GDP per capita (constant 2005 US$) (data.worldbank. org); International Monetary Fund, Data and Statistics, External debt, total debt service (imf. org); James K. Boyce and Léonce Ndikumana, "Capital Flight from Sub-Saharan African Countries: Updated Estimates, 1970-2010," Political Economy Research Institute, University of Massachusetts-Amherst (October 2012); Léonce Ndikumana and James K. Boyce, *Africa's Odious Debts: How Foreign Loans and Capital Flight Bled a Continent* (Zed Books, 2011).

Article 3.6

# THE "EMERGING ECONOMIES" TODAY

## AN INTERVIEW WITH JAYATI GHOSH
May/June 2016

The terms "emerging markets" and "emerging economies" have come into fashion, especially to refer to countries supposedly poised to make the leap from "developing" to "developed" economies. There's no definitive list, but Brazil, India, Indonesia, Mexico, Russia, South Africa, Turkey, and China are among the large countries that often headline articles on "emerging economies." Economic growth rates—as well as the drop-off in growth during the global Great Recession and the recovery since—vary widely between countries typically placed in this group.

China is by far the most prominent of the emerging economies—the most populous country in the world, with an extraordinary period of industrial growth since the 1980s, and with an enormous impact (not only as an exporter of manufactured goods but also as an importer of raw-material and intermediate inputs to manufacturing) on the world economy. The "secular stagnation" of the high-income capitalist economies and resulting growth slowdown in China, therefore, has much wider implications for the developing world. In this interview, economist Jayati Ghosh addresses the current challenges for China and other countries—and possible paths toward inclusive and sustainable development. – Eds.

**Dollars & Sense:** You've written about the "retreat" of emerging-market economies, which until recently had been held up as examples of robust growth, in contrast to the stagnant economies of the so-called capitalist "core." What's driving the slowdown of economic growth in the emerging economies today?

**Jayati Ghosh:** The emerging economies are really those that have integrated much more into the global financial system, not just the global trade system. And I think what happened during the period of the economic boom is that many people forgot that their growth was still ultimately driven by what was happening in the North. That is, the engine of demand was still the northern economies. So whether you're talking about China in particular or the range of emerging economies that was seen as more prominent in the first half of the 2000s, all of them depended on exports to the North and particularly to the United States.

It was the U.S. boom that drew in more and more of the exports from developing countries. When it came to an end—as it inevitably had to—these economies had to look for other sources of demand. There are two ways of doing this. One is to try and do a domestic demand-driven expansion based on higher domestic incomes because of wage and employment growth. And the other is the model which unfortunately seems to be the more popular one, which is to have a debt-driven kind of growth, based on both consumption and accumulation that is essentially led by taking on more and more debt. This is, of course, also what the U.S. did in the 2000s, which unraveled in 2007 and 2008. But it's also what a number of European economies did, and they're paying the price now.

Remarkably, developing countries that don't need to take this path, and can see all the problems associated with it, also took this path in the wake of the global financial crisis. In China there was a doubling of the debt-to-GDP ratio between 2007 and 2014. This reflected increases in debt to every single sector, but it was dominantly for investment. In a range of other important developing countries, from Mexico to Indonesia, Malaysia, South Korea, etc., there was a dramatic expansion of household debt, particularly real estate and housing debt. We all know that these real-estate and housing bubbles that are led by taking on more debt, these end in tears. And that's really what has been happening.

In these "emerging" economies, financial integration allowed them to break the link between productive investment and growth. It fueled a debt-driven pattern of expansion, which inevitably has to end. It's ending now. The problem is that it's ending at a time when demand from the North is slowing dramatically. So there is a double whammy for these emerging economies. The slowdown in northern markets means that China—which had become the major driver of expansion—can no longer continue to export at the same rate. That means its imports have also come down. In the past year, China's exports fell by 5%, but its imports fell by 20%. That has affected all the other developing countries. And that's in combination with this end of the debt-driven expansion model.

*D&S:* A number of economists have argued for quite some time that China's export-oriented growth model would inevitably reach its limits. Are we seeing it finally reach an impasse now, and if so, is there a prospect for China to make a transition from a low-wage export-oriented model to a domestic demand-driven model that would necessarily require higher wages?

*JG:* I think it's indisputable that the export-driven model is over for the time being, for sure, certainly for the next five years, probably the next decade. That's not a bad thing, because one of the problems with that export-driven model is that it persists in seeing wages as costs rather than as a source of internal demand that you can use to your benefit. It encourages massive degradation of nature and taking on environmental costs that are now recognized to be completely unsustainable and socially undesirable. And, overall, we know that these can't last—these export-driven models can't last.

So, yes, it has ended. It does mean that the Chinese government and authorities have to look for an alternative. Many of us have been arguing that the alternative necessarily requires much more emphasis on increasing consumption, not through debt, but by increasing real incomes. And that means encouraging more employment of a desirable type—"decent work" as it's been called—and increasing wages. Now, this doesn't mean that the rates of growth will continue as high as they have been, but that doesn't matter.

In fact, the obsession with GDP growth is becoming a real negative now in the search for alternatives. The Chinese authorities, like all the financial analysts across the world who are constantly looking at China, are obsessed with GDP: Is it going to be 6.5% annual growth? Is it going to be 6.1%? Is it going to fall below 6%? As if that's all that matters. What they should really be looking at is the incomes of, let us say, the bottom 50 or 60%. Are these growing? If these are growing at about 4 or 5%, that's fantastic. That's wonderful. And that's really what the economy needs in a sustainable way. If these are growing in combination with patterns of production and consumption that are more sustainable, that are environmentally friendly, that are less carbon-emitting, then that is of course even more desirable.

But that means the focus has to shift away from GDP growth, and away from just pushing up GDP by any means whatsoever—to one which looks at how to improve the real incomes and the quality of life of the majority of the citizens. Unfortunately, the Chinese government doesn't seem to be choosing that path just yet. There have been some moves—in terms of increasing health spending, in terms of some attempts to increase wages and social protection for some workers—but overall the focus is still once again on more accumulation, on more investment, usually driven by more debt.

**D&S:** When you say the export-oriented model is "over," does that mean you think sticking to this approach will no longer deliver what policymakers and elites are aiming for, in terms of growth and accumulation? (And perhaps that this will lead to an elite-driven restructuring in the near term?) Or is it that this approach just cannot plausibly deliver in terms of inclusive development—the improvement in the quality of life for the majority?

**JG:** Both, really. The conditions of the global economy at present are such that an economy as large as that of China (and many other smaller economies as well) cannot expect much stimulus from external demand Significant increases in exports would only be possible by increasing markets share; that is, eating into some other country's exports. So the past pattern of accumulation based on external demand is unlikely to work in the near future.

But in addition, this approach has not delivered in terms of inclusive growth over the past decade except to some extent in China, which has been able to use it to generate a "Lewisian" process (theorized by economist Arthur Lewis in the 1950s) of shifting labor out of lower productivity activities. Even in China it was successful because wages increased much less than productivity and so export prices could fall or remain low. In many other countries, export-led expansion has actually been associated stagnant or lower wages and greater fragility of incomes, along with very substantial environmental costs that are typically not factored in.

**D&S:** Is it possible that that kind of transition is not going to happen in China until we see the development of a robust labor movement that's capable of winning a higher share of the national income in the form of wages, and pushing up mass consumption in that way?

**JG:** There is probably much greater public concern about all this in China than is often depicted in the media, certainly in the Chinese media, but even abroad. We know that there are thousands, literally, tens of thousands of protests in China—often about land grabs and so on in the peasantry, but also many, many workers' protests, and many other protests by citizens about environmental conditions. They have mostly been suppressed, but I don't think you can keep on suppressing these.

I do believe the Chinese elite has recognized that there are a couple of things that are becoming very important for them to maintain their political legitimacy. One is, of course, inequality and, associated with that, corruption. That is why the anti-corruption drive of President Xi Jinping retains a lot of popularity. Then there is the fact of the environmental unsustainability. Both India and China have created monstrosities in urban areas, in terms of the pollution, congestion, degradation, which are really making many of our cities and towns unlivable. There is widespread protest about that, and about the pollution of water sources, of the atmosphere, of land quality. And there is real concern that ordinary Chinese citizens are not continuously experiencing the better life that they have grown accustomed to expect.

So I think, even without a very large-scale social mobilization, there is growing awareness in China—among officialdom, as well—that they can't carry on as before. It is likely that there's a tussle at the very higher echelons of the leadership and in the Communist Party, between those who are arguing for the slower but more sustainable and more wage-led path, and those who just want to keep propping up growth by more financial liberalization, by encouraging investors to jump in and invest even in projects that are unlikely to continue, and somehow keep that GDP growth going. It's a political tussle but of course that will determine the direction of the economy as well.

**D&S:** In the midst of this period of stagnation of the very high-income capitalist economies, and a resulting slowdown of growth in the so-called emerging economies, we also have an effect on countries that had primarily remained raw-material (or "primary-product") exporters. Is that boom in commodities exports now also over for the foreseeable future, and do you see those countries as now reinventing their economic development models?

**JG:** I think that the period of the boom was really a bit of an aberration. Since the early 20th century, these periods of relatively high commodity prices have always been outliers, and they don't last very long. They last for about five, six, maybe eight years at most, and then they they you come back to this more depressed situation relative to other prices. I have a feeling this is now going to continue, and that boom is, for the time being, over. It definitely means that the manna from heaven that many countries experienced has reduced, and therefore you have to think of other ways of diversifying your economies.

Many countries actually tried to do this but, you know, when you're getting so much income from the primary product exports it's very hard to diversify. It's actually easier to diversify when primary product prices are lower. So, once again, I think it's important for these countries to stop thinking of this as a huge loss, and start thinking of it as an opportunity—as an opportunity to use cheap primary commodities as a means of industrializing for domestic and regional markets. So it means a different strategy. The export-led obsession has to end. Without that, we're not going to get viable and sustainable strategies.

I'd like to make one other point, though, about the slowdown in China and the impact on developing countries, which is that it's also going to affect manufacturing exporters. China had become the center of a global production chain that was heavily exporting to the North but was drawing in more and more raw material and intermediate products from other developing countries. So almost every country had China become their main trade partner in both imports and exports. Many of these manufacturing economies are now going to face, once again, a double whammy. They will face a reduction, from China, in terms of lower Chinese imports of raw materials and intermediate goods for final export, and they're going to face greater competition from China in terms of their own export markets and their own domestic markets. Because China is now devaluing its currency, even though thus far it has been minor. It is looking to cheapen its exports even further, and this will definitely impact on both export markets and internal markets in developing countries.

So I think both primary exporters and manufacturing exporters are in for a bit of a bad time. They need to think of creative ways of dealing with the situation. It is not helped by believing that integration into global value chains is the only option, because these global value chains basically reduce the incomes of the actual producers. If you look at it, the emergence of global value chains and the associated trade treaties—not just the World Trade Organization (WTO) but the proliferation of regional trading agreements and things like the Trans-Pacific Partnership (TPP)—increase competition and reduce the value of the actual production stage of all commodities and goods. And they simultaneously increase the pre-production and post-production value. That is, all of the aspects that are driven by intellectual property monopolies—their values increase. So whether it is design elements or it is the marketing and branding and all of that—the intellectual property rights over which are retained by companies in the North—all of those are getting more and more value. And the actual production is getting less value because of the greater competitive pressure unleashed by these various trade agreements.

Developing countries that are seeking to get out of this really have to think of alternative arrangements—possibly regional arrangements, more reliance on domestic demand and South-South trade, which is more possible today than it has ever been—and moving away from a system that allows global and northern-led multinationals to capture all the rents and most of the profits of production everywhere.

**D&S:** So, in the course of this discussion, I think two major questions emerge about the way forward in so-called developing economies. One is how to square economic development—in terms of raising the quality of life for the majority—with environmental sustainability. The other is how to ensure the economic development of some countries isn't at odds with development in others. Are there ways of mutually fostering development—and in particular sustainable development—across the developing economies?

**JG:** Yes, I think we need to really move away from the traditional way of looking at growth and development, which is ultimately still based on GDP. As long as we keep doing that, we're going to be caught in this trap. We have to be focusing much more on quality of life and ensuring what we would call the basic needs or minimum re-quirements for a civilized life among all the citizenry. If we do that, then we're less in competition with one another and we're less obsessed with having to be the cheapest show in town. We then see wages and employment growth as a means of expansion of economic activity. We will see social policies as delivering not just better welfare for the people but also more employment, and therefore a better quality of life.

If we look for regional trading arrangements that recognize this, if we look to increase the value of domestic economic activity by encouraging the things that matter for ordinary people (especially, let's say, the bottom half of the population), if we focus on new technologies that are adapted to specific local requirements—in terms of being more green, more environmentally sustainable, as well as recognizing the specific availability of labor in these economies—I think we can do a lot more. It may be slower in terms of GDP growth, but really that doesn't mean anything. So we have to move away from GDP growth as the basic indicator of what is desirable. I think that's the ultimate and most essential issue. ❑

# Chapter 4

# UNEMPLOYMENT AND INFLATION

## INTRODUCTION

In an introductory macroeconomics course, students are likely to hear that two key macroeconomic outcomes are the rates of unemployment and inflation, and that there is a trade-off between the two. In recent years, we have seen the see-saw of unemployment and inflation tilt very heavily in one direction. Unemployment in the United States and other countries reached rates not seen since the Great Depression, while many countries experienced not only very low inflation but even deflation for the first time in living memory. Unemployment has gradually come down over years of slow economic "recovery," but job growth remains sluggish and inflation very low.

Economist Robert Pollin delves into why the textbook trade-off between inflation and unemployment affects the returns of stockholders and other investors. The answer, Pollin points out, is "all about class conflict" (Article 4.1). Higher unemployment rates and fewer jobs eat away at the bargaining power of workers, keeping wage growth and inflation in check and corporate profit margins wide. As Pollin sees it, the unemployment rate consistent with price stability—the so-called "natural rate"—declined dramatically in the 1990s because workers' economic power eroded during the decade.

John Miller and Jeannette Wicks-Lim take on the claim that the persistently high unemployment in the U.S. economy is due to a "skills deficit" among those looking for work. They examine the data on job openings, hires, and unemployment, and find that there are plenty of experienced workers still looking for work even in the industries doing most of the hiring. For them, a jobs deficit, not a skills deficit, is the cause of today's unemployment problems (Article 4.2).

Meanwhile, Dean Baker tackles arguments that excessive regulation is stifling job growth. Baker argues that these claims have clear implications about what industries will be affected and how they will respond. The data, he argues, simply do not bear out the regulation-bashing story (Article 4.3).

Economist Gerald Friedman details the rise of temporary, contingent, insecure work in the U.S. economy (Article 4.4). His article, "The Gig Economy," focuses not just on whether people are employed or unemployed, but on the terms under which people are employed, especially in regards to job security. The macroeconomic implications, in regards to unemployment and inflation, may be important. Low unemployment is usually associated with higher workers' bargaining power, as they have less fear of losing their jobs and are bolder in pressing wage and other demands on their employers, But is this the case if people are increasingly working at insecure "gig" jobs?

In the next article, Evita Nolka takes us to Greece, where unemployment remains at stratospheric levels (Article 4.5). She describes not only the obvious costs of unemployment—loss of incomes and production—but also the human toll for young people seeing the primes of their lives fritter away, looking at a bleak future, and sometimes feeling compelled to leave their country in search of better opportunities. To be sure, disillusionment and cynicism about the political system are high, but Nolka also shows the resilient spirit of Greeks who are still fighting for economic change that will benefit the majority.

Finally, in "Keynes, Wage and Price 'Stickiness,' and Deflation" (Article 4.6), Alejandro Reuss turns to the writings of John Maynard Keynes and arguments about whether declining money wages are the cure for unemployment. He outlines Keynes' classic arguments—against conservative economists who believed that wage declines were part of the economy's "self-correction" during a depression—that wage declines could actually worsen depression conditions.

## Discussion Questions

1. (Article 4.1) What is the concept of the non-accelerating inflation rate of unemployment (the NAIRU, or natural rate of unemployment)? Why do some economists consider it problematic to call this the "natural rate"? What kinds of factors determine the level of the NAIRU?

2. (Article 4.1) The economists who first posited the idea of a "natural rate or unemployment" certainly did not think they were devising a class-conflict theory. Yet Pollin says the "natural rate" is "all about class conflict." Why?

3. (Article 4.2) What data support the case that today's high unemployment rates can be attributed to a mismatch between job openings and workers' skills? How do Miller and Wicks-Lim respond to these arguments?

4. (Article 4.3) What are the five implications of the view that regulation is to blame for weak job creation? Do the data show what we would expect if this hypothesis were correct? What conclusions does Baker reach?

5. (Article 4.4) Why do you think "contingent" labor arrangements have grown more prevalent in recent years? How might these reasons be related to employers' desire to adjust to the ups and downs of macroeconomic cycles?

6. (Article 4.5) What might be some of the costs of unemployment, to the unemployed worker and to the society as a whole, besides the worker's loss of income?

7. (Article 4.6) Deflation means a decrease in the overall price level. Lower prices sound good to most people. So what's not to like about deflation?

*Article 4.1*

# THE "NATURAL RATE" OF UNEMPLOYMENT
*It's all about class conflict.*

**BY ROBERT POLLIN**
*September/October 1998*

In 1997, the official U.S. unemployment rate fell to a 27-year low of 4.9%. Most orthodox economists had long predicted that a rate this low would lead to uncontrollable inflation. So they argued that maintaining a higher unemployment rate—perhaps as high as 6%—was crucial for keeping the economy stable. But there is a hitch: last year the inflation rate was 2.3%, the lowest figure in a decade and the second lowest in 32 years. What then are we to make of these economists' theories, much less their policy proposals?

Nobel prize-winning economist Milton Friedman gets credit for originating the argument that low rates of unemployment would lead to accelerating inflation. His 1968 theory of the so-called "natural rate of unemployment" was subsequently developed by many mainstream economists under the term "Non-Accelerating Inflation Rate of Unemployment," or NAIRU, a remarkably clumsy term for expressing the simple concept of a threshold unemployment rate below which inflation begins to rise.

According to both Friedman and expositors of NAIRU, inflation should accelerate at low rates of unemployment because low unemployment gives workers excessive bargaining power. This allows the workers to demand higher wages. Capitalists then try to pass along these increased wage costs by raising prices on the products they sell. An inflationary spiral thus ensues as long as unemployment remains below its "natural rate."

Based on this theory, Friedman and others have long argued that governments should never actively intervene in the economy to promote full employment or better jobs for workers, since it will be a futile exercise, whose end result will only be higher inflation and no improvement in job opportunities. Over the past generation, this conclusion has had far-reaching influence throughout the world. In the United States and Western Europe, it has provided a stamp of scientific respectability to a whole range of policies through which governments abandoned even modest commitments to full employment and workers' rights.

This emerged most sharply through the Reaganite and Thatcherite programs in the United States and United Kingdom in the 1980s. But even into the 1990s, as the Democrats took power in the United States, the Labour Party won office in Britain, and Social Democrats won elections throughout Europe, governments remained committed to stringent fiscal and monetary policies, whose primary goal is to prevent inflation. In Western Europe this produced an average unemployment rate of over 10% from 1990-97. In the United States, unemployment rates have fallen sharply in the 1990s, but as an alternative symptom of stringent fiscal and monetary policies, real wages for U.S. workers also declined dramatically over the past generation. As of 1997, the average real wage for nonsupervisory workers in the United States was 14% below its peak in 1973, even though average worker productivity rose between 1973 and 1997 by 34%.

Why have governments in the United States and Europe remained committed to the idea of fiscal and monetary stringency, if the natural rate theory on which such policies are based is so obviously flawed? The explanation is that the natural rate theory is really not just about predicting a precise unemployment rate figure below which inflation must inexorably accelerate, even though many mainstream economists have presented the natural rate theory in this way. At a deeper level, the natural rate theory is bound up with the inherent conflicts between workers and capitalists over jobs, wages, and working conditions. As such, the natural rate theory actually contains a legitimate foundation in truth amid a welter of sloppy and even silly predictions.

## The "Natural Rate" Theory Is About Class Conflict

In his 1967 American Economic Association presidential address in which he introduced the natural rate theory, Milton Friedman made clear that there was really nothing "natural" about the theory. Friedman rather emphasized that: "by using the term 'natural' rate of unemployment, I do not mean to suggest that it is immutable and unchangeable. On the contrary, many of the market characteristics that determine its level are man-made and policy-made. In the United States, for example, legal minimum wage rates ... and the strength of labor unions all make the natural rate of unemployment higher than it would otherwise be."

In other words, according to Friedman, what he terms the "natural rate" is really a social phenomenon measuring the class strength of working people, as indicated by their ability to organize effective unions and establish a livable minimum wage.

Friedman's perspective is supported in a widely-read 1997 paper by Robert Gordon of Northwestern University on what he terms the "time-varying NAIRU." What makes the NAIRU vary over time? Gordon explains that, since the early 1960s, "The two especially large changes in the NAIRU... are the increase between the early and late 1960s and the decrease in the 1990s. The late 1960s were a time of labor militancy, relatively strong unions, a relatively high minimum wage and a marked increase in labor's share in national income. The 1990s have been a time of labor peace, relatively weak unions, a relatively low minimum wage and a slight decline in labor's income share."

In short, class conflict is the spectre haunting the analysis of the natural rate and NAIRU: this is the consistent message stretching from Milton Friedman in the 1960s to Robert Gordon in the 1990s.

Stated in this way, the "Natural Rate" idea does, ironically, bear a close family resemblance to the ideas of two of the greatest economic thinkers of the left, Karl Marx and Michal Kalecki, on a parallel concept—the so-called "Reserve Army of Unemployed." In his justly famous Chapter 25 of Volume I of *Capital*, "The General Law of Capitalist Accumulation," Marx argued forcefully that unemployment serves an important function in capitalist economies. That is, when a capitalist economy is growing rapidly enough so that the reserve army of unemployed is depleted, workers will then utilize their increased bargaining power to raise wages. Profits are correspondingly squeezed as workers get a larger share of the country's total income. As a result, capitalists anticipate further declines in profitability and they therefore reduce their investment spending. This then leads to a fall in job creation, higher unemployment, and a replenishment of the reserve army. In other words, the reserve army of the unemployed is the instrument capitalists use to prevent significant wage increases and thereby maintain profitability.

Kalecki, a Polish economist of the Great Depression era, makes parallel though distinct arguments in his also justly famous essay, "The Political Aspects of Full Employment." Kalecki wrote in 1943, shortly after the 1930s Depression had ended and governments had begun planning a postwar world in which they would deploy aggressive policies to avoid another calamity of mass unemployment. Kalecki held, contrary to Marx, that full employment can be beneficial to the profitability of businesses. True, capitalists may get a smaller share of the total economic pie as workers gain bargaining power to win higher wages. But capitalists can still benefit because the size of the pie is growing far more rapidly, since more goods and services can be produced when everyone is working, as opposed to some significant share of workers being left idle.

But capitalists still won't support full employment, in Kalecki's view, because it will threaten their control over the workplace, the pace and direction of economic activity, and even political institutions. Kalecki thus concluded that full employment could be sustainable under capitalism, but only if these challenges to capitalists' social and political power could be contained. This is why he held that fascist social and political institutions, such as those that existed in Nazi Germany when he was writing, could well provide one "solution" to capitalism's unemployment problem, precisely because they were so brutal. Workers would have jobs, but they would never be permitted to exercise the political and economic power that would otherwise accrue to them in a full-employment economy.

Broadly speaking, Marx and Kalecki do then share a common conclusion with natural rate proponents, in that they would all agree that positive unemployment rates are the outgrowth of class conflict over the distribution of income and political power. Of course, Friedman and other mainstream economists reach this conclusion via analytic and political perspectives that are diametrically opposite to those of Marx and Kalecki. To put it in a nutshell, in the Friedmanite view mass unemployment results when workers demand more than they deserve, while for Marx and Kalecki, capitalists use the weapon of unemployment to prevent workers from getting their just due.

## From Natural Rate to Egalitarian Policy

Once the analysis of unemployment in capitalist economies is properly understood within the framework of class conflict, several important issues in our contemporary economic situation become much more clear. Let me raise just a few:

1. Mainstream economists have long studied how workers' wage demands cause inflation as unemployment falls. However, such wage demands never directly cause inflation, since inflation refers to a general rise in prices of goods and services sold in the market, not a rise in wages. Workers, by definition, do not have the power to raise prices. Capitalists raise prices on the products they sell. At low unemployment, inflation occurs when capitalists respond to workers' increasingly successful wage demands by raising prices so that they can maintain profitability. If workers were simply to receive a higher share of national income, then lower unemployment and higher wages need not cause inflation at all.

2. There is little mystery as to why, at present, the so-called "time-varying" NAIRU has diminished to a near vanishing point, with unemployment at a 25-year low while inflation remains dormant. The main explanation is the one stated by Robert Gordon—that workers' economic power has been eroding dramatically through the 1990s. Workers have been almost completely unable to win wage increases over the course of the economic expansion that by now is seven years old.

3. This experience over the past seven years, with unemployment falling but workers showing almost no income gains, demonstrates dramatically the crucial point that full employment can never stand alone as an adequate measure of workers' well-being. This was conveyed vividly to me when I was working in Bolivia in 1990 as part of an economic advising team led by Keith Griffin of the University of California-Riverside. Professor Griffin asked me to examine employment policies.

I began by paying a visit to the economists at the Ministry of Planning. When I requested that we discuss the country's employment problems, they explained, to my surprise, that the country *had no employment problems.* When I suggested we consider the situation of the people begging, shining shoes, or hawking batteries and Chiclets in the street just below the window where we stood, their response was that these people *were* employed. And of course they were, in that they were actively trying to scratch out a living. It was clear that I had to specify the problem at hand far more precisely. Similarly, in the United States today, we have to be much more specific as to what workers should be getting in a fair economy: jobs, of course, but also living wages, benefits, reasonable job security, and a healthy work environment.

4. In our current low-unemployment economy, should workers, at long last, succeed in winning higher wages and better benefits, some inflationary pressures are likely to emerge. But if inflation does not accelerate after wage increases are won, this would mean that businesses are not able to pass along their higher wage costs to their customers. Profits would therefore be squeezed. In any case, in response to *either* inflationary pressures or a squeeze in profitability, we should expect that many, if not most, segments of the business community will welcome a Federal Reserve policy that would slow the economy and raise the unemployment rate.

Does this mean that, as long as we live in a capitalist society, the control by capitalists over the reserve army of labor must remain the dominant force establishing the limits of workers' strivings for jobs, security, and living wages? The challenge for the progressive movement in the United States today is to think through a set of policy ideas through which full employment at living wages can be achieved and sustained.

Especially given the dismal trajectory of real wage decline over the past generation, workers should of course continue to push for wage increases. But it will also be crucial to advance these demands within a broader framework of proposals. One important component of a broader package would be policies through which labor and capital bargain openly over growth of wages and profits after full employment is achieved. Without such an open bargaining environment, workers, with reason, will push for higher wages once full employment is achieved, but capitalists will then respond by either raising prices or favoring high unemployment. Such open bargaining policies were conducted with considerable success in Sweden and other Nordic countries from the 1950s to the 1980s, and as a result, wages there continued to rise at full employment, while both accelerating inflation and a return to high unemployment were prevented.

Such policies obviously represent a form of class compromise. This is intrinsically neither good nor bad. The question is the terms under which the compromise is achieved. Wages have fallen dramatically over the past generation, so workers deserve substantial raises as a matter of simple fairness. But workers should also be willing to link their wage increases to improvements in productivity growth, i.e., the rate at which workers produce new goods and services. After all, if the average wage had just risen at exactly the rate of productivity growth since 1973 and not a penny more, the average hourly wage today for nonsupervisory workers would be $19.07 rather than $12.24.

But linking wages to improvements in productivity then also raises the question of who controls the decisions that determine the rate of productivity growth. In fact, substantial productivity gains are attainable through operating a less hierarchical workplace and building strong democratic unions through which workers can defend their rights on the job. Less hierarchy and increased workplace democracy creates higher morale on the job, which in turn increases workers' effort and opportunities to be inventive, while decreasing turnover and absenteeism. The late David Gordon of the New School for Social Research was among the leading analysts demonstrating how economies could operate more productively through greater workplace democracy.

But improvements in productivity also result from both the public and private sector investing in new and better machines that workers put to use every day, with the additional benefit that it means more jobs for people who produce those machines. A pro-worker economic policy will therefore also have to be concerned with increasing investments to improve the stock of machines that workers have at their disposal on the job.

In proposing such a policy approach, have I forgotten the lesson that Marx and Kalecki taught us, that unemployment serves a purpose in capitalism? Given that this lesson has become part of the standard mode of thinking among mainstream economists ranging from Milton Friedman to Robert Gordon, I would hope that I haven't let it slip from view. My point nevertheless is that through changing power relationships at the workplace and the decision-making process through which investment decisions get made, labor and the left can then also achieve a more egalitarian economy, one in which capitalists' power to brandish the weapon of unemployment is greatly circumscribed. If the labor movement and the left neglect issues of control over investment and the workplace, we will continue to live amid a Bolivian solution to the unemployment problem, where full employment is the by-product of workers' vulnerability, not their strength. ❏

*Sources:* A longer version of this article appears as "The 'Reserve Army of Labor' and the 'Natural Rate of Unemployment': Can Marx, Kalecki, Friedman, and Wall Street All Be Wrong?," *Review of Radical Political Economics*, Fall 1998. Both articles derive from a paper originally presented as the David Gordon Memorial Lecture at the 1997 Summer Conference of the Union for Radical Political Economics. See also Robert Pollin and Stephanie Luce, *The Living Wage: Building a Fair Economy*, 1998; David Gordon, *Fat and Mean*, 1997; David Gordon, "Generating Affluence: Productivity Gains Require Worker Support," *Real World Macro*, 15th ed., 1998.

*Article 4.2*

# UNEMPLOYMENT: A JOBS DEFICIT OR A SKILLS DEFICIT?

## BY JOHN MILLER AND JEANNETTE WICKS-LIM
*January/February 2011*

Millions of Americans remain unemployed nearly a year and a half after the official end-date of the Great Recession, and the nation's official unemployment rate continues at nearly 10%.

Why? We are being told that it is because—wait for it—workers are not qualified for the jobs that employers are offering.

Yes, it's true. In the aftermath of the deepest downturn since the Great Depression, some pundits and policymakers—and economists—have begun to pin persistently high unemployment on workers' inadequate skills.

The problem, in this view, is a mismatch between job openings and the skills of those looking for work. In economics jargon, this is termed a problem of "structural unemployment," in contrast to the "cyclical unemployment" caused by a downturn in the business cycle.

The skills-gap message is coming from many quarters. Policymaker-in-chief Obama told Congress in February 2009: "Right now, three-quarters of the fastest-growing occupations require more than a high school diploma. And yet, just over half of our citizens have that level of education." His message: workers need to go back to school if they want a place in tomorrow's job market.

The last Democrat in the White House has caught the bug too. Bill Clinton explained in a September 2010 interview, "The last unemployment report said that for the first time in my lifetime, and I'm not young … we are coming out of a recession but job openings are going up twice as fast as new hires. And yet we can all cite cases that we know about where somebody opened a job and 400 people showed up. How could this be? Because people don't have the job skills for the jobs that are open."

Economists and other "experts" are most likely the source of the skills-gap story. Last August, for instance, Narayana Kocherlakota, president of the Federal Reserve Bank of Minneapolis, wrote in a Fed newsletter: "How much of the current unemployment rate is really due to mismatch, as opposed to conditions that the Fed can readily ameliorate? The answer seems to be a lot." Kocherlakota's point was that the Fed's monetary policy tools may be able to spur economic growth, but that won't help if workers have few or the wrong skills. "The Fed does not have a means to transform construction workers into manufacturing workers," he explained.

The skills-mismatch explanation has a lot to recommend it if you're a federal or Fed policymaker: it puts the blame for the economic suffering experienced by the 17% of the U.S. workforce that is unemployed or underemployed on the workers themselves. Even if the Fed or the government did its darndest to boost overall spending, unemployment would be unlikely to subside unless workers upgraded their own skills.

The only problem is that this explanation is basically wrong. The weight of the evidence shows that it is not a mismatch of skills but a lack of demand that lies at the heart of today's severe unemployment problem.

## High-Skill Jobs?

President Obama's claim that new jobs are requiring higher and higher skill lev-els would tend to support the skills-gap thesis. His interpretation of job-market trends, however, misses the mark. The figure that Obama cited comes from the U.S. Department of Labor's employment projections for 2006 to 2016. Specifi-cally, the DOL reports that among the 30 fastest growing occupations, 22 of them (75%) will typically require more than a high school degree. These occupations include network systems and data communications analysts, computer software engineers, and financial advisors. What he fails to say, however, is that these 22 occupations are projected to represent less than 3% of all U.S. jobs.

What would seem more relevant to the 27 million unemployed and underem-ployed workers are the occupations with the *largest* growth. These are the occupa-tions that will offer workers the greatest number of new job opportunities. Among the 30 occupations with the largest growth, 70%—21 out of 30—typically do not require more than a high school degree. To become fully qualified for these jobs, workers will only need on-the-job training. The DOL projects that one-quarter of all jobs in 2016 will be in these 21 occupations, which include retail salespeople, food-preparation and food-service workers, and personal and home care aides.

In fact, the DOL employment projections estimate that more than two-thirds (68%) of the jobs in 2016 will be accessible to workers with a high school degree

---

### LABOR MARKET MUSICAL CHAIRS

To understand the data discussed here, try picturing the U.S. labor market as a game of musical chairs, with a few twists. At any time, chairs (job openings) can be added to the circle and players can sit down (get hired). When the music stops at the end of the month, not all the chairs are filled. Still, many people—far more people than the number of empty chairs—are left standing.

Each month, the Bureau of Labor Statistics reports on what happened in that month's game of labor market musical chairs in its various measures of unemploy-ment and in the Job Openings and Labor Turnover Survey (JOLTS). Here's how the BLS scorecard for labor market musical chairs works.

- **Job openings** is a snapshot of the number of jobs available on the last day of the month—the number of empty chairs when the music stops.
- **Hires** are all the new additions to payroll during the month—the number of people who found a chair to sit in while the music was playing. Because many chairs are added to the circle and filled within the same month, the number of hires over a month is typically greater than the number of openings available on the last day of that month.
- **Unemployed persons** are those who looked for a job that month but couldn't find one—the number of people who played the game but were left standing when the music stopped at the end of the month.

or less. Couple this with the fact that today, nearly two-thirds (62%) of the adult labor force has at least some college experience, and an alleged skills gap fails to be convincing as a driving force behind persistent high unemployment.

## Low-Skill Workers?

If employers were having a hard time finding qualified workers to fill job openings, you'd think that any workers who are qualified would be snapped right up. But what the unemployment data show is that there remains a substantial backlog of experienced workers looking for jobs or for more hours in their existing part-time jobs in those major industries that have begun hiring—including education, healthcare, durable goods manufacturing, and mining.

Most telling are the *underemployed*—those with part-time jobs who want to work full-time. Today there are more underemployed workers in each of the major industries of the private economy than during the period from 2000 to 2007, as Arjun Jayadev and Mike Konczal document in a recent paper published by the Roosevelt Institute. Even in the major industries with the highest number of job openings—education and health services, professional and business services, transportation and utilities, leisure and hospitality, and manufacturing—underemployment in 2010 remains at levels twice as high or nearly twice as high as during the earlier period (measured as a percentage of employed workers).

Purveyors of the mismatch theory would have a hard time explaining how it is that underemployed workers who want full-time work do not possess the skills to do the jobs full time that they are already doing, say, 20 hours a week.

More broadly, workers with a diverse set of skills—not just construction workers—lost jobs during the Great Recession. Workers in manufacturing, professional and business services, leisure and hospitality, transportation and utilities, and a host of other industries were turned out of their jobs. And many of these experienced workers are still looking for work. In each of the 16 major industries of the economy unemployment rates in September 2010 were still far higher than they had been at the onset of the Great Recession in December 2007. In the industries with a large number of (cumulative) job openings during the recovery—education and health services, professional and business services, and manufacturing—experienced workers face unemployment rates twice what they were back in December 2007.

There are plenty of experienced workers still looking for work in the industries with job openings. To be faithful to the data, Kocherlakota and the other mismatch proponents would need to show that experienced workers no longer possess the skills to work in their industry, even though that industry employed them no more than three years ago. That seems implausible.

## Statistical Errors

Still, the statistical oddity that Bill Clinton and many economists have pointed to does seem to complicate the picture. If the number of job openings is rising at a good clip yet the number of new hires is growing more slowly and the unemployment rate is stagnant, then maybe employers *are* having trouble finding qualified folks to hire.

Once you take a closer looks at the numbers, though, there is less here than meets the eye.

First, the *rate* at which job openings and new hires numbers change over time is not the right place to look. What we really need to know is how the number of unfilled job posts compares to the number of qualified workers employers hire over the same month. If employers in today's recovery are having a hard time finding workers, then the job openings left unfilled at the end of the month should be relatively high compared to the number of newly hired workers that month. In other words, if the number of positions left unfilled at the end of the month relative to the number of new hires rises *above* what we've seen during past recoveries, this would mean that employers are finding it harder to fill their positions with the right workers this time around.

But it turns out that the ratio of unfilled job openings to new hires is approximately the same during this recovery as in the recovery from the 2001 recession. In September 2010, fifteen months into the current economic recovery, the ratio of job posts left unoccupied at the end of the month to the number of monthly new hires stood at 69%—very close to its 67% level in February 2003, fifteen months into the

## WHERE MISMATCHES MAY MATTER

The skills-mismatch theory does not go very far toward explaining stubbornly high U.S. unemployment. Still, there are unquestionably some unemployed and underemployed workers whose job prospects are limited by "structural" factors.

One kind of structural unemployment that does seem to fit the contours of the Great Recession to at least some degree is that caused by a mismatch of geography: the workers are in one part of the country while the jobs they could get are in another. The housing crisis surely has compromised the ability of unemployed workers to unload their single largest asset, a house, and move to another part of the country. Plus, job losses have been particularly heavy in regions where the housing crisis hit hardest.

But at the same time, lost jobs have been widespread across industries and there is little real evidence of geographic mismatch between job openings and unemployed workers. As labor economist Michael Reich reports, "economic decline and the growth of unemployment have been more widespread than ever before, making it unclear where the unemployed should migrate for greater job opportunities."

Even where there is a skills mismatch, that doesn't mean the government shouldn't get involved. On the contrary, government policies to boost economic demand can help significantly. When demand is high, labor markets become very tight and there are few available workers to hire. Workers previously viewed as "unemployable" get hired, get experience and on-the-job training, and see their overall career prospects brighten.

And, of course, government can fund expanded job-training programs. If the economy continues to slog along with low growth rates and persistent unemployment, the ranks of the long-term unemployed will rise. As they go longer and longer without work, their skills will atrophy or become obsolete and they will face a genuine skills-mismatch problem that will make job-training programs more and more necessary.

last recovery. In other words, today's employers are filling their job openings with the same rate of success as yesterday's employers.

Comparisons that focus on the unemployment rate rather than on the number of new hires are even less meaningful. As hiring picks up at the beginning of an economic recovery, workers who had given up the job search start looking again. This brings them back into the official count of the unemployed, keeping the unemployment rate from dropping even as both job openings and new hires rise.

## Not Enough Jobs

The reality of the situation—the widespread job losses and the long, fruitless job searches of experienced workers—make it clear that today's employment problem is a jobs deficit across the economy, not a skills deficit among those looking for work.

While it's true that any given month ends with some number of unfilled job openings, the total number of jobs added to the economy during this recovery has simply been inadequate to put the unemployed back to work. In fact, if every job that stood open at the end of September 2010 had been filled, 11.7 million officially unemployed workers would still have been jobless.

This recovery has seen far fewer job openings than even the so-called "jobless" recovery following the 2001 recession. Economists Lawrence Mishel, Heidi Shierholz, and Kathryn Edwards of the Economic Policy Institute report that cumulative job openings during the first year of this recovery were roughly 25% lower than during the first year of the recovery following the 2001 recession—that's 10 million fewer jobs. Even in the industries generating the most job openings in the current recovery—education and health services, professional and business services, leisure and hospitality, and manufacturing—the cumulative number of job openings has lagged well behind the figure for those industries during the first year of the recovery from the 2001 recession. (Only the mining and logging category, which accounted for just 0.5% of employment in 2007, has had more job openings during the first year of this recovery than during the first year of the 2001 recovery.)

Why has the pick-up in jobs following the Great Recession been worse than usual? The simple answer is that the recession was worse than usual. The sharp and extreme decline of output and employment in the Great Recession has severely dampened demand—that is, people have not had money to buy things. With the resulting lack of sales, businesses were not willing to either invest or hire; and this in turn has meant a continuing lack of demand.

If businesses have barely resumed hiring, it has not been for lack of profits. By the middle of 2010, corporate profits (adjusted for inflation) were about 60% above their low point at the end of 2008, well on their way back to the peak level of mid-2006. Also, in early 2010 non-financial firms were sitting on almost $2 trillion in cash. There was no lack of ability to invest and hire, but there was a lack of incentive to invest and hire, that is, a lack of an expectation that demand (sales) would rise. As is well known, small businesses have generally accounted for a disproportionately large share of job growth. Yet, since the onset of the Great Recession, small business owners have consistently identified poor sales as their single most important problem—and thus, presumably, what has prevented them from expanding employment.

## LONG-TERM UNEMPLOYMENT RISES EVEN AFTER RECESSION

Record job losses and persistent unemployment have left the U.S. economy out of order and forced those looking for a job to longer and longer without work.

When the Great Recession hit at the end of 2007 jobs disappeared, unemployment rose, and its duration lengthened. By the official end of the recession in midyear 2009 the unemployed who had gone 27 weeks or longer without work, what economists call long-term unemployment, had nearly doubled to 29% of those job seekers.

But as the anemic economic recovery that followed did little to put people back to work, long term unemployment rate continued to climb reaching a peak of 45% of the unemployed in April 2010. In February 2012, more than two and half years into this "97 pound weakling of a recovery," as Time Magazine called it, more than 5.4 million job-seekers had gone more than a half of year without work and the long term unemployment rate still stood at 42.6% of the unemployed.

Long-term unemployment in the current period is more pervasive than any time on record, with data available in 1948. During the typical downturn of the last 60 years less than one fifth of the unemployed went more than 27 weeks without a job.

As long-term unemployment increases so too does the economic suffering inflicted on those without work and their families. At the beginning of 2012, more than 2 million of the unemployed had gone 99 weeks or more without work, exhausting their unemployment benefits. Also, as the Congressional Research Service confirms, when unemployment spells lengthen the prospects for finding employment diminishes. Finally the long-term unemployed are at increasing risk of drop out the labor force (by not actively searching for a job) and joining those without work who go uncounted in this data even though they want a job.

Long-term unemployment hits older workers and black workers especially hard. While the official unemployment rates for older workers are lower than those of younger workers, older workers who lose their jobs find it particularly difficult to find another. In February 2012, more than half (52.4%) of the unemployed 55 to 64 year olds had gone more than 27 weeks without a job. For black workers conditions are considerably worse. Nearly the same share of the black unemployed had been out of work for 27 months or more as for older workers. (In February 2012 the long-term unemployment stood at 46.7% for unemployed black men and 51.8% for unemployed black women.) But the official unemployment rate for blacks was 14.1% in February 2012, while the rate for workers 55 and older was 5.9%.

—*John Miller*

*Sources:* Bureau of Labor Statistics, "The Employment Situation – February 2012," Table A-2, Table A-12, Table A-36; The 97-lb. Recovery," by Rana Foroohar and Bill Saporito. Time Magazine, April 12, 2012; "The Trend in Long-Term Unemployment and Characteristics of Workers Unemployed for More than 99 Weeks," by Gerald Mayer, Congressional Research Service, December 20, 2010; and, "Long-Term Hardship in the Labor Market," by John Schmitt and Janelle Jones, Center for Economic and Policy Research, March 2012.

## The Role of Demand

Regardless of the lack of evidence to support it, the skills-mismatch story has seeped into media coverage of the economy. Take, for example, National Public Radio's recent Morning Edition series titled "Skills gap: holding back the labor market." In one segment, reporter Wendy Kaufman presents anecdotes about employers turning down record numbers of applicants and leaving job openings unfilled. Economist Peter Capelli then comes on and remarks, "You know, a generation ago you'd never expect that somebody could come into a reasonably skilled, sophisticated position in your organization and immediately make a contribution. That's a brand new demand." Now, that comment does not point to today's workers possessing fewer skills or qualifications. Rather, it suggests that employers have raised the bar: they are pickier than in the past.

That makes sense. We've seen that employers are successfully filling positions at about the same rate as in the recent past. What's different this time around is that employers have had up to six unemployed workers competing for every job opening left vacant at the close of the month. This is by far the highest ratio on record with data back to 2000. During the 2001 recession, that ratio rose to just over two unemployed workers for each opening. (In the first years of the "jobless recovery" following the 2001 recession, the ratio continued to rise, but it remained below three to one.) Clearly, these numbers favor the alternative explanation. Unfortunately, Kaufman doesn't even consider it.

That's too bad. Recognizing that a lack of demand for goods and services is to blame for the severe crisis of unemployment puts the focus squarely back on the federal government and on the Fed, which could help to remedy the problem —*if* they had the political will to do so. Millions of unemployed workers, organized and armed with an accurate diagnosis of the problem, could create that political will— unless they are distracted by a wrong-headed diagnosis that tries to blame them for the problem. ❑

**Sources:** Bureau of Labor Statistics Table A-14, Unemployed persons by industry and class of workers, not seasonally adjusted, historical data (bls.gov); Lawrence Mishel, Heidi Shierholz, and Kathryn Anne Edwards, "Reasons for Skepticism About Structural Unemployment," Economic Policy Institute, Briefing Paper #279, September 22, 2010 (epi.org); Arjun Jayadev and Mike Konczal, "The Stagnating Labor Market," The Roosevelt Institute, September 19, 2010 (rooseveltinstitute. org); Bureau of Labor Statistics, Job Openings and Labor Turnover (JOLTS) Highlights, September 2010 (bls.gov); Michael Reich, "High Unemployment after the Great Recession: Why? What Can We Do?," Policy Brief from the Center on Wage and Employment Dynamics, Institute for Research on Labor and Employment, University of California, Berkeley, June 2010 (irle.berkeley.edu/cwed); Narayana Kocherlakota, President Federal Reserve Bank of Minneapolis, "Inside the FOMC," Marquette, Michigan, August 17, 2010 (minneapolisfed.org); Lawrence Mishel and Katherine Anne Edwards, "Bill Clinton Gets It Wrong," Economic Policy Institute, Economic Snapshot, September 27, 2010 (epi.org); "Remarks of President Barack Obama—Address to Joint Session of Congress," February 24, 2009 (whitehouse.gov); "The Skills Gap: Holding Back the Labor Market," Morning Edition, National Public Radio, November 15, 2010 (npr.org).

*Article 4.3*

# BADGE OF IGNORANCE: THE NOTION THAT REGULATION IS THE CAUSE OF UNEMPLOYMENT

## BY DEAN BAKER
*October 2011*; Al Jazeera English

Politicians pushing right-wing positions in public debate now operate with the assumption that they can get away with saying anything without getting serious scrutiny from the media. That is why right-wing politicians repeatedly blame government regulation for the failure of the economy to generate jobs. Even though there is no truth whatsoever to the claim, right-wing politicians know that the media will treat their nonsense respectfully in news coverage.

If political reporters did their job, they would make an effort to determine the validity of the regulation-killing-jobs story and expose the politicians making the claim as either ignorant or dishonest, just as if a politician were going around claiming that September 11 was an inside job. However, today's reporters are either too lazy or incompetent to do their homework. What follows is a bit of a how-to manual to make reporters' jobs easier.

The first step in assessing the right-wingers' claim about regulation killing jobs is to figure out what it is. The argument is usually that companies have enough demand for labor that they would be hiring now, but because of existing or expected regulations, such as President Obama's health care plan that mostly takes effect in January of 2014, they are declining to hire more workers.

Governor Romney was kind enough to spell this argument out explicitly in the presidential debate on the economy. He told the audience that businesses have to look two or three years ahead when they make hiring decisions, not just a few months.

With this in mind, there are some clear implications of the regulations-cost-jobs story. First, we would expect that firms would be looking to increase hours per workers as an alternative to hiring. If employers can't hire more workers due to regulations, then they would look to get more labor out of each of the workers that they already have.

Second, employers would hire temporary workers as an alternative to hiring permanent employees. Temporary workers can be easily dismissed if regulations make it unprofitable to keep employees on staff.

Third, the companies that are most affected by the regulations should see the largest impact on their hiring. If costly regulations are keeping companies from hiring, then we should see that expect that the companies that are most affected by these regulations will have the sharpest reduction in employment.

Fourth, industries with longer-term employment should have the greatest reduction in employment. It may make sense for a company to not hire today because of a regulation that only kicks in two years from now if they expect the new hires to still be with them in two years. However, if a company has frequent turnover, then hiring workers today will not increase their employment in two years, unless they decide to replace workers as they leave.

Finally, if regulations are preventing firms from hiring, then we would expect them to complain about regulation when asked in employer surveys.

If we look at the data, we find that none of these conditions hold. The length of the average workweek was 34.3 hours in September. This is up from 33.7 hours at the low-point of the downturn in 2009, but it is still down by 0.4 hours from its pre-recession peaks. With average workweeks still shorter than before the downturn, there is no evidence that employers are requiring each worker to put in longer hours as an alternative to hiring new workers.

The same story applies to temp workers. Temp employment is up by 550,000 from the trough of the downturn, but it is still down by almost 400,000 from its pre-recession peak. If employers are hesitant to hire because of regulations, they clearly are not turning to temps as alternative. They hired far more temp workers before the big bad Obama let the regulators run wild.

The third point is that we should see more of an impact on hiring in the firms that are most affected by the regulation. The right's biggest villain here is Obamacare. This would have the greatest impact on hiring at mid-size firms. There is little in the legislation that affects firms of less than 50 and most of the biggest firms already provide care that exceeds what is required under the bill. So, we should see the largest falloff in hiring in firms that exceed the 50-employee limit but don't already provide health care.

In fact it is impossible to find any clear pattern in hiring by firm size. In 2010, hiring by firms that employ 50-100 workers was down by 14.5 percent from pre-recession levels, while hiring by firms that employ 100-250 workers was down by 13.3 percent. By comparison, hiring by the largest firms (over 1,000 workers) was down by only 11.4 percent, but hiring by firms that employ 10-19 workers was down by 15.8 percent.

There is a similar story when we look at industry groups. Manufacturing and health care, where industries workers often hold jobs for long periods of time, are both adding jobs more rapidly than before the downturn. By contrast, restaurants, where turnover is frequent, are adding jobs at just over half of their pre-recession pace.

Finally, employers themselves don't list regulation as major factor when asked in surveys. The National Federation of Independent Businesses, an association of small businesses, has fielded a survey for close to three decades that asks its members what are the biggest obstacles they face. Only around 14 percent list regulation, not much different than in the years before President Obama was elected.

In short, there is no evidence that is consistent with the regulation-impeding-job-growth story. When politicians repeat this line, they are just making things up and reporters should call them on it. ❑

Article 4.4

# THE GIG ECONOMY
*The Rise of the Insecure Labor in the United States*

## BY GERALD FRIEDMAN
*March/April 2014*

Growing numbers of Americans no longer hold a regular "job" with a long-term connection to a particular business. Instead, they work "gigs" where they are employed on a particular task or for a defined time, with little more connection to their employer than a consumer has with a particular brand of chips. Borrowed from the music industry, the word "gig" has been applied to all sorts of flexible employment (otherwise referred to as "contingent labor," "temp labor," or the "precariat"). Some have praised the rise of the gig economy for freeing workers from the grip of employers' "internal labor markets," where career advancement is tied to a particular business instead of competitive bidding between employers. Rather than being driven by worker preferences, however, the rise of the gig economy comes from employers' drive to lower costs, especially during business downturns. Gig workers experience greater insecurity than workers in traditional jobs and suffer from lack of access to established systems of social insurance.

## FIGURE 1: DISTRIBUTION OF THE LABOR FORCE BY CONTRACT TYPE, 1999

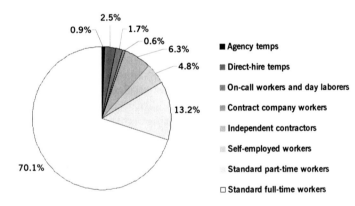

Special surveys by the Bureau of Labor Statistics in 1995, 2001, and 2005, and by the General Accounting Office in 1999, yielded widely varying estimates of the scale of the gig economy. The GAO estimated that as many as 30% of workers were on some type of contingent labor contract, including some categories of workers (self-employed and part-time workers) who are not counted as contingent workers by the BLS. Using the narrower BLS definition, 12% of workers were on contingent contracts in 1999 (similar to the number estimated from more recent surveys).

FIGURE 2: SHARE OF WORKERS ON CONTINGENT CONTRACTS,
BY INDUSTRY, 2005

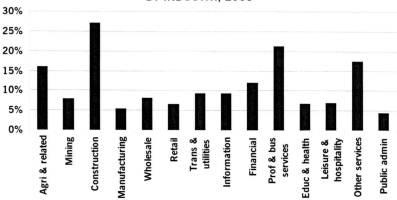

Contingent workers are employed throughout the economy, in all industries and in virtually all occupations. Using the BLS definition, which includes independent contractors, temporary workers, on-call workers, and workers provided by contract firms, contingent workers made up over 11% of the labor force in 2005. Some contingent workers do low-wage work in agriculture, construction, manufacturing, retail trade, and services; others are employed as highly paid financial analysts, lawyers, accountants, and physicians.

FIGURE 3: CONTINGENT LABOR, COLLEGE AND UNIVERSITY FACULTY

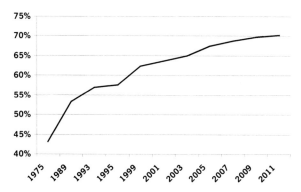

While many people may think of "day laborers" in construction or office "temps" when they think of contingent workers, few occupations have seen as sharp an increase in contingent labor as teaching in higher education. Adjunct and part-time professors now account for the great majority of college faculty nationwide. Tenured and tenure-track faculty now comprise less than a third of the teaching staff, and teach barely half of all classes. Colleges and universities hire adjunct faculty because they make it possible to more precisely match faculty to the demand for classes, and because adjuncts are paid substantially less.

## FIGURE 4: AVG. EARNINGS, TRADITIONAL VS. CONTINGENT EMPLOYMENT

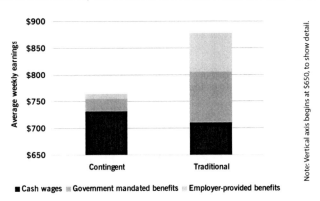

Note: Vertical axis begins at $650, to show detail.

■ Cash wages ▨ Government mandated benefits ▨ Employer-provided benefits

Employers prefer contingent labor because it is more "flexible." Workers can be laid off at any time in response to a decline in sales. Employers can also pay contingent workers less by not offering benefits. By treating many contingent workers as independent contractors, employers avoid paying for government-mandated benefits (the employer's half of Social Security, unemployment insurance, workers' compensation, etc.). They also usually exclude contingent workers from employer-provided benefits such as health insurance and pensions. Counting wages and benefits, contingent workers are paid substantially less than workers in traditional jobs and are left much more vulnerable to illness or economic downturns.

## FIGURE 5: NEW JOBS, TRADITIONAL VS. CONTINGENT, 1995-2013

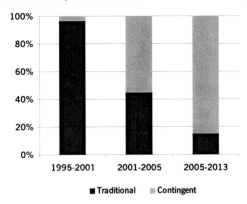

■ Traditional ▨ Contingent

While a solid majority of workers is still employed under traditional arrangements, most new jobs since 2001 have been under contingent arrangements. This is in sharp contrast to the late 1990s, when unemployment rates were low and employers had to offer workers more desirable long-term contracts. With the economic recession of the early 2000s, followed by the Great Recession and the anemic recovery (2007 to the present), however, employers have shunned long-term employment contracts and workers have had to settle. ❏

***Sources:*** General Accounting Office (GAO), Contingent Workers: Incomes and Benefits Lag Behind Those of Rest of Workforce (gao.gov); Bureau of Labor Statistics (BLS), Contingent and Alternative Employment Arrangements, February 2005 and February 2001 (bls.gov); Sharon Cohany, "Workers in Alternative Employment Arrangements." *Monthly Labor Review* (October): 31–46; U.S. Department of Education, National Center for Education Statistics, National Study of Postsecondary Faculty; John Curtis, "Trends in Faculty Employment Status, 1975-2011" (aaup.org).

*Article 4.5*

# THE HUMAN TOLL OF GREEK AUSTERITY

## BY EVITA NOLKA
*March/April 2016*

Giannis and Lena, both in their early 30s and with MBA degrees, consider themselves lucky to be employed. Living in Thessaloniki, Greece's second largest city, located in the heart of Macedonia, Giannis is a merchandise buyer at a company that imports household items. Lena works in the export department of a pasta-producing enterprise.

"Every Greek family is experiencing the crisis their own way," Lena tells me. "Unemployment, wage and pension cuts, taxes, and increases in prices of basic goods have caused despair to millions of people."

Giannis shares a bit more. His family's income has taken a real hit. His father's wages have been reduced by one third and his mother got laid off three years ago. She used to work at a ready-made garments factory that went bankrupt soon after. For a year and a half, she hasn't been paid and she is still claiming the money she is owed.

Like so many others, Giannis had been unemployed for years. There was nothing he could do other than hope to get accepted at one of the five-month temporary work programs in the country funded by the European Union (EU). "You're being deprived of the opportunity to work during the most productive years of your life," Giannis tells me as he explains the psychological burden of unemployment. "There's a feeling that you're standing still even though the whole world keeps moving and after a while you feel numb. You accept that's how things are and you are unable to get out of the rut."

## Sticking with Austerity

For six years now, Greece has lived under unprecedented austerity policies demanded by its lenders and accepted by a succession of governments. The social and political reality created by austerity was demonstrated sharply by two events on the same day in October 2015.

First, Eurostat, the European statistical service, released a report on poverty and social exclusion in Greece. The report showed that, in 2014, 22.1% of the Greek population lived in conditions of poverty, 21.5% were severely materially deprived, and 17.2% lived in families with very low work intensity. (Economists define "work intensity" as the total number of months that all working-age household members have worked as a percentage of the total number of months they theoretically could have worked. Households under 20% are considered to have "very low" work intensity.) Altogether, 36% of the population faced one or more of these terrible conditions. That figure was 7.9% percentage points higher than in 2008.

Second, the Greek parliament approved a new piece of legislation imposing further austerity measures as demanded by its creditors—primarily the EU and the International Monetary Fund (IMF)—to meet the terms of Greece's most recent (third) bailout agreement. The new package involves cutting public spending by 14.32 billion euros, while raising taxes by 14.09 billion euros, over the next five years. The measures will primarily affect privately owned businesses, homeowners, and employees close to retirement.

Austerity policies were first adopted in 2010 as a "solution" to the economic crisis that erupted in 2009–10. Severe cuts in public spending, deep reductions in wages and pensions, enormous tax increases, and a stripping back of labor protections were imposed—ostensibly—to stabilize the economy and gain the confidence of financial markets. In practice, the measures have plunged the Greek economy into a prolonged recession that has led to the disastrous results outlined by Eurostat. Unfortunately, the current Greek government, formed by the left-wing SYRIZA party, appears determined to keep the country on the same path.

## The Crushing Burden of Unemployment

In the course of the recession, the Greek economy has shrunk by more than 25%. At present, more than one out of four workers is unemployed (one out of two among the nation's youth), and more than one million jobs have disappeared. The prospects for improvement, given the austerity policies imposed under the third bailout agreement, are dim at best. "No legislation can guarantee even the most basic labor rights," Lena says in describing the way employers have used the specter of unemployment to further reduce wages. "It's no wonder," she adds, "that so many well-educated young people choose to leave the country."

Since the unemployment rate for people with higher education is nearly 20%—the highest in the world—more than 200,000 young Greeks have left the country in search of better opportunities abroad. I discussed Greece's brain drain with Victoria, 18, a first-year electrical and computer engineering student at the University of Thessaly. "Don't be mistaken," she says, "all those young people that seek a better life abroad care deeply for Greece and won't hesitate to return once things have improved." Victoria herself is already considering leaving Greece once she finishes her studies. Who can blame her? She is highly unlikely to find a job in her field after graduation.

## Collapse of Production

Austerity policies have also led the country's productive sector to near collapse, with industrial production in 2015 down by a staggering 35% compared to its level in 2008. Industrial production currently represents less than 10% of Greece's GDP, an exceptionally low level historically for the country, as well as for the eurozone today.

To be sure, the deindustrialization of the Greek economy started a lot earlier, in the early 1980s. The country's new development model, after its integration into the European Community and the emerging Single Market, systematically favored the tertiary (services) sector and ignored the primary (agriculture, mining, etc.) and secondary (manufacturing) sectors. Greek industries, accustomed to the heavy protectionist measures of the post-war period and poorly prepared for the requirements of market integration and the liberalization of trade, failed to adapt. The massive influx of European funds to the tertiary sector (mainly tourism) shaped a services-centered economy (the services sector contributes over 80% to the country's GDP), while weakening the country's competitiveness and contributing decisively to the dismantling of its industrial base.

Things got immeasurably worse after 2009. During the recession, about 250,000 small and medium-sized enterprises closed down. Many more have been forced to the verge of closure due to reduced revenues and increased financial obligations to social security funds, tax offices, and banks. Thousands of small business owners have opted to relocate to neighboring Balkan countries, which offer lower labor costs and corporate tax breaks.

"Reality has shown that the austerity measures applied across Europe are not the most effective response to the crisis," says Costas, a civil engineer from Patra, Greece's third largest city, in the southern region of the Peloponnese. Costas is 45 years old and a former member of SYRIZA, the current governing party. "No other country in the eurozone has had to impose such far-reaching austerity programs," he says, "and I just don't see how Greek society can sustain the burden of yet another bailout."

The policy is simply not working, even on its own terms. After five years of austerity and three bailout agreements, Greece's national debt of 320 billion euros is right where it was in 2010. But its debt-to-GDP ratio has shot up to 175% (compared to 150% in 2010), and the European Commission projects that it will rise to 200% in 2016. The country's destroyed economy will never be able to repay this huge volume of debt.

## SYRIZA U-Turn, Popular Disillusionment

Originally elected in January 2015 on a vehement anti-austerity platform, Greek Prime Minister Alexis Tsipras subsequently made a complete U-turn. Ignoring the popular outcry against austerity, loudly expressed in a referendum on July 5, he has given in to the creditors' demands. In August, SYRIZA and the creditors signed a new bailout agreement, including not only another round of austerity measures but also neocolonial restrictions on Greece's national sovereignty. No legislation related to the objectives of the bailout, however minor, can be taken by Greece's political institutions without the prior approval of its creditors. The creditors thus have the right to monitor the Greek government and to wield veto power over virtually all policy measures in Greece.

And yet, on September 20, Tsipras won a new election, again forming a government. The result seemed to vindicate his capitulation. It appears that Greek voters, confronted with a narrative presenting the new agreement as inescapable, opted to give the governing party a second chance. "This wasn't a vote of hope," says Costas, the civil engineer from Patra, "but a vote for the 'lesser evil' within the limits of a 'nothing can really change' mentality."

Costas is even convinced that if there were another general election soon, the governing party would still emerge victorious. Greek voters appear to think that there is no credible alternative to austerity. "Ever since the PM marginalized any voices in SYRIZA that tried to show a different way and declared there was no alternative," he says, "Greek society, having lost its morale, has come to accept its fate."

## Defeat and Apathy

To fully understand the popular mood, one must look at the abstention rates in the recent election. Turnout plummeted, with a record-high abstention rate of 45%. In addition, blank ballots reached an extraordinary 2.5%. The message is quite clear:

the Greek people's disappointment has led to a massive rejection of the political process altogether. Victoria tells me that most of her friends either cast a blank ballot or didn't bother to vote at all since "they didn't believe any of the existing political parties could actually make a difference."

The low turnout was not an isolated incident. During the past few years, social unrest and frustration over the austerity measures have given rise to widespread discontent and large-scale demonstrations. But the decline of the struggle as unemployment began to bite and, especially, SYRIZA's betrayal of popular hopes have led to a wholesale rejection of politics by broad layers of the population. The sense of defeat and indifference is pronounced among workers, and especially the young.

"Wishful thinking," says Costas about SYRIZA's hopes to overturn austerity by creating a domino effect in the countries of the European periphery. The balance of power has proven not that easy to change and now people feel that Greece is being punished for daring to question Europe's neoliberal policies.

European Union officials have categorically ruled out any possibility of a debt write-down. Restructuring in the form of a lengthening of maturity or perhaps a lowering of interest rates is still on the table, but it would have very debatable long-term results. Greece would probably be given more time to get back on its feet, but this would not eliminate short-term financing problems. Besides, even though Greek aid loans are very long-term (over thirty years) and interest rates have already been lowered several times (lower than 1%), the country's national debt is still considered unsustainable.

As for the SYRIZA government's current promise to implement a "parallel" social program that would ease the burden of harsh new austerity policies on poorer Greeks, it has already been forced to withdraw the intended bill following severe objections by the country's creditors. Many of the proposed measures lacked required budget-impact estimates. There were also concerns about the program's compatibility with the conditions of the third bailout agreement. "Parallel" programs running alongside austerity measures are not what the EU has in mind, nor would they be possible to implement within the strict framework of the latest bailout.

## The Prospect of Change

The only real question for Greece at the moment is: Could there be an alternative path?

Not everyone has given in to despondency and apathy. In a school building in central Athens, I meet Georgia, a young teacher and mother of three, who offers extra classes to underprivileged students free of charge. "People would take to the streets because they hoped they could make an actual difference," she says. "Now it is clear that our hopes were false." Nonetheless, she tells me, the economic crisis has made her more politically aware. She now chooses to spend much of her time and energy in political and social movements and social solidarity structures, where she can actually feel useful.

Popular Unity, a new political front including SYRIZA's left wing, which split from the party by refusing to accept the new bailout, has so far offered the only coherent argument about how Greece could adopt an anti-bailout strategy. Its radical program includes the introduction of a new national currency, a deep national debt write-off, a lifting of austerity measures, and a restructuring of the productive sector

### ENKLO: Life, Death—and Rebirth?

A case in point of Greece's manufacturing decline is provided by United Textiles (ENKLO), a 140-year-old company operating in Central Macedonia and Thrace with a strong presence in international markets, a skilled workforce, advanced technology, and excellent product quality. The company closed down in 2009, sinking under a debt burden of 350 million euros due mostly to poor management decisions and the expansion of its business activities beyond the textiles industry.

Ever since its shutdown, the laid-off workers, unable to find other jobs and refusing to accept that the company would never operate again, have been maintaining the equipment and guarding the buildings in order to prevent theft. "We are here night and day to make sure that the machines remain unharmed," says Petros, who has worked as an electrician for 25 years.

Instead of the scheduled liquidation of the company's property, the workers now propose its revival by converting its debts into stockholders' equity, taking advantage of the country's bankruptcy code. It is an ambitious business plan that aspires to utilize the existing equipment and the invaluable expertise of the workers.

No public funds are needed to re-start production. All that's required is a government intervention that would settle any legal complications that may arise. With the government's support, Petros argues, the company could operate the very next day.

and the welfare state. However, Popular Unity has so far failed to convince Greek voters, and did not gain parliamentary representation in the last elections.

Social injustice has spurred new modes of resistance far from political parties and trade unions. As the state becomes ever more hostile to the Greek people, many choose to self-organize by forming neighborhood assemblies and solidarity networks that support basic human rights, organizing micro-economies without middle-men, and setting up "solidarity clinics" providing free health care.

This is a period of reflection and finding alternative forms of resistance that could potentially be the basis for something new to emerge in the future. All hope is not yet lost that Greece may regain some economic stability and find a development policy in the interest of its people. "People feel exhausted, defeated and betrayed," says Georgia, "but many refuse to give up." ❏

**Sources:** Eurostat news release 181/2015 (ec.europa.eu/eurostat/documents); Eurostat dataset (ec. europa.eu/eurostat), "Youth unemployment rate," "Long-term unemployment rate," "Production in industry—manufacturing," "Production in industry—total (excluding construction)," "Production in industry—annual data, percentage change," "General government gross debt—annual data"; "Young, gifted and Greek: Generation G—the world's biggest brain drain," *The Guardian* (theguardian.com); C. Pitelis & N. Antonakis (2003), "Manufacturing and competitiveness: the case of Greece," *Journal of Economic Studies*, Vol. 30, Issue 5, pp. 535—547; H. Louri and I. Pepelasis Minoglou (2002), "A hesitant evolution: industrialisation and de-industrialisation in Greece over the long run", *Journal of European Economic Studies*, Vol. 31, No. 2, pp. 321-348; M. Nence, "Greek entrepreneurship after crisis—investment abroad, the easiest solution" (pecob.eu); Kathimerini, "Crisis wipes out a quarter of Greece's SMEs" (ekathimerini.com); September 2015 official election results (ekloges.ypes.gr)..

Article 4.6

# KEYNES, WAGE AND PRICE "STICKINESS," AND DEFLATION

## BY ALEJANDRO REUSS

*August 2009*

Most people are accustomed to worrying about inflation, which has been a durable fact of life in the United States for half a century. The overall price level in the U.S. economy (a sort of average of prices across the economy), as measured by the Consumer Price Index, has increased every calendar year since 1957. Or, rather, had increased every year since 1957, until 2008. Last year, as the U.S. economy went into its most severe recession since the Great Depression, the CPI declined by 0.2%. For the first time in decades, there is reason in the United States to worry about the dangers of deflation.

## Deflation: What's Not to Like?

Lower prices may sound appealing, but deflation can make a bad recession worse. Deflation can bring down overall demand. If individuals and firms expect prices to decline, they may postpone purchases. Why buy today, if the price will be lower tomorrow? Declining prices and wages can exacerbate firms' negative expectations about future sales and profits, discouraging current investment. If a firm does not think it will be able to sell future output at a sufficient profit, it will not make purchases of new plant and equipment now. Deflation can also make the cost of borrowing higher, and increase the burden of past debt. This can ruin debtors and bankrupt firms, as each dollar owed becomes harder to come by as prices drop. Over the three years with the sharpest drop in output and employment during the Great Depression, 1930-1933, the Consumer Price Index dropped by over 25%. More broadly, a study by economists Michael Bruno and William Easterly of over 100 countries from the 1960s to 1990s showed that rates of deflation between 0% and 20% were associated with lower rates of economic growth than low to moderate rates of inflation (up to 30%) were.

Such concerns about deflation run sharply counter to the "mainstream" or neoclassical view of recessions. Neoclassical economists argue that the economy is "self-correcting," and that if it dips into recession it will quickly return itself to "full employment" without any need for deliberate government action. One of their main arguments for this view is that prices—including wages (the price of labor) and interest rates (the price of money)—are flexible. If there is excess supply of labor (unemployment), workers will reduce their wage demands, causing employers to want to hire more labor and workers to offer less labor for sale, until the surplus is eliminated. Likewise, if there is excess saving, the interest rate will decline, causing people to save less and borrow more, until that surplus is eliminated. In this view, a recovery (from a period of low employment and output) involves a decrease in the price level. Deflation, in other words, is the cure for what ails us.

## What Is Price "Stickiness"?

One response to the neoclassical argument is that, in fact, prices are not perfectly flexible (they exhibit "stickiness"). For this reason, the economy is not self-correcting, at least not in the short run. Wages and prices may be "too high" (and, therefore, result in suppliers offering larger quantities for sale than demanders are able and willing to buy), but not come down quickly and eliminate the market surplus. This view has been widely attributed to John Maynard Keynes, and is, in fact, a key argument in what is known as "New Keynesian" economic theory. But this was not Keynes' argument.

Keynes expressed, in numerous passages in *The General Theory*, the view that wages were "sticky" in terms of money. He noted, for example, that workers and unions tended to fight tooth-and-nail against any attempts by employers to reduce money wages (the actual sum of money workers receive, as opposed to the real purchasing power of these wages, taking account of changes in the cost of living), even by a little bit, in a way they did not fight for increases in wages every time there was a small rise in the cost of living eroding their "real wages." Keynes argued emphatically, however, against the idea that the stickiness of money wages was the cause of unemployment, or that full flexibility of money wages (in particular, a decline in money wages) was likely to be a cure for depressions.

## Is Wage Flexibility the Solution?

Keynes was careful to describe many different possible effects of declining money wages, some pointing towards increased consumption or investment (and therefore an increase in total output and incomes), and some pointing in the opposite direction. He pointed out two fundamental errors in the conventional view that lower money wages would necessarily result in increased employment. First, he noted that, while one worker could gain employment (at the expense of someone else) by accepting a lower wage, this did not automatically mean that lower money wages across the board would cause overall employment to increase. Second, he argued that, while decreased money wages would result in increased employment if total ("aggregate") demand were unchanged, there was no reason to believe that would be the case.

Keynes made at least four major arguments that declining money wages were not the cure for unemployment (and depressions) that classical economists thought.

1. Workers do not decide their level of real wages, and so cannot reduce these to a level that will ensure full employment. Keynes pointed out that particular workers (or groups of workers) and employers bargained not over real wages, but money wages. Real wages depended not only on these money-wage bargains but also on the overall price level. The price level, in turn, depended on money-wage bargains made between many different groups of workers and employers across the economy as a whole. Keynes argued that, if workers in general were to accept lower money wages, the overall price level could not possibly remain unchanged. The price level, instead, would decline by a similar proportion, so real wages might not change very much at all. In that case, employers would not have an incentive to hire more workers, and overall employment would change very little.

2. Reductions in workers' money wages may result in decreased consumption, and therefore can result in lower incomes and output. Keynes argued that declines in money wages change the distribution of income—increasing the incomes of owners of other factors of production (capitalists and landowners) at the expense of workers, and those of rentiers (owners of money capital) at the expense of entrepreneurs (owners of businesses). These changes in distribution could result in a decrease in the "marginal propensity to consume" (the amount spent on consumption out of each additional dollar of income). Declining money wages (and the resulting decline in the price level) would tend to redistribute income from lower-income individuals (who tend to consume a very large proportion of their incomes) to higher-income individuals (who tend to consume lower proportions of their incomes, and to save higher proportions).

3. Declining wages can create incentives for employers to postpone purchases of durable equipment. Keynes argued that the effects of the reduction in money wages on the incentive for capitalists to invest (purchase durable equipment) depended on the expectations of future changes in money wages. If money wages declined, but capitalists expected them to go up in the immediate future (that is, money wages were thought to have "bottomed out"), Keynes argued, the effect on investment would be positive, since the cost of producing durable equipment now would be lower than in the future. However, if the decline in money wages made capitalists expect continued future declines, the effect on investment would be negative. Durable equipment purchased in the current period would, in Keynes' words, have to "compete ... with the output from equipment produced [in the future] ... at a lower labor cost." Owners of the more expensive equipment would have to cut their prices and accept lower profits to match the prices that owners of the less expensive equipment would be willing to accept (having the advantage of lower costs). This would produce an incentive to put off purchases of such equipment into the future.

4. A decline in the price level creates increased real burdens for debtors. When the price level goes down, the purchasing power of the currency increases. We would say, "A dollar becomes more valuable." Since most debts take the form of a specific sum of money owed, and the real purchasing power of this sum increases as the price level decreases, the real purchasing power that the debtor has to hand over also increase. Looked at another way, across-the-board deflation means that the debtor cannot charge as much for whatever she sells, but the amount of money she has to pay to the creditor does not change. Therefore, she now has to sell more units (of whatever it is she sells) to pay back the debt. Debt service will swallow up an increasing proportion of her gross income. "If the fall of wages and prices goes far ... those entrepreneurs who are heavily indebted," Keynes argues, "may soon reach the point of insolvency." That is, deflation can result in an epidemic of bankruptcies.

Keynes' arguments on the effects of declining wages and prices during a recession were part of his case, contrary to the mainstream economics of his time (and ours), that capitalist economies were not inherently "self-correcting." Depression conditions, Keynes argued, would not necessarily set off a chain of events pulling the economy back to its "full employment" level of output. Declining money wages and prices could, in fact, lead to a downward spiral deeper into recession. Capitalist economies could get stuck in a low-output, high-unemployment condition. Keynes believed that government action was necessary to guarantee a return to and maintenance of full employment. For this reason, he argued that the complacent attitude of conventional economists toward economic crises—that, eventually, the problem would solve itself—was not of much use. "Economists set them too easy, too useless a task," he wrote, "if in tempestuous seasons they can only tell us that when the storm is over the ocean is flat again." ❑

**Resources**: John Maynard Keynes, *The General Theory of Employment, Interest, and Money* (New York: Harcourt, Inc., 1964); John Maynard Keynes, *A Tract on Monetary Reform* (London: MacMillan, 1923); Consumer Price Index, All Urban Consumers (CPI-U), Economagic; Michael Bruno and William Easterly, "Inflation Crises and Long-Run Growth," Policy Research Working Paper, World Bank, September 1995.

# Chapter 5

# WEALTH, INEQUALITY, AND POVERTY

## INTRODUCTION

Wealth and inequality are both end products of today's patterns of economic growth. But while all macroeconomics textbooks investigate wealth accumulation, most give less attention to wealth disparities. The authors in this chapter fill in the gap by looking at who makes out, and who doesn't, in the accumulation of wealth.

Economist Chris Tilly debunks the myth that today's inequality is inevitable or (as many mainstream economists would have it) actually desirable (Article 5.1). He argues that rampant inequality is not necessary for economic growth, showing that among both developing and industrial economies and across individual countries' distinct regions, there is no correlation between higher inequality and faster economic growth. He argues that greater equality actually supports economic growth by bolstering spending, raising productivity, and reducing social conflict.

John Miller ("Inequality and Our Economic Problems") (Article 5.2) argues that some prominent economists have badly misunderstood rising income inequality. It is not a growing divide between the college-educated and those with less education, but between the very rich and everyone else. It is not just that market incomes have grown more unequal, but also that taxes now do less to reduce income inequality. And it is not the case that income inequality has been a minor factor in our recent sluggish economic growth. Rather, it has reduced demand and output.

The next article focuses on changes in inequality, rooted in changes in labor relations, between the mid 20th century and the present. As Arthur MacEwan points out, the income share of the richest 1% rose when the share of workers who were union members fell. To MacEwan it seems clear that restoring union size and strength would go a long way toward reducing inequality (Article 5.3).

Next, Jeannette Wicks-Lim (Article 5.4) describes another dimension of inequality, the racial wealth gap. This gap, already large before the Great Recession, has been exacerbated by the devastating effects of the crisis on black families' wealth.

What has happened to world income inequality is a matter of intense debate. Many analysts claim that globally, incomes have converged, leading to a sharp reduction in world inequality in the second half of the twentieth century.

Many others report that the gaps between the poorest and the richest people and between countries have continued to widen over the last two decades. Arthur MacEwan (Article 5.5) unpacks the trends, both in terms of rising inequality within most large economies and some reduction of the income gaps between different countries.

Rounding out the chapter, Steven Pressman (Article 5.6) analyzes the celebrated work of French economist Thomas Piketty on the growth of income inequality over the history of capitalism. Pressman summarizes Piketty's arguments that rising inequality is not a short-term anomaly, but a deep long-term trend in capitalist societies, then turns to a thoughtful discussion of Piketty's proposed policy responses.

## Discussion Questions

1. (General) The authors of this chapter believe that income and wealth distribution is as important as income and wealth creation, and consider greater economic equality an important macroeconomic goal. What are some arguments for and against this position? Where do you come down in the debate?

2. (General) "A rising tide lifts all boats," proclaimed John F. Kennedy as he lobbied for pro-business tax cuts in the early 1960s. Have recent periods of economic growth (or "booms") lifted all boats? How have stockholders fared versus wage earners? How has the distribution of income and wealth by income group and by race changed?

3. (Article 5.1) Why do conservatives argue that inequality is good for economic growth? What counterarguments does Tilly use to challenge this traditional view of the "tradeoff" between inequality and growth? What evidence convinces Tilly that equality is good for economic growth? Does that evidence convince you?

4. (Article 5.2) Some economists hypothesize that unequal access to college education is driving the rise of income inequality in the United States. Why does Miller disagree with this view?

5. (Article 5.3) MacEwan shows that union strength and economic inequality are negatively associated (when one is high, the other is low). What possible explanations does MacEwan offer? Is there good reason to believe that higher unionization was the cause of greater equality in the past, and the decline of unions explains increased inequality in recent years?

6. (Article 5.4) Why is there a racial wealth gap in the United States? How, according to Wicks-Lim, have the housing crash and Great Recession exacerbated this problem? What do you think about the policy responses Wicks-Lim proposes?

7. (Article 5.5) MacEwan argues that income inequality within most large countries has widened in recent decades, while income inequality between countries had narrowed somewhat? Which of these trends would you consider more significant?

8. (Article 5.6) Economist Thomas Piketty proposes a global tax on wealth as a response to rising inequality. Do you think that his solution is feasible? Is it desirable?

*Article 5.1*

# GEESE, GOLDEN EGGS, AND TRAPS
*Why inequality is bad for the economy.*

## BY CHRIS TILLY
*July/August 2004*

Whenever progressives propose ways to redistribute wealth from the rich to those with low and moderate incomes, conservative politicians and economists accuse them of trying to kill the goose that lays the golden egg. The advocates of unfettered capitalism proclaim that inequality is good for the economy because it promotes economic growth. Unequal incomes, they say, provide the incentives necessary to guide productive economic decisions by businesses and individuals. Try to reduce inequality, and you'll sap growth. Furthermore, the conservatives argue, growth actually promotes equality by boosting the have-nots more than the haves. So instead of fiddling with who gets how much, the best way to help those at the bottom is to pump up growth.

But these conservative prescriptions are absolutely, dangerously wrong. Instead of the goose-killer, equality turns out to be the goose. Inequality stifles growth; equality gooses it up. Moreover, economic expansion does not necessarily promote equality—instead, it is the types of jobs and the rules of the economic game that matter most.

## Inequality: Goose or Goose-Killer?

The conservative argument may be wrong, but it's straightforward. Inequality is good for the economy, conservatives say, because it provides the right incentives for innovation and economic growth. First of all, people will only have the motivation to work hard, innovate, and invest wisely if the economic system rewards them for good economic choices and penalizes bad ones. Robin Hood-style policies that collect from the wealthy and help those who are worse off violate this principle. They reduce the payoff to smart decisions and lessen the sting of dumb ones. The result: people and companies are bound to make less efficient decisions. "We must allow [individuals] to fail, as well as succeed, and we must replace the nanny state with a regime of self-reliance and self-respect," writes conservative lawyer Stephen Kinsella in *The Freeman: Ideas on Liberty* (not clear how the free woman fits in). To prove their point, conservatives point to the former state socialist countries, whose economies had become stagnant and inefficient by the time they fell at the end of the 1980s.

If you don't buy this incentive story, there's always the well-worn trickle-down theory. To grow, the economy needs productive investments: new offices, factories, computers, and machines. To finance such investments takes a pool of savings. The rich save a larger fraction of their incomes than those less well-off. So to spur growth, give more to the well-heeled (or at least take less away from them in the form of taxes), and give less to the down-and-out. The rich will save their money and then invest it, promoting growth that's good for everyone.

Unfortunately for trickle-down, the brilliant economist John Maynard Keynes debunked the theory in his *General Theory of Employment, Interest, and*

*Money* in 1936. Keynes, whose precepts guided liberal U.S. economic policy from the 1940s through the 1970s, agreed that investments must be financed out of savings. But he showed that most often it's changes in investment that drive savings, rather than the other way around. When businesses are optimistic about the future and invest in building and retooling, the economy booms, all of us make more money, and we put some of it in banks, 401(k)s, stocks, and so on. That is, saving grows to match investment. When companies are glum, the process runs in reverse, and savings shrink to equal investment. This leads to the "paradox of thrift": if people try to save too much, businesses will see less consumer spending, will invest less, and total savings will end up diminishing rather than growing as the economy spirals downward. A number of Keynes's followers added the next logical step: shifting money from the high-saving rich to the high-spending rest of us, and not the other way around, will spur investment and growth.

Of the two conservative arguments in favor of inequality, the incentive argument is a little weightier. Keynes himself agreed that people needed financial consequences to steer their actions, but questioned whether the differences in payoffs needed to be so huge. Certainly state socialist countries' attempts to replace material incentives with moral exhortation have often fallen short. In 1970, the Cuban government launched the Gran Zafra (Great Harvest), an attempt to reap 10 million tons of sugar cane with (strongly encouraged) volunteer labor. Originally inspired by Che Guevara's ideal of the New Socialist Man (not clear how the New Socialist Woman fit in), the effort ended with Fidel Castro tearfully apologizing to the Cuban people in a nationally broadcast speech for letting wishful thinking guide economic policy.

But before conceding this point to the conservatives, let's look at the evidence about the connection between equality and growth. Economists William Easterly of New York University and Gary Fields of Cornell University have recently summarized this evidence:

- Countries, and regions within countries, with more equal incomes grow faster. (These growth figures do not include environmental destruction or improvement. If they knocked off points for environmental destruction and added points for environmental improvement, the correlation between equality and growth would be even stronger, since desperation drives poor people to adopt environmentally destructive practices such as rapid deforestation.)
- Countries with more equally distributed land grow faster.
- Somewhat disturbingly, more ethnically homogeneous countries and regions grow faster—presumably because there are fewer ethnically based inequalities.
- In addition, more worker rights are associated with higher rates of economic growth, according to Josh Bivens and Christian Weller, economists at two Washington think tanks, the Economic Policy Institute and the Center for American Progress.

These patterns recommend a second look at the incentive question. In fact, more equality can actually strengthen incentives and opportunities to produce.

## Equality as the Goose

Equality can boost growth in several ways. Perhaps the simplest is that study after study has shown that farmland is more productive when cultivated in small plots. So organizations promoting more equal distribution of land, like Brazil's Landless Workers' Movement, are not just helping the landless poor—they're contributing to agricultural productivity!

Another reason for the link between equality and growth is what Easterly calls "match effects," which have been highlighted in research by Stanford's Paul Roemer and others in recent years. One example of a match effect is the fact that well-educated people are most productive when working with others who have lots of schooling. Likewise, people working with computers are more productive when many others have computers (so that, for example, e-mail communication is widespread, and know-how about computer repair and software is easy to come by). In very unequal societies, highly educated, computer-using elites are surrounded by majorities with little education and no computer access, dragging down their productivity. This decreases young people's incentive to get more education and businesses' incentive to invest in computers, since the payoff will be smaller.

Match effects can even matter at the level of a metropolitan area. Urban economist Larry Ledebur looked at income and employment growth in 85 U.S. cities and their neighboring suburbs. He found that where the income gap between those in the suburbs and those in the city was largest, income and job growth was slower for everyone.

"Pressure effects" also help explain why equality sparks growth. Policies that close off the low-road strategy of exploiting poor and working people create pressure effects, driving economic elites to search for investment opportunities that pay off by boosting productivity rather than squeezing the have-nots harder. For example, where workers have more rights, they will place greater demands on businesses. Business owners will respond by trying to increase productivity, both to remain profitable even after paying higher wages, and to find ways to produce with fewer workers. The CIO union drives in U.S. mass production industries in the 1930s and 1940s provide much of the explanation for the superb productivity growth of the 1950s and 1960s. (The absence of pressure effects may help explain why many past and present state socialist countries have seen slow growth, since they tend to offer numerous protections for workers but no right to organize independent unions.) Similarly, if a government buys out large land-holdings in order to break them up, wealthy families who simply kept their fortunes tied up in land for generations will look for new, productive investments. Industrialization in Asian "tigers" South Korea and Taiwan took off in the 1950s on the wings of funds freed up in exactly this way.

## Inequality, Conflict, and Growth

Inequality hinders growth in another important way: it fuels social conflict. Stark inequality in countries such as Bolivia and Haiti has led to chronic conflict that hobbles economic growth. Moreover, inequality ties up resources in unproductive uses such as paying for large numbers of police and security guards—attempts to prevent individuals from redistributing resources through theft.

Ethnic variety is connected to slower growth because,on the average, more ethnically diverse countries are also more likely to be ethnically divided. In other words, the problem isn't ethnic variety itself, but racism and ethnic conflict that can exist among diverse populations. In nations like Guatemala, Congo, and Nigeria, ethnic strife has crippled growth—a problem alien to ethnically uniform Japan and South Korea. The reasons are similar to some of the reasons that large class divides hurt growth. Where ethnic divisions (which can take tribal, language, religious, racial, or regional forms) loom large, dominant ethnic groups seek to use government power to better themselves at the expense of other groups, rather than making broad-based investments in education and infrastructure. This can involve keeping down the underdogs—slower growth in the U.S. South for much of the country's history was linked to the Southern system of white supremacy. Or it can involve seizing the surplus of ethnic groups perceived as better off—in the extreme, Nazi Germany's expropriation and genocide of the Jews, who often held professional and commercial jobs.

Of course, the solution to such divisions is not "ethnic cleansing" so that each country has only one ethnic group—in addition to being morally abhorrent, this is simply impossible in a world with 191 countries and 5,000 ethnic groups. Rather, the solution is to diminish ethnic inequalities. Once the 1964 Civil Rights Act forced the South to drop racist laws, the New South's economic growth spurt began. Easterly reports that in countries with strong rule of law, professional bureaucracies, protection of contracts, and freedom from expropriation—all rules that make it harder for one ethnic group to economically oppress another—ethnic diversity has no negative impact on growth.

If more equality leads to faster growth so everybody benefits, why do the rich typically resist redistribution? Looking at the ways that equity seeds growth helps us understand why. The importance of pressure effects tells us that the wealthy often don't think about more productive ways to invest or reorganize their businesses until they are forced to. But also, if a country becomes very unequal, it can get stuck in an "inequality trap." Any redistribution involves a tradeoff for the rich. They lose by giving up part of their wealth, but they gain a share in increased economic growth. The bigger the disparity between the rich and the rest, the more the rich have to lose, and the less likely that the equal share of boosted growth they'll get will make up for their loss. Once the gap goes beyond a certain point, the wealthy have a strong incentive to restrict democracy, and to block spending on education which might lead the poor to challenge economic injustice—making reform that much harder.

## Does Economic Growth Reduce Inequality?

If inequality isn't actually good for the economy, what about the second part of the conservatives' argument—that growth itself promotes equality? According to the conservatives, those who care about equality should simply pursue growth and wait for equality to follow.

"A rising tide lifts all boats," President John F. Kennedy famously declared. But he said nothing about which boats will rise fastest when the economic tide comes in.

Growth does typically reduce poverty, according to studies reviewed by economist Gary Fields, though some "boats"—especially families with strong barriers to participating in the labor force—stay "stuck in the mud." But inequality can increase at the same time that poverty falls, if the rich gain even faster than the poor do. True, sustained periods of low unemployment, like that in the late 1990s United States, do tend to raise wages at the bottom even faster than salaries at the top. But growth after the recessions of 1991 and 2001 began with years of "jobless recoveries"— growth with inequality.

For decades the prevailing view about growth and inequality within countries was that expressed by Simon Kuznets in his 1955 presidential address to the American Economic Association. Kuznets argued that as countries grew, inequality would first increase, then decrease. The reason is that people will gradually move from the low-income agricultural sector to higher-income industrial jobs—with inequality peaking when the workforce is equally divided between low- and high-income sectors. For mature industrial economies, Kuznets's proposition counsels focusing on growth, assuming that it will bring equity. In developing countries, it calls for enduring current inequality for the sake of future equity and prosperity.

But economic growth doesn't automatically fuel equality. In 1998, economists Klaus Deininger and Lyn Squire traced inequality and growth over time in 48 countries. Five followed the Kuznets pattern, four followed the reverse pattern (decreasing inequality followed by an increase), and the rest showed no systematic pattern. In the United States, for example:

- incomes became more equal during the 1930s through 1940s New Deal period (a time that included economic decline followed by growth);
- from the 1950s through the 1970s, income gaps lessened during booms and expanded during slumps;
- from the late 1970s forward, income inequality worsened fairly consistently, whether the economy was stagnating or growing.

The reasons are not hard to guess. The New Deal introduced widespread unionization, a minimum wage, social security, unemployment insurance, and welfare. Since the late 1970s, unions have declined, the inflation-adjusted value of the minimum wage has fallen, and the social safety net has been shredded. In the United States, as elsewhere, growth only promotes equality if policies and institutions to support equity are in place.

## Trapped?

Let's revisit the idea of an inequality trap. The notion is that as the gap between the rich and everybody else grows wider, the wealthy become more willing to give up overall growth in return for the larger share they're getting for themselves. The "haves" back policies to control the "have-nots," instead of devoting social resources to educating the poor so they'll be more productive.

Sound familiar? It should. After two decades of widening inequality, the last few years have brought us massive tax cuts that primarily benefit the wealthiest, at the expense of investment in infrastructure and the education, child care, and income supports that would help raise less well-off kids to be productive adults. Federal and state governments have cranked up expenditures on prisons, police, and "homeland security," and Republican campaign organizations have devoted major resources to keeping blacks and the poor away from the polls. If the economic patterns of the past are any indication, we're going to pay for these policies in slower growth and stagnation unless we can find our way out of this inequality trap. ❏

*Sources:* William Easterly, *The Elusive Quest for Growth*, MIT Press 2001; Gary S. Fields, *Distribution and Development*, MIT Press 2001; Josh Bivens and Christian Weller, "Rights make might: Ensuring workers' rights as a strategy for economic growth," Economic Policy Institute 2003.

*Article 5.2*

# INEQUALITY AND OUR ECONOMIC PROBLEMS

## BY JOHN MILLER
*November/December 2013*

> ... President Obama and his supporters have been talking about "an econ-
> omy that grows from the middle out." ...
> The key causal factor of the middle-out view is that a wider income distri-
> bution slows economic growth by lowering consumption demand. The data for
> the recovery since mid-2009 do not support this view.
> Moreover, data do not support the view that tax cuts in the past 30 years
> are responsible for the widening income distribution.
> —John B. Taylor, "The Weak Recovery Explains Rising Inequality, Not
> Vice Versa," Wall Street Journal, Sept. 9, 2013.

Vice versa back at you, John Taylor. Rising inequality is not just bad for us, but is the root cause of today's economic problems. A Stanford economist and Senior Fellow at the conservative Hoover Institute, Taylor readily admits that inequality is on the rise. But he never spells out the degree to which the widening gulf between the best off and the rest of us has concentrated economic gains nearly exclusively among the super rich. Had he done so, he would have found it far harder to dismiss the roles that pro-rich economic policies and worsening inequality have played in causing today's economic maladies.

The most recent data, drawn from a variety of highly credible sources, show what the concentration of income "more at the upper end," as Taylor puts it, has meant in practice. As of 2012, the richest 1% of families, all with incomes above $394,000, receive more than one-fifth of the income of the nation, some 22.5%, according the latest data compiled by economists Emmanuel Saez and Thomas Piketty. That's nearly equal to their 23.5% share of income in 2007, before the onset of the Great Recession, and their 24% share during the late 1920s, on the eve of the Great Depression—the two highest concentrations of income since 1913. And, as Saez and Piketty document, a stunning 95% of what income gains there have been during the current recovery (from 2009 to 2012) have gone to richest 1%.

Not surprisingly, by 2012 only the income of the top 5% had returned to its pre-recession level in 2007, as the latest figures from the Bureau of the Census confirm. The inflation-adjusted income of the median family, on the other hand, was still 8.3% below its pre-recession level, and no higher than in 1989, nearly a generation earlier.

## College Grads and the Super-Rich

What accounts for today's staggering inequality? Taylor claims that changes in the private economy have driven up the wages of the well-educated and have left those with fewer years of education behind. The distance between the economic position of workers with college degrees and those without has, indeed, widened considerably over the last three decades. In 1979, the "college premium" was 1.41. That is, the median wage of a college graduate was 41% greater than that of a worker with only a high-school diploma. By 2007, the college premium had reached 1.75. In addition, since the onset of the Great Recession in December 2007, the number of jobs held by college graduates has increased, while the number of jobs held by those without a college degree has fallen.

But that is hardly enough evidence to support Taylor's claim. First off, nearly all of the increase in the college premium occurred before the last decade, but inequality has continued to worsen. In addition, the inequality among wage earners, especially between the top wage earners and the rest of the workforce, a large and increasing number of whom hold a college degree, is far greater than the college premium data suggest. For instance, looking at the ranking of wage and salary earners between 1979 and 2007, the wages and salaries of the top 1% rose by 156%, while those of the bottom 90% went up by just 17%. At the end of that period, the ratio of the wages and salaries of the top 1% to those of the bottom 90% stood at over 20-to-1, more than double the 9.7-to-1 ratio in 1979.

When investment income is added to wage and salary income, the economic gulf between the elites and the vast majority becomes even greater and increases even more quickly than the wage gap alone. Over the same 1979-to-2007 period, the ratio of total income of the top 1% to that of the bottom 90% tripled from 14-to-1 to 42-to-1. And even among the richest 1% income became considerably more concentrated. In 1979, the ratio of income of the top one-tenth of 1% to that of the top 1% was 3.4-to-1 in 1979 but reached to 5.2-to-1 by 2007.

These vast differences cannot be attributed solely, or even primarily, to differences in years of education among wage earners.

## Pro-Rich Tax Cuts and Inequality

Taylor also emphatically disagrees with the "middle-out view" that the pro-rich tax cuts and economic policies that began in the early 1980s are the cause of the ever-widening gulf between the haves and the have-nots. But the very evidence he uses to support his position suggests otherwise.

Taylor's argument rests on data published by the Congressional Budget Office (CBO) showing that "the distribution of market income before taxes widened in the 1980s and '90s by about as much as the distribution of income after taxes." But that hardly makes his case. Rather, the fact that after-tax income and before-tax income are widening at about the same rate offers powerful testimony to how pro-rich tax cuts have wiped out whatever government taxing policies had done in the past to mitigate the effects of widening economic differences in the private sector. "Market income inequality rose almost continually over the period [from 1979 to 2009]," write CBO tax analysts Ed Harris and Frank Sammartino. "Taxes and transfers did not offset market inequality."

Federal taxes are considerably less progressive than in the past and no match for three decades of widening inequality. In 1979, the richest 1% paid an effective federal tax rate of 35%—handing over a little over one-third of their total income in federal taxes. By 2009, the effective tax rate of the top 1% had fallen to 28.9%, according to the CBO. And when a less progressive federal tax code was combined with a regressive state and local tax code, taxes could no longer combat widening inequality.

## Inequality and Economic Growth

Finally, there are also several reasons to reject Taylor's claim that inequality is not the cause of the weak recovery and sluggish economic growth since the official end of the Great Recession in June 2009.

Taylor's argument is that inequality has not retarded spending because today's saving rate of 5.4% is not especially high by historical standards. That's true. But after the 1980s, the saving rate dropped steadily as consumption, boosted by a stock market boom, rose during the 1990s and, fueled by a housing bubble, rose still more during the last decade. Today's savings rate is considerably higher than the 3% savings rate that prevailed in the middle of the last decade.

While spending by the rich, if high enough, could hypothetically power economic growth, several prominent economists are convinced that the redistribution of income toward the upper end has diminished spending and stood in the way of more rapid economic growth. Alan Krueger, current chair of the Council of Economic Advisors, thinks the drag on spending from this upwards redistribution "could be substantial." He estimates that, by 2007, increased income inequality put an additional $1.1 trillion a year into the hands of the top 1%, who spend only about one-half of additional income. Had that $1.1 trillion remained in the hands of the bottom 99%, who have a general savings rate of about 10%, Krueger calculates that total consumption spending would have been 5% higher.

On top of its retarding effect on consumer spending, the concentration of income enhanced the political power of the super rich. Political scientists Adam Bonica, Nolan McCarty, Keith Poole, and Howard Rosenthal report that the share of individual campaign contributions made by the richest 0.01% rose from about 15% in 1980 to 40% in 2012.

And the political outcomes of the last three decades have surely conformed to the political interests of the most well-to-do—from the deregulation of the financial sector to pro-rich taxes to constraints on federal spending since the end of the Great Recession. Government spending and investment have been falling since 2010. Cuts in discretionary spending have reduced economic growth by 0.7 percentage points since 2010 and raised the unemployment rate by 0.8 percentage points, according to a recent report prepared for the conservative Peter G. Peterson Foundation. Taylor claims that three decades of rising inequality are explained by market forces. The lesson here, as Joseph Stiglitz has argued, is that "market forces don't exist in a vacuum—we shape them." In the last three decades, the very policies Taylor is determined to absolve have, in fact, shaped market forces in a way that has brought us ever-widening economic inequality, economic crisis, and now unrelenting economic stagnation. ❑

***Sources:*** Lawrence Mishel and Josh Bivens, "Occupy Wall Streeters Are Right About Skewed Economic Rewards in the United States," Economic Policy Institute Briefing Paper, Oct. 26, 2011; Congressional Budget Office, "The Distribution of Household Income and Federal Taxes, 2008 and 2009," July 2012; Adam Bonica, Nolan McCarty, Keith T. Poole, and Howard Rosenthal, "Why Hasn't Democracy Slowed Rising Inequality?" *Journal of Economic Perspectives,* Summer 2013; Emmanuel Saez, "Striking it Richer," University of California-Berkeley, Sept. 3, 2013; Ed Harris and Frank Sammartino, "Trends in the Distribution of Household Income, 1979-2009," Congressional Budget Office, Aug. 6, 2012; Jonathan James, "The College Wage Premium," *Economic Commentary,* Aug. 8, 2012; Carmen DeNavas-Walt, Bernadette D. Proctor, Jessica C. Smith, Income, Poverty, and Health Insurance Coverage in the United States: 2012, September 2013; Paul Krugman, "The Damage Done," *New York Times,* Oct. 17, 2013; Joseph Stiglitz, "Inequality Is Holding Back the Recovery," *New York Times,* Jan. 19, 2013; Dean Baker, "Krugman versus Stiglitz on Inequality and Economic Growth," Center for Economic and Policy Research, Jan. 20, 2013; Macroeconomic Advisers, LLC, The Cost of Crisis-Driven Fiscal Policy, Peter G. Peterson Foundation; Alan Krueger, "The Rise and Consequence of Inequality in the United States," White House Council of Economic Advisors, Jan. 12, 2012.

*Article 5.3*

# UNIONS AND INCOME INEQUALITY

### BY ARTHUR MacEWAN
*November/December 2011*

> Dear Dr. Dollar:
> *I know unions have shrunk in the United States, but by how much? And how best to respond to my right-wing friends who claim that unions are bad for the economy?* —Rich Sanford, Hardwick, Mass.

Take a look at the graph below. The two lines on the graph show for the period 1917 through 2007 (1) labor union membership as a percentage of the total U.S. work force and (2) the percentage of all income obtained by the highest 1% of income recipients. So the lines show, roughly, the strength of unions and the distribution of income for the past century. (John Miller and I developed this graph for our book *Economic Collapse, Economic Change.*)

The picture is pretty clear. In periods when unions have been strong, income distribution has been less unequal. In periods when unions have been weak, income distribution has been more unequal. In the post-World War II era, union members were about 25% of the labor force; today the figure is about 10%. In those postwar years, the highest-income 1% got 10% to 12% of all income; today they get about 25%.

**UNION MEMBERSHIP AND INCOME INEQUALITY, 1917-2007**

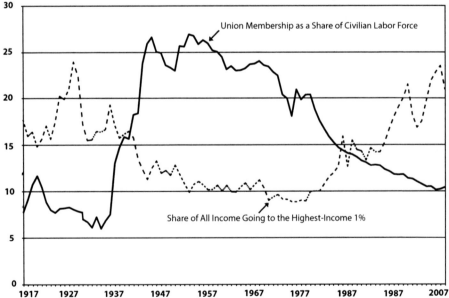

*Source:* Arthur MacEwan and John A. Miller, *Economic Collapse, Economic Change: Getting to the Root of the Crisis* (M.E. Sharpe, 2011).

The causation between union strength and income distribution is not simple. Nonetheless, there are some fairly direct connections. For example, when unions are strong, they can push for higher wages and thus we see a more equal distribution of income. Also, strong unions can have an impact on the political process, bringing about policies that are more favorable to workers.

But causation can work in the other direction as well. Great income inequality puts more power in the hands of the rich, and they can use that power to get policies put in place that weaken unions—for example, getting people who are hostile to unions appointed to the National Labor Relations Board.

And then there are other factors that affect both union strength and income distribution—for example, the changing structure of the global economy, which places U.S. workers in competition with poorly paid workers elsewhere. Yet the structure of the global economy is itself affected by the distribution of political power. For example, the "free trade" agreements that the United States has established with other countries generally ignore workers' rights (to say nothing of the environment) and go to great lengths to protect the rights of corporations. So, again, causation works in complex ways, and there are certainly other factors that need to be taken account of to explain the relationship shown in the graph.

However one explains the relationship, it is hard to imagine that we can return to a more equal distribution of income while unions remain weak. This means, at the very least, that the interests of unions and of people at the bottom of the income distribution are bound up with one another. Building stronger unions is an important part of fighting poverty—and the hunger and homelessness that are the clear manifestations of poverty.

One important thing to notice in the graph: In the post-World War II years, economic growth was the best we have seen. Certainly no one can claim that it is impossible for strong unions and a more equal distribution of income to co-exist with fairly rapid economic growth. Indeed, we might even argue that strong unions and a more equal distribution of income create favorable conditions for economic growth!

Stronger unions, it turns out, could be good preventive medicine for much of what ails our economy. ❏

*Article 5.4*

# THE GREAT RECESSION IN BLACK WEALTH

**BY JEANNETTE WICKS-LIM**
*January/February 2012*

The Great Recession produced the largest setback in racial wealth equality in the United States over the last 25 years. In 2009 the average white household's wealth was 20 times that of the average black household, nearly double that in previous years, according to a 2011 report by the Pew Research Center.

Driving this surge in inequality is a devastating drop in black wealth. The typical black household in 2009 was left with less wealth than at any time since 1984 after correcting for inflation.

It's important to remember wealth's special role—different from income—in supporting a household's economic well-being. Income pays for everyday expenses—groceries, clothes, and gas. A family's wealth, or net worth, includes all the assets they've built up over time (e.g., savings account, retirement fund, home, car) minus any money they owe (e.g., school loans, credit card debt, mortgage). Access to such wealth determines whether a layoff or medical crisis creates a bump in the road, or pushes a household off a financial cliff. Wealth can also provide families with financial stepping-stones to advance up the economic ladder—such as money for college tuition, or a down payment on a house.

Racial wealth inequality in the United States has always been severe. In 2004, for example, the typical black household had just $1 in net worth for every $11 of a typical white household. This is because families slowly accumulate wealth over their lifetime and across generations. Wealth, consequently, ties the economic fortunes of today's households to the explicitly racist economic institutions in America's past—especially those that existed during key phases of wealth redistribution. For example, the Homesteading Act of 1862 directed the large-scale transfer of government-owned land nearly exclusively to white households. Also starting in the 1930s, the Federal Housing Authority made a major push to subsidize home mortgages—for primarily white neighborhoods. On top of that, Jim Crow Laws—in effect until the mid-1960s—and racial violence severely curtailed efforts by the black community to start their own businesses to generate their own wealth.

The housing market crisis and the Great Recession made racial wealth inequality yet worse for two reasons. First, the wealth of blacks is more concentrated in their

## MEDIAN HOUSEHOLD NET WORTH (2009 DOLLARS)

|  | 1984 | 1988 | 1991 | 1993 | 1995 | 2004 | 2009 |
|---|---|---|---|---|---|---|---|
| White | $76,951 | $75,403 | $68,203 | $67,327 | $68,520 | $111,313 | $92,000 |
| Black | $6,679 | $7,263 | $7,071 | $6,503 | $9,885 | $9,823 | $4,900 |
| Ratio of White to Black | 12 | 10 | 10 | 10 | 7 | 11 | 19 |

*Source:* Taylor et al., *Twenty-to-One: Wealth Gaps to Rise to Record High Between Whites, Blacks and Hispanics,* Pew Research Center.

homes than the wealth of their white counterparts. Homes of black families make up 59% of their net worth compared to 44% among white families. White households typically hold more of other types of assets like stocks and IRA accounts. So when the housing crisis hit, driving down the value of homes and pushing up foreclosure rates, black households lost a much greater share of their wealth than did white households.

Second, mortgage brokers and lenders marketed subprime mortgages specifically to black households. Subprime mortgages are high-interest loans that are supposed to increase access to home financing for risky borrowers—those with a shaky credit history or low income. But these high-cost loans were disproportionately peddled to black households, even to those that could qualify for conventional loans. One study estimated that in 2007 nearly double the share of upper-income black households (54%) had high-cost mortgages compared to low-income white households (28%).

Subprime mortgages drain away wealth through high fees and interest payments. Worse, predatory lending practices disguise the high-cost of these loans with initially low payments. Payments then shoot up, often leading to default and foreclosure, wiping out a family's home equity wealth. In 2006, Mike Calhoun, president of the Center for Responsible Lending, predicted that the surge of subprime lending within the black community would "…likely be the largest loss of African-American wealth that we have ever seen, wiping out a generation of home wealth building." It was a prescient prediction.

To reverse the rise in racial wealth inequality, we need policies that specifically build wealth among black households, such as the "baby bonds" program proposed by economists William Darity of Duke University and Darrick Hamilton of The New School. Baby bonds would be federally managed, interest-bearing trusts given to the newborns of asset-poor families, and could be as large as $50,000 to $60,000 for the most asset-poor. By using a wealth means-test, this program would disproportionately benefit black communities, while avoiding the controversy of a reparations policy. When recipients reach age 18, they could use the funds for a house down payment, tuition, or to start a business. This program would cost about $60 billion per year, which could easily be covered by letting the Bush-era tax cuts expire for the top 1% of income earners. ❏

*Sources:* Amaad Rivera, Brenda Cotto-Escalera, Anisha Desai, Jeannette Huezo, and Dedrick Muhammad, *Foreclosed: State of the Dream 2008*, United for a Fair Economy, 2008; Citizens for Tax Justice, "The Bush Tax Cuts Cost Two and a Half Times as Much as the House Democrats' Health Care Proposal," CTJ Policy Brief, September 9, 2009; Darrick Hamilton and William Darity, Jr., "Can 'Baby Bonds' Eliminate the Racial Wealth Gap in Putative Post-Racial America?" *Review of Black Political Economy*, 2010; Paul Taylor, Rakesh Kochhar, Richard Fry, Gabriel Velasco, and Seth Motel, *Twenty-to-One: Wealth Gaps to Rise to Record High Between Whites, Blacks and Hispanics*, Washington DC: Pew Research Center, 2011.

*Article 5.5*

# INEQUALITY IN THE WORLD

## BY ARTHUR MACEWAN
*November/December 2014*

> Dear Dr. Dollar:
> *I had thought that neoliberal globalization was making the world more un-equal. But recently I have seen claims that the distribution of income in the world has become more equal. Is this true?*
> —Evan Swinerton, Brookline, Mass.

The answer to these questions depends on what you mean by "in the world." In many countries in the world—including most of the high-income countries and the most populous lower-income countries—the distribution of income has become more unequal. If we look at the income differences among countries, however, the situation has become more equal because per capita income has generally increased more rapidly in lower-income countries than in higher-income countries—though with important exceptions. And if we look at income distribution among all the people in the world—accounting for inequality both within and between countries—it seems that in recent decades the very high degree of inequality has remained about the same. (Before proceeding, please see the warning in the box below.)

## Distribution *Within* Countries

Take a look at Figures 1 and 2, which show the changes in the distribution of income within selected countries, several high-income and several low- or middle-in-

---

### Warning!

There are many problems in determining the extent of income inequality. The results can differ depending on which measure of inequality we use. Also, there are data difficulties. While some of these difficulties arise from poor reporting, plenty arise from the complexity of the issues. Also, different countries collect income data in different ways and do so in different years. With one exception (explained below), I will not detail the difficulties here, but readers should keep in mind that such difficulties exist.

How we compare incomes in different countries, where relative prices differ, currencies differ, and exchange rates (e.g., the number of Mexican pesos it takes to buy a dollar) often do not tell us accurately the buying power of income in different countries. The income data here are reported in terms of purchasing power parity (PPP) and reported in relation to the U.S. dollar. Comparing incomes in different countries using the PPP method gives us a comparison of the real buying power of income in the different countries. Calculating PPP data is complex and not precise, but the PPP figures are the best we have.

## FIGURE 1: INCOME RATIO, TOP 10% TO BOTTOM 10%, SELECTED HIGH-INCOME COUNTRIES

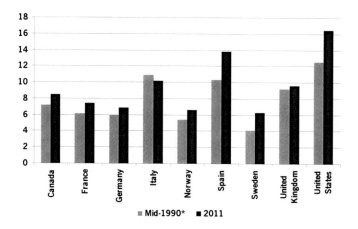

**Source:** OECD. *For the U.K. the figure is for 1999; for Spain the figure is for 2004; for France the figure is for 1996. For all others the earlier figures are for 1995. The later U.S. figure is for 2012.

come, over roughly the last two decades. The measure of income distribution used in these graphs is the ratio of the total income of the highest-income tenth of the population to the total income of the lowest-income tenth of the population.

The first thing that stands out in Figure 1 is that the U.S. income distribution is substantially more unequal than those of any of the other countries. Also, the absolute increase by this measure of inequality is greatest in the United States. However, with the sole exception of Italy, all the countries in Figure 1 experienced *rising income inequality.*

Things are different in Figure 2, which includes the ten most populous lower-income countries (ten of the twelve most populous countries in the world, the United States and Japan being the other two). The degree of inequality is quite high in some of the countries in the graph. Brazil is the extreme case. However, Brazil and most of the other countries in Figure 2 experienced a *reduction of inequality* in this period—though several are still highly unequal. The most populous countries in Figure 2—China, India, and Indonesia—though, experienced rising inequality. These countries are the first, second, and fourth most populous countries in the world (with the United States third).

The data in Figures 1 and 2 illustrate the widespread rise of income inequality *within* countries, especially among high-income countries. Among lower-income countries, the picture is mixed. Although Brazil remains highly unequal, the reduction of inequality in Brazil is important because it has been achieved, at least in part, by policies directed at reducing poverty. Brazil's redistributive policies represent a trend in many Latin American countries—a backlash against the neoliberal policies of preceding decades.

## Distribution *Among* Countries

Figure 3 illustrates what has been happening to income distribution *among* countries and indicates that the situation has become more equal because, in general, lower-in-

FIGURE 2: INCOME RATIO, TOP 10% TO BOTTOM 10%,
MOST POPULOUS LOW- AND MIDDLE-INCOME COUNTRIES

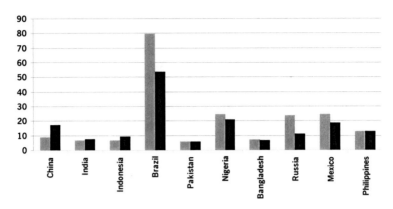

*Source:* World Bank. *Note:* These countries along with the United States and Japan are the twelve most populous countries in the world. The combined population of these ten accounts for 55% of the world's population in 2014.

FIGURE 3: PER CAPITA GDP, MOST POPULOUS LOW- AND MIDDLE-INCOME
COUNTRIES, AS PERCENTAGE OF U.S. GDP (PPP)

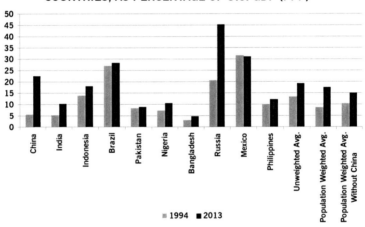

*Source:* World Bank.

come countries have grown more rapidly during the last two decades than have higher-income countries. For 1994 and 2013, the two columns in Figure 3 show Gross Domestic Product (GDP) per capita in the ten most populous low- and middle-income countries (listed by population) compared to GDP per capita in the United States. The comparison is in terms of purchasing power parity (PPP).

For nine of these ten countries—Mexico is the exception—GDP per capita rose more rapidly than in the United States. Taken as a group and using an average weighted by population, these ten countries in 1994 had an average GDP per capita 9% of that in the United States, but by 2013 this figure had risen to 17%. The basic result is not due simply to the remarkably rapid economic growth in China. When China is removed from the group, the weighted average still increases over this time period, from 10% to 15%. (This general phenomenon is certainly not a universal phenomenon; several very low-income countries have fallen further and further behind.)

So, if countries are our units of observation, Figure 3 illustrates how things have become more equal since the early 1990s. Going back further in time, comparing countries' incomes weighted by population shows inequality dropping pretty much continuously since 1960, and especially sharply since the early 1990s. But if the average is not weighted by population—thus removing the dominance of China, India, and some other very populous countries—the situation among countries only started to become more equal from 2000. Nonetheless, many low-income countries have been left behind in this period, most notably several countries of Africa. The dominant trend is not the exclusive trend.

## Global Distribution Among People

To obtain a truly global estimate of the distribution of income, it is necessary to compare the incomes of people (or families or households) in the world. Availability of data (as well as other data problems) makes such an estimate rough, but useful nonetheless. Branko Milanovic, perhaps the leading expert on these issues, has shown that, from the mid-1980s to 2011, global inequality remained roughly constant, with a slight decline toward the end of this period—likely explained by the greater slowdown of high-income countries compared to low-income countries in the Great Recession. The relative stability of income distribution would seem to result from a rough balance between the reduction of inequality among countries (Figure 3) and the rise of inequality within countries (Figure 1 and the most populous countries of Figure 2).

Milanovic's estimate uses the Gini coefficient, a standard measure of income inequality. The Gini takes account of incomes of the whole population, unlike the measure used in Figures 1 and 2, which focuses on extremes. The Gini can vary from 0 (everyone has the same income) to 1 (all the income goes to one person). For income distribution in almost all countries, the Gini ranges from about 0.27 (Norway) to about 0.65 (South Africa).

For the global population, over the period of Milanovic's estimates, the Gini varies around 0.70—a higher figure, showing a more unequal distribution, than for any single country. However, if inequality were measured by a comparison of extremes, it is likely that inequality would be rising. There remains a large share of the world's population that continues to live in extreme poverty, while incomes at the very top have sky-rocketed in recent years. But whether the measure is the Gini or a comparison of extremes, the distribution among people in the world is very unequal.

## What Matters?

Each of these measures of income inequality "in the world" matters in one way or another. For example, to understand political conflicts within countries, the changes in the distribution within countries is probably most important. To understand how the changing structures of the global economy have affected people's lives in various parts of the world, it is useful to consider all of these measures. And to understand the dynamics of international politics, the measures that focus on inequalities among countries are probably paramount.

The measurements show both some positive and negative changes in the world. On the one hand, the rapid growth of several low-income and middle-income countries has, in spite of the high (and sometimes rising) level of inequality in these countries, pulled many people out of abject poverty. On the other hand, we know that rising inequality within a country tends to undermine social cohesion and generate stress at virtually all levels of society—with damaging effects on health, education, the natural environment, and crime. Even in this era of increased globalization, it is in the national context that inequality has the primary impact on people's behavior and how they judge their well-being.

And no matter how we look at the situation, the world has long been and remains a very unequal place. ❑

**Sources:** Branko Milanovic, *Worlds Apart: Measuring International and Global Inequality*, Princeton University Press, 2005; Branko Milanovic, *Global Income Inequality by the Numbers: in History and Now—An Overview*, The World Bank, Development Research Group, Poverty and Inequality Team, November 2012; Christoph Lakner and Branko Milanovic, *Global Income Distribution: From the Fall of the Berlin Wall to the Great Recession*, The World Bank, Development Research Group, Poverty and Inequality Team, December 2013, WPS6719; Richard Wilkinson and Kate Pickett, *The Spirit Level: Why Greater Equality Makes Societies Stronger*, Bloomsbury Press, 2009.

*Article 5.6*

# WEALTH INEQUALITY AND WEALTH TAXATION
*A Primer on Piketty*

## BY STEVEN PRESSMAN
*May 2014*

Great works in economics address important issues head-on, adopt a broad per-spective, and change our views regarding how economies work. Make no mis-take about it: Thomas Piketty's *Capital in the Twenty-First Century* is a great work. As an added bonus, it is extremely well written (and translated).

Given decades of rising inequality and its negative consequences and public concern about a disappearing middle class, this book is particularly timely. It re-lies on a wide array of data, collected by the author, showing long-term trends in income and wealth distribution. It explains the causes of these trends and finishes by setting forth some bold policy solutions.

Still, the most important aspect of *Capital in the Twenty-First Century* is that it changes how we view the world. The following parallel might provide some his-torical perspective on the book, and help understand its importance and the emo-tional reaction it has elicited.

Thomas Robert Malthus became one of the most controversial figures in economics following the publication of his *Essay on Population* in 1798. De-spite much optimism at the time that ordinary people's lives could be improved, for Malthus poverty was inevitable due to the relationship between population growth and the growth of the food supply. His *Essay* argued (based on some em-pirical data) that population growth would outstrip food supply growth, result-ing in famine and misery.

Piketty can best be understood as a sort of modern-day Malthus. Both doubt-ing Thomases sought to refute popular beliefs that life could easily be improved for most people, both used simple growth rates to do this, and both were criticized for their pessimistic conclusions.

Optimism regarding the future distribution of income stems from the work of Nobel laureate Simon Kuznets. In the 1950s, Kuznets examined U.S. income-tax data and saw income inequality improving over several decades. According to the standard interpretation of his work, he hypothesized that as capitalist econo-mies develop, inequality first increases and then decreases. This message fit Amer-ica's economic experience during the post-war years and its geo-political needs during the Cold War. Most economists came to accept this message of hope.

But times have changed. Inequality is rising in the United States and other high-income capitalist countries. Piketty explains why economists got it wrong. He argues that greater equality between World War I and the 1960s was not part of some positive long-term trend; rather, it stemmed from a unique set of factors—two wars (that destroyed much wealth), the very high marginal tax rates imple-mented to pay for these wars, plus a stock-market crash and Great Depression. Starting in the 1970s or 1980s (dates differ by country) the moneyed class revolted and began to influence policy. Top income-tax rates fell; income and wealth inequality rose rapidly. As a result, we seem headed toward another Gilded Age, similar to the late 19th century, where the fabulously wealthy live charmed lives and everyone else struggles to survive.

Piketty, like Malthus, draws his dismal conclusion from the relationship between two growth rates. In Piketty's case, they are the rate of return to wealth or capital (r) and the growth rate of the economy (g). When r exceeds g, more money flows to those at the top and inequality increases; when r is less than g, more benefits of economic growth flow to workers, making income and wealth distribution more equal.

One great virtue of Piketty's book is that it explains why income inequality has grown of late. First, the ratio of wealth to GDP declined in Europe from 6:1 or 7:1 around World War I to 2:1 in the 1960s. It has since rebounded to nearly 6:1. The United States experienced a smaller decline, since its factories were not destroyed by the two wars, but has also experienced a growing wealth-to-GDP ratio of late. Second, r has averaged around 5% over long periods of time in many different countries, while g cannot be expected to grow by much more than 1%.

Together these results create a distribution problem, which may be easiest to comprehend in personal terms.

Suppose you receive a $200,000 inheritance (your wealth) and you make $100,000 a year. If your wealth grows at 5% per year and your wages grow by 1%, after 35 years (a typical working life) your wages would be around $140,000 and your wealth (assuming no spending down of this wealth) over $1 million. After several generations, around 100 years, your great grandchild would have labor income of $268,000 and have $25 million in capital assets. With a 5% return, their capital income ($1.25 million) would dwarf their labor income. If some income from wealth gets consumed, which is likely, this process just takes a little longer to work out. At some point income from wealth will far exceed income from labor.

The problem is that we don't all begin with equal amounts of capital. Some start with large inheritances; most people begin with nothing. As a result, the incomes of the haves grow much more rapidly than those of the have-nots—and wealth inequality soars.

Piketty's story is far superior to standard economic explanations of rising inequality, such as technological change and globalization. He rightly rejects these theories because they cannot explain national differences in rising inequality—technological change and globalization should have similar impacts on all developed nations.

Compiling the data to make this case has been a heroic endeavor. Piketty uses income tax returns to get data on the share of national income going to the top 10%, the top 1%, and the top 0.1% of households. Estate tax returns enable him to estimate wealth inequality. Substantial evidence supports Piketty's conclusion that income and wealth inequality have risen in the United States and elsewhere since the late 20th century.

Similar to Malthus's *Essay*, Piketty's *Capital* contains virtually no economic theory. It does not address what determines economic growth or the return to wealth. Its dismal conclusion stems from historic trends and Piketty's explanation of why high rates of return to wealth increase inequality.

## So Where Do We Go From Here?

The last part of Piketty's book discusses how to deal with rising inequality. Piketty is skeptical that institutional policies such as raising the minimum wage, or more generous government spending programs, will help much. It is not that he opposes such efforts. Rather, he thinks they are inadequate when wealth is so unevenly distributed and grows so rapidly. Government spending programs can help, but they cannot increase labor income by 5% annually over the long run.

Tax policy is all that is left (no pun intended). Piketty favors a more progressive individual income tax, with a 70% top rate. Corporations, he argues, also need to be taxed based on where they pay wages so they cannot book profits to subsidiaries in low-tax countries.

These policies would reduce income inequality and slow down, but not reverse, the more pressing issue of greater wealth inequality. To deal with this latter problem, Piketty advocates an annual wealth tax, imposed at very low rates—one or two percent on wealth in excess of 1 million euros (around $1.1 million at mid-2015 exchange rates). And it must be a global tax, so that it cannot be escaped by moving wealth abroad.

Those on the right object to the tax rates that Piketty proposes as excessively high. The worst of these objections engage in name-calling, deeming anyone a socialist who proposes higher taxes for whatever reason. Almost as bad have been the objections that higher taxes would give the government more money to waste—as if businesses never, ever wasted money and consumers always spent their money cautiously and rationally (e.g., they would never buy homes or be able to obtain mortgages that they couldn't possibly afford to repay). The more thoughtful and reasonable objections from the right have focused on the bad incentives to work hard, earn money, accumulate wealth, and provide for one's children and grandchildren as a result of higher taxes.

Those on the left and toward the center of the political spectrum have been fairly consistent in maintaining that the main policy proposal of Piketty was impractical because a global wealth tax would never get enacted. After making this point, the next sentence of these critiques typically push other policies (invariably the personal favorites of those criticizing Piketty), which are just as unlikely to get enacted given the current political situation in the United States and elsewhere.

I find all these criticisms both disturbing and a little bit off the mark. But before looking at Piketty's wealth tax proposals in greater detail, it is worth examining what he has to say regarding monetary policy and fiscal policy, something which was not discussed in most of the prominent reviews of his book. Piketty downplays monetary policy in favor of fiscal policy. Monetary policy, he contends, cannot deal with the problem of rising inequality. In fact, he contends that we cannot know the impact of monetary policy on income and wealth distribution, although there is no argument for this. My gut instinct is that this is true, but I would have liked to see some data that supports this contention—say, looking at how income and wealth distribution vary based on interest rates. Such a study would make for a great thesis or doctoral dissertation, to say nothing about a nice professional paper.

Regarding fiscal policy, Piketty is fairly critical of government deficits. He spends a good deal of time focusing on the need to tax wealth so that we can repay existing government debt, but he fails to address the issue of whether government deficits and debt may be necessary at times. He also doesn't address the issue of whether government debt does any actual harm to overall macroeconomic performance. Rather, the focus is mainly (Surprise! Surprise! Surprise!) on the impact of debt on income distribution. Piketty's main point is that the large majority of government bonds created when the government goes into debt is owned by the very wealthy. They benefit greatly from government debt. With little risk, they receive positive returns on their money. This income generates part of their 5% rate of return on wealth or capital.

Unfortunately, the passages on fiscal policy and distribution are too brief. There are two key reasons I wish Piketty had written a good deal more on the relationship between fiscal policy and inequality. First, he argues throughout *Capital* that one main reason inequality declined from World War I through the 1950s was that there were high marginal tax rates on top incomes. This reduced the after-tax gains from owning wealth. Second, fiscal policy is central to Piketty's major policy proposals.

Writing more on fiscal policy and distribution would not have been all that difficult to do. Moreover, his entire case for changes in tax policy would have been considerably stronger had Piketty spent more time on this topic and then related it to the beginnings of the revolt of the rentiers in the United Kingdom and the United States, when Margaret Thatcher and Ronald Reagan were elected heads of government.

The story in both cases is rather similar and involved several policy changes. There was a sharp cut in government spending (that hurt the poor and middle class more than wealthy households, which can provide their own benefits) and a sharp cut in taxes focused at the top of the income distribution. Overall, the cuts in government expenditures were less than the tax cuts, and the government had to borrow money by selling bonds. Abstracting a little from the overall process, the Reagan and Thatcher governments gave large tax breaks to the wealthy, and then borrowed the money back from them to pay for the tax cuts. Everyone else got small tax cuts that were funded by cutting the government benefits they received. Or in slightly bolder and simpler terms, the Reagan and Thatcher governments decided to fund a good deal of government spending by borrowing money from the wealthy rather than taxing the wealthy.

As Piketty's data demonstrate, these changes led to sharply rising inequality in the UK and United States over the past several decades. And it is no wonder why this occurred. Those earning high incomes got to keep a lot more of their income. Yet they had to do something with all this additional money. It could not be kept under the mattress, earning nothing. Bank deposits were insured, but not for balances of the sort that the very wealthy possessed. The result could only be that all this additional disposable income fueled rising asset prices, which also primarily benefited the wealthy.

According to the gospel of "supply-side" economics, which was used to justify these policy changes, the whole process should have resulted in much greater economic growth and enormous tax collections by the government so that there would be no deficit. However, this claim ignored the "balanced budget multiplier" described by the great 20th century U.S. economist Paul Samuelson. Samuelson showed that an equal cut in taxes and in government spending would slow economic growth or reduce GDP by an amount equal to the tax cut (or cut in government spending). The reason for this is very simple. A dollar less in government spending is a dollar less in spending while a dollar tax cut is not an additional dollar in spending since some of the added disposable income will be saved. Overall, this will reduce spending and economic growth. Yet ideology triumphed over economic knowledge. So, the U.S. and UK governments gave huge tax cuts to the wealthy, and then borrowed the money back from them in order to fund the tax cuts. Economic growth slowed as the balanced budget multiplier predicted it would. This made distributional matters even worse because it increased the gap between r and g—by lowering g.

One last thing is worth additional comment before getting to the issue of income and wealth taxes, especially since this has been one of the most frequent criticisms of Piketty. Many commentators complained that Piketty ignored alternative policies such as supporting unions and raising the minimum wage—but Piketty actually does discuss these policies. Chapter 9 of the book includes an extensive discussion of the minimum wage. The data Piketty presents and the written text both make it very clear that the distribution of wages has remained relatively equal in France because the French have continually increased the minimum wage and the French minimum wage is rather high compared to average wages. Piketty even discusses why this happened—French President Charles de Gaulle (in office 1958-1969) was worried about the crisis of May 1968 and used higher minimum wages to deal with a problem that was more cultural and social than economic. Moreover, Piketty clearly supports raising the minimum wage and even provides several justifications for doing so. So it is puzzling that so many people would criticize Piketty for not supporting higher minimum wages.

The real problem Piketty has with raising the minimum wage is not that it won't help equalize wage income, but that it won't deal with the problem of rising capital income in the long run. He is also skeptical that the minimum wage can be increased enough (5% per year in real terms) over the long haul without generating substantial unemployment. To try to make Piketty's point as simple and clear as possible, even if wages (and we can add rising union power here) were made completely equal across the board, inequality would be high and would continue to increase because of the immense wealth that is possessed by a few people.

It is wealth inequality for Piketty that is the main force driving the rise in inequality to under capitalism. A higher minimum wage can slow the process down. So can stronger unions. So, too, can government spending policies that equalize after-tax incomes, such as paid parental leave, child allowances, generous unemployment insurance programs, and a large and sturdy social safety net. These are all policies that Piketty, I imagine, would support. But the key insight of *Capital* is this: the driving force of inequality is that we start with great wealth inequality and the high returns to wealth make things worse over time. Policies that equalize income distribution will help a little, but they ignore the main problem.

Piketty argues, first, for a progressive income tax because this (along with inheritance taxes) is the only progressive form of taxation that governments have. Sales taxes or indirect taxes are regressive in nature and social-insurance taxes (for retirement and for unemployment) tend to be proportional or regressive. Again, Piketty does not make either a strong or forceful case for this policy. I wish he had put a little more emphasis on the fact that high marginal tax rates during the World War II years and in the decade or so after contributed to falling inequality in this era. Historically, he contends that high marginal income tax rates have led to lower (before-tax) inequality. It is in the data; it should have been stressed more in the policy section of the book.

Piketty also worries about current trends in individual income taxation. In particular, by exempting capital income from the income tax (or taxing it at lower rates) the income tax becomes regressive at the very top (because that is where they get most of their income) and tends to make the entire tax system regressive in developed countries. But, again, the big issue for Piketty is that progressive income taxes cannot solve the wealth inequality problem. Like progressive spending programs, a progressive income tax would help reduce income inequality, but it does not solve the problem that wealth inequality tends to rise because of the high returns to wealth—much of it, such as stocks and homes that are not sold, are not taxed at all.

In a couple of pages that were pretty much ignored in the reviews of *Capital*, Piketty calls for reforming corporate taxation. He proposes that corporate income taxes be assessed based on wages paid in different countries rather than on where in the world the multi-national firm declares its profits to come from (typically the country that has the lowest corporate income tax rate). This is not headline grabbing, and tax reform is never as exciting as proposing a new type of tax (this is why there are so many articles on the flat tax and the Tobin Tax and why reviews of *Capital* focused on the global wealth tax), but it is something that needs to receive serious consideration and should be pushed more.

Again, the fact that Piketty does not focus a lot of attention on this proposal probably stems from the fact that (like higher marginal income tax rates) it will affect income distribution but not wealth distribution. When corporations pay higher taxes to governments there is less profit to distribute to the owners as dividends. This will reduce current incomes. However, higher corporate income taxes also reduce future profits after-taxes, which should affect the value of corporate stock. This will lower the price of shares of stock. Since it is mainly the very wealthy who own large amounts of stock, and whose wealth portfolios contain a higher percentage of stock compared to middle-income households, this policy should have significant and substantial effect on wealth inequality.

## Piketty and the Global Tax on Wealth

At last, we come to Piketty's main policy conclusion, his claim that the way to keep more and more income from going to those at the very top of the distribution is a global wealth tax. The tax needs to be global in order to keep wealth from moving to tax havens where it is not subject to the tax. Piketty also wants to keep the tax rate low (1-2%) in order to mitigate negative disincentives. His particular plan is that net assets worth between 1 million euros ($1.1 million) and 5 million euros ($5.5 million) be taxed at 1% and net assets worth more than 5 million euros be taxed at 2%. The goal in all this, Piketty makes clear, is not to raise money for social programs but to tame the inequality that inevitably results under capitalism.

Piketty provides several different arguments for his progressive and global wealth tax.

First, he resorts to an appeal to authority. He invokes the 1918 American Economic Association Presidential address by Irving Fisher, in which Fisher worried about the fact that only 2% of the U.S. population owned more than 50% of the nation's wealth while two-thirds of the population had no net wealth. Fisher then went on to suggest a steeply progressive wealth tax to remedy this situation.

Second, Piketty argues that the rewards going to the very top are not justified by traditional economic arguments (that they depend on the marginal productivity of the worker). Instead, Piketty makes the case that CEO pay is due to luck to a large degree and that a bargaining model fits the data better than marginal productivity theory. He argues that when the government takes a very large chunk of any extra income, it is not worth it for a CEO to bargain with a compensation committee or shareholders to get higher pay. And he points to empirical evidence that high marginal tax rates keep down CEO pay while not hurting the economic performance of the firm.

Finally there is the main argument—that a global wealth tax is the only way to limit the growth of wealth accumulation and a return to 19th-century levels of inequality. Or, this is the only way we can avoid the negative economic, social, and political consequences of great inequality. A tax on income will not achieve this end because much income is tied up in stocks and bonds and real estate that generally do not get taxed. The gains from these investments are taxed when assets are sold. This allows the gains to accumulate at the top and to keep doing so. Only a wealth tax can stop this process.

Of this I am rather skeptical. There are well-known problems with wealth taxation, including how to value assets that aren't regularly traded and liquidity issues for those with little cash assets. In addition, cash (and many other assets) are relatively easy to hide from tax authorities. I also worry about the consequences of letting every government in the world have access to everyone's wealth tax returns, which would be required with a global wealth tax. Last, but not least, past historical attempts to tax wealth (such as the infamous UK window tax) were universally detested, led to undesirable consequences (people bricked up their windows), and were soon abolished.

On the other hand, I find Piketty's other solutions are more promising—a strengthened corporate income tax, a more progressive individual income tax, and greater use of estate and inheritance taxes. We have substantial knowledge and experience with these forms of taxation. The high tax rates on corporate and individual incomes during most of the 20th century kept inequality from rising. And as argued above, higher income taxes on the returns to wealth will reduce wealth and wealth inequality. Moreover, substantial estate and inheritance taxes can break up large wealth holdings. One of the most important achievements of *Capital* is its demonstration that wealth inequality and income inequality are closely related. By controlling either one, we will be able to control the other one. ❏

Chapter 6

# FISCAL POLICY, DEFICITS, AND AUSTERITY

## INTRODUCTION

Most textbooks, at least to the extent that they are influenced by Keynesian economics, depict a macroeconomy stabilized by government intervention. They look at ways the government can use fiscal policy—government spending and taxation—to bolster a flagging economy. Today's economy, yet to recover fully from the worst economic crisis since the Great Depression, is still flagging. Worse yet, this lingering crisis comes on the heels of a feeble economic expansion that created fewer jobs and did less to raise wages than any other economic expansion since World War II.

What is the role of fiscal policy in this context? As the crisis worsened in the fall of 2008, the federal government dramatically increased spending. First, Congress passed the Troubled Asset Relief Program (TARP), which bailed out giant investment banks and insurance companies. It then passed the Obama stimulus package and budget, which provided some much-needed domestic spending but also boosted military spending. At the same time, the Federal Reserve ("the Fed") and the Federal Deposit Insurance Corporation (FDIC) issued loans, lines of credit, and loan guarantees, and pledged an emergency fund to clean up losses on Wall Street. All told, the federal government, the Fed, and FDIC sank nearly the value of a year's total U.S. national output into propping up the failed financial sector and rescuing the economy. That was enough to prevent a repeat of the Great Depression, but not enough to ignite the rapid economic growth necessary to put those who lost their jobs back to work.

While the increased spending played a role, it was mainly the collapse of the economy and the Bush administration's tax cuts and war spending that pushed the federal budget far into the red. The surge in government deficits and debt somehow became the focus of macroeconomic policy debates in the United States, despite the persistence of historically high unemployment. The articles in this chapter contest the orthodox view that short-term deficit-reduction should be the focus of macroeconomic policy, arguing that fiscal stimulus is necessary to tackle the still-raging unemployment crisis.

In Article 6.1, economist Marty Wolfson debunks the widespread myth, parroted by mainstream politicians and media commentators, that government spending cannot create jobs. He sees this as part of a conservative ideological campaign to prevent government from doing just that. Government spending, he argues, need

165

not be wasteful, and in fact is not necessarily less valuable than private spending. The government, he concludes, can and should be creating jobs.

Alejandro Reuss (Article 6.2) takes a close look at what Keynes actually had to say about the efficacy of fiscal policy in his most famous book, *The General Theory of Employment, Interest, and Money*. Keynes was a strong advocate of fiscal policy, especially government spending, as a response to business-cycle downturns. Reuss explains how Keynes challenged the "Treasury view" that government spending could not get the economy going because it would "crowd out" private investment, the same argument conservatives have invoked against fiscal stimulus policies today.

Gerald Friedman shows that cutting taxes on the very rich, as the U.S. government has been doing for decades, has not led to the investment or economic growth that conservative economists promised (Article 6.3).

Economist Marty Wolfson (Article 6.4) clarifies the link between Social Security benefit payments and the gross federal debt. Of the $17 trillion in federal debt, $2.7 trillion are in the form of treasury bonds held by the Social Security Trust Fund. That slice of the federal debt is not a result of overly generous benefits that we cannot afford. Rather, an entire generation of workers paid more into Social Security than they have withdrawn in benefits, and the surplus has been invested in federal government bonds.

Finally, economist Harry Konstantinidis analyzes the depths of the economic crisis in Greece (Article 6.5)—especially the successive rounds of painful austerity imposed by the country's creditors—and the reasons that the anti-austerity Syriza government never genuinely contemplated an exit from the euro. Konstantinidis does not only diagnose Greece's current problems, but also outlines a program for the "productive reconstruction" of the Greek economy along principles of worker self-management and participatory budgeting.

## Discussion Questions

1. (Article 6.1) What are the main arguments made by opponents of government "stimulus" spending? How does Wolfson refute each of these points?

2. (Article 6.2) Why did Keynes think that the dollar-for-dollar crowding-out argument (the "Treasury view") was mistaken? And how might Keynes respond to the arguments conservatives leveled against fiscal stimulus policies during the Great Recession?

3. (Article 6.3) When it comes to promoting investment and economic growth, what is the track record of tax cuts for high-income individuals? If Friedman is right, and these policies had done little to promote investment and growth, why do advocates of such tax cuts persist in arguing that they do?

4. (Article 6.4) Why is the $17 trillion figure for gross federal debt a misleading measure of our future obligations? Wolfson argues that reducing Social Security benefits would actually *increase* the federal debt. How could this be so?

5. (Article 6.5) Many observers of the eurozone crisis have argued that the common currency put member countries into a fiscal straitjacket. When they got into debt, they had no alternative but painful "austerity" policies. Why, then, did the anti-austerity government of Greece not call for an exit from the euro?

*Article 6.1*

# THE IDEOLOGICAL ATTACK ON JOB CREATION
*Responding to Anti-Government Arguments*

**BY MARTY WOLFSON**
*May/June 2012*

> "Government doesn't create jobs. It's the private sector that creates jobs."
> —presidential candidate Mitt Romney, speaking at Wofford College,
> Spartenburg, S.C., January 18, 2012

I t is jarring to hear pundits say that the government can't create jobs. It is even more jarring to hear the same refrain from someone whose job was created by the government! Perhaps Mr. Romney has forgotten, or would like to forget, that he used to have a government job as governor of Massachusetts.

But surely those currently on the government payroll have not forgotten, like the chairman of the House Republican Policy Committee, Rep. Tom Price (R-Ga.). He used the same talking points, "The government doesn't create jobs. It's the private sector that creates jobs," speaking on MSNBC's "Andrea Mitchell Reports" last June.

Rep. Price apparently thinks he doesn't have a real job, but what about teachers, firefighters, police officers, and school cafeteria workers? And what about the 2 to 4.8 million jobs—in both the public and private sectors—the U.S. Congressional Budget Office estimated were created by the 2009 U.S. economic stimulus package?

The "government doesn't create jobs" mantra is part of a coordinated right-wing campaign to *prevent* the government from creating jobs and promoting the interests of working families, and to instead encourage a shift in the distribution of income towards the wealthy. It is supported by ideologically motivated arguments and theories from conservative economists and anti-government think tanks. In what follows, these arguments are addressed and criticized, in the hopes of clearing away some of the confusion undermining a vigorous government program to put people back to work.

## The Argument That Government Spending Can't Increase Jobs

A Senior Fellow at the Cato Institute says the idea that government spending can create jobs "has a rather glaring logical fallacy. It overlooks the fact that, in the real world, government can't inject money into the economy without first taking money out of the economy." This argument is wrong for several reasons.

First, the government *can* inject money into the economy. It does so whenever it finances its spending by selling bonds to the Federal Reserve. In this case, money is created by the Federal Reserve when it buys the bonds. It creates a reserve account on its books; money is thus created without any reduction in money elsewhere in the economy.

Alternatively, the government can finance its spending by taxes or by selling bonds to the public. This is the case envisioned by the Cato analysis. The argument is that the money spent by the government is exactly balanced by a reduction in money in the pockets of taxpayers of bond buyers. However, if the taxpayers' or the bond buyers' money would otherwise have been saved and not spent, then there is a net injection into the economy of funds that can put people to work.

The argument made by the Cato Institute is actually a variation of another theory, known as "crowding out." In this theory, government spending creates competition for real resources that "crowds out," or displaces, private investment; private companies are unable to obtain the workers and capital they need for investment, so that any jobs due to government spending are offset by a decrease of jobs in the private sector.

This theory is valid only when there is full employment because there would be no idle resources, labor or capital, to put to use. In that case, though, neither the government nor the private sector would be able to create net new jobs. In contrast, in a situation of unemployment, it is precisely because the government can access otherwise idle resources that it can create jobs.

And, of course, that is exactly the situation we are in. As of March, the official unemployment rate stood at 8.2 %. Adjusted for underemployment, e.g., by counting those discouraged workers who have dropped out of the labor force and those workers who are working part-time but would like to work full-time, the more accurate unemployment rate was 14.5%.

## The Argument That Cutting Government Spending Creates Jobs

Consistent with anti-government ideology, conservative economics asserts not only that government spending can't create jobs, but also that cutting government spending creates jobs. Here's how the argument goes: less government spending will reduce the government deficit; smaller deficits will increase the confidence of businesses that will invest more and in that way create more jobs. According to John B. Taylor, an economist affiliated with Stanford's conservative Hoover Institution, "Basic economic models in which incentives and expectations of future policy matter show that a credible plan to reduce gradually the deficit will increase economic growth and reduce unemployment by removing uncertainty and lowering the chances of large tax increases in the future." (Interestingly, an analysis by economist Robert Pollin of the Political Economy Research Institute at the University of Massachusetts-Amherst finds that Taylor's empirical model concludes that the stimulus bill was ineffective—but only because it included too much in tax cuts as opposed to direct government spending.)

This assertion is based more on wishful thinking than empirical validity, and has been criticized by Paul Krugman as depending on belief in a "confidence fairy." But it is not just liberal economists like Krugman who are critical of this theory. A confidential report prepared for clients by the investment bank Goldman Sachs concluded that a $61 billion cut in government spending from a bill passed by the House of Representatives in February 2011 (but not enacted into law) would lead to a decline in economic growth of 2%. And economist Mark Zandi, formerly an advisor to Republican presidential candidate John McCain, concluded that this $61 billion reduction in government spending could result in the loss of 700,000 jobs by 2012.

Ben Bernanke, chairman of the Board of Governors of the Federal Reserve System, stated that "the cost to the recovery [of steep reductions in government outlays now] would outweigh the benefits in terms of fiscal discipline." Even the International Monetary Fund, in its semiannual report on the world economic outlook, concluded that "the idea that fiscal austerity triggers faster growth in the short term finds little support in the data."

Also, in a review of studies and historical experience about the relationship between budget-cutting and economic growth, economists Arjun Jayadev and Mike Konczal concluded that countries historically did not cut government spending and deficits in a slump and that there is no basis to conclude that doing so now, "under the conditions the United States currently faces, would improve the country's prospects."

## The Argument That Private Spending Is Always Better than Public Spending

Another way that right-wing economics tries to discredit the idea that the government can create jobs is to assert that private spending is always to be preferred to public spending. There are several rationalizations for this view.

One is that private spending is more efficient than public spending. This ideological refrain has been repeated consistently, and gained a following, over the past thirty years. But repetition does not make it correct. Of course, the proponents of this argument can point to examples of government mismanagement, such as that following Hurricane Katrina. However, government bungling and inefficiency by an administration that did not believe in government does not prove the point. A much more grievous example of inefficiency and misallocation of resources is the housing speculation and financial manipulation—and eventual collapse that brought us to the current recession—due to a deregulated private financial system. Yet for free-market ideologues, this somehow does not discredit the private sector.

Some people think that economists have "proven" that "free" markets are efficient. The only thing that has been proven, however, is that you can arrive at any conclusion if your assumptions are extreme enough. And the assumptions that form the basis for the free-market theory are indeed extreme, if not totally unrealistic and impossible. For example: orthodox free-market economics assumes perfectly competitive markets; perfect information; no situations, like pollution, in which private decision-makers do not take account of the societal effects of their actions; even full employment. But none of these assumptions hold true in the real world. Also, the distribution of income is irrelevant to the conclusions of this theory. The distribution of income is simply taken as given, so that the results of the theory are consistent with a relatively equal distribution of income as well as a very unequal distribution. As economist Joseph Stiglitz has said, "Today, there is no respectable intellectual support for the proposition that markets, by themselves, lead to efficient, let alone equitable outcomes."

A second reason for supposing that private spending is to be preferred to public spending is the notion that public spending is less worthwhile than private spending. This means, for many people, reducing government spending as much as possible. For example, Grover Norquist, founder and president of Americans for Tax Reform and author of the anti-tax pledge signed by many members of Congress, said that he wanted to "shrink [the government] down to the size where we can drown it in the bathtub." The anti-tax, anti-spending crusade has in many cases been successful in reducing government budgets, on the national as well as the local level. This has resulted in a significant decrease in government services. Although some people are attracted to the view that government spending should always be reduced, they probably at the same time don't want to drive on roads and bridges that aren't repaired and they probably want fire trucks to arrive if their house is on fire. Perhaps, too, they wouldn't automatically prefer twelve kinds of toothpaste to schools, parks, and libraries.

## The Argument That Government Spending Is Wasteful

Another argument contends that public spending is wasteful. Discussions of government accounts generally do not take account of public investment, so all public spending is essentially treated as consumption. As such, it is considered unproductive and wasteful by those who wish to disparage government spending. In other words, the government budget does not make a distinction between long-term investments and other spending as corporate budgets do.

One implication of treating all government spending as consumption is the notion that the federal government should maintain a balanced budget. To put this in accounting terms, on this view government accounts are considered to only have an income statement (which shows current revenues and current expenditures), not a balance sheet (which shows assets and liabilities).

Corporations, in contrast, maintain balance sheets. They don't balance their budgets in the way that the budget hawks want the government to do. Private investment in plant and equipment, for example, is accounted for on the asset side of the balance sheet; borrowing to finance this investment is accounted for on the liability side. Interest on the debt is accounted for on the income statement, and it is only the interest, not the outstanding debt balance, that has to be covered by current revenues. The assumption behind this accounting is that borrowing to finance productive investment will generate the revenue to pay off the borrowing.

In other words, corporations borrow on a regular basis to finance investment. So they only attempt to balance their current expenditures and revenues and not their capital budget.

Much confusion about private and public spending, and also about budget deficits, could be avoided if discussion focused on a federal government balance sheet. In that way, current spending that needs to be balanced with current revenue could be separated from long-term investments that will increase the productivity of the American economy. Such investments, in areas like infrastructure and education, can increase future economic growth and income, and thus generate more tax revenue to pay off the debt. Just like a private company's investments, they are legitimately financed by borrowing.

## Government Can Indeed Create Jobs

The main point, though, is this: whether financed by borrowing or taxes, whether consumption or investment, government spending that increases the demand for goods and services in the economy is not wasteful. It has the ability to employ underutilized resources and create jobs.

Ultimately, a job is a job, whether created by the private or public sector. A job has the potential to enable workers to support themselves and their families in dignity. We should not let ideological arguments keep us from using every available means to promote the basic human right of employment. ❏

**Sources:** Congressional Budget Office, "Estimated Impact of the American Recovery and Reinvestment Act on Employment and Economic Output From April 2010 Through June 2010," August 2010; Daniel J. Mitchell, "The Fallacy That Government Creates Jobs," The Cato Institute, 2008; John B. Taylor, "Goldman Sachs Wrong About Impact of House Budget Proposal," Economics One blog, February 28, 2011; Paul Krugman, "Myths of austerity," *The New York Times*. July 1, 2010; Jonathan Karl, "Goldman Sachs: House Spending Cuts Will Hurt Economic Growth," The Note, 2011; Mark Zandi, "A federal shutdown could derail the recovery," Moody's Analytics, February 28, 2011; Pedro da Costa and Mark Felsenthal, "Bernanke warns against steep budget cuts," Reuters, February 9, 2011; International Monetary Fund, *World Economic Outlook: Recovery, Risk, and Rebalancing*, 2010; Arjun Jayadev and Mike Konczal, "When Is Austerity Right? In Boom, Not Bust," *Challenge*, November-December 2010, pp. 37-53; Joseph Stiglitz, Foreword, in Karl Polanyi, *The Great Transformation: The Political and Economic Origins of Our Times*, 2001; David Aschauer, "Is Public Expenditure Productive?" *Journal of Monetary Economics*, 1989, pp. 177-200; Robert Pollin, "US government deficits and debt amid the great recession: what the evidence shows, *Cambridge Journal of Economics*, 2012, 36, 161-187; Kelsey Merrick and Jim Horney, "Chairman Ryan Gets 62 Percent of His Huge Budget Cuts from Programs for Lower-income Americans," Center on Budget and Policy Priorities, March 23, 2012; Paul Ryan, The Path to Prosperity, March 20, 2012; Ethan Pollack, "Ryan's Budget Would Cost Jobs," The Economic Policy Institute, March 21, 2012.

Article 6.2

# FISCAL POLICY AND "CROWDING OUT"

## BY ALEJANDRO REUSS

*May/June 2009*

In response to the deepest recession in the United States since the Great Depression, the Obama administration proposed a large fiscal "stimulus" plan. (Fiscal policies involve government spending and taxation. A fiscal stimulus involves increases in government spending or tax cuts, or both.) The current stimulus plan, after some compromises between the Obama administration and Republicans in Congress, included both substantial tax cuts and increases in government spending. Together, they would increase the federal government deficit by over $700 billion.

A fiscal stimulus is a standard "Keynesian" response to a recession. The logic behind these policies is that recessions can be caused by insufficient total demand for goods and services. If saving (a "leakage" from demand) exceeds investment (an "injection" of demand), there will not be enough demand to buy all the goods and services that the economy is capable of producing at the "full employment" level. Some goods will go unsold, and firms will reduce output. They will cut jobs, cancel supply orders, and even close production facilities. The economy will spiral into a recession.

In standard Keynesian models, either tax cuts or increased government spending can increase total demand, and therefore total output and employment. An initial increase in spending (by either the government or the recipients of the tax cuts) results in new income for other individuals, who then go on to spend part (not all) of this income, which results in new income for still other individuals, and so on. Ultimately, this series of additions to income results in a total increase in GDP greater than the original increase in government spending or reduction in taxes. The increase in real GDP divided by the initial spending increase is called the "multiplier." The standard Keynesian view implies a multiplier greater than one.

## The Conservative Critique

Conservative economists, whose intellectual heritage includes decades-old attempts to refute Keynesian theory, disagree with this view. They argue that government spending cannot possibly increase overall economic activity, and that the stimulus plan is therefore doomed to fail. This position is sometimes known as the "Treasury view" (because it mirrors the arguments of the British Treasury Department during the Great Depression) or the theory of "crowding out." The new government spending, these economists argue, "has to come from somewhere," either from higher taxes or increased government borrowing. Either way, the increase in government spending will come at the expense of private spending.

If the spending is financed by tax increases, conservative economists argue, this will reduce individuals' after-tax incomes and therefore reduce their spending. If it is financed through borrowing, the increased government demand for loans will drive up interest rates, and this will "crowd out" private investment. (Some private investment projects that would have been profitable at lower interest rates would not be profitable at the higher rates, and therefore would not be undertaken.) Extreme versions of this theory, known as "dollar-for-dollar" crowding out, argue that the decrease in private investment will exactly offset the increase in government spending, and there will be no change in the overall output of goods and services.

Government intervention is not only incapable of pulling the economy out of a recession, conservative economists argue, it is also unnecessary. If there is more saving than investment, the quantity of funds people are willing to loan out will exceed the quantity that people are willing to borrow at the current interest rate. The surplus of loanable funds will drive down the interest rate. People will save less (since the reward to saving is lower) and borrow more and invest more (since the cost of borrowing is lower), until the injection of investment and the leakage of saving are equal. In short, if insufficient demand ever caused a recession, the economy would quickly pull itself back to full employment without any need for government intervention.

## Keynes' Rejoinder

Keynes agreed with the idea that saving equals investment. In his view, however, this is true not only when the economy is producing at its full-employment capacity, but also when it is producing at far less than its capacity. Keynes argued that the "classical" economists (as he called the conservative orthodoxy of his time) had an incorrect view of the relationship between interest rates and savings, and that this was at the heart of their errors about the possibility of prolonged recessions.

The classicals believed that as interest rates increased, savings would increase, and that as interest rates declined, savings would decline. Keynes agreed that this was true at "a given income," but that a change in the interest rate would also affect the amount investment and therefore the level of income. A higher interest rate, he argued, was associated with lower investment, lower incomes, and therefore lower saving; a lower interest rate, with higher investment, higher incomes, and therefore higher saving. (As people's incomes increase, they spend more *and* save more; as their incomes decline, they spend less *and* save less.) In Keynes' view, saving will equal investment whether investment and saving are both high (at or near the full employment level of output) or if investment and saving are both low (in a low-output, high-unemployment economy). In the latter case, Keynes believed, there was no guarantee that the economy would pull itself back to full employment.

Keynes was also well aware, long before his critics, that government borrowing could crowd out some private investment. In *The General Theory* itself, he noted that the effects of the government directly increasing employment on public works may include "increasing the rate of interest and so retarding investment in other directions." This does not imply, however, dollar-for-dollar crowding out. Keynes still believed, and the empirical evidence confirms, that under depression conditions an increase in government spending can result in an increase in total output larger than the initial spending increase (a multiplier greater than one).

## Of Spending and Multipliers

In a January 2009 article in the *Wall Street Journal*, conservative economist Robert Barro declares, as a "plausible starting point," that the multiplier actually equals zero. That's what the dollar-for-dollar crowding-out theory means—an increase in government spending will be matched by equal decreases in private spending, and so will have zero effect on real GDP. When it comes to estimating the multiplier, based on historical data from 1943-1944, however, Barro finds that it is not zero, but 0.8.

First, contrary to Barro's intent, this is actually a disproof of dollar-for-dollar crowding out. It means that increased government spending brought about increased real GDP, though not by as much as the spending increase. It increased the production of public-sector goods by (much) more than it reduced the production of private-sector goods. Unless one views private-sector goods as intrinsically more valuable than public-sector goods, this is not an argument against government spending.

Second, Barro chose to base his study on two years at the height of the U.S. mobilization for World War II. When the economy is at or near full employment, the multiplier is bound to be small. If all resources are already being used, the only way to produce more of some kinds of goods (say, tanks and war planes) is to produce less of some others (say, civilian cars). Keynesian economists certainly understand this. Their point, however, is that government spending creates a large multiplier effect when the economy is languishing in a recession, not when it is already at full employment.

Economist Mark Zandi of Moody's Economy.com reports much higher multipliers for government spending. Zandi estimates multipliers between 1.3 and 1.6 for federal aid to states and for government infrastructure expenditures. The multipliers are even larger for government transfers (such as food stamps or unemployment compensation) to the hardest-hit, who are likely to spend all or almost all of their increase in income. Zandi estimates these multipliers at between 1.6 and 1.8. Tax cuts for high income individuals and corporations, who are less likely to spend their additional disposable income, have the lowest multipliers—between 0.3 and 0.4.

## Why the *General* Theory?

The conservative case against standard Keynesian fiscal stimulus policy rests on the assumption that all of the economy's resources are already being used to the fullest. Keynes titled his most important work *The General Theory* because he thought that the orthodox economics of his time confined itself to this special case, the case of an economy at full employment. He did not believe that this was generally the case in capitalist economies, and he sought to develop a theory that explained this.

The argument conservatives make against government spending—"it has to come from somewhere"—is actually no less true for private investment. If dollar-for-dollar crowding out were true, therefore, it would be just as impossible for private investment to pull the economy out of a recession. This, of course, would be nonsense unless the economy was already at full employment (and an increase in one kind of production would have to come at the expense of some other kind of production).

If the economy were already operating at full capacity—imagine a situation in which all workers are employed, factories are humming with activity 24/7, and no unused resources would be available to expand production if demand increased—the argument that increased government spending could not increase overall economic output might be plausible. But that is manifestly not the current economic situation.

Real GDP declined at an annual rate of 6.3% in the fourth quarter of 2008. The official unemployment rate surged to 8.5%, the highest rate in 30 years, in March 2009. Over 15% of workers are unemployed, have given up looking for work, or can only find part-time work. Employment is plummeting by more than half a million workers each month. A theory that assumes the economy is already at full employment can neither help us understand how we got into this hole—or how we can get out. ❏

**Sources**: John Maynard Keynes, *The General Theory of Employment, Interest, and Money*, 1964; Associated Press, "Obama: Stimulus lets Americans claim destiny," Feb. 17, 2009; Paul Krugman, "A Dark Age of macroeconomics (wonkish)," Jan. 27, 2009 (krugman.blogs.nytimes.com); J. Bradford DeLong, "More 'Treasury View' Blogging," Feb. 5, 2009 (delong.typepad.com); J. Bradford DeLong, "The Modern Revival of the 'Treasury View,'" Jan. 18, 2009 (delong.typepad.com); Robert J. Barro,"Government Spending is No Free Lunch," *Wall Street Journal*, Jan. 22, 2009 (wsj.com); Paul Krugman, "War and non-remembrance," Jan. 22, 2009 (krugman.blogs.nytimes.com); Paul Krugman, "Spending in wartime," Jan. 23, 2009 (krugman.blogs.nytimes.com); Mark Zandi, "The Economic Impact of a $750 Billion Fiscal Stimulus Package," Moody's Economy.com, March 26, 2009; Bureau of Labor Statistics, Alternative measures of labor underutilization; Bureau of Labor Statistics Payroll Employment.

*Article 6.3*

# THE GREAT TAX-CUT EXPERIMENT
*Has cutting tax rates for the rich helped the economy?*

## BY GERALD FRIEDMAN
*January/February 2013*

Since the late 1970s, during the Carter Administration, conservative economists have been warning that high taxes retard economic growth by discouraging productive work and investment. These arguments have resonated with politicians, who have steadily cut income taxes, especially those borne by the richest Americans. The highest marginal tax rate, which stood at 70% by the end of the 1970s, was cut to less than 30% in less than a decade. (The marginal rate for a person is the one applied to his or her last dollar of income. A marginal rate that applies to, say, the bracket above $250,000, then, is paid only on that portion of income. The portion of a person's income below that threshold is taxed at the lower rates applying to lower tax brackets.) Despite increases in the early 1990s, the top marginal rate remained below 40%, when it was cut further during the administration of George W. Bush. These dramatic cuts in tax rates, however, have not led to an acceleration in economic growth, investment, or productivity.

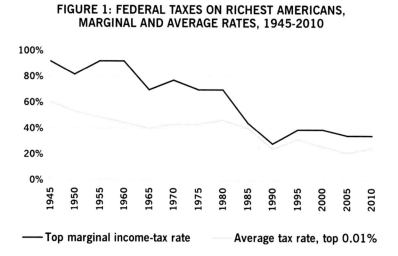

**FIGURE 1: FEDERAL TAXES ON RICHEST AMERICANS, MARGINAL AND AVERAGE RATES, 1945-2010**

The federal government has been cutting taxes on the richest Americans since the end of World War II. The average tax paid by the richest taxpayers, as a percentage of income, is typically less than the top marginal rate. Some of their income (the portion below the threshold for the top marginal rate, any capital-gains income, etc.) is taxed at lower rates. Some is not subject to federal income tax because of deductions for state and local taxes, health-care costs, and other expenses. The decline in the average tax rate for the richest, however, does follow the cuts in the top marginal income-tax rate.

## FIGURE 2: TAX REVENUE AS A PERCENTAGE OF GDP, 2008

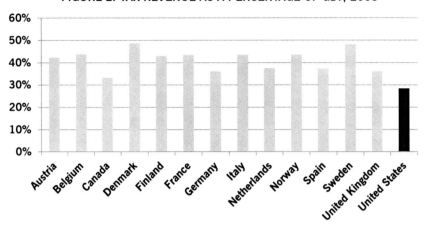

Americans pay a smaller proportion of total income in taxes than do people in any other advanced capitalist economy. As recently as the late 1960s, taxes accounted for as high a share of national income in the United States as in Western European countries. After decades of tax cuts, however, the United States now stands out for its low taxes and small government sector.

## FIGURE 3: AVERAGE TAX RATES ON RICHEST AND REAL GDP GROWTH, BY PRESIDENT, 1947-2010

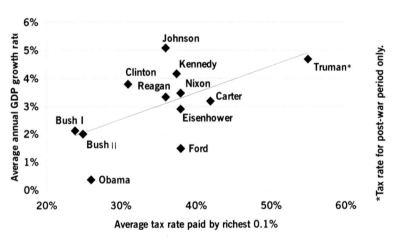

On average, the economy has grown faster during presidential administrations with higher tax rates on the richest Americans. Growth was unusually slow during George W. Bush's two terms (Bush II) and during Obama's first term, when the Bush tax cuts remained in effect. On average, every 10 percentage-point rise in the average tax rate on the richest has been associated with an increase in annual GDP growth of almost one percentage point.

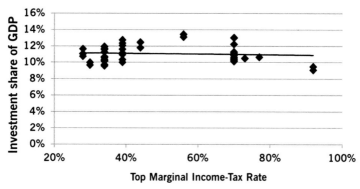

FIGURE 4: TOP MARGINAL TAX RATE AND INVESTMENT,1963-2011

Cutting taxes on the richest Americans has not led them to invest more in plant and equipment. Over the past 50 years, as tax rates have declined, there has been no increase in investment spending as a percentage of GDP. (The flat trend line shows that changes in the highest marginal income-tax rate have not affected investment much, one way or the other.) Instead, the investment share of the economy has been determined by other factors, such as aggregate demand, rather than tax policy.

FIGURE 5: TAX SHARE OF GDP AND PRODUCTIVITY GROWTH

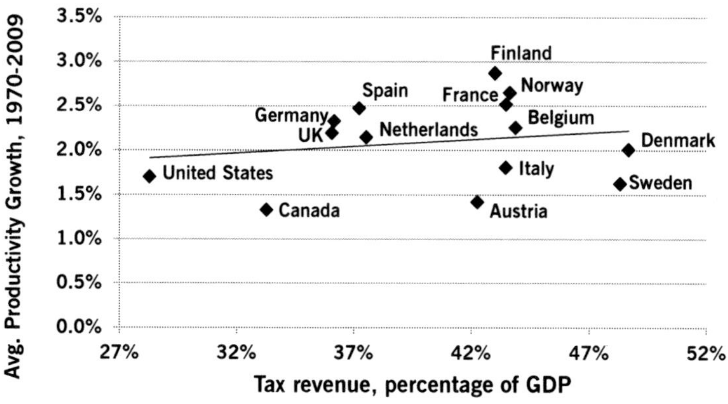

Despite lower and declining tax rates, especially on the rich, the United States has had slower productivity growth over the last several decades than other advanced economies. Overall, lower taxes are associated with slower growth in GDP per hour worked. A 10 percentage point increase in taxes as a share of GDP is associated with an increase in the productivity growth rate of 0.2 percentage points. ❑

*Sources:* Tom Petska and Mike Strudler, "Income, Taxes, and Tax Progressivity: An Examination of Recent Trends in the Distribution of Individual Income and Taxes" (Statistics of Income Division, Internal Revenue Service, 1997); Thomas Hungerford, "Taxes and the Economy: An Economic Analysis of the Top Tax Rates Since 1945" (Congressional Research Service, 2012); Economic Report of the President, 2012; Bureau of Economic Analysis (bea.gov); Organization of Economic Cooperation and Development, OECD STAT.

*Article 6.4*

# THE $17 TRILLION DELUSION

**BY MARTY WOLFSON**
*January/February 2014*

$17,000,000,000,000

President Obama boasted last week that he had signed legislation to lift "the twin threats" to our economy of government shutdown and default. But what was done to fix the problem of growing debt that leads Washington to repeatedly raise the debt ceiling?

Nothing. In fact, by Friday, the U.S. debt had rocketed past $17 trillion. What does this mean?

At $17 trillion, this number has passed total U.S. gross domestic product (GDP), the measure of all that is produced in the economy.

Since Obama took office, the national debt has increased from about $10.6 trillion to more than $17 trillion—a 60 percent increase.

. . . Meanwhile, entitlement spending—the key driver of spending and debt—remains unaddressed.

—"Debt Hits $17 Trillion," The Foundry: Conservative Policy News Blog from the Heritage Foundation, Oct. 21, 2013

Shortly after the ceiling on federal debt was raised on October 17, 2013, the conservative Heritage Foundation notified its readers that the outstanding debt of the United States had "rocketed past $17 trillion," and that "entitlement spending—the key driver of spending and debt—remains unaddressed." The three assumptions in that statement—that the true measure of our debt is $17 trillion, that the cause of the buildup of debt is entitlement spending, and that therefore the appropriate policy to "address" this problem is to cut Social Security benefits and other "entitlements"— are endorsed by many politicians and policy pundits in Washington. But they're all wrong as economic analysis and disastrous as policy recommendations.

Seventeen trillion dollars certainly sounds like a big, scary number, especially when national debt clocks tell us that this translates into more than $53,000 for every person in the United States. But it is the wrong number to focus on.

The $17 trillion figure is a measure of "gross debt," which means that it includes debt owed by the U.S. Treasury to more than 230 other U.S. government agencies and trust funds. On the consolidated financial statements of the federal government, this intragovernmental debt is, in effect, canceled out. Basically, this is money the government owes itself. What is left is termed "debt held by the public." It is this measure of debt that is relevant to a possible increase in interest rates due to competition for funding between the private and public sectors. It is also the category of government debt used by the Congressional Budget Office and other analysts. (Of course, the full economic significance of any debt measure needs to be considered in context, in relationship to the income available to service the debt.) The total debt held by the public is $12 trillion.

The Social Security Trust Fund owns $2.7 trillion of the $5 trillion of Treasury securities held in intragovernmental accounts. In fact, Social Security is the largest single owner of Treasury securities in the world, surpassing even China's significant holdings of $1.3 trillion.

Social Security accumulated all these Treasury securities because of the way that its finances are organized. Social Security benefits to retirees (and to the disabled) are paid for by a payroll tax of 12.4 % on workers' wages (with 6.2% paid by the worker and 6.2% paid by the employer), up to a limit, currently $113,700. If, in any year, Social Security revenue is greater than what is needed to pay current retiree benefits, the surplus must, by law, be invested in Treasury securities (most of which are "special obligation bonds" issued only to the Social Security Trust Fund).

Since 1983, workers have been paying more in Social Security taxes than what was needed to pay retiree benefits. A special commission, appointed by President Reagan and chaired by future Federal Reserve Chair Alan Greenspan, recommended several changes to increase the revenue received by the Social Security Trust Fund. Most prominent among these changes was an increase in the payroll tax rate to its current level of 12.4%, although the Commission also recommended reductions in benefits, including a gradual increase in the retirement age from 65 to 67. The effect of the changes would be to create significant surpluses in the Social Security Trust Fund. The thinking was that, if in the future payroll taxes fell below benefits, the Trust Fund could draw upon the accumulated surpluses to pay benefits.

Therefore, the $2.7 trillion of Treasury securities held by the Trust Fund came about not because entitlements are out of control and the government has been forced to borrow to meet retiree benefits, but rather because future retirees have paid more taxes than necessary to meet benefit obligations. Workers have essentially been prepaying into the Trust Fund in order to provide for their future benefits.

So it makes no sense to try to solve the supposed problem of too much government debt by cutting benefits for current and future Social Security recipients. These workers were asked to help keep Social Security solvent by paying increased payroll taxes. As a result, the gross federal debt increased. It would be totally unfair and irrational to cut benefits now because these workers had sacrificed in the past. That would be hitting them with a double burden, the second burden of benefits cuts incurred because there was the first burden of overpaying payroll taxes into the Trust Fund.

What's more, the strategy the Heritage Foundation advocates would make the alleged problem they are claiming to address even worse. That's because cutting benefits would mean that payroll taxes would more easily meet retiree benefits, and so the surplus accumulating in the Social Security Trust Fund would be greater. Since the Trust Fund is required by law to invest its surpluses in Treasury securities, a greater surplus translates into more bonds being accumulated by the Trust Fund, and therefore a higher gross federal debt (assuming that Treasury borrowing from other sources remains the same). So cutting Social Security benefits in order to reduce the $17 trillion debt would produce the contradictory result that the debt would be even higher than it would have been without the benefit cuts. Even if Congress decided to reduce overall borrowing in step with lower Social Security benefits, there would still be no positive effect on federal debt: the lower borrowing would be balanced by the increase in Treasury securities held by the Trust Fund. Thus, in neither case would the goal of reducing outstanding gross federal debt be achieved.

Despite the 1983 changes to Social Security, the Trustees, the board that oversees Social Security, stated in their 1995 annual report that the 75-year projection of Social Security finances was no longer in "close actuarial balance" and that the long-range deficits should be "addressed." In 2002, they began to be more specific: "Bringing Social Security into actuarial balance over the next 75 years could be achieved by either a permanent 13-percent reduction in benefits or a 15-percent increase in payroll tax income, or some combination of the two."

Of course, the assumptions used by the Trustees, their policy approach, and the need for benefit cuts are all a matter of dispute. However, had benefits been cut by 13% beginning in 1996, total reductions would have totaled $1.2 trillion by 2012. So the Trust Fund would have accumulated that much more in Treasury securities, and the gross debt would actually have increased to $18.2 trillion.

In reality, the bonds in the Social Security Trust Fund are primarily a political accounting device to remind us that we as a society have promised a certain level of benefits to Social Security retirees. It is true that at some point the Trust Fund will most likely need to redeem the bonds in order to pay full benefits to retirees. And it is true that the government will need to raise the funds to do this, either by borrowing from the public (selling Treasury bonds) or through increased tax revenue. But this is the case because we promised benefits to these retirees, not because there is a certain level of bonds in the Trust Fund. The benefits would be due retirees whether or not there are bonds in the Trust Fund.

So the real issue is whether or not society will keep its commitment to retirees. The agenda of those who say we have to cut benefits is really that they don't want to meet this commitment. We should recognize that this is their agenda, and not let them hide behind the smokescreen of supposedly out-of-control federal debt. ❏

*Sources:* Congressional Budget Office, "Federal Debt and the Statutory Limit," November 20, 2013; Financial Management Service, United States Department of the Treasury, "Monthly Treasury Statement," October 2013; United States Department of the Treasury, "Treasury International Capital System, Monthly Foreign Holders of Treasury Securities," October 2013; The Annual Report of the Board of Trustees of the Federal Old-Age and Survivors Insurance and Federal Disability Insurance Trust Funds, various years; Office of the Chief Actuary, Social Security Administration, Statistical Tables, Benefit Payments by Calendar Year.

*Article 6.5*

# WHAT'S NEXT FOR GREECE?

## BY HARRY KONSTANTINIDIS
*September/October 2015*

M ost readers already probably know the sequence of events between Greece and
its creditors over the last month: a fruitless and frustrating negotiation; a take-
it-or-leave-it offer from the creditors; the announcement of a referendum (the first in
more than 40 years) for the people of Greece to decide whether to accept the offer;
a triumph of the "No" vote (61.3% rejecting the offer, despite a visceral campaign
in favor of the "Yes" by the Greek media and foreign politicians); the resignation of
Finance Minister Yanis Varoufakis; a retreat by the governing Syriza coalition offering austerity in exchange for a deal; the creditors' outrageous demands in an open
attempt to push Greece or Syriza towards exit from the euro (€); a harsh deal that
neither the Greek government nor its European partners believe in; the ratification
of the ensuing economic adjustment program by the Greek parliament despite almost one-fourth of Syriza MPs voting against, abstaining, or absent, rendering Syriza effectively a minority government; the government's resignation, and triggering a
snap election in the fall; finally, the creation of a leftist anti-euro political formation
(Popular Unity) by Syriza dissenters who claim adherence to the principles Syriza
upheld before its rise to power.

The terms of the agreement between Greece and its lenders reflect the creditors' attempt to make Syriza renege on all its promises and cross all its "red lines,"
except for the promise to maintain eurozone membership. Sharp value-added tax
(VAT) increases, the establishment of a privatization fund including €50 billion
worth of assets, no restoration of collective bargaining rights or minimum wages,
vetting of all legislation by the Troika (European Commission, European Central
Bank, and IMF), and the "depoliticization" of Greek public administration, extending the model of the "independent" central bank to other aspects of government. How could Syriza have agreed to such a deal? Wouldn't Greece be better
off introducing its own currency, rather than conceding both fiscal and monetary
policy sovereignty?

In order to answer this question, one has to understand the political identity of
Syriza. Syriza has historically been a "Europeanist" party—differing from the Communist Party of Greece in its adherence to the notion that it is possible to change
existing European institutions. Synaspismos, the predecessor of Syriza, even voted
in favor of the Maastricht Treaty that laid the foundations of the European Union
and the eurozone in 1992, viewing the treaty as a first—albeit incomplete—step towards a more solidaristic and unified Europe. Most of the Syriza MPs, even to this
date, believe that Europe, rather the nation-state, is the locus on which to improve
conditions for workers and achieve positive social change. The rise of Syriza also
came with support from "Eurosceptic" leftists, as well as increasing disillusionment
of some Syriza factions with European Union and Eurozone institutions. However,
for the Syriza leadership, the goal was not to exit the European Union, but to change

---

### Leave the Euro but Stay in the EU?

Technically, all EU countries are required to aim towards eurozone membership, aside from the UK and Denmark, which have received exception clauses in the relevant EU treaties. Greece does not currently have such an exception—which also explains why an EU-28 summit was originally called for mid-July, before being canceled at the last minute, i.e., to accommodate a "temporary" Greek exit from the Eurozone within the European Union.

However, it is important to note that the Greek media and European politicians were suggesting that a voluntary eurozone exit would also necessitate an exit from the EU. This was a powerful fear for Greece, and the fact that all this is uncharted water makes that fear hard to contradict.

---

it in favor of working people. Furthermore, Syriza never suggested that its goal was to abandon the euro: the closest the Syriza leadership ever came to proposing eurozone exit was Prime Minister Alexis Tsipras' saying in 2012 that "the euro is not a fetish." In 2015, such ambivalences were abandoned.

After the electoral victory of 2015, Syriza's strategy focused on showing that the magnitude of the crisis was not Greece's own doing, but a direct outcome of the eurozone's flawed architecture and the catastrophic austerity policies imposed by the Troika. Exiting the euro would let the EU off the hook for its mistakes. However, both Syriza finance ministers, Yanis Varoufakis and now Euclid Tsakalotos, have openly stated that they were surprised at the lack of European willingness to engage in a substantive debate about the crisis and the remedies: Other finance ministers even chastised Varoufakis for "lecturing macroeconomics" to them. Despite making little headway with its European "partners," Syriza never chose to exit the European terrain.

Herein lies the weakness of the strategy: a weakness of political imagination. Syriza never opened a public discussion about the euro in Greece. How does the euro help or detract from the project of productive reconstruction that Syriza promised the Greek electorate? Is the euro a tool for workers or for financial capital? What would happen to Greek citizens' deposits and debts if Greece were to leave the euro? Would there be shortages of fuel, medicine, or food if Greece were to return to a national currency?

The Greek oligarch-controlled media, which are now celebrating the agreement and praising "Tsipras, the statesman," set the political terrain domestically by equating the euro with progress and a return to the drachma with catastrophe. The Greek collective imagination still clings to the euro as something beyond dispute, and significant parts of the left hold the same position. When—especially after the announcement of the referendum—the Greek media, the Greek opposition, and European politicians equated Syriza's support of the "No" vote with the return to a national currency, Syriza attempted to close down the discussion, essentially embracing the discourse of catastrophe associated with leaving the euro. Even after signing the deal on July 13, Tsipras has said that Greece was not in a position to leave the euro without foreign reserves, while Varoufakis equated leaving the euro to becoming "North Korea." Could the Greek government have chosen to leave the euro at that time? Realistically, the answer is no. Despite what various critics may claim, a significant part of Greek voters would have been unprepared for it.

However, no one can claim ignorance any longer. By following a consistent pro-Europe agenda, Syriza managed to point out the inconsistencies of the European currency union and its "democratic deficit." When even Ben Bernanke, the former chairman of the Fed, comes out in support of the Greek position and the IMF categorically rejects the viability of the Greek debt without debt relief, it is bizarre to call Syriza a "radical" or "extreme" left-wing party. One has to look elsewhere for zealots. Now, Greece needs to take actions to stake out a stronger bargaining position in future negotiations. Given that the deal with the partners is not complete yet, and that Berlin politicians and their satellites will do their best to prevent any debt relief and stop the deal from materializing, it is time for a leftist government to take actions that will both undermine the effects of the neoliberal policies imposed on Greece and allow Greece to be better prepared for the next round of negotiations.

What does Syriza need to do in the very short-run, assuming that it maintains power after the fall elections? The Greek government, first of all, needs to (finally) attack the Greek oligarchy and tackle the web of intertwining relations between the media, banks, and other big business in Greece. Over the last five years, the Greek public has been taking out loans to recapitalize the Greek banks in exchange for preferred (nonvoting) stock: thus, the management of Greek banks has stayed in private hands. While lending had generally come to a standstill, the banks continued to make loans to insolvent private media, owned by a small number of Greek families with strong political ties. At the same time, the Bank of Greece (the national central bank), whose governor was appointed by the previous government and was both an architect and a staunch defender of austerity, has posed obstacles to Syriza's attempts to shed light on these corrupt relationships, refusing to provide information about these loans on the grounds of bank secrecy. These relationships need to stop.

Furthermore, Syriza needs to start the productive reconstruction of the Greek economy. The negotiations with the creditors have dragged on for a long time, and have detracted attention from domestic issues. If the Greek economy has any chance of recovering—either inside or outside the eurozone—Syriza needs to build and foster the productive structures that provide employment and allow the people of Greece to cover their basic needs. Even in the absence of fiscal space to pursue a traditional expansionary Keynesian policy, a productive reconstruction based on self-management, new food systems striving towards food sovereignty, and increased

---

*Three Points for a Program of Reconstruction]*

**Self-management:** The management of firms by workers. Workers get to decide how their workplace will be run, the payment of salaries, and the distribution of profits.

**Food sovereignty:** An alternative movement to the corporate neoliberal food regime, food sovereignty revolves around smallholder agriculture and agroecological principles. It promotes healthy and culturally appropriate food, as well as ecological and social sustainability.

**Participatory budgeting:** A democratic process for allocating public funds. Citizens get to decide how public funds will be spent through regular participation in open forums, during which they determine collectively and transparently what goals and needs to prioritize.

public participation (through local assemblies and participatory budgeting) are imperative (see box). In addition, perhaps spurred by the creation of the new anti-euro Popular Unity formation, Syriza must engage in an open and frank discussion about how productive reconstruction can (or cannot) take place within existing European economic and political institutions.

Is this an easy task? No. But in the absence of fiscal and monetary policy, Greece doesn't really have any traditional options left. If Greece wants to increase its leverage when the negotiations come to the next impasse, instead of just being a laboratory of austerity, it has to quickly become a laboratory of experimentation and radical imagination. ❑

# Chapter 7

# MONEY AND MONETARY POLICY

## INTRODUCTION

**E**conomist Ben Bernanke took over as the man behind the curtain of the Federal Reserve ("the Fed") just in time to oversee the worst financial crisis since the Great Depression.

Bernanke could have used all the wizard-like powers the business press sometimes attributed to his predecessor, "maestro" Alan Greenspan, given that it was now his job to pull the economy's fat out of the fire. Just how unenviable was the situation? In October 2008, Greenspan confessed before Congress that he had "made a mistake in presuming that banks ... were capable of protecting their own shareholders" and that the financial crisis had left him "in a state of shocked disbelief."

Under Bernanke, the Fed arguably did help to avert a complete economic meltdown. Limited steps were undertaken to resolve the nearly intractable mortgage debt crisis and to put in place the measures that might prevent another financial crash. Still, working people fared no better under Bernanke than they did under Greenspan. Even before the financial crisis, Greenspan worried that, under his tenure, inequality had worsened to levels that threatened our democratic institutions, and that the unprecedented level of U.S. reliance on foreign borrowing had become unsustainable. Bernanke acknowledged the seriousness of both problems as well, but seemed just as incapable as his predecessor of seriously addressing them. Now, he has been succeeded as Fed chair by Janet Yellen. Economic stagnation, slow job growth, and severe inequality, however, remain the order of the day.

Why should it matter who chairs the Federal Reserve? The Fed is charged with using monetary policy to keep inflation in check and provide liquidity to keep the economy going (or bolster a flagging economy). The Fed is supposed to use its three tools—the reserve requirement, the discount rate, and open-market operations—to manipulate banking activity, control the money supply, and direct the economy to everyone's benefit.

It all sounds value-free. But what the Fed really does is serve those who hold financial assets. So when it comes to making monetary policy, the Fed puts the interests of bondholders first, well before those of workers or job seekers. Investors look to the Fed to protect the value of their stocks and bonds by keeping inflation low—and if that means keeping a lid on employment growth, so be it.

To begin the chapter, two articles take us through the basics of money and the monetary system. We use money every day, but usually do not stop to think about how money is defined, how it has evolved historically, or how it is created today. Economist Doug Orr explains in everyday language what money is and how the Fed attempts to control the money supply (Article 7.1). Next, Arthur MacEwan explains how a "fractional reserve banking" system works, and whether it is at the root of our current economic troubles (Article 7.2).

The next several articles go into the ways that governments use monetary policy, especially in response to economic downturns.

Gerald Friedman confirms, based on the explosion in excess reserves held by U.S. banks, that the Fed can do little to get the economy going using conventional monetary policy if banks just won't make loans (Article 7.3).

Dean Baker questions the dire predictions bankers made about what would happen if they didn't get their way (Article 7.4). During the financial crisis, Wall Street insisted that without a massive intervention by the Federal Reserve to save them from the consequences of their own reckless lending, we would fall into a Second Great Depression. That was not a warning of an inevitable consequence, argues Baker. It was a threat.

Next, in his article on the Federal Reserve's recently announced interest-rate hike (Article 7.5), Marty Wolfson explains that the Fed is planning on paying banks billions of dollars in interest even though it doesn't really have to. The Fed's conduct of monetary policy is channeled through private banks and beholden to their interests. More, its decision-makers see it as their sacred mission to act as protectors and benefactors to high finance.

The final two articles of the chapter step back to take a broader view of monetary policy historically.

Gerald Epstein analyzes the transition, over the last few decades, toward "inflation targeting"—central bank policies prioritizing the achievement of very low inflation above all other policy goals—in high-income and developing economies alike (Article 7.6). He considers, too, alternative goals that central banks have pursued in the past, and could again in the future, like full employment and economic development.

To round out the chapter, Alejandro Reuss (Article 7.7) looks at the key arguments made by John Maynard Keynes, in *The General Theory of Employment, Interest, and Money*, on the *limitations* of monetary policy as a tool for reviving economies mired in depression conditions. Reuss applies lessons from Keynes' work to current problems in the U.S. economy.

## Discussion Questions

1. (Article 7.1) What are the mechanisms the Fed uses to "control" the creation of money by the banking system? Why, according to Orr, is the Fed's control over the creation of money "limited"?

2. (Article 7.2) What is "fractional reserve banking"? Do banks "create money out

of thin air"? In what ways, according to MacEwan, do U.S. economic problems go deeper than the monetary system?

3. (Article 7.3) Why does Friedman, like others before him, liken monetary policy to "pushing on a string"? What evidence does Friedman offer to show that this analogy is an apt description of monetary policy today?

4. (Article 7.4) At the height of the financial crisis, we heard dire warnings of the potential for a Second Great Depression. Since we experienced "only" a severe recession, not a depression on the scale of the 1930s, should we conclude that the bailout worked? Or was there an alternative response that could have been better?

5. (Article 7.5) Does it make sense for the Fed to pay banks interest for their reserves, so that they will not lend at interest rates that are too low? Why or why not?

6. (Article 7.6) Why have central banks moved from prioritizing goals like full employment and economic development to championing very low inflation? Do you agree with Epstein that it would be better if central banks abandoned single-minded "inflation targeting" in favor of a broader set of macroeconomic goals?

7. (Article 7.7) What, according to Keynes, were the key limitations of monetary policy, as a response to an economic downturn? If these were well described many decades ago, why did governments rely on monetary policy anyway, in responding to the Great Recession?

# WHAT IS MONEY?

## BY DOUG ORR
*November/December 1993; revised October 2010*

We all use money every day. Yet many people do not know what money actually is. There are many myths about money, including the idea that the government "prints" all of it and that it has some intrinsic value. But actually, money is less a matter of value, and more a matter of faith.

Money is sometimes called the universal commodity, because it can be traded for all other commodities. But for this to happen, everyone in society must believe that money will be accepted. If people stop believing that it will be accepted, the existing money ceases to be money. Recently in Poland, people stopped accepting the zloty, and used vodka as money instead.

In addition to facilitating exchanges, money allows us to "store" value from one point in time to another. If you sell your car today for $4,000, you probably won't buy that amount of other products today. Rather, you store the value as money, probably in a bank, until you want to use it.

The "things" that get used as money have changed over time, and "modern" people often chuckle when they hear about some of them. The Romans used salt (from which we get the word "salary"), South Sea Islanders used shark's teeth, and several societies actually used cows. The "Three Wise Men" brought gold, frankincense and myrrh, each of which was money in different regions at the time.

If money does not exist, or is in short supply, it will be created. In POW camps, where guards specifically outlaw its existence, prisoners use cigarettes instead. In the American colonies, the British attempted to limit the supply of British pounds, because they knew that by limiting the supply of money, they could hamper the development of independent markets in the colonies. Today, the United States uses a similar policy, through the International Monetary Fund, in dealing with Latin America.

To overcome this problem, the colonists began to use tobacco leaves as money. This helped the colonies to develop, but it also allowed the holders of large plots of land to grow their own money! When the colonies gained independence, the new government decreed gold to be money, rather than tobacco, much to the dismay of Southern plantation owners. Now, rather than growing money, farmers had to find or buy it.

To aid the use of gold as money, banks would test its purity, put it in storage, and give the depositor paper certificates of ownership. These certificates, "paper money," could then be used in place of the gold itself. Since any bank could store gold and issue certificates, by the beginning of the Civil War, over 7,000 different types of "paper money" were in circulation in the United States, none of it printed by the government.

While paper money is easier to use than gold, it is still risky to carry around large amounts of cash. It is safer to store the paper in a bank and simply sign over its ownership to make a purchase. We sign over the ownership of our money by writing a check. Checking account money became popular when, in an unsuccessful attempt to control the amount of money created by banks, the government outlawed the printing of paper money by private banks in 1864.

## How Banks Create Money

Banks are central to understanding money, because in addition to storing it, they help to create it. Bankers realize that not everyone will withdraw their money at the same time, so they loan out much of the money that has been deposited. It is from the interest on these loans that banks get their profits, and through these loans the banking system creates new money.

If you deposit $100 cash in your checking account at Chase Manhattan Bank, you still have $100 in money to use, because checks are also accepted as money. Chase must set aside some of this cash as "reserves," in case you or other depositors decide to withdraw money as cash. Current regulations issued by the Federal Reserve Bank (the Fed) require banks to set aside an average of three cents out of each dollar. So Chase can make a loan of $97, based on your deposit. Chase does not make loans by handing out cash but instead by putting $97 in the checking account of the person, say Emily, taking out the loan. So from your initial deposit of $100 in cash, the economy now has $197 in checking account money.

The borrower, Emily, pays $97 for some product or service by check, and the seller, say Ace Computers, deposits the money in its checking account. The total amount of checking account money is still $197, but its location and ownership have changed. If Ace Computer's account is at Citibank, $97 in cash is transferred from Chase to Citibank. This leaves just $3 in cash reserves at Chase to cover your original deposit. However, Citibank now has $97 in "new" cash on hand, so it sets aside three cents on the dollar ($2.91) and loans out the rest, $94.09, as new checking account money. Through this process, every dollar of "reserves" yields many dollars in total money.

If you think this is just a shell game and there is only $100 in "real" money, you still don't understand money. Anything that is accepted as payment for a transaction is "real" money. Cash is no more real than checking account money. In fact, most car rental companies will not accept cash as payment for a car, so for them, cash is not money!

As of June 2010, there was $883 billion of U.S. currency, i.e. "paper money," in existence. However, somewhere between 50% to 70% of it is held outside the United States by foreign banks and individuals. U.S. $100 bills are the preferred currency of choice used to facilitate illegal international transactions, such as the drug trade. The vast majority of all money actually in use in the United States is not cash, but rather checking account money. This type of money, $1,590 billion, was created by private banks, and was not "printed" by anyone. In fact, this money exists only as electronic "bits" in banks' computers. (The less "modern" South Sea Islanders could have quite a chuckle about that!)

The amount of money that banks can create is limited by the total amount of reserves, and by the fraction of each deposit that must be held as reserves. Prior to

1914, bankers themselves decided what fraction of deposits to hold as reserves. Since then, this fraction has been set by the main banking regulator, the Fed.

Until 1934, gold was held as reserves, but the supply of gold was unstable, growing rapidly during the California and Alaska "gold rushes," and very slowly at other times. As a result, at times more money was created than the economy needed, and at other times not enough money could be created. Starting in 1934, the U.S. government decided that gold would no longer be used as reserves. Cash, now printed by the Fed, could no longer be redeemed for gold, and cash itself became the reserve asset.

Banks, fearing robberies, do not hold all of their cash reserves in their own vaults. Rather, they store it in an account at a regional Fed bank. These accounts count as reserves. What banks do hold in their vaults is their other assets, such as Treasury bonds and corporate bonds.

## The Fed and Bank Reserves

The only role of the government in creating money is indirectly through the Fed, which is controlled by neither the Congress nor the executive branch. If the Fed wants to expand the money supply, it must increase bank reserves. To do this, the Fed buys Treasury bonds from a bank, and pays with a check drawn on the Fed itself. By depositing the check in its reserve account at the Fed, the bank now has more reserves, so the bank can now make more loans and create new checking account money.

By controlling the amount of reserves, the Fed attempts to control the size of the money supply. But as recent history has shown, this control is limited. During the late 1970s, the Fed tried to limit the amount of money banks could create by reducing reserves, but banks simply created new forms of money, just like the POW camp prisoners and colonial farmers. In 1979, there was only one form of checking account money. Today, there are many, with odd names such as NOWs, ATSs, repos, and money market deposit accounts. If there is a profit to be made creating money, banks will find a way.

In 2010, we have the opposite problem. The Fed is trying to expand the money supply, but banks are refusing to create new money. In good times, banks hold as few reserves as possible, so they can profit from making loans. In times of crisis, banks fear that we will lose faith in the commercial banking system and all try to take out our "money" as cash. Since there is far more electronic money than cash, this is impossible. But if the bank cannot give us our money in the form we want it, the bank fails and ceases to exist. Since the start of 2007, over 300 banks, with assets totally more than $637 billion, have failed.

Since all banks fear they will be next, they want as many reserves as possible. Excess reserves are any reserves above those required by the Fed. During the 1990s, these averaged about $1 billion for the entire banking system. During the crisis of 2001, they spiked to the then unheard of level of $19 billion. As of June 2010, excess reserves in the banking system were $1,035 billion! This is the classic case of trying to push on a string. The Fed can create reserves, but only banks can create money and they are not yet willing to make any new loans.

These amorphous forms of money function only because we believe they will function, which is why the continued stability of the banking system is so critical. While it is true that the bailout of the banking system was not handled very well, and that many people who created the crisis are still profiting from it, the bailout was a necessary evil. In a modern market economy, banks create the money, and no market economy can function without its money. Money only exists if we believe in it, so we have to maintain the faith. To maintain the faith we need more democratic control over money creation, which can only come if regulation of the financial system is greatly expanded. ❏

*Sources:* Money supply: Federal Reserve Board, www.federalreserve.gov/releases/h6/current/; excess reserves: St. Louis Federal Reserve Bank, research.stlouisfed.org/fred2/series/EXCRESNS; bank failures: Federal Deposit Insurance Corporation (FDIC), www.fdic.gov/bank/individual/failed/banklist.html.

*Article 7.2*

# SHOULD WE BLAME "FRACTIONAL RESERVE" BANKING?

## BY ARTHUR MacEWAN
*May/June 2013*

> Dear Dr. Dollar:
> *I have seen various arguments (on the Internet, for example) that a prime cause of our economic problems (inequality, crises, mass unemployment, the immense power of the banks, etc.) is our monetary system. In particular, that it is a "fractional reserve system," in which "money is created out of thin air." Could you comment?*
> —Mike Smith, New York, NY

The last several years, when banks and the whole financial system have been at the core of economic disruption, could easily lead one to see the monetary system as central to our economic problems.

Keep in mind, however, that we have had essentially the same monetary system for decades, the Federal Reserve has existed for a hundred years, and the "fractional reserve" system existed before the Fed. During these earlier eras, including periods when we relied on the gold standard as the basis of our monetary system, we have had depressions, inflation, severe inequality, and excessive power in the hands of finance and large corporations generally. We have also had some relatively good times—periods of stable economic growth, less economic inequality, lower unemployment, and less power and profits for the banks. So, whatever is wrong with our monetary system (and there are certainly things wrong), the explanation of our economic problems must be more complex.

But what is the fractional reserve system? Basically, it is the system by which banks keep as reserves only a fraction of the amount of deposits that their customers have with the banks. Banks can do this because at any time their customers will demand only a fraction of those total obligations. When, for example, you deposit $100 in the bank, the bank will loan out to someone else perhaps $90 of that $100. This $90 is new money that the bank has created. The person or business taking this loan then deposits the $90 in another account with the bank or another bank, allowing a new loan of $81 to be generated by the banking system; the remaining $9 (10% of the deposit) will be kept as reserves. And so on.

By this process, if people are willing to take out the loans, the banks can create an additional $900 of money based on an original deposit of $100. This is sometimes called "creating money out of thin air." In fact, it is creating money on the basis of 10% reserves.

If banks were left to their own devices, competition would create pressure to push down the reserve ratio—they could, for example, make twice the amount of loans were they to reduce their reserves from 10% to 5% of obligations. However, the Federal Reserve has a great deal of authority over what the banks can do. It sets the reserve ratio. Banks cannot simply lower the amount of reserves to make more loans. (The actual reserve ratio varies depending on type of obligation; 10% is just an example that makes calculations easy.) Most frequently, the Fed affects the supply of money by buying bonds from the banks, thus increasing the banks' reserves (and enabling them to lend more), or selling bonds to the banks, thus reducing the banks' reserves.

That's the formal way it works. Although critics of a fractional reserve system claim it "debases the currency" (i.e., leads to inflation), it does not automatically allow the banks to create more and more money without limits, which could indeed generate severe inflation. The U.S. economy has experienced mild inflation for most of the last century (averaging 3.2% annually), but fractional reserve banking is not generally associated with high "runaway" inflation. Ironically, in light of the claims of the critics, the Fed has often followed policies that work in exactly the opposite direction—restricting the banks' ability to create money, thus restricting the loans they can make, and restraining economic growth and employment. (After all, neither banks nor other large corporations like severe inflation.)

But of course the formal way the system works is not the whole story. The banks themselves and other big firms have a great deal of influence over what the Fed does. So the Fed usually regulates the banks with a very light hand. In the Great Recession, in particular, the Fed (along with the U.S. Treasury) provided the banks with funds to meet their obligations when many of those banks would have otherwise failed. In this respect, the way the Fed works is not so different from the way the government works in general—money has a great deal of influence over policy.

It would be nice if our economic problems were so simple that they could be solved by some reorganization of our monetary system. But the problems are bigger and deeper. ❏

*Article 7.3*

# PUSHING ON STRINGS
*The explosion of U.S. banks' excess reserves since last fall
illustrates the dramatic failure of monetary policy.*

## BY GERALD FRIEDMAN
*May/June 2009*

Monetary policy is not working. Since the economic crisis began in July 2007, the Federal Reserve has dramatically cut interest rates and pumped out over a trillion dollars, increasing the money supply by over 15% in less than two years. These vast sums have failed to revive the economy because the banks have been hoarding liquidity rather than lending.

The Federal Reserve requires that banks hold money on reserve to back up deposits and other bank liabilities. In the past, beyond these required reserves, banks would hold very small amounts of excess reserves, holdings that they minimized because reserves earn very little or no interest. Between the 1950s and September 2008, U.S. banks held over $5 billion in total excess reserves only once, after the September 11 attacks. This changed with the collapse of Lehman Brothers. Beginning with less than $2 billion in August 2008, excess reserves soared to $60 billion in September and then to $559 billion in November before peaking at $798 billion in January 2009. (They had dropped to $644 billion by the time this article was written.)

This explosion of excess reserves represents a signal change in bank policy that threatens the effectiveness of monetary policy in the current economic crisis. Aware of their own financial vulnerability, even insolvency, frightened bank managers

## BANK EXCESS RESERVES SINCE 1999

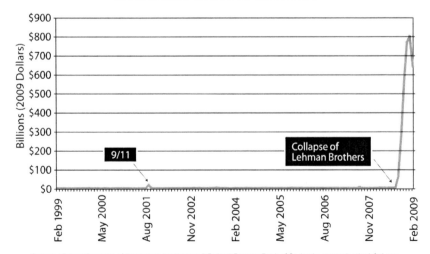

*Source:* "Excess Reserves of Depository Institutions," Federal Reserve Bank of St. Louis, research.stlouisfed.org.

responded to the collapse of major investment houses like Lehman Brothers by grabbing and hoarding all the cash that they could get. At the same time, a general loss of confidence and spreading economic collapse persuaded banks that there are few to whom they could lend with confidence that the loans would be repaid. Clearly, our banks have decided that they need, or at least want, the money more than consumers and productive businesses do.

Banks could have been investing this money by lending to businesses needing liquidity to buy material inputs or pay workers. Had they done so, monetarist economists would be shouting from the rooftops, or at least in the university halls, about how monetary policy prevented another Great Depression. Instead, even the *Wall Street Journal* is proclaiming that "We're All Keynesians Again" because monetary policy has failed. Monetary authorities, the *Journal* explains, can create money but they cannot force banks to lend or to invest it in productive activities. The Federal Reserve confronts a reality shown in the graph above: it can't "push on a string," as Fed Chair Marriner Eccles famously put it in testimony before Congress in 1935, in the depths of the Great Depression.

If the banks won't lend, then we need more than monetary policy to get out of the current crisis. No bailout, no TARP program, can revive the economy if banks hoard all the cash they receive. The Obama stimulus was an appropriate response to the failure of string-pushing. But much more government stimulus will be needed to solve a crisis this large, and we will need programs to move liquidity from bank vaults to businesses and consumers. It may be time to stop waiting on the banks, and to start telling them what to do with our money. ❑

*Article 7.4*

# THE FINANCIAL CRISIS AND THE SECOND GREAT DEPRESSION MYTH

## BY DEAN BAKER
*September 2013, Truthout*

All knowledgeable D.C. types know that the TARP and Fed bailout of Wall Street banks five years ago saved us from a second Great Depression. Like most things known by knowledgeable Washington types, this is not true.

Just to remind folks, the Wall Street banks were on life support at that time. Bear Stearns, one of the five major investment banks, would have collapsed in March of 2008 if the Fed had not been able to arrange a rescue by offering guarantees on almost $30 billion in assets to J.P. Morgan. Fannie Mae and Freddie Mac both went belly up in September. The next week Lehman, another of the five major investment banks did go under. AIG, the country's largest insurer was about to follow suit when the Fed and Treasury jerry-rigged a rescue.

Without massive government assistance, it was a virtual certainty that the remaining three investment banks, Goldman Sachs, Morgan Stanley, and Merrill Lynch, were toast. Bank of America and Citigroup also were headed rapidly for the dustbin of history. It is certainly possible, if not likely, that the other two giant banks, Wells Fargo and J.P. Morgan, would have been sucked down in the maelstrom.

In short, if we allowed the magic of the market to do its work, we would have seen an end to Wall Street as we know it. The major banks would be in receivership. Instead of proffering economic advice to the president, the top executives of these banks would be left walking the streets and dodging indictments and lawsuits.

This was when they turned socialist on us. We got the TARP and infinite money and guarantees from the Fed, FDIC, and Treasury to keep the Wall Street crew in their expensive suits. All the politicians told us how painful it was for them to hand out this money to the wealthy, but the alternative was a Second Great Depression.

It's not clear what these people think they mean, but let's work it through. Suppose that we did see a full meltdown. The commercial banks that handle checking and saving accounts and are responsible for most personal and business transactions would then be under control of the FDIC.

The FDIC takes banks over all the time. This would be more roadkill than it was accustomed to, but there is little reason to think that after a few days most of us would not be able to get to most of the money in our accounts and carry through normal transactions.

Credit conditions would likely be uncertain for business loans for some time, as in fact was the case even with the bailouts. Mortgage credit would have been provided by Fannie Mae and Freddie Mac, as has been the case since September of 2008.

One item deserving special attention in this respect is the commercial paper market. This is the market that most major businesses rely upon to meet regular payments like payroll and electric bills. When he was lobbying Congress for the TARP, Federal Reserve Board Chair Ben Bernanke said that this market was shutting down, which would in fact be disastrous for the economy.

What Bernanke neglected to mention was that he unilaterally had the ability to support the commercial paper market through the Fed. In fact he announced a special lending facility for exactly this purpose, the weekend after Congress approved the TARP.

It is also worth ridiculing people who say the government made a profit on its bailout loans. It's true that most loans were repaid with interest. However these loans were made to favored borrowers (Wall Street banks) at far-below-the-market interest rates at the time.

The Congressional Oversight Panel commissioned a study on the subsidies involved in just the first round of TARP loans. The study put the subsidies at a bit more than 30 percent of the money lent out, implying bank subsidies of almost $80 billion from just this small segment of the bailout. Adding in other loans and various implicit and explicit guarantees would certainly increase this number considerably.

But suppose we hadn't opened the government's wallet and instead let the banks drown in their own greed. Would we have faced a decade of double-digit unemployment? From an economic standpoint there would be no reason for concern. We know from the last Great Depression, the key to recovery from a period of weak demand is to have the government spend lots of money. We eventually got out of the Great Depression by spending huge amounts of money on World War II. To get the economy jump-started this time we could have had massive spending on education, child care, rebuilding the infrastructure and making the economy more energy efficient. As Paul Krugman has repeatedly joked, if we need a political rationale for this spending we can say it is necessary to protect the United States from a Martian invasion.

Of course as a political matter, such massive spending could prove a tough sell given the present day politics. But that is a political argument, not an economic one.

Since we would be in uncharted water following this sort of collapse, no one can with a straight face claim they know how the politics would play out. We can separate out three camps.

First we have the folks who would like the government to spend enough to restore full employment, but argue the political opposition would be too great. These people have a coherent second Great Depression story, but based on politics, not economics. The bad guys would have forced us to endure a decade of double-digit unemployment if we didn't rescue Wall Street.

Then we have the people who don't like government spending and would oppose efforts to boost the economy back to full employment. These people are saying that we would have faced a second Great Depression if we didn't rescue Wall Street because they would have insisted upon it.

Finally, there are Washington Very Serious People types like the *Washington Post* editorial page, who would go along with restarting the economy but only if accompanied by sharp cuts to programs like Social Security and Medicare. These people are hostage takers who are saying that if the country didn't bailout Wall Street, they would force it to endure a second Great Depression, unless it eviscerated essential programs that working people need.

So the long and short is that we only need to have worried about a Second Great Depression if the bad guys got their way. And most of the people who warn about a Second Great Depression were on the list of bad guys. The prospect of a second Great Depression was not a warning, it was a threat. ❑

*Article 7.5*

# THE FED RAISES INTEREST RATES ... BY PAYING THE BANKS

**BY MARTY WOLFSON**
*January/February 2016*

The business and financial press has been abuzz with speculation about when the Federal Reserve would begin raising interest rates. After the meeting of its Federal Open Market Committee (FOMC) on December 15-16, the Fed ended the suspense by announcing that it was raising its target federal funds rate by a quarter of a percentage point (to a range of 0.25 to 0.50%). Flying under the radar, though, was the Fed's use of a dramatically different method of raising interest rates. The new method involves paying billions of dollars to banks, primarily by paying interest on banks' reserves held at the Fed. The payments will reduce the amount of money that the Fed remits to the Treasury and, ultimately, to taxpayers.

## Why Is the Fed Paying the Banks?

This new method is best understood when viewed in the context of the recent financial crisis. The collapse of the housing bubble in 2007 threatened both the financial system and the broader economy. The Federal Reserve began a campaign of aggressively reducing interest rates, lowering the interest rate that it controls, the federal funds rate, from its peak of 5.25% in September 2007 to just 2% in April 2008. The federal funds rate is an interest rate that banks pay when borrowing from other banks. Lower costs for the banks in turn lead to lower interest rates for business and consumer borrowing, thus encouraging greater spending, output, and employment.

In making these changes to the federal funds rate, the Fed used its classic method of changing the level of bank reserves. (See sidebar, below.) It is this method that the Fed jettisoned when it announced its new procedures.

After the failure of Lehman Brothers in September 2008, financial markets became unsettled and many of the traditional funding sources for financial institutions dried up. Into this void stepped the Federal Reserve, which dramatically increased its lending and other interventions to help the banks. In the process, it pumped money into the banking system and expanded bank reserves, significantly beyond the level of reserves necessary to maintain its target for the federal funds rate.

On October 1, 2008, the Federal Reserve began to pay interest on bank reserves. Then-Fed Chair Ben Bernanke, in his recent memoir, gave this reason for the change: "The concern in 2008 was that emergency lending would lead short-term interest rates to fall below our federal funds target and thereby cause us to lose control of monetary policy."

In other words, without paying interest on reserves, banks would have so many excess reserves that did not earn any interest, and be so eager to gain at least some return on them, that the Fed would be unable to prevent them from lending at rates below the Fed's target for the federal funds rate (2% at that time). By paying interest on reserves, the Fed would eliminate banks' incentive to lend at rates below those it was receiving from the Fed.

This, however, is a curious explanation. The Fed dropped its target federal funds rate by 0.5% on October 8, 2008, and then by another 0.5% on October 29. On December 16, it lowered its target all the way to zero (a band of 0 to 0.25%), where it has stayed for seven years. Why was it concerned about the federal funds rate falling below its target rate when it was in the process of dropping its target rate to zero?

Moreover, in October 2008 the economy was moving into free fall. Real gross domestic product (GDP) fell at an annual rate of 8.2% in the fourth quarter of 2008 and unemployment was increasing rapidly. The Fed explained that it reduced the federal funds rate to zero "in order to provide stimulus to household and business spending and so support economic recovery." So why was the Fed giving the banks an incentive to keep their excess reserves at the Fed rather than lend them out?

The Fed's action can perhaps be understood by examining how it interprets its objectives. In addition to its mandates affecting employment and inflation, the Fed is also responsible for promoting financial stability. For the Fed, this means easing panic in financial markets, but also protecting the viability and profitability of the banks, especially those judged to be systemically important.

Promoting financial stability in the fall of 2008 meant the necessary step of intervening aggressively to prevent the collapse of the global financial system. But the Fed also interpreted it to mean bailing out large banks, even if the process did not sufficiently curtail the banks' power and risky practices. And it meant paying interest on reserves. Such payments directly boosted bank profitability, even if they may have come at the expense of the broader economy.

### The Classic Method of Affecting Interest Rates: Change the Level of Bank Reserves

Banks are required to hold cash in proportion to the amount of their deposits. This cash is termed bank reserves. (Currently, the reserve requirement is 10% of the total amount deposited in checking accounts.) Banks hold some of this cash in their vaults in order to meet requests for withdrawals, but typically much of it is held as deposits with the Fed.

Some banks hold more reserves than they need to satisfy reserve requirements, but some find themselves with a deficit. Those banks needing reserves typically borrow them from banks with a surplus. The interest rate that banks charge to lend their reserves to other banks is called the federal funds rate.

When the Fed wants to lower the federal funds rate, as it did in 2007-08, it buys government securities and writes a check to the seller. When the seller deposits the check in a bank, the bank sends the check to the Fed, which then credits the bank with more reserves. A greater amount of reserves in the banking system reduces the need for borrowing to meet reserve requirements, and the federal funds rate falls.

Likewise, when the Fed wants to increase the federal funds rate, it sells government securities. The buyer gives a check to the Fed written on the buyer's bank, and the Fed reduces the amount of reserves the bank has on deposit with the Fed. The bank, now short of reserves, seeks to borrow them from other banks and is willing to pay an increased federal funds rate in order to do so.

The reserves not needed to meet reserve requirements are called excess reserves. Up to 2008, the Fed did not pay any interest on excess reserves. To earn interest, banks lent out the cash to businesses and consumers and thereby encouraged greater spending. In this way, excess reserves were usually kept relatively low.

# The Implications of Quantitative Easing

With the federal funds rate at zero, the Federal Reserve began its program of "quantitative easing." This involved buying longer-term assets, U.S. Treasury securities as well as mortgage-backed securities. The Fed's stated objective was to reduce long-term interest rates so as to stimulate spending in housing and business investment.

There were three stages of quantitative easing, and interest rates did indeed fall. But, again, the Fed also had its eye on the banks. After the financial crisis, the demand for mortgage-backed securities fell, since massive numbers of mortgages were in default and payments on the securities were therefore down. As demand fell, the prices of the mortgage-backed securities plummeted. Many of the banks held large quantities of these securities. By purchasing so many of them, the Fed supported their prices and increased their value on the banks' balance sheets.

As a result of its quantitative easing programs, the Fed dramatically expanded its holding of assets. At the end of 2008, it owned less than half a trillion dollars in Treasury securities and no mortgage-backed securities. By November 2015, it held $2.5 trillion in Treasuries and $1.8 trillion in mortgage-backed securities. Because buying all these securities meant that the Fed's checks became reserves for the banks, and because the banks were paid for keeping these reserves with the Fed, excess reserves ballooned to $2.5 trillion.

The Fed's announcement on December 16 that it is raising its target for the federal funds rate does bring to the fore Bernanke's concern in 2008: how to increase the federal funds rate when there are so many excess reserves. The Fed ruled out any largescale reduction of excess reserves when it also announced on December 16 that it would not be reducing its large holdings of securities. By not selling securities, the Fed would not be accepting checks from bank accounts and thus not reducing the reserves the banks hold on deposit with the Fed.

The Fed's solution, instead, is to double down and increase the payment of interest on bank reserves. It announced that it will begin paying interest on reserves at 0.5%. This procedure won't reduce reserves, but will give banks an incentive not to make loans at interest rates below the amount they can get from the Fed.

However, this will not totally solve the Fed's problem. Even when it was paying the banks 0.25% interest on reserves, the effective federal funds rate (the rate at which reserves at the Fed were actually being traded) was below 0.25%. This is why the Fed adopted a range for the federal funds rate of 0-0.25%.

The reason the Fed could not keep the federal funds rate at 0.25% was because financial institutions other than banks participate in the federal funds market. In particular, government-sponsored enterprises (GSEs) like Fannie Mae, Freddie Mac, and the Federal Home Loan Banks are allowed to keep funds at the Fed but are not paid interest on them. In recent years the Home Loan Banks have become the main lender in the federal funds market. (They were established during the Depression to lend to savings and loan associations to support housing, but now lend mainly to banks.)

The Home Loan Banks were able to lend federal funds at interest rates below 0.25% and still make a profit. In turn, banks were able to take the borrowed funds and deposit them with the Fed at 0.25%, making a profit as well.

So when the Fed on December 16 established a range of 0.25-0.50% for the federal funds rate, it also announced a new procedure designed to keep the federal funds rate from falling below 0.25%. The new procedure is to conduct overnight reverse repurchase agreements (ON RRP) with the Home Loan Banks (as well as with banks, other GSEs, and money market mutual funds, which are important lenders in short-term markets).

ON RRP is an imposing-sounding term, but reflects a relatively simple process: the Fed sells government securities to the financial institutions on one day and then buys them back the next. The financial institutions are essentially making an overnight loan to the Fed, with the securities as collateral.

But here's the point: the money the Fed pays to buy back the securities is not only a repayment of the original loan. It also includes an interest payment. And the Fed plans to pay interest at 0.25%, the bottom of its target for the fed funds rate, thus giving the Home Loan Banks an incentive not to lend at less than 0.25%. Although it plans to use ON RRP as a secondary tool to its main focus of paying interest on bank reserves, it anticipates that both of these tools will keep the fed funds rate within its target range of 0.25-0.5%.

It seems that the Fed has backed itself into a corner, where the only way to raise the federal funds rate is to increase its payments to financial institutions. With reserves held at the Fed equal to $2.6 trillion, even a 0.5% payment to the banks would cost $13 billion. And, of course, including the expense of the ON RRP program and increasing the fed funds rate in the future would add even more to the cost.

To add insult to injury, 25 minutes after the Fed's announcement on December 16, Wells Fargo Bank reported that it is raising its prime rate (an interest rate tied to business and consumer loans) by 0.25% but not the rates it pays to depositors. Later in the day other large banks, including JP Morgan Chase and Bank of America, made similar declarations.

## Is There an Alternative?

Could the Fed, instead, choose not to pay interest to the banks and other financial institutions? This would have the effect of reducing excess reserves, but it would also mean that the Fed would have to delay raising interest rates.

That would, in fact, be a good policy decision. Although the unemployment rate is 5.0%, inflation is still below the Fed's 2% target. In the late 1990s, under then-Chair Alan Greenspan, the Fed allowed unemployment to fall below 4% without an appreciable increase in inflation. If the Fed waits, it could see how far excess reserves would fall without the payment of interest on reserves and how far the unemployment rate would fall without pushing inflation above 2%.

But what if a growing economy and a falling rate of unemployment edged the inflation rate past 2%, say, to 3 or 4%? The top 1% of the income distribution would not like inflation to eat away at their accumulated wealth. However, during times of very low unemployment the demand for workers can be strong enough to push money wages up faster than prices, so workers without a job and those who haven't seen a raise in many years would probably not be unhappy.

Under current Chair Janet Yellen, the Federal Reserve has shown a genuine concern about unemployment, but it is still trapped in its assumptions: There is a "maximum feasible" level of employment. Above that level (or below the corresponding rate of unemployment) inflation will exceed its 2% target. The conclusion from these assumptions is that the Fed should raise interest rates to prevent employment from exceeding the "maximum feasible" level.

Instead, the Fed should adopt a real full-employment target: a job for everyone who wants to work. It should adopt a "minimum feasible" target for inflation: the lowest possible rate compatible with full employment. We need a policy perspective in which economic justice for workers is a higher priority than paying the banks. ❑

Article 7.6

# INFLATION TARGETING AND NEOLIBERALISM

## BY GERALD EPSTEIN
May 2016

**I**n recent decades, central banks in both high-income ("developed") and lower-income ("developing") countries have turned increasingly towards "inflation targeting" monetary policy—the emphasis on very low inflation, to the exclusion of other policy objectives. In this interview, Gerald Epstein, a professor of economics at UMass-Amherst and a founding co-director of the Political Economy Research Institute (PERI) explains the causes behind the rise of inflation targeting, its effects in practice, and possible alternative approaches. —Eds.

**Dollars & Sense:** When we talk about central banks and monetary policy, what precisely is meant by the phrase "inflation targeting"? And how does that differ from other kinds of objectives that central banks might have?

**Gerald Epstein:** Inflation targeting is a relatively new but very widespread approach to central bank policy. It means that the central bank should target a rate of inflation—sometimes it's a range, not one particular number, but a pretty narrow range—and that should be its only target. It should use its instruments—usually a short-term interest rate—to achieve that target and it should avoid using monetary policy to do anything else.

So what are some of the other things that central banks have done besides try to meet an inflation target? Well, the United States Federal Reserve, for example, has a mandate to reach two targets—the so-called "dual mandate"—one is a stable price level, which is the same as an inflation target, and the other is high employment. So this is a dual mandate. After the financial crisis there's a third presumption, that the Federal Reserve will look at financial stability as well. Other central banks historically have tried to promote exports by targeting a cheap exchange rate. Some people have accused the Chinese government of doing this but many other developing countries have targeted an exchange rate to keep an undervalued exchange rate and promote exports. Other countries have tried to promote broad-based development by supporting government policy. So there's a whole range of targets that, historically, central banks have used.

**D&S:** Has inflation targeting gone hand-in-hand not only with prioritizing price stability over other kinds of objectives, but also an emphasis on very low rates of inflation?

**GE:** That's right. In practice, what inflation-targeting advocates have argued for is an extremely low rate of inflation. For example, the European Central Bank has a 2% target, or to keep inflation in fact just below 2%, and typically what is called for is inflation in the low single digits. In developing countries, targets have ranged from 4% to 8%. So these are targets for inflation that are very low compared to broad historical experience. These days, very low inflation and indeed the threat of deflation in some countries have raised all kinds of issues about this inflation targeting approach.

I see this as part of a whole neoliberal approach to central banking. That is, the idea that the economy is inherently stable, it will inherently reach full employment and stable economic growth on its own, and so the only thing that the macro policymakers have to worry about is keeping a low inflation rate and everything else will take care of itself. Of course, as we've seen, this whole neoliberal approach to macroeconomic policy is badly mistaken.

**D&S:** Why have we seen inflation targeting become more prevalent in monetary policy making, both in high-income and lower-income countries, in recent years? What are the key arguments that are made by advocates of inflation targeting in favor of that approach? And what might be some underlying political and economic causes, even apart from those arguments?

**GE:** It's been a real revolution in central bank policy and, as I said earlier, it's in my view part and parcel of the whole neoliberal trend in macroeconomic policy. The essential thing underlying this, in my view, is to try to reduce the power of government and social forces that might exercise some power within the political economy—workers and peasants and others—and put the power primarily in the hands of those dominating in the markets. That's often the financial system, the banks, but also other elites.

The idea of neoliberal economists and policymakers is that you don't want the government getting too involved in macroeconomic policy. You don't want them promoting too much employment because that might lead to a raise in wages and, in turn, to a reduction in the profit share of the national income. So, sure, this might increase inflation, but inflation is not really the key issue here. The problem, in their view, is letting the central bank support other kinds of policies that are going to enhance the power of workers, people who work in agricultural areas, and even sometimes manufacturing interests. Instead, they want to put power in the hands of those who dominate the markets, often the financial elites.

That is, of course, not what the advocates of inflation targeting say publicly. What the advocates say is, "Look, inflation is harmful. We've got to keep a low and stable rate of inflation in order to promote economic growth." They build on the neoclassical, New Keynesian, or even New Classical approaches to macroeconomic policy that say the market economy is stable in and of itself, so government intervention can only mess things up. So there's only one thing left to do—there's only one thing on the "to do" list for macroeconomic policy—and that is to keep a stable inflation rate, so let's assign the central bank to do that and not to do anything else, and the capitalist economy will take care of itself.

This approach, I think, really has contributed to enormous financial instability. Notice that this inflation targeting targets commodity inflation. But what about asset bubbles, that is, asset inflation? There's no attempt to reduce asset bubbles like we had in subprime or in real estate bubbles in various countries. That is another kind of inflation that could have been targeted.

Of course, we know that the capitalist economy does not achieve full employment on its own. So why not target higher employment? In South Africa, for example, they have unemployment rates of 25 or 26%. They have an inflation-targeting regime to keep inflation in the low single digits, rather than targeting employment. It makes no sense at all.

The other argument that inflation-targeting advocates make is a government failure argument. Even if you concede that the economy won't do perfectly on its own, any time the government gets involved in the market economy they just mess it up. So, they argue, let's just have a minimalist kind of government intervention and at least the government will do no harm. I think this is a common argument as well. But as we know, there have been many successful government interventions in South Korea and China and elsewhere where governments working with a financial system and other actors in the economy have played a crucial role in economic development. The government-failure arguments, I think, have now been shown to be pretty fallacious. Olivier Blanchard, who was the chief economist at the IMF said we had this beautiful illusion that all we needed is one target, that is low inflation, and one interest rate, that is a short-term interest-rate, and everything would be OK. Well, after the crisis, we now know that we need multiple targets and we need multiple tools to achieve our goals.

*D&S:* Hasn't it been a central concern on the part of elites in capitalist countries, at least in those where there is representative government, that the majority could impose its will and force policymakers to prioritize full employment and wage growth (as opposed to, say, "sound money")? Has the transition toward inflation targeting been accompanied by institutional changes to "wall off" monetary policy from those kinds of popular pressures?

**GE:** Yeah, I think that's a very important point here. Inflation targeting ideas have also been often accompanied by the idea that central banks should be "independent"—that is, independent from the government. I think you'll find that these two things go hand-in-hand.

If you look at the whole list of central bank rules that the International Monetary Fund (IMF) and others have advocated for developing countries, the argument goes like this: You want to have an independent central bank. Well, what should this independent central-bank do? It should target inflation. Well, isn't this anti-democratic? No, what we're really saying is that central bankers should have instrument independence, that is, the ability to decide how they'll achieve their target. The government should set the target, but what should target be? Well, the consensus is that the target should be a low rate of inflation. So that's a nice little package designed to prevent the central bank from doing such things as helping to finance government infrastructure investment or government deficits. It's designed to prevent the central bank from keeping interest rates "too low," which might actually contribute to more rapid economic growth or more productivity growth, but might lead to somewhat higher inflation.

Where do they get this low inflation rate from? There's no economic evidence, in fact—and there have been lots of studies—to demonstrate that an inflation rate in the low single digits is optimal for economic growth in most countries, certainly not in developing countries. Some early studies—and this has been replicated many times—have suggested that inflation rates of up to 15%, even 20%, as long as they're relatively steady, don't harm economic growth. They might even contribute to it. So this is a kind of strait-jacket that these forces are trying to put the central bank in, in order to prevent them from making policies in the interest of a broader part of the economy. And it's just one plank in the macroeconomic neoliberal straitjacket. The other plank, of course, is no fis-cal deficits. So you limit what government can do—no fiscal deficits or low fiscal defi-cits—you limit what the central bank can do—only target low inflation—and you've pretty much made it impossible for the government to engage in macroeconomic policy that's going to have a broad-based supportive effect on the economy.

**D&S:** What is the record of inflation targeting policy in practice, in terms of eco-nomic outcomes we can actually observe, in both developing and so-called devel-oped countries?

**GE:** The first thing to realize, I think, is that inflation-targeting approaches have been devastating in the reaction to the financial crisis of 2007-2008, particularly in Europe. There you had, an extreme case where the European Central Bank (ECB) mandate was to target inflation—period—and nothing else. And indeed to keep inflation in the low single digits, less than 2%. And what this did—along with other rules, other problems in Europe, not just this—was give the ECB the cover to do very little in terms of fighting the crisis when it hit, to in fact raise interest rates within the first year after the crisis hit. And it took the ECB several years before it finally realized the disaster that had befallen Europe and, when Mario Draghi finally came in as president of the ECB in 2011, to do whatever it takes to keep the euro going. It took a break from this kind of orthodoxy for them to begin to turn around Europe. (As we can now see Europe is still in ter-rible shape.)

Second, the single-minded focus on inflation in Europe and in other countries made them ignore the financial bubble, the asset bubbles that were occurring. Cen-tral bankers said, "Well, you know, that's not my department. I'll just worry about commodity inflation. I won't worry about other kinds of inflation because that's not my mandate." They had this tunnel vision, not seeing what else was going on around them in the economy.

In developing countries, there's pretty strong evidence that real interest rates have been higher than they would have been otherwise. There's some evidence that economic growth is lower in a number of developing countries than it would have been otherwise, because real interest rates have been so high. And there is some evi-dence that this has contributed to a redistribution of income towards the rentiers, that is, to the bankers and the financiers, and away from others because real interest rates have been so high and inflation has been relatively low. Most of the evidence suggests that it has had a negative consequence for working people and others in de-veloping countries as well.

In the end, the negative impacts have been mitigated to some extent by the fact that a lot of central banks, in developing countries particularly, claim to be following a very strict inflation-targeting regime but in fact they've been "cheating." Almost all of them target exchange rates to some extent because they know they can't let their exchange rates get too overvalued or otherwise that is going to hurt their exports and cause other problems. They've been fiddling with the inflation data, or exactly what kind of inflation target they use, etc. In some ways it's a bit of a ruse. For developing countries, it's saying to the IMF, "OK, we're doing what you're telling us." Saying to the global financial markets, to the global investors, "OK we're doing this orthodox thing, but (wink wink) if we really did this all the time in a strict way it would be suicide so we're not going to really do this completely." So they're finally is a recognition, I think, that inflation targeting is a very destructive practice.

**D&S:** In your view, then, what would be a preferable approach to central bank policy—what priorities should central banks have and how should they go about achieving these aims?

**GE:** Central banks should be free and open, in conjunction with their governments, to identify the key problems facing their own countries, the key obstacles to social and economic development, and developing tools and targets that are appropriate to dealing with those problems. And these are going to differ from country to country. So, for example, in South Africa, my colleague Bob Pollin, James Heintz, Leonce Ndikumana, and I did a study a number of years ago: We proposed an employment-targeting regime for the central bank. The Reserve Bank of South Africa, in conjunction with the government of South Africa, would develop a set of policies and tools—such as credit allocation policies, subsidized credit, lower interest rates, capital controls to keep the capital in the country, more expansionary and targeted fiscal policy—so that monetary policy and fiscal policy would work hand-in-hand to lower the massively high unemployment rate in South Africa. That's an example of an alternative structure for monetary policy and one that has worked for other developing countries. So, for example, in South Korea in the 1950s ,1960s, and 1970s, the central bank supported the government's industrial policy—by lending to development banks that would lend to export industries, by subsidizing credit for export industries, and they would do this as part of the government plan to develop the economy. I call this developmental central banking, that is, central banking that in combination with the government is oriented to developing the country using a variety of tools—interest rates, credit allocation tools, etc.

Not all countries would do the same thing. It not only depends on the country, but also on the problems of the historical conjuncture. So take the United States for example. Right now we do have for the Federal Reserve a dual mandate, which some Republicans are trying to get rid of, for high employment and stable prices. But the financial intermediation system is broken because of what happened in the crisis. Interest rates are down to zero but banks aren't lending to the real economy. People aren't able to borrow from banks for small businesses and so forth. The Federal Reserve, through quantitative easing, bought a lot of financial assets but it's probably time for the Fed to develop new tools, to give direct credit to small businesses, for infrastructure development, etc.

It is the case now, with the crisis and with negative interest rates, or very low interest rates, central banks are being much more experimental trying to develop new tools, new approaches. But they're all doing it under the guise of inflation targeting. European central bankers were doing all these wild monetary experiments, but their goal was really just to get inflation up to 2%. In fact, what's happening is that this inflation targeting is no longer the guiding post for central banks. They need to have much broader sets of tools and targets to get out of this terrible slump that most of these economies are in. ❑

*Article 7.7*

# KEYNES AND THE LIMITS OF MONETARY POLICY

## BY ALEJANDRO REUSS
*April 2009*

As the United States has plunged into financial crisis and the deepest recession since the Great Depression, the U.S. Federal Reserve (the "Fed") has pursued an aggressively "expansionary" monetary policy. Monetary policy refers to government policies affecting the money supply or interest rates. Expansionary monetary policy is aimed at increasing the money supply or lowering interest rates. The idea is that, by lowering interest rates, the government can stimulate investment (such as firms' purchases of new equipment and construction of new plant). Projects that would not be profitable for a company if it had to borrow at a higher interest rate could be profitable if borrowing were less costly. Fed policymakers hope, then, that lower interest rates will encourage investment and bring about renewed economic growth.

The main interest rate the Fed targets is the "federal funds rate," the interest rate that banks charge each other for overnight loans. For all of 2006 and 2007, the federal funds rate stood at over 4%. In the course of 2008, as the financial crisis and recession grew deeper, the Fed moved aggressively to cut interest rates. By the end of the year, the federal funds rate was 0.0-0.25%, where it remains today. Even with the federal funds rate basically at zero, however, the economy has spiraled deeper into recession. GDP shrank at an annual rate of 6.2% in the fourth quarter of 2008 and the official unemployment rate climbed to 8.5% by March 2009.

## Are Interest Rates Coming Down?

Firms and consumers cannot borrow at the federal funds rate. Then why does the Fed try to bring down the federal funds rate when it wants to stimulate economic activity? Fed policymakers hope that by pulling down very short-term interest rates that do not directly affect firms and consumers, they can indirectly pull down longer-term interest rates that are important to firms and consumers.

Interest rates on 30-year fixed-rate mortgages have declined, reaching historic lows under 5% in March 2009. The low mortgage rates, however, may be deceptive. Mortgage lenders have generally tightened lending standards, and the low rates are only available to borrowers that banks consider very safe. Other borrowers may pay rates several percentage points higher, or be unable to borrow at all. Meanwhile, banks have raised credit-card interest rates and dramatically tightened borrowing limits.

Key corporate interest rates have not come down as the Fed hoped. Moody's AAA bond rate, an index of the interest rates on long-term bonds for low-risk corporate borrowers, was about the same in March 2009 as in January 2008 (about 5.3%). Moody's Baa bond rate, the equivalent index or higher-risk corporate borrowers, has gone from about 6.5% in January 2008 to over 8% in March 2009. The spreads between these rates and the federal funds rate have increased dramatically as the federal funds rate has fallen.

That would come as no surprise to John Maynard Keynes. Keynes argued, in *The General Theory of Employment, Interest, and Money* (1936), that during boom periods the general estimation of risk by both lenders and borrowers is "apt to become unusually and imprudently low." Lenders loan out money freely, even recklessly, accepting a low rate of interest relative to the risk involved. During crisis periods, on the other hand, lenders often become much more risk-averse, parting with their money less freely, and insisting on a higher rate of interest in exchange for the risk of not being paid back. This is sometimes known as the "flight to liquidity" or "flight to safety." Keynes' analysis suggests that during economic crises the interest rates on assets that are considered very safe—like government bonds—are apt to go down, since people are looking to avoid losses and willing to accept a low rate of return to do so. But the interest rates on riskier assets may go up. A rise in the interest rates that firms or consumers pay would tend to deepen—rather than correct—an economic downturn.

## Can't the Fed Do More?

If interest rates are not low enough to turn the economy around, then why doesn't the Fed increase the money supply some more—until interest rates *are* low enough? The answer is that nominal interest rates can reach a lower bound below which they cannot decline further. (The "nominal" interest rate, in contrast to the "real" interest rate, does not account for changes in the purchasing power of the dollar due to inflation.) This lower bound can be greater than 0%, but cannot be lower than 0%. The federal funds rate is now about 0%. When interest rates reach this lower limit, the economy is commonly described as being caught in a "liquidity trap."

People hold their wealth in the form of bonds rather than money because they can earn interest on bonds. For example, you may be able to buy a bond for $100 that promises a payment of $110 in one year. That gives you a 10% annual interest rate (you loaned the bond issuer $100 for a year, and at the end of the year get your $100 back plus $10 interest). That is the incentive to buy the bond instead of just holding money.

Suppose the Fed wants to lower interest rates to stimulate spending. It offers to buy government bonds (previously sold to the public) at a higher price, driving down the interest rate. For instance, the Fed might offer $110 for bonds that promise $110 in one year. If you were to buy such a bond at the new price of $110, you would receive the same amount of money back a year later. The interest rate on that bond is now 0%. The idea of the policy is that banks will sell their government bonds to the Fed at the new higher price, take the money and buy other bonds (such as those issued by corporations), driving up their price and lowering the interest rate on those bonds.

Imagine that the Fed, however, decided that an interest rate of 0% was not low enough, and decided instead to pay banks $120 for bonds that promise $110 in a year. The banks would gladly sell their bonds, so the money supply would increase. But they would not loan out the money they received at a negative interest rate (paying consumers or firms to borrow from them). They would be better off just keeping the money in their vaults. In other words, once the interest rate reaches 0%, there is nothing more that the government can do with conventional expansionary monetary policy. That is the liquidity trap—any extra liquidity (money) the Fed makes available gets trapped, instead of being loaned out.

## Monetary Policy and Interest Rates Today

Economic journalists and commentators have inaccurately described "interest rates" as being at or near 0% these days. The federal funds rate has hit rock bottom, but other interest rates clearly have not. Keynes was acutely aware that, when monetary authorities limit themselves to buying short-term securities, the "effect may ... be mainly confined to the very short-term rate of interest and have but little reaction on the much more important long-term rates of interest."

In a famous passage in *The General Theory*, Keynes notes the possibility that "after the rate of interest has fallen to a certain level ... almost everyone prefers cash to holding a debt which yields so low a rate of interest." This passage is often taken to be Keynes' description of the liquidity trap. He goes on to say that he did not know of any case when this had actually happened and notes that it is not likely to happen "owing to the unwillingness of most monetary authorities to deal boldly in debts of long term." It is clear from this passage that Keynes was not describing merely a situation in which certain short-term interest rates targeted by the government (such as the federal funds rate) were pushed to their lower limits, but rather one in which all interest rates hit rock bottom—a different situation from what is commonly referred to as a "liquidity trap" today.

Keynes viewed monetary policymakers' focus on certain short-run interest rates not as an inherent limitation in monetary policy, but as a limitation in the ways monetary policy was conventionally practiced. He notes that governments did not usually buy long-term bonds and drive down long-term interest rates, but that there was no reason they could not. In March, the Fed actually began to do just that, buying billions in long-term government securities in an attempt to bring down long-term rates. The 10-year Treasury bond rate dropped dramatically (from about 3% to 2.5%) the day the purchases began. It has increased somewhat since then, but remains lower than it was before November 2008.

Any attempt to revive private investment by manipulating interest rates, however, faces at least two additional barriers:

First, the interest rates consumers and firms pay do not move in lockstep with interest rates on government securities, either short-term or long-term. The contrast between short-term and long-term bonds is not the same as the difference between relatively safe government bonds and riskier corporate bonds or consumer loans. As we have seen, interest rates on corporate bonds have failed to decline, even as rates on long-term government bonds have declined. Banks' consumer lending standards, likewise, have tightened even as the Fed has driven down interest rates on government bonds.

Second, economic activity simply may not change dramatically in response to changes in interest rates, especially during a recession. Expectations of future sales and profits are extremely negative, so firms are dramatically slashing payrolls and investment spending. Total employment has decreased by over ½ million people for each of five consecutive months from November 2008 to March 2009. Nonresidential fixed investment decreased by over 20% in the last quarter of 2008; investment in nonresidential structures by nearly 10%. Firms have inventories they cannot sell, are laying off workers, and are producing below their existing productive capacity. Most of them are not going to make large investments in new plant and equipment under such conditions.

For these reasons, Keynesian economists have advocated a very large fiscal stimulus. Fiscal policy, in contrast to monetary policy, involves government spending and taxation. A fiscal stimulus program involves increases in government spending or reductions in taxes. Keynesian economists, believing that monetary policy is not adequate to pull the economy out of its current crisis, have argued especially for a dramatic increase in government spending as the surest way to revive overall spending, production, and employment. ❑

*Sources:* John Maynard Keynes, *The General Theory of Employment, Interest, and Money*, First Harvest/Harcourt, 1964; The Federal Reserve Bank, Intended federal funds rate, Change and level, 1990 to present; Bureau of Economic Analysis, News Release: Gross Domestic Product (GDP) and Corporate Profits, March 26, 2009; Bureau of Labor Statistics, Table A-12, Alternative measures of labor underutilization; Luke Mullins, "Banks Tighten Mortgage Lending Standards," *U.S. News and World Report*, Feb. 2, 2009; Jeannine Aversa and Alan Zibel, "Mortgage rates down, but standards remain high," Associated Press, Press-Telegram (Long Beach, CA), March 19, 2009; Bob Tedeschi, "Mortgages: 'Cashing Out' is Now Harder," *New York Times*, March 19, 2009; Kathy Chu, "Changing credit card terms squeeze consumers," *USA Today*, Dec. 16, 2008; Jane J. Kim, "BofA to Boost Rates on Cards With Balances," *Wall Street Journal*, April 9, 2009; Federal Reserve Bank of St. Louis, Moody's Seasoned Aaa Corporate Bond Yield; Federal Reserve Bank of St. Louis, Moody's Seasoned Baa Corporate Bond Yield; Paul Krugman (blog), "Spreads," Jan. 19, 2009; Jon Hilsenrath, "Fed in Bond-Buying Binge to Spur Growth," *Wall Street Journal*, March 19, 2009; Paul Krugman (blog), "Return of depression economics," March 4, 2009; Federal Reserve Bank of St. Louis, Ten-Year Treasury Constant Maturity Rate; Bureau of Labor Statistics, Payroll Employment; Bureau of Economic Analysis, News Release: Gross Domestic Product (GDP) and Corporate Profits, March 26, 2009.

# Chapter 8

# SAVINGS, INVESTMENT, AND FINANCE

## INTRODUCTION

In the orderly world of classical macroeconomics, capital markets—governed by all-powerful interest rates—work seamlessly to assure that saving is matched by investment, fueling growth in the private economy, which in turn guarantees full employment. Should the flow of saving exceed the uptake of investment, falling interest rates automatically solve the problem.

In the real world, economies are far messier than classical macroeconomics suggests. Keynes argued that there is no neat connection, or "nexus," between savings and investment in a modern financial economy. Savings often sit, hoarded and uninvested. And interest rates, no matter how low, seldom coax balky investors to lay out their money in a weak economy. In the Keynesian world, economies regularly suffer from investment shortfalls that lead to recessions and cost workers their jobs.

Ramaa Vasudevan provides a primer on the increased importance of financial markets, financial institutions, and financial elites in today's economy and its governing institutions. The fact that failed financial corporations have received massive bailouts, for Vasudevan, only underlines the power they wield in the era of "financialization" (Article 8.1).

Gerald Epstein (Article 8.2) discusses not only the dramatic growth in the size of the financial sector, but also the transformation from regulated "boring" banking to deregulated "roaring" banking. Epstein argues that the current system has ill-served the economy and society, and calls for regulation of private finance and development of alternative financial institutions as two parts of the needed solution.

Economist Marty Wolfson gives a down-to-earth description of the financial instruments and deregulatory measures at the heart of the current economic crisis. He calls for a regulatory structure that puts limits on financial risk and manipulation (Article 8.3).

Alejandro Reuss (Article 8.4) takes a look back at economist John Maynard Keynes' understanding of financial instability—especially financial "bubbles"— a major problem in the U.S. economy. Reuss argues that bubbles have been a key driver of demand in the U.S. economy in recent decades, and so it will require deeper changes than just financial regulation to solve this problem.

Robert Pollin reviews the insights of economist Hyman Minsky on the tendency toward excessive financial risk-taking during economic booms (Article 8.5).

Minsky pointed to government regulation as a substitute for the discipline of the market (which reins in risk-taking only through ruinous financial crashes).

Finally, Nina Eichacker explains how the boom-and-bust cycle of capitalist economies has been adrenalized by the deregulation of finance (Article 8.6). As Eichacker argues in her study of Iceland's financial collapse, no country has the institutional capacity to cope with the instability inherent in a deregulated and "supercharged" financial system.

## Discussion Questions

1. (Article 8.1) What is "financialization"? How does it manifest itself in today's economy? How did it contribute to the recent financial crisis?

2. (Article 8.2) "Roaring" sounds better than "boring." Why does Epstein believe that "boring" banking is better than "roaring" banking?

3. (Article 8.3) What exactly is a "derivative" and what role did derivatives play in the financial crisis?

4. (Article 8.4) Some economists argue that financial market instability is the result of "irrational" investor behavior. Did Keynes agree?

5. (Article 8.5) Why do financial companies tend to engage in excessive risk-taking during economic booms? If financial crashes are too harmful to tolerate, and bailouts (to prevent or contain a crash) only encourage further risky behavior, what are the alternatives?

6. (Article 8.6) Why did government, business media, and international institutions all profess that Iceland's financial deregulation posed little threat to the country's economic stability? Was this a simple "mistake," or was there more to it than that?

*Article 8.1*

# FINANCIALIZATION: A PRIMER

## BY RAMAA VASUDEVAN
*November/December 2008*

You don't have to be an investor dabbling in the stock market to feel the power of finance. Finance pervades the lives of ordinary people in many ways, from student loans and credit card debt to mortgages and pension plans.

And its size and impact are only getting bigger. Consider a few measures:

- U.S. credit market debt—all debt of private households, businesses, and government combined—rose from about 1.6 times the nation's GDP in 1973 to over 3.5 times GDP by 2007.
- The profits of the financial sector represented 14% of total corporate profits in 1981; by 2001-02 this figure had risen to nearly 50%.

These are only a few of the indicators of what many commentators have labeled the "financialization" of the economy—a process University of Massachusetts economist Gerald Epstein succinctly defines as "the increasing importance of financial markets, financial motives, financial institutions, and financial elites in the operation of the economy and its governing institutions."

In recent years, this phenomenon has drawn increasing attention. In his latest book, pundit Kevin Phillips writes about the growing divergence between the real (productive) and financial economies, describing how the explosion of trading in myriad new financial instruments played a role in polarizing the U.S. economy. On the left, political economists Harry Magdoff and Paul Sweezy had over many years pointed to the growing role of finance in the operations of capitalism; they viewed the trend as a reflection of the rising economic and political power of "rentiers"—those whose earnings come from financial activities and from forms of income arising from ownership claims (such as interest, rent, dividends, or capital gains) rather than from actual production.

## From Finance to Financialization

The financial system is supposed to serve a range of functions in the broader economy. Banks and other financial institutions mop up savings, then allocate that capital, according to mainstream theory, to where it can most productively be used. For households and corporations, the credit markets facilitate greatly increased borrowing, which should foster investment in capital goods like buildings and machinery, in turn leading to expanded production. Finance, in other words, is supposed to facilitate the growth of the "real" economy—the part that produces useful goods (like bicycles) and services (like medical care).

In recent decades, finance has undergone massive changes in both size and shape. The basic mechanism of financialization is the transformation of future streams of income (from profits, dividends, or interest payments) into a tradable asset like a stock or a bond. For example, the future earnings of corporations are transmuted into equity stocks that are bought and sold in the capital market. Likewise, a loan, which involves certain fixed interest payments over its duration, gets a new life when it is converted into marketable bonds. And multiple loans, bundled together then "sliced and diced" into novel kinds of bonds ("collateralized debt obligations"), take on a new existence as investment vehicles that bear an extremely complex and opaque relationship to the original loans.

The process of financialization has not made finance more effective at fulfilling what conventional economic theory views as its core function. Corporations are not turning to the stock market as a source of finance for their investments, and their borrowing in the bond markets is often not for the purpose of productive investment either. Since the 1980s, corporations have actually spent more money buying back their own stock than they have taken in by selling newly issued stock. The granting of stock options to top executives gives them a direct incentive to have the corporation buy back its own shares—often using borrowed money to do so—in order to hike up the share price and allow them to turn a profit on the sale of their personal shares. More broadly, instead of fostering investment, financialization reorients managerial incentives toward chasing short-term returns through financial trading and speculation so as to generate ballooning earnings, lest their companies face falling stock prices and the threat of hostile takeover.

What is more, the workings of these markets tend to act like an upper during booms, when euphoric investors chase the promise of quick bucks. During downturns these same mechanisms work like downers, turning euphoria into panic as investors flee. Financial innovations like collateralized debt obligations were supposed to "lubricate" the economy by spreading risk, but instead they tend to heighten volatility, leading to amplified cycles of boom and bust. In the current crisis, the innovation of mortgage-backed securities fueled the housing bubble and encouraged enormous risk-taking, creating the conditions for the chain reaction of bank (and other financial institution) failures that may be far from over.

## Financialization and Power

The arena of finance can at times appear to be merely a casino—albeit a huge one—where everyone gets to place her bets and ride her luck. But the financial system carries a far deeper significance for people's lives. Financial assets and liabilities represent claims on ownership and property; they embody the social relations of an economy at a particular time in history. In this sense, the recent process of financialization implies the increasing political and economic power of a particular segment of the capitalist class: rentiers. Accelerating financial transactions and the profusion of financial techniques have fuelled an extraordinary enrichment of this elite.

This enrichment arises in different ways. Financial transactions facilitate the reallocation of capital to high-return ventures. In the ensuing shake-up, some sectors of capital profit at the expense of other sectors. More important, the capitalist class as a whole is able to force a persistent redistribution in its favor, deploying its newly expanded wealth to bring about changes in the political-economy that channel even more wealth its way.

The structural changes that paved the way for financialization involved the squashing of working-class aspirations during the Reagan-Thatcher years; the defeats of the miners' strike in England and of the air traffic controllers' (PATCO) strike in the United States were perhaps the most symbolic instances of this process. At the same time, these and other governments increasingly embraced the twin policy mantras of fighting inflation and deregulating markets in place of creating full employment and raising wages. Corporations pushed through legislation to dismantle the financial regulations that inhibited their profitmaking strategies.

Financialization has gathered momentum amid greater inequality. In the United States, the top 1% of the population received 14.0% of the national after-tax income in 2004, nearly double its 7.5% share in 1979. In the same period the share of the bottom fifth fell from 6.8% to 4.9%.

And yet U.S. consumption demand has been sustained despite rising inequality and a squeeze on real wages for the majority of households. Here is the other side of the financialization coin: a massive expansion of consumer credit has played an important role in easing the constraints on consumer spending by filling the gap created by stagnant or declining real wages. The credit card debt of the average U.S. family increased by 53% through the 1990s. About 67% of low-income families with incomes less than $10,000 faced credit card debt, and the debt of this group saw the largest increase—a 184% rise, compared to a 28% increase for families with incomes above $100,000. Offered more and more credit as a privatized means of addressing wage stagnation, then, eventually, burdened by debt and on the edge of insolvency, the working poor and the middle class are less likely to organize as a political force to challenge the dominance of finance. In this sense, financialization becomes a means of social coercion that erodes working-class solidarity.

As the structures created by financial engineering unravel, the current economic crisis is revealing the cracks in this edifice. But even as a growing number of U.S. families are losing their homes and jobs in the wake of the subprime meltdown, the financial companies at the heart of the crisis have been handed massive bailouts and their top executives have pocketed huge pay-outs despite their role in abetting the meltdown—a stark sign of the power structures and interests at stake in this era of financialization. ❏

*Sources:* Robin Blackburn, "Finance and the Fourth Dimension," *New Left Review* 39 May-June 2006; Robert Brenner, "New Boom or Bubble," *New Left Review* 25 Jan-Feb 2004; Tamara Draut and Javier Silva, "Borrowing to make ends meet," *Demos*, Sept 2003; Gerald Epstein, "Introduction" in G. Epstein, ed., *Financialization and the World Economy*, 2006; John Bellamy Foster, "The Financialization of Capitalism," *Monthly Review*, April 2007; Gretta Krippner, "The financialization of the US economy," *Socio-Economic Review* 3, Feb. 2005; Thomas Palley, "Financialization : What it is and why it matters," Political Economy Research Institute Working Paper #153, November 2007; A. Sherman and Arin Dine, "New CBO data shows inequality continues to widen," Center for Budget Priorities, Jan. 23, 2007; Kevin Phillips, *Bad Money: Reckless Finance, Failed Politics, and the Global Crisis of American Capitalism*, 2008.

*Article 8.2*

# FROM "BORING" BANKING TO "ROARING" BANKING
*How the Financial Sector Grew Out of Control, and How We Can Change It*

## AN INTERVIEW WITH GERALD EPSTEIN
May/June 2015

**G**erald Epstein is a professor of economics and a founding co-director of the Political
Economy Research Institute (PERI) at the University of Massachusetts-Amherst. He has
*written extensively about U.S. and global finance and recently delivered the Distinguished*
*Faculty Lecture at UMass-Amherst titled "When Big is Too Big: Do the Financial System's*
*Social Benefits Justify Its Size?" In April, he sat down with* Dollars & Sense *co-editor Ale-*
*jandro Reuss to discuss major themes in his current research—the dramatic growth in the fi-*
*nancial sector, the transformation from regulated "boring" banking to deregulated "roaring"*
*banking, the ways the current system has ill-served the economy and society, and the need for*
*regulation of private finance and development of alternative financial institutions.*

**Dollars & Sense:** What should we be looking at as indicators that the financial sector has grown much larger in this most recent era, compared to what it used to be?

**Gerald Epstein:** There are a number of different indicators and dimensions to this.
The size of the financial sector itself is one dimension. If you look at the profit share
of banks and other financial institutions, you'll see that in the early post-war period,
up until the early 1980s, they took down about 15% of all corporate profits in the
United States. Just before the crisis, in 2006, they took down 40% of all profits,
which is pretty astonishing.

Another measure of size is total financial assets as a percentage of gross domestic
product. If you look at the postwar period, it's pretty constant from 1945 to 1981, with
the ratio of financial assets to the size of the economy—of GDP—at about 4 to 1. But
starting in 1981, it started climbing. By 2007, total financial assets were ten times the size
of GDP. If you look at almost any metric about the overall size of the financial sector—
credit-to-GDP ratios, debt-to-GDP ratios, etc.—you see this massive increase starting
around 1981, going up to a peak just before the financial crisis, in 2006.

Two more, related, dimensions are the sizes of the biggest financial firms and
the concentration of the industry. For example, the share of total securities-industry
assets held by the top five investment banks was 65% in 2007. The share of the total
deposits held by the top seven commercial banks went from roughly 20% in the
early postwar period to over 50%. If you look at derivatives trading, you find that
the top five investment banks control about 97% of that. So there's a massive concentration in the financial system, and that hasn't declined—in some ways, it's gotten worse—since the financial crisis.

**D&S:** Could you describe the qualitative changes in financial institution behavior in
this same era, and the origins of these changes? When we hear that year 1981, we immediately think of deregulation. Is it just deregulation, or is there more to it than that?

**GE:** We can roughly think about two periods of banking and finance in the post-World War II era. Coming out of the Great Depression, when there was a lot of financial regulation, the Glass-Steagall Act separated investment from commercial banking, there were rules governing the issuing of complex and risky securities, rules for different kinds of financial institutions in terms of what kinds of assets they could hold. Savings and loans could mostly focus on housing, commercial banks primarily on business loans, investment banks couldn't take deposits and mostly engaged in underwriting and those kinds of activities. There were interest-rate ceilings, high capital requirements, leverage requirements. During this period, most of the activity of banks, commercial banks particularly, was in terms of taking in deposits and making individual loans—business loans, mortgages, real-estate loans. Many people call this the age of "boring banking." It was also called the age of "3-6-3" banking—bankers paid 3% interest, lent out at 6%, and got to the golf course by 3:00 in the afternoon.

Then starting in the late 1970s and early 1980s, their activities really changed, partly as a result of financial deregulation, partly as a result of increased competition from other kinds of financial institutions. Relatively unregulated banks could pay depositors higher interest rates, could charge higher interest rates on their loans, and could engage in new kinds of financial innovation—such as securitization, which is placing a bunch of loans into a bundle, such as an asset-backed security or mortgage-backed security, and selling these things off. "Boring banking" could no longer compete, so instead of engaging in one-to-one lending, they started engaging in more activities with the capital markets—bundling up or securitizing loans, selling them off, using derivatives to hedge risks but also to make bets. They kind of became like hedge funds in the sense of doing a lot of trading, buying and selling a lot of derivatives, engaging with the securities and capital markets. But they still had the government guarantees like they were banks.

---

### How the Banks Broke Out of Regulations

*D&S:* You talk about banks that had been comfortably and profitably engaging in highly regulated "boring" activities coming under competitive pressure. How much of this coming from new players and how much is it the banks themselves finding those niches to evade the regulations that existed at the time?

GE: It's both, for sure. I can't really tell you about the relative weights of those two factors, but certainly both are going on. So for example, one of the key restrictions that commercial banks were working under was the "Regulation Q ceiling." There were limits on what they could pay for deposits. In the late 1960s and 1970s, when inflation began taking off, savers were finding that the real interest rates they were getting from their deposits with banks were turning negative, banks couldn't raise the interest rates they paid to keep depositors. And these aren't small savers. We're talking about big corporations and wealthy people. Financial institutions were able to find niches outside the regulations, particularly money market mutual funds and other innovations. Fidelity Investments, for example, was

*D&S:* How does finance measure up, during this most recent era of deregulated finance, against the key claims that are made about its socially constructive role?

**GE:** If you look at the textbook description of the positive roles that finance plays, basically it comes down to six things: channel savings to productive investment, provide mechanisms for households to save for retirement, help businesses and households reduce risk, provide stable and flexible liquidity, provide an efficient payments mechanism, and come up with new financial innovations, that will make it cheaper, simpler, and better to do all these other five things. If you go through the way finance operated in the period of "roaring" banking, one can raise questions about the productive role of banking in all of these dimensions.

Taking the first role, channeling finance to productive investment, in the early postwar period, nonfinancial corporations on average got about 15-20% of their funding for productive investment from outside sources, from banks and from the capital markets. For the rest, they used retained earnings. In the latter period, after around 1980 or so, this was cut more or less in half—to 7–10%. So finance didn't really provide a huge percentage of funds for nonfinancial corporate investment in the age of roaring banking. So you have this paradoxical situation where the income going to finance grew significantly while the real contribution to providing funding for investment went down. During the 1960s, finance got about 40 cents for every dollar they gave to nonfinancial corporations for investment. By the 2000s, it was up to 66 cents.

What was finance doing instead? As Juan Montecino, Iren Levina, and I point out in a paper we wrote, they started lending to each other, instead of to the real economy or nonfinancial corporations. So we looked at intra-financial sector lending as a share of total lending from 1950 to 2010 and we found that, from 1950 up to around 1980 or so, they were only doing about 10% of total lending to each other. Just before the crisis in 2008 or so, they were doing almost 30% of all lending to

---

able to create a checking account based on a money market mutual fund. They could start offering much higher interest rates.

But the banks themselves also found out ways of breaking out of this, primarily through the Eurodollar market that developed in the mid-1960s. Citibank, Bank of America, and all these other banks were able to develop these same kinds of financial products overseas, where they weren't subject to the same kinds of restrictions. Of course, it wasn't really overseas, it was just accounting changes on their books. One set of accounts was the Eurodollar market and another set of accounts was domestic, but they were all really in the same place, in New York or wherever. They were able to develop these kinds of new products and able to keep their commercial customers and others by setting up in the Eurodollar market rather than in New York.

Citibank was one of the examples of a bank that started pushing the envelope in various ways, to set up these accounts in the United States. The Federal Reserve essentially looked the other way—gave them an administrative pass—in the late 1970s. This just started opening up a floodgate. So it was a combination of new players coming in and developing these kinds of things and the old players figuring out ways around restrictions, primarily by booking all of this in overseas accounts.

each other. This lending to each other really was a way of providing finance for derivatives trading and other kinds of betting, rather than financing real investment.

The second role is providing mechanisms for households to save for retirement. There are a lot of studies that show that banks didn't do a very good job in the period of roaring banking. Part of the problem is that the savings vehicles that finance provides for households come at a very high cost. If you put your money in a mutual fund, say, with Fidelity or one of these other companies, oftentimes the fees that you have to pay are very high, and the returns that you get aren't any better—sometimes worse—than if you put your money in a broad portfolio of stocks, like the S&P 500 or something like that. There are a lot of studies that show that the returns that you get from putting your money in these active funds is more than 2% less than if you just put it into a broad stock portfolio. Well, this 2% is going directly to the company, to Fidelity and the people who work for them, so it's a way that finance is overcharging.

The way in which finance has failed in helping households save for retirement is even more stark if you realize that, for most households in the United States, most of the wealth that people have is in their homes. If you think about what the financial sector did to people's savings in their houses in that period, it's a pretty dismal record—especially for African American and Hispanic and other minority households, much more so than for white households. Already, African Americans' wealth is just a fraction of white wealth, and most of their wealth was in their houses. The financial crisis of 2006-2007 pretty much wiped out a large percentage of African American wealth during this period. So clearly, roaring banking didn't do much to help households save for retirement.

The third role is to reduce risk. You just need to look at the kinds of financial products that banks were selling under the guise of reducing risk—like credit default swaps, mortgage-backed securities, asset-backed securities, etc. These products lost enormous amounts of value during the financial crisis, and would have lost almost all of their value if the government hadn't bailed them out. The financial sector was a source of enormous risk, rather than a source of reducing risk.

The same can be easily said of the fourth function, providing stable and flexible liquidity. If you look at the housing bubble and the tremendous run-up in asset prices provided by the tremendous increase in liquidity from the financial sector—through asset-backed securities, subprime lending, and so forth—you realize that it was not stable. It was actually what led to the asset bubble and crash. So private banking does not provide stable or flexible liquidity. In the end, in 2008, the Federal Reserve had to come in and provide enormous amounts of liquidity to the system to keep it from melting down entirely.

For the fifth role, to provide an efficient payments mechanism, we see a similar kind of thing. The only thing that kept the payments system operating after the financial crisis was the enormous amounts of liquidity that the Federal Reserve flooded into the financial system. Moreover, if anyone has ever tried to transfer money from one bank to another, or overseas, you realize that our payments mechanism—even in normal times—is very inefficient. Banks can hold onto your funds for two or three or four days before making them available to you, when you try to transfer from one bank to another, just as a way of extracting more money from households.

Both in abnormal times and in normal times, the payments mechanism in the period of roaring banking is very poor.

Finally, that brings us to banking innovations. Paul Volcker famously told a group of bankers in 2009 that the only financial innovation that he could see in the last 20 years that had been at all efficient was the ATM. There's no evidence that financial innovations have led to more economic growth. Jim Crotty and I did a literature survey that showed that at the minimum 30-40% of financial innovations over the last 20 years or so are used at least to some extent, if not largely, to evade regulations or to evade taxes—that is, to shift around pieces of the pie from the public to the banks, rather than to increase the size of the pie.

In short, roaring banking has done a pretty dismal job of providing any of these functions that the textbook case says finance should provide.

***D&S:*** Of course, bubbles burst and exacerbate the severity of downturns. One of the amazing things about the aftermath of the recent crisis has been the apparent imperviousness of the financial sector to serious reform—especially in contrast to the Great Crash of 1929 and the Great Depression. How do you make sense of that?

**GE:** You have to use a political economy approach to understand the sources of political support for finance. I call these multilayered sources of support the "bankers' club."

The lead group in the bankers' club is the bankers themselves, and the politicians that they're able to buy off with financial contributions and so forth. Their ability to do that, of course, has become much greater with changes in the campaign finance reform laws and Citizens United and so forth, so it makes it much easier for the banks to throw enormous amounts of money at politicians and prevent significant reform. This is true for both parties, for the Republicans and for the Democrats. We know how important finance was to Bill Clinton's political coalition in raising money. That's been true for Democrats for many years, not just Republicans.

The bankers have a lot of other support as well. Historically, the Federal Reserve has been one of the main orchestrators of the bankers' club. You can clearly see that in the role that Timothy Geithner played—when he was at the New York Fed, and then after he became Treasury Secretary under Obama—in fighting tooth-and-nail against any significant reform. He was one of the main figures in the opposition to tough reform through the Dodd-Frank Act. The Federal Reserve, through many mechanisms—the "revolving door" mechanism, the fact that they regulate banks, and so on—is a very strong member of the bankers' club.

A perhaps surprising group in the bankers' club has been many economists, especially academic economists who work on finance. Some of them take quite a bit of money from financial firms as consulting fees or are on the boards of directors of financial firms. Jessica Carrick-Hagenbarth and I studied this, looking at a group of 19 well-known academic economists who were working with two groups, the Pew Charitable Trusts Financial Reform Project and the Squam Lake Working Group on Financial Regulation, on financial reform issues. And they were coming up with financial reforms that, while some of them were OK, a lot really lacked teeth. We found that many of them, if not most of them, had some kind of association with financial firms, but were not disclosing this when they would write their academic papers speak on the radio or on TV or give testimony.

An important source of power of the bankers' club is that bankers can threaten to fail if we don't bail them out. They can threaten to leave—to move to London, Frankfurt, Hong Kong, or Shanghai—if we don't give them what they want. So this threat is the ultimate "club" that the bankers hold over our heads, and they use that all the time in the fight over financial reform.

On top of that, there's an important member of the bankers' club that in the 1930s wasn't a member—nonfinancial corporations. This time around, if you look at the fight over Dodd-Frank, you find very little opposition to banks from other members of the capitalist class. They were either silent or supported the banks. This is a big contrast to the 1930s when a lot of industrial firms did not support the banks, and in fact joined with FDR on financial regulation. Why is this? Why didn't we see more opposition from other capitalists to what the banks had done? After all, what the banks did led to this massive recession and hurt profits, at least initially, created all sorts of problems for nonfinancial corporations—and yet they supported the banks. Part of the answer may be that nonfinancial corporations have now become financialized themselves. The CEOs of these corporations get a lot of their incomes and wealth through stock options and other kinds of financial activities. Some nonfinancial firms have large financial components themselves. GE, for example, is now spinning off its financial subsidiary, GE Capital. But for many years it was getting quite a lot of income from GE Capital. And it's not just GE but also many other large nonfinancial corporations.

So there was a united front among the capitalists to oppose strong financial reform. Finance had plenty of money to buy off politicians. And while there was strong and valiant effort on the part of Americans for Financial Reform, Better Markets, some academic economists who were opposing what the banks did, and important roles played by Elizabeth Warren and some other senators—it just wasn't enough, given this united front of capitalists, the money machine, and the academic economists who were giving legitimacy to what the banks were doing.

**D&S:** That brings us to the question of a reform agenda for now. We've heard a lot about the need for re-regulation of finance, with an eye toward the restoration of the boring banking of the 1950s-1970s. The other question is whether the functions of finance require capitalist banks at all, even within a capitalist economy. Could all the functions of finance be done better by public and cooperative financial institutions, rather than private capitalist banks?

**GE:** The way I've been thinking about it is that we need both—that they're complements to each other. Short of complete overthrow of capitalism, and having a totally socialist economy, which is unlikely to happen in the immediate future, what I think we should argue for is both re-regulation of private finance and a much stronger push for what I call "banks without bankers." We need to have re-regulation of private finance as long as it continues to exist, for two reasons.

First, as we've seen—and as John Maynard Keynes and Hyman Minsky and others argued—private finance can create a lot of problems if it's not regulated. As

---

### Did the U.S. Economy Rely on a Financial "Bubble Machine"?

*D&S:* What would you think of the characterization that—within the context of U.S. capitalism becoming reliant on asset bubbles for achieving anything close to full-employment output—finance played the role of being the "bubble machine"? So, finance as an essential cog of a bigger dysfunctional system.

*GE:* My colleague Bob Pollin wrote a great book about this called *Contours of Descent*, about the Clinton administration and its role in creating this bubble machine. One of the impacts of all this roaring banking and this "pro-cyclical" liquidity creation—massive liquidity on the way up and then withdrawal of liquidity on the way down—was that it did have a huge levitating effect on wealth and, through this wealth effect, led to significant consumption particularly among the wealthy. And that helped to propel the economy forward in the 1990s.

Sometimes, people talk about this as if capitalism needed this to survive and that's why it's happened that way. I don't like that type of thinking methodologically. The question is: What is the counterfactual? What would have happened if the bubble machine weren't operating? Would the economy have slid into a long period of stagnation, or would there have been economic and political forces that would have generated a much healthier type of growth? These are things that we can't know, though which are certainly worth asking. But the characterization that bubbles had that kind of effect—of generating these booms, particularly during the Clinton years—is certainly correct.

---

Keynes put it, when "enterprise is a bubble on a whirlpool of speculation," we're in big trouble. You have to bring private finance under control so that it can't continue to generate these massive bubbles and then crashes, which create enormous problems for workers and for households all over the world.

Second, as long as there's private finance out there and the bankers are making enormous profits and incomes, not only does that generate a worsening of the income distribution—it's an engine for inequality—it also makes it hard to have a stable and productive public financial sector. If you have public or cooperative banks, and you have people running those institutions and they think of themselves as financiers or bankers, and they realize that they could jump ship and work for the private financial sector and make five, ten, fifteen, twenty times what they're making in the public interest, this can be extremely tempting. Or it can get them to reorient the activities that they engage in to make them more profitable and look more like private banks. This is what happened to a number of public financial institutions around the world in the run-in up to the financial crisis. The first financial institution that really got into trouble, or one of the first, was a Landesbank, a regional provincial public bank in Germany that was supposed to be making boring banking investments, but instead was making roaring banking investments, because they wanted to keep up with the private financial institutions.

You can't let there be too big a gap between the activities and the incomes and pay between the public sector and the private sector if the public sector is going to do the job it needs to do. Of course, you can have a gap, and it can be somewhat large, but it can't get as big as it got in the 2000s. So for both of those reasons I do think that we do need to control private finance.

But in order to break up the bankers' club and to provide the real kind of finance that society needs, we do need to promote more cooperative finance and public finance. How do you do that? Well, there are a bunch of different ways. For example, there's the State Bank of North Dakota, and there are a number of organizations that are trying to promote state banks in other states. I know there's been an organization in Massachusetts, for example, that's been trying to do this. There are credit unions all over the country, so building the credit unions by having a national credit union bank to support them. These are all things that should be done.

The government should stop subsidizing the "too big to fail" banks by bailing them out. This lowers the cost of funds for these banks, allows them to grow larger and squeeze out cooperative and other kinds of community banks. So the government should end too big to fail as a way to make more room for these other kinds of public and cooperative banks. The Federal Reserve could serve as a backstop for these types of banks, by agreeing to act as a lender of last resort, to let them use their securities as collateral for borrowing. So there are all different kinds of ways that the government could support the creation or expansion of these sorts of institutions.

I think that's necessary for us to get out of the trap that we're in. ❏

*Article 8.3*

# DERIVATIVES AND DEREGULATION

## BY MARTY WOLFSON
*November/December 2008*

It has become commonplace to describe the current financial crisis as the most serious since the Great Depression. Although we have more tools now to avoid a depression, the current crisis presents in some ways more significant challenges than did the banking crises of the 1930s.

And it's not over.

The form of the current crisis is similar to others we have seen in the past: a speculative increase in asset prices, overly optimistic expectations, and an expansion of debt sustainable only if the speculative bubble continues. Then the bubble pops, debt can't be repaid, and losses mount at financial institutions. The risk of bank failures rises and lenders get scared. They panic, refuse to lend to anyone that seems at all risky, and seek safety in cash or super-safe assets.

In the early 1930s, there was no federal deposit insurance and little federal government intervention. Depositor runs took down the banking system.

In more recent crises, though, the Federal Reserve successfully developed and used its powers as a lender of last resort. Deposit insurance helped to reassure small depositors and, if needed, the Federal Deposit Insurance Corporation stepped in and bailed out threatened banks. It could guarantee all liabilities of a failing bank and arrange mergers with healthier banks. These tools generally worked to reduce panicked reactions and prevent the freezing up of credit.

But this time, after the collapse of the speculative bubble in housing prices, the course of events has been different. The Federal Reserve was forced to expand the concept of a lender of last resort in unprecedented ways. It has lent to investment banks and insurance companies, not just regulated depository institutions. It has taken all kinds of assets as collateral for its loans, not just the high-grade securities it traditionally accepted. It has even lent to nonfinancial corporations (by buying their commercial paper).

What is surprising is that these dramatic actions and expensive bailouts of financial institutions, such as American International Group (AIG) and even Fannie Mae and Freddie Mac, were insufficient to reassure lenders about the ability of financial institutions to honor their repayment commitments. Treasury Secretary Paulson's plan to use $700 billion to buy "toxic assets" from financial institutions, signed into law by President Bush on October 3rd, failed to stop what had become by then a generalized panic and freeze-up of credit. It took a coordinated global initiative to inject capital directly into financial institutions, plus a federal guarantee on bank debt and unlimited FDIC insurance on non-interest-bearing (mostly business) accounts at banks, announced on October 12th, to begin to have an effect on unfreezing credit markets.

The "TED spread," a widely watched measure of credit risk that had spiked sharply during the panic, began to reverse its path following the October 12 announcement. The TED spread measures the difference between an interest rate that banks charge when lending to each other (the London Interbank Offered Rate, or Libor) and the interest rate on U.S. Treasury bills. Because the Treasury is assumed to be "risk-free," the difference between it and Libor measures the perceived relative risk of lending to banks.

Why has this panic been so much more difficult to control? The answer has to do with the widespread use of complicated and opaque securities, known as derivatives, in a deregulated, interconnected, and global financial system.

A derivative is a financial contract that derives its value from something else, such as an asset or an index. At the root of the current crisis are derivatives known as mortgage-backed securities (MBSs). MBSs are claims to payments from an underlying pool of mortgages. The ability of MBS issuers to repay their debt, and thus the value of the MBS, is derived from the ability of homeowners to meet their mortgage payments.

In the process leading up to the crisis, a mortgage broker typically extended a mortgage to a borrower, and then turned to a commercial bank to fund the loan. The bank might sell the loan to Fannie Mae, which would pool a group of mortgages together and sell the resulting MBS to an investment bank like Lehman Brothers. Lehman, in turn, repackaged the MBS in various ways, and issued even more complicated derivatives called collateralized debt obligations (CDOs). Buyers of the CDOs might be other banks, hedge funds, or other lenders.

At the base of this complicated pyramid of derivatives might be a subprime borrower whose lender did not explain an adjustable-rate loan, or another borrower whose ability to meet mortgage payments depended on a continued escalation of home prices. As subprime borrowers' rates reset, and especially as housing price speculation collapsed, the whole house of cards came crashing down.

Why were mortgage loans made that could not be repaid? And why did supposedly sophisticated investors buy MBSs and CDOs based on these loans? First of all, the mortgage brokers and commercial banks that made and funded these loans quickly sold them off and no longer had any responsibility for them. Second, rating agencies like Moody's and Standard & Poor's gave these derivatives stellar AAA ratings, signifying a credit risk of almost zero. Recent Congressional hearings have highlighted the conflict of interest that these rating agencies had: they were being paid by the issuers of the derivatives they were rating. Third, financial institutions up and down the line were making money and nobody was limiting what they could do. In the deregulated financial environment, federal regulators stood aside as housing speculation spun out of control and did little to regulate, or even document, the growth of complicated derivatives.

Finally, financial institutions' concerns about the creditworthiness of the derivatives they held were eased because they thought they could protect themselves against possible loss. For example, by using another type of derivative known as a credit default swap, holders of MBSs and CDOs could make periodic premium payments to another financial institution, like American International Group (AIG), to insure themselves against default by the issuers of the MBSs and CDOs. (This insurance contract was technically classified as a derivative rather than insurance in order to escape regulation.) However, if an insurer like AIG is unable to honor all its insurance contracts, then the protection against loss is illusory.

The total value of all the securities insured by credit default swaps at the end of 2007 was estimated by the Bank of International Settlements to be $58 trillion, and by the International Swaps and Derivatives Association to be $62 trillion. (The estimates could vary by as much as $4 trillion because unregulated credit default swaps do not have to be officially reported to regulatory agencies. Moreover, even greater ambiguity surrounds these contracts because insurers can transfer their liability to other parties, and the insured party may be unaware of the creditworthiness or even the identity of the new insurer.)

Surprisingly, though, the value of the actual securities that form the basis of these credit default swaps was only about $6 trillion. How could $6 trillion worth of assets be insured at ten times that amount? The discrepancy is due to the fact that it is possible to speculate on the likelihood of default of a security without actually owning the security: all the speculator has to do is enter into a credit default swap contract with an insurer. The total volume of "insured securities" can thus escalate dramatically.

Because derivatives are so complex, because so much speculation and debt are involved, and because it is so hard to know how much is at risk (and exactly who is at risk), regulators are unsure of the implications of the failure of a particular financial institution. That is why they have been so fearful of the consequences of letting a troubled institution fail.

The exception that did indeed prove the rule was Lehman Brothers. The Federal Reserve and Treasury did not bail it out, and its failure led to an intensification of the problems in credit markets. A money market fund, the Reserve Primary Fund, announced that it would only pay 97 cents on the dollar to its investors, because its investments in Lehman Brothers could not be redeemed. The Treasury moved quickly to announce that it would insure money market funds, in order to prevent a run on the funds. However, the Lehman failure raised further concerns that lenders had about the derivatives portfolios of other banks, and about the possibility that the banks would not have enough capital to cover potential losses.

Secretary Paulson's initial plan to buy "toxic" assets (including MBSs and CDOs) from financial institutions was designed to address these concerns about bank capital. However, his plan was probably also negatively affected by uncertainty. Because these "toxic" assets are complex and nobody wants to buy them, there is no market for them and their value is uncertain. And because the Paulson plan's unstated objective was to boost bank capital by overpaying for these assets, the difficulties in pricing the assets raised the prospects of long delays and questions about whether the plan to increase bank capital would be successful. Lenders continued to hold back. They may also have hesitated because of concern about a political backlash against a taxpayer subsidy for the very banks that many people blamed for the crisis.

By injecting capital directly into the banks, the global initiative announced on October 12, 2008 raised the prospect of returns on the capital investment for taxpayers. It also avoided the uncertainties of buying individual assets and helped to reduce the panic.

But the crisis isn't over. Reducing the panic is only the first step. There is now likely to be a longer-term credit crunch that will continue to threaten the broader economy. Banks and other lenders will be wary for quite some time. Losses on mortgage-related assets will continue as years of housing speculation—financed with heaps of borrowed money—continues to unwind. Bank lending will lag as banks rebuild their capital and overcome their pessimistic expectations.

It will be up to the federal government to pick up the slack that the banks will leave. We will need programs to enable people to stay in their homes and stabilize their communities. We will need to create jobs by investing in infrastructure, renewable energy, and education. We will need a "trickle-up" approach that puts people first and raises living standards and opportunities.

At the same time, we need a regulatory structure for the financial system that puts limits on risk and manipulation. It is clear that deregulation, and the entire neoliberal model that has dominated economic policy for the past 30 years, has run aground. It has sown the seeds of financial crisis, and this crisis has led us to the edge of an abyss. Only by dramatically reorienting our economic and financial structure can we avoid the abyss and create the kind of society that meets our needs. The nature of that new structure should be the subject of intensive democratic discussion and debate in the days to come. ❏

*Article 8.4*

# BUBBLE, BUBBLE, TOIL, AND TROUBLE
*Keynes and Financial Instability*

## BY ALEJANDRO REUSS
*October 2013*

In recent years, the United States has experienced major "bubbles"—increases in asset prices fueled by nothing more than the expectation that in the future others will be willing to pay even more—in the stock market and in real-estate markets. The S&P Composite Index, a broad index of stock prices, stood at less than 850 in early 2003, after the "dot.com" crash. By 2007, it had ballooned to over 1500. The real-estate bubble saw the Case-Shiller 20-City Housing Price Index, the main index of U.S. housing prices, more than double from 100 at the beginning of 2000 to over 206 in the middle of 2006. Both have crashed since then. The Case-Shiller Index fell to less than 150 by January 2008. The S&P lost about half its value, down to a little more than 750, between its 2007 peak and March 2009.

## Sources of Market Volatility

In the words of former Federal Reserve chair Alan Greenspan, a wave of "irrational exuberance" fueled the stock market boom. It is easy to believe that daredevil risk-taking, an unreasoning faith that prices will keep rising and rising, and possibly testosterone intoxication, are responsible for asset "bubbles." That may not be entirely false, but we chalk up bubbles exclusively to irrational behavior at the peril of ignoring the element of individual rationality in joining into a bubble and fueling its growth. In *The General Theory*, Keynes argued that financial-market instability, in particular, was due not merely to some "wrong-headed propensity" on the part of the individuals involved, but to the organization of financial markets themselves.

Conventional economic theory of asset markets is dominated by the "efficient markets hypothesis." Proponents of this view argue that the price of a financial asset at any given moment reflects all the available information about its true value (e.g., stock prices at any given moment reflect all the available information about the value of a company, or real-estate prices about the value of those properties). When new information becomes available, either about a particular asset or about the national or world economy, this causes market participants to revalue the asset, and the price goes up or down accordingly. If it were possible to know now that a stock's price would, say, go up to a specific level the next day, people would buy it now in anticipation of the rise, bidding up the price today. We would not have to wait until tomorrow to get to the new, higher price. In this view, stock prices reflect the real values of the assets being traded, so far as the available information allows, and price fluctuations on the stock market and other asset markets originate from outside the markets themselves.

Critics of the efficient markets hypothesis have argued that it underestimates the instability generated within asset markets. Price fluctuations are caused not only by newly available information, but by market participants' reactions to previous price fluctuations and prediction of how other participants will react to those fluctuations. Market participants are concerned, in Keynes' view, not with correctly ascertaining the long-term value of an asset, but primarily with guessing what others will be willing to pay for it in the short-run. They buy and sell, Keynes argued, not on the basis of "what an investment is really worth to [someone] who buys it 'for keeps'," but on the basis of "what the market will value it at … three months or a year hence."

## Keynes' Beauty Contest

In *The General Theory*, Keynes famously compared financial markets to a strange sort of beauty pageant run by London newspapers in his time. The papers published an array of photos, and readers could enter a contest in which the winner was the reader who guessed which faces would be chosen by the most other readers. (Keynes was not commenting, one way or another, about the existence of these or other "beauty contests." In fact, he was not focused on this as a contest between the women pictured, but as a contest between the readers doing the guessing.) As Keynes pointed out, it would not do to simply choose the photo that one found most attractive, for one's own tastes might not match those of other entrants. Neither, however, should one choose the photo that one thought other entrants would find most attractive (for they would not themselves be choosing the one they found most attractive). Each entrant would, rather, be trying to guess what other entrants would guess about which photos most other entrants would choose.

In the same way, participants in the stock market, Keynes argued, did not generally attempt to estimate the likely returns from a company's investments (often referred to these days as its "fundamentals"), but to "guess better than the crowd how the crowd will behave." If other market participants are, for whatever reason, buying a particular kind of asset and driving up its price, rational participants would decide to buy as well (to benefit from the short-run increase in prices) as long as they expected that the price would continue to rise.

This makes sense, from the standpoint of an individual buyer, even if the buyer, in some sense, knows better—that is, believes that the company in question has bad long-term prospects, that "the market" has overpriced the stock, that other buyers are acting unwisely, and so on. For example, you may not think that Springfield Nuclear Power is a very well-run company, but as long as you think other people are (unwisely) going to buy its stock, pushing up the stock price, it makes sense for you to buy the stock and profit from these future price increases. As more people buy in to take advantage of a crowd-induced rise in prices, of course, they further fuel the growth of the bubble. These price increases, in turn, may induce still others to buy the stock in anticipation of further increases, and so on.

This process can dramatically unhitch the price of an asset from its "fundamentals," at least for a time. To show that the price of a stock, of houses, or of some other asset has grown out of all due proportion, however, we must have some basis for estimating the "correct" value. For stocks, one comparison is the "price-earnings (P/E) ratio" (the ratio of the stock price to the corporation's profits, on which stocks ultimately are a claim). For housing, one can use a ratio between housing prices and "owner's equivalent rent" (how much it would cost to rent a similar house), or the "price-rent ratio." By these measures,

U.S. stocks and housing have been grossly overvalued during the bubbles of recent years. Economist Robert Shiller, a leading authority on asset bubbles, notes that price-earnings ratios in the mid 20s are above historical norms. In 2007, the P/E ratio peaked over 27. (It had peaked at over 44 in late 1999, during the dot.com bubble.) The price-rent ratio, likewise, went way above historical norms in 2007. The national average for the 15 preceding years was less than 17. In mid 2007, it was nearly 23.

## Bubbles and the Real Economy

Some people will profit in any bubble. But bubbles do not go on forever. Some end with a fizzle (prices stop rising, and inflation gradually erodes the value of the asset); others, with a dramatic crash, as in the U.S. stock market and housing markets did in 2008. As a bubble bursts, however, the price may not simply return to the "right" level. Instead, market participants may believe that price declines now mean that prices are likely to continue to fall in the future (in effect, this is a bubble in reverse, known as a "panic selloff"). As the price of an asset declines, more and more people sell to avoid getting stuck with it, fueling a further decline, and so on. Falling asset prices may, in short, overshoot the mark in the other direction.

Keynes was concerned that the "daily revaluations of the Stock Exchange … inevitably exert a decisive influence of the rate of current investment"—that fluctuations in stock prices affect real economic activity. Rising stock prices, which make it possible for a company to raise capital cheaply by issuing new shares, have the same effects as falling interest rates. Some investment projects, which would be unprofitable if the cost of capital were greater, will be undertaken. Plummeting stock prices, on the other hand, are like increasing interest rates. They make it more expensive for companies to raise capital, and may therefore result in decreased real investment.

The collapse of the stock and housing bubbles reverberated on real economic activity in at least two more ways.

First, people's consumption spending is affected not only by their current incomes, but also their wealth (the value of the assets they own, minus their debts, at any given time). As people's wealth increases, they spend more freely; if their wealth decreases, they curtail their spending. This is known as the "wealth effect." Keynes described this phenomenon in *The General Theory*, writing that the "consumption of the wealth-owning class may be extremely susceptible to unforeseen changes in the money-value of its wealth." The stock-market and real-estate bubbles certainly fueled increased consumption. Many people simply spent more freely because they felt financially secure. Some borrowed against the rising values of their homes, often for consumption spending. As the values of these assets have plummeted, people have cut back dramatically on spending.

Second, the collapse of the housing market detonated a major financial crisis. Banks had bet heavily on the continued rise in real-estate prices. They extended mortgage loans indiscriminately. They bought enormous amounts of mortgage-backed securities (which pay returns to their owners based on payments made on an underlying set of mortgages). When real-estate prices plummeted and mortgage defaults skyrocketed, banks were left holding assets that were plummeting in value and were basically unsellable. Many curtailed their lending dramatically, trying to build their cash reserves as a guard against bankruptcy. The resulting tightening of credit made it difficult for consumers and firms to borrow, further dragging down spending and contributing to the deepening recession.

## Is Regulation the Answer?

In the parts of *The General Theory* focused on financial instability, Keynes argued that the speculative short-term speculative buying and selling of securities disconnected financial markets from any real evaluation of the long-term prospects of different investments. While this was, in Keynes' view, harmless enough if the speculation existed on the surface on a "steady stream of enterprise," it could be very harmful if enterprise became the surface on top of a "whirlpool of speculation."

It's easy to see the relevance of this analysis to the current economic crisis. From the 1940s to the 1970s, banks, insurance companies, and other financial institutions were highly regulated, and financial crises were relatively rare. Since the deregulation of finance, in the 1980s, the nonregulation of ever-more-exotic financial securities, and the creation of a vast world of "shadow banking," they have become much more frequent. Enterprise (that is, the real economy) seems to have been dragged down, as Keynes foresaw, into the whirlpool.

The chain-reaction of excessive financial risk-taking, the eruption of the financial crisis, and the deepest recession since the 1930s has resulted in calls for renewed financial regulation. As of yet, only partial and inadequate measures have been adopted, and the largest banks are flying higher than ever. Even if there were robust new financial regulation, however, that would not solve the problems that cause the Great Recession in the first place—since these problems went way beyond just excessive financial speculation or risk-taking.

Economic growth in capitalist economies depends on growing demand for goods and services to match the growing productive capacity of an economy. From the late 1940s to the early 1970s, the rate of productivity growth was matched by the rate of real wage growth. Ordinary workers, then, largely created the demand for the goods that they were producing in ever-greater abundance. Since then, however, real wage growth has stagnated, while productivity and total output have kept right on rising. The demand for these goods and services had to come from somewhere. In part, it came from the wealthy who, enjoying a growing share of the total income, spent more. In part, it came from working families that made up for stagnant wages with more hours of paid work (especially by women) and more and more debt. In large measure, though, it also came from bubbles! Remember, growing asset prices encourage people to spend more. Unsustainable asset bubbles are not just a way that the U.S. economy has *failed* over the last few decades—they are a way that it has *worked*.

This way of structuring a capitalist economy, however, is prone to periodic crises that inflict an enormous human toll. Creating an economy that does not depend on the next bubble, however, requires much more than just an overlay of financial regulation. ❏

*Sources:* John Maynard Keynes, *The General Theory of Employment, Interest, and Money* (New York: Harcourt, Inc., 1964); S&P/Case-Shiller Home Price Indices; "Stock Market Winners Get Big Payoff—In Testosterone," *Scientific American*; Robert Shiller, Online Data; Robert Shiller, *Irrational Exuberance*, 2nd ed.; "Where Housing is Heading," *Fortune*.

*Article 8.5*

# WE'RE ALL MINSKYITES NOW

## BY ROBERT POLLIN
*October 2008; The Nation*

As the most severe financial crisis since the 1930s Depression has unfolded over the past eighteen months, the ideas of the late economist Hyman Minsky have suddenly come into fashion. In the summer of 2007, the *Wall Street Journal* ran a front-page article describing the emerging crisis as the financial market's "Minsky moment." His ideas have since been featured in the *Financial Times, BusinessWeek* and *The New Yorker*, among many other outlets. Minsky, who spent most of his academic career at Washington University in St. Louis and remained professionally active until his death, in 1996, deserves the recognition. He was his generation's most insightful analyst of financial markets and the causes of financial crises.

Even so, most mainstream economists have shunned his work because it emerged out of a dissident left Keynesian tradition known in economists' circles as post-Keynesianism. Minsky's writings, and the post-Keynesian tradition more generally, are highly critical of free-market capitalism and its defenders in the economics profession—among them Milton Friedman and other Nobel Prize-winning economists who for a generation have claimed to "prove," usually through elaborate mathematical models, that unregulated markets are inherently rational, stable and fair. For Friedmanites, regulations are harmful most of the time.

Minsky, by contrast, explained throughout his voluminous writings that unregulated markets will always produce instability and crises. He alternately termed his approach "the financial instability hypothesis" and "the Wall Street paradigm."

For Minsky, the key to understanding financial instability is to trace the shifts that occur in investors' psychology as the economy moves out of a period of crisis and recession (or depression) and into a phase of rising profits and growth. Coming out of a crisis, investors will tend to be cautious, since many of them will have been clobbered during the just-ended recession. For example, they will hold large cash reserves as a cushion to protect against future crises.

But as the economy emerges from its slump and profits rise, investors' expectations become increasingly positive. They become eager to pursue risky ideas such as securitized subprime mortgage loans. They also become more willing to let their cash reserves dwindle, since idle cash earns no profits, while purchasing speculative vehicles like subprime mortgage securities that can produce returns of 10% or higher.

But these moves also mean that investors are weakening their defenses against the next downturn. This is why, in Minsky's view, economic upswings, proceeding without regulations, inevitably encourage speculative excesses in which financial bubbles emerge. Minsky explained that in an unregulated environment, the only way to stop bubbles is to let them burst. Financial markets then fall into a crisis, and a recession or depression ensues.

Here we reach one of Minsky's crucial insights—that financial crises and recessions actually serve a purpose in the operations of a free-market economy, even while they wreak havoc with people's lives, including those of tens of millions of innocents who never invest a dime on Wall Street. Minsky's point is that without crises, a free-market economy has no way of discouraging investors' natural proclivities toward ever greater risks in pursuit of ever higher profits.

However, in the wake of the calamitous Great Depression, Keynesian economists tried to design measures that could supplant financial crises as the system's "natural" regulator. This was the context in which the post-World War II system of big-government capitalism was created. The package included two basic elements: regulations designed to limit speculation and channel financial resources into socially useful investments, such as single-family housing; and government bailout operations to prevent 1930s-style depressions when crises broke out anyway.

Minsky argues that the system of regulations and the bailout operations were largely successful. That is why from the end of World War II to the mid-1970s, markets here and abroad were much more stable than in any previous historical period. But even during the New Deal years, financial market titans were fighting vehemently to eliminate, or at least defang, the regulations. By the 1970s, almost all politicians—Democrats and Republicans alike—had become compliant. The regulations were initially weakened, then abolished altogether, under the strong guidance of, among others, Federal Reserve chair Alan Greenspan, Sen. Phil Gramm (R-TX), and Clinton Treasury Secretary Robert Rubin.

For Minsky, the consequences were predictable. Consider the scorecard over the twenty years before the current disaster: a stock market crash in 1987; the savings-and-loan crisis and bailout in 1989-90; the "emerging markets" crisis of 1997-98—which brought down, among others, Long-Term Capital Management, the super-hedge fund led by two Nobel laureates specializing in finance—and the bursting of the dot-com market bubble in 2001. Each of these crises could easily have produced a 1930s-style collapse in the absence of full-scale government bailout operations.

Here we come to another of Minsky's major insights—that in the absence of a complementary regulatory system, the effectiveness of bailouts will diminish over time. This is because bailouts, just like financial crises, are double-edged. They prevent depressions, but they also limit the costs to speculators of their financial excesses. As soon as the next economic expansion begins gathering strength, speculators will therefore pursue profit opportunities more or less as they had during the previous cycle. This is the pattern that has brought us to our current situation—a massive global crisis, being countered by an equally massive bailout of thus far limited effectiveness.

Minsky's Wall Street paradigm did not address all the afflictions of free-market capitalism. In particular, his model neglects the problems that arise from the vast disparities of income, wealth and power that are just as endemic to free-market capitalism as are its tendencies toward financial instability, even though he fully recognized that these problems exist. Yet Minsky's approach still provides the most powerful lens for understanding the roots of financial instability and developing an effective regulatory system.

Minsky understood that his advocacy of comprehensive financial regulations made no sense whatsoever within the prevailing professional orthodoxy of free-market cheerleading. In his 1986 magnum opus, *Stabilizing an Unstable Economy*, he concluded that "the policy failures since the mid-1960s are related to the banality of orthodox economic analysis.... Only an economics that is critical of capitalism can be a guide to successful policy for capitalism." ❑

*Article 8.6*

# LESSONS FROM ICELAND'S FINANCIAL CRISIS

## BY NINA EICHACKER
*March/April 2016*

In a span of just three days in 2008—between October 7 and October 9—Iceland's three largest banks, Landsbanki, Glitnir, and Kaupthing, all failed. The banks' debts amounted to over 15 times Iceland's GDP at the time. Iceland residents, British and Dutch account holders, bank shareholders, and, soon, the rest of the world learned that those banks were completely insolvent, and that the Icelandic government could not afford to bail them out (at an estimated price tag of $300 billion).

Following these events, the people of Iceland began the "Kitchenware Revolution," gathering in front of parliament while banging pots and pans. They successfully demanded the resignation of the ruling right-wing Independence Party, which had implemented the financial deregulation that had led to the implosion of Iceland's financial system. In addition, they laid the groundwork for the rejection in a national referendum of the next government's plan to pay loan guarantees, for one of the country's three big banks, to the governments of the UK and the Netherlands. In December 2008, the Icelandic government created the Special Inquiry Commission, which produced an exhaustive report of the causes and consequences of the financial crisis. The government authorized a special prosecutor to investigate and bring charges against guilty parties—including prominent political figures such as the former minister of finance, financial figures including the president and CEO of Glitnir, the president and chairman of Kaupthing, and the president and managing director of Landsbanki.

The crisis, years in the making, was a consequence of the Icelandic government's rapid deregulation and privatization of Iceland's banking system back in the 1990s and early 2000s, and of the banks' embrace of large-scale and risk-heavy investment banking. With little or no supervision, and relying on the widespread belief globally in the integrity of Iceland's government and financial system, bankers got away with murder—until the fall of the U.S. investment bank Lehman Brothers in 2008, after which Iceland's banks could no longer rely on cheap and easy credit from U.S. investment banks.

## Foreseeable, But Not Foreseen

Policymakers, academics, and business reporters should have seen it coming. By 2006, Icelandic banking and economic data described an overheating financial sector and overall economy. Foreign banks' lending to Iceland increased from just over 50% of Icelandic GDP in 1999 to nearly 80% in 2003 to over 400% in 2007. Icelandic credit intermediation—the share of loans held by financial corporations compared to borrowing by non-financial firms, the general government, households, and non-profits—also increased in this period, from 64% in 2004 to 80% in 2007. This trend of a rapidly growing financial sector relative to the "real" sector of the economy was by no means unique to Iceland, but the scale was. Financial firms' debt rose from less than four times Iceland's GDP in 2003, to over nine times in 2007, to over 15 times in 2008. The net negative financial worth of Iceland's financial corporations rose from 4% of GDP in 2003, to 147% in 2007, to 649% in 2008.

Economist Anne Sibert and finance expert Gudrun Johnsen have written about "love-letters"—debt securities issued by Icelandic banks and then used as collateral for borrowing from other Icelandic banks, the Central Bank of Iceland, and even the European Central Bank. Icelandic banks' developed this fraudulent practice as they found it more difficult to borrow in global capital markets from 2006 onward. Economist and former banking regulator William K. Black has argued that the rapid acceleration of the banks' debts just before the collapse of Iceland's banking system was the result, not of desperate attempts to resurrect the banks, but of fraud: bank officers were trying to loot as much money as possible while they still could. In the years that Icelandic banks engaged in these practices, Frederic Mishkin (Columbia University), Richard Portes (London Business School), and Fridrik Baldursson (Reykjavik University) all wrote reports celebrating the integrity of the Icelandic financial system.

Perhaps as a consequence of these reports, top Icelandic officials, like the then prime minister and head of the central bank, were still surprised by the onset of the country's financial crisis, as were reporters with major media outlets like the *New York Times*, *Fortune*, and *BusinessWeek*. Top economists who had promoted the Icelandic strategy of financial deregulation, like Arthur Laffer (formerly economic advisor in the Reagan administration), Mishkin, Portes, and Baldursson were quiet in the immediate aftermath.

These events point to the dominance of neoliberal theories about the necessity of financial deregulation, and an assumption that a northern European country would have the institutional sophistication to avoid financial crises like those observed in developing countries that had rapidly deregulated. Neoclassical economists with outsize faith in the efficiency of financial markets and integrity of the Icelandic state believed that little could go wrong in Iceland—the crisis in October of 2008 proved otherwise. A wider understanding of the theories of John Maynard Keynes and Hyman Minsky (see Reuss, p. 234; Pollin, p. 238) would have helped policymakers and other observers foresee Iceland's crisis, and to prevent future such episodes. Keynes and Minsky understood—as Icelandic government officials, academic economists, and the financial press did not— that financial actors will engage in risky behavior in the pursuit of profits, making financial crises inevitable in the absence of regulation to prevent such behavior. Governments therefore must regulate financial sectors for the greater economic good.

## Underproduction of Criticism, Overproduction of Praise

The lack of financial-market transparency was one integral reason that Iceland's crisis went unforeseen. Organizations that could have reported on the conditions of the Icelandic financial marketplace and the state of the Icelandic economy simply did not. The Icelandic state threatened to defund public institutions and agencies that published reports contradicting the narrative of a robust financial infrastructure and growth.

Iceland's Chamber of Commerce paid economists, like Columbia University's Mishkin, hundreds of thousands of dollars to write favorable reports—including one titled "Financial Stability in Iceland"—about the country's financial sector and overall economic growth prospects. Mishkin would later become infamous, in the documentary "Inside Job," for that report and for changing its title to "Financial Instability in Iceland" on his curriculum vitae after Iceland's collapse.

The Icelandic news media consistently underpublicized reports critical of the Icelandic financial sector, while publishing many stories that praised Iceland's big three banks. Iceland's center-right party historically had large ownership stakes in several Icelandic media companies; the shared interest of Iceland's right and center-right parties in promoting the financial sector explains some of the media's lack of coverage of financial malfeasance.

Another cause of this disparity was the cross-ownership of media-company shares by Icelandic financial actors and institutions, and financial-corporation shares by Icelandic media institutions. The chair of the board of directors of Baugur Group, a large stakeholder in Kaupthing Bank, also owned 365—parent company of *Frettabladid*, Iceland's largest-circulation daily newspaper—as well as DV, another large media company. Björgólfur Guðmundsson, the former majority owner and chairman of Landsbanki, acquired Arvakur, the company that publishes *Morgunbladid*, the other major Icelandic newspaper, only to sell in 2009 after declaring bankruptcy. The interconnectedness of these industries created conflicts of interest for all involved.

Credit-rating agencies, meanwhile, also contributed to the notion that Iceland's financial markets were safer than they were. The sub-prime mortgage crisis of 2007 revealed a host of problems with how the three largest global credit-rating agencies—Moody's, Standard & Poor's, and Fitch—operate. It used to be that parties interested in investing in a particular class of assets paid for reports evaluating their riskiness. Since the 1970s, however, the setup as shifted, to one in which institutions issuing securities paid for ratings. This gave the agencies an incentive to rate securities as safer than they were. In other words, it created huge conflicts of interest.

In 2007, Fitch, the smallest of the big three rating agencies, downgraded Iceland's credit rating on the basis of its overextension. But Moody's, one of the two bigger agencies, upgraded it, on the premise that Iceland was so financially leveraged that its central bank would, as the lender of last resort, bail out the big three banks. This move paradoxically increased broad confidence in Icelandic financial stability, despite the fact that the rationale for the improved rating was the excessive leverage of Iceland's financial sector. This further lulled international investors and retail banking customers into trusting Icelandic financial actors with their money and spurred still greater leverage and risky behavior. The feedback effects increased the scale of the financial system relative to the Icelandic economy as a whole, placed more and more actors throughout Iceland at risk in the likely event of failure, and increased the severity of the imminent collapse of Iceland's financial system.

In short, the underproduction of criticism and the overproduction of praise for Iceland's banks skewed public understanding of the country's financial sector.

## Governments and International Institutions

The Icelandic Central Bank's decision to change from stability-promoting to inflation-targeting monetary policy led to rising interest rates, precipitous increases in capital inflows, and asset bubbles in the housing market.

Prior to the early 1990s, the Icelandic Central Bank had pursued economic stability above all else. It charged very low interest rates in order to promote lending to local banks, and to hedge against possible bank failures at the local level. Bank employees at all levels were compensated in ways that would not encourage risky behavior.

The shift to inflation-targeting monetary policy resulted in a rapid increase in Icelandic interest rates. Inflation targeting is designed to prevent an increase in the price level, typically through high interest rates, which make it more difficult for banks and other institutions to borrow. High interest rates, however, attracted capital flows from investors in the United States and Western Europe, two financial markets with low interest rates in the early 2000s. This, in turn, had the perverse consequence of raising the value of the Icelandic krona relative to other global currencies. As the krona grew stronger, Iceland's exports fell and its imports rose, leading to a large trade deficit. The financial inflows also provided Icelandic bankers with a ready source of funding for financial speculation. The government's promotion of non-financial firms' and households' purchase of shares in the banks created perverse incentives for them to raise share prices, and increased the scope of losses in the event of the banks' failure. Bank employees now had motivation to boost share prices by whatever means; households with little understanding of the activities of the banking sector would be increasingly vulnerable to the fate of the banks' performance.

Global financial institutions, meanwhile, seemed to forget that Argentina and Chile had liberalized their financial markets in the 1970s and 1980s with bad results: banks became more risk-taking, without becoming more efficient. Argentina's Central Bank offered guarantees on bank deposits, which encouraged more capital inflows. Though Chile's government initially stated that it would not insure deposits, its Central Bank ultimately guaranteed them after several panics early in the liberalization process. The big banks that had been privatized in the 1970s had to be re-nationalized during the crisis of the early 1980s, despite the "free market" views of the University of Chicago economists (or "Chicago Boys") who made economic policy for Chile's military dictatorship.

Foreign governments' economic and political pressure for governments and central banks to insure their investments guaranteed what economists call "moral hazard" problems: if businesses and banks trust that a government will bail them out in times of crisis, they will likely engage in riskier behavior, since they will profit more in the event of success, and not pay as much (or perhaps not pay anything) in the event of failure. Private financial institutions around the world, but particularly in Europe, trusted in Iceland's supposedly robust financial governance, despite Iceland's short history of financial liberalization. Many followed the advice of economists like Mishkin and Portes, who argued that Iceland should not be assumed to have the same financial risks as developing economies, despite the newness of its supercharged financial system. Outside investors' continued willingness to lend to Iceland increased the leveraged state of Icelandic banks and the scope of the eventual financial crisis.

## Heading Off the Next Crisis

Iceland's crisis reveals the inherent instability created by rapid financialization. When a country deregulates banks, encourages international capital inflows, and promotes wide-scale acquisition of those financial institutions' securities (by households, non-financial firms, government, and other banks), financial firms appear to be artificially profitable. Conflicts of interest develop that weaken the stability of the financial sector and the economy as a whole.

Mainstream economists failed to recognize this. However, this was well understood by heterodox figures like Keynes and Minsky, who argued that financial systems without adequate regulatory apparatuses are inherently prone to crisis. A number of current scholars, absorbing the lessons of Keynes and Minsky, argued that Iceland's financial sector was due for a collapse given the changes that had occurred in banking practices and economic orientation of the country. These processes increased Icelandic instability and the costs of the inevitable crisis.

Irrational exuberance and moral hazard overcame the ample evidence that Iceland was dangerously over-leveraged. Investors had access to data demonstrating the risks of investing in Iceland's financial system and economy, yet turned headlong into the storm. National and international unwillingness to compare Iceland's policy actions and history to that of developing economies like Argentina and Chile reflected the faulty assumption that Icelandic institutions were ready for the job of supervising a radically transformed financial sector. The Icelandic government's repression of data demonstrating instability, and the Icelandic media's unwillingness to publish unflattering stories, gave the lie to the notion that western European states' financial institutions and governments were robust enough for highly liberalized financial sectors.

Iceland's crisis demonstrates the need for the radically different policies: States and social movements must promote widespread financial literacy, so that ordinary people are aware of changes in the financial landscape and better able to protect themselves. If it is to be undertaken, financial deregulation, like cigarette packages, should come with large and impossible-to-miss warnings about its inherent dangers. These warnings should alert the public to the risks of purchasing large shares in globally active banks or other under-regulated financial products, and should warn less sophisticated financial intermediaries like pension funds about the riskiness of different financial assets. In Iceland, as in the United States, the financial system's default setting was to push households into excessive risk-taking; a public counterweight that prioritizes stability over risk would be valuable. "Nudges" encouraging safer approaches to personal wealth management—like insured deposits, defined-benefit retirement plans, and manageable mortgage loans—would still allow financially savvy or risk-loving individuals to engage in riskier transactions, while protecting the broader public. Stability-minded monetary policy is another means to ensuring greater financial and economic well-being. Greater regulatory vigilance against the excesses of financialization and shadow banking, too, would benefit most.

More broadly, given Iceland's experiences and those of other countries before it, states should reject financial deregulation and finance-led growth strategies. The costs of financialization, in the presence of moral hazard and irrational exuberance, expand rapidly in the absence of meaningful oversight. Iceland's experience illustrates this to the rest of the world. The country's policy responses to the crisis—starting with a systematic inquiry and prosecution of guilty bankers—also provide a worthy model for the world. Other countries would be wise to follow its example: The renationalization of banks that could have bankrupted the Icelandic government and central bank, implementation of capital controls (regulations on international capital flows) to stabilize an out-of-control financial system, and enforcement of new financial regulations to protect banks, firms, and households from the consequences of another financial bubble. ❑

*Sources:* Robert Aliber, "Monetary Turbulence and the Icelandic Economy," in Robert Aliber and Gylfi Zoega, eds., *Preludes to the Icelandic Financial Crisis* (Palgrave MacMillan, 2011); Anna Andersen, "The Watchdog That Didn't Bark," Reykjavik Grapevine, October 2010 (grapevine.is); Daniel Chartier, *The End of Iceland's Innocence: The Image of Iceland in the Foreign Media During the Financial Crisis* (University of Ottawa Press, 2011); V. Corbo and J. De Melo, "Lessons from the Southern Cone Policy Reforms." *The World Bank Research Observer*, 2(2), 1987; Jon Danielsson and Gylfi Zoega, "The Collapse of a Country," Working Paper 09:03, Institute of Economic Studies (hhi.hi.is); C. Diaz-Alejandro, "Good-Bye Financial Repression, Hello Financial Crash." *Journal of Development Economics*, 19(1), 1985; Gudrun Johnsen, Bringing Down the Banking System (Palgrave MacMillan, 2014); John Maynard Keynes, "National Self-Sufficiency," *The Yale Review* 22, 1933; Charles Kindleberger and Robert Aliber, *Manias, Panics, and Crashes: A History of Financial Crises* (Wiley, 2005); E. G. Mendoza and M.E. Terrones, *An Anatomy of Credit Booms and Their Demise* (No. w18379), National Bureau of Economic Research, 2012 (nber.org); Hyman Minsky, *Stabilizing An Unstable Economy* (McGraw-Hill, 2008); Hyman Minsky, "The Financial Instability Hypothesis," The Levy Institute, Working Paper No. 74, May 1992 (levyinstitute. org); Hyman Minsky, *Can 'It' Happen Again? Essays on Instability and Finance* (M.E. Sharpe, Inc., 1982); Frederic Mishkin and Tryggvi Herbertsson, "Financial Stability in Iceland," Iceland Chamber of Commerce Publication, 2006 (vi.is); F. S. Mishkin, *Inflation Targeting in Emerging Market Countries* (No. w7618), National Bureau of Economic Research (nber.org); D. Rodrik, "Growth Strategies," in P. Aghion and S.N. Durlauf, eds., *Handbook of Economic Growth*, Volume 1 (Elsevier, 2005); Throstur Sigurjonsson, "Privatization and Deregulation: A Chronology of Events," in Robert Aliber and Gylfi Zoega, eds., *Preludes to the Icelandic Financial Crisis* (Palgrave Macmillan, 2011); Robert Wade, "Iceland as Icarus," *Challenge* 52, 2009; Robert Wade and Silla Sigurgeirsdottir, "Lessons from Iceland," *New Left Review* 65, 2010; Robert Wade and Silla Sigurgeirsdottir, "Iceland's Rise, Fall, Stabilization, and Beyond," *Cambridge Journal of Economics* 36, 2011; Gylfi Zoega, "A Spending Spree," in Robert Aliber and Gylfi Zoega, eds., *Preludes to the Icelandic Financial Crisis* (Palgrave Macmillan, 2011).

Chapter 9

# THE GLOBAL ECONOMY

## INTRODUCTION

When it comes to the global economy, most textbooks line up behind the "Washington Consensus"—a package of free-trade and financial-liberalization policies that the U.S. Treasury Department, the International Monetary Fund (IMF), and the World Bank have prescribed for the world's developing economies. Mainstream textbook discussions of exchange rates, international trade, and economic-development policies almost always promote a market-dictated integration into the world economy. Outside the classroom, however, popular discontent with the Washington Consensus has spawned worldwide movements calling into question the myth of self-regulating markets on which these policies rest.

While the doctrines of free trade and international financial deregulation are seldom questioned in mainstream economics textbooks, both are scrutinized here. Economist Arthur MacEwan shows how industrialized economies developed by protecting their own manufacturing sectors—never preaching the "gospel of free trade" until they were highly developed. Today, he argues, the United States government prescribes free trade not because it's the best way for others to develop, but because it gives U.S. corporations free access to the world's markets and resources, which in turn strengthens the power of businesses against workers (Article 9.1).

Next, MacEwan follows with an overview of the changing place of the dollar in the global economy—especially its "dominance" as the key currency in which international trade is conducted and reserves are held—over the span of over seventy years (Article 9.2). He describes three critical moments: The first, near the end of the Second World War, when the Bretton Woods conference clearly established the dollar as the most important world currency; the next, in early 1970s, when the "dollar crisis" led to the United States abandoning the convertibility of dollars for gold at a fixed rate (the "gold standard"), yet the dollar remained the dominant currency. The third is happening right now, with the United States' dominant position in the global economy slipping, and the future role of the dollar unclear.

The next three articles look at international trade-and-investment agreements.

Over twenty years after the passage of the North American Free Trade Agreement (NAFTA), Dean Baker looks at its consequences for wage growth in the United States (Article 9.3). He argues that NAFTA—not incidentally, but deliberately—dragged down wages for U.S. workers. This is not because of any inherent fact that causes some to thrive and others to flounder in the global economy. Rather,

Baker argues that the treaty, like other trade and investment treaties that followed, deliberately exposed some workers to global competition while other groups (with more political power) remained insulated from competition.

Next, John Miller argues that the Trans-Pacific Partnership (TPP), a proposed "trade agreement" encompassing a dozen countries around the Pacific Rim, including the United States, is not really about trade at all (Article 9.4). Rather, like other so-called trade agreements, it is really about tilting the playing field of the global economy in favor of big corporations. Dean Baker makes a similar argument about the proposed Transatlantic Trade and Investment Partnership (Article 9.5). Its true purpose, in his view, is to create a political structure, above national governments, that will be dominated by big business. This structure will, in turn, be used to reduce consumer-protection and environmental regulations at the national level. The result, Baker argues, would be large profits for corporations in the telecommunications, pharmaceuticals, petrochemical, and other industries.

Marie Christine Duggan (Article 9.6) points to a failure of political institutions to deal with trade and debt imbalances, except in ways that are extremely costly and painful for ordinary people. Europe's main policy-making institutions have pushed—especially on Greece—austerity policies sure to inflict great suffering on the people and likely to undermine economic growth across Europe. Duggan points out that John Maynard Keynes developed a better solution way back in the 1940s: make surplus or creditor countries spend their surpluses (rather than hoarding them), which will boost demand for goods in the deficit countries, allowing the latter to grow their way out of debt.

In the final article in this chapter, Sirisha C. Naidu describes a gigantic shift of women out of the wage labor force in India in recent years (Article 9.7). Naidu argues for a new development program prioritizing job creation, living-wage and labor-conditions regulation, and essential public services. Government action against gender discrimination and sexual harassment, too, is necessary for inclusive development.

## Discussion Questions

1. (Article 9.1) MacEwan claims that the "infant industry" argument for trade protection is much more widely applicable than standard theory suggests. To what countries and industries might it apply in today's world economy? Explain your answer.

2. (Article 9.1) "Free trade" policies, MacEwan argues, give business greater power relative to labor. Why is this so? Is this a good reason to oppose such policies?

3. (Article 9.2) What does it mean to say that the dollar is the "dominant" currency in the world? Why has this been the case for nearly three quarters of a century? Consider economic and political factors.

4. (Article 9.3) Baker reports that NAFTA has contributed to wage suppression and to lower prices on many goods. What is the net effect on income distribution within the United States? Could a trade agreement be structured in a different way, and result in different distributional outcomes?

5. (Article 9.4) According to Miller, "with lost manufacturing jobs unlikely to return to the United States," labor union opposition to the TPP is not about protecting manufacturing industry from import competition or about protecting union jobs in manufacturing. Then what is it about?

6. (Article 9.5) According to advocates of international "trade agreements," increased global competition will be good for consumers. Baker argues that the TTIP would have opposite effects. Why?

7. (Article 9.6) Duggan argues that the ideas of John Maynard Keynes about how to deal with international financial imbalances in the 1940s can be applied to the problems of Europe today. Do you think the kinds of policies Keynes proposed then, and that Duggan proposes now, would be better than the "austerity" policies that have been pursued so far?

8. (Article 9.7) According to Naidu, why has there been such a large decline in women's labor force participation in India? What do you think of her proposed policy responses?

*Article 9.1*

# THE GOSPEL OF FREE TRADE: THE NEW EVANGELISTS

## BY ARTHUR MacEWAN
*November 1991; updated July 2009*

Free trade! With the zeal of Christian missionaries, for decades the U.S. government has been preaching, advocating, pushing, and coercing around the globe for "free trade."

As the economic crisis emerged in 2007 and 2008 and rapidly became a global crisis, it was apparent that something was very wrong with the way the world economy was organized. Not surprisingly, as unemployment rose sharply in the United States, there were calls for protecting jobs by limiting imports and for the government to "buy American" in its economic stimulus program. Similarly, in many other countries, as unemployment jumped upwards, pressure emerged for protection—and some actual steps were taken. Yet, free trade missionaries did not retreat; they continued to preach the same gospel.

The free-traders were probably correct in claiming that protectionist policies would do more harm than good as a means to stem the rising unemployment generated by the economic crisis. Significant acts of protectionism in one country would lead to retaliation—or at least copying—by other countries, reducing world trade. The resulting loss of jobs from reduced trade would most likely outweigh any gains from protection.

Yet the argument over international economic policies should not be confined simply to what should be done in a crisis. Nor should it simply deal with trade in goods and services. The free-traders have advocated their program as one for long-run economic growth and development, yet the evidence suggests that free trade is not a good economic development strategy. Furthermore, the free-traders preach the virtue of unrestricted global movement of finance as well as of goods and services. As it turns out, the free flow of finance has been a major factor in bringing about and spreading the economic crisis that began to appear in 2007—as well as earlier crises.

## The Push

While the U.S. push for free trade goes back several decades, it has become more intense in recent years. In the 1990s, the U.S. government signed on to the North American Free Trade Agreement (NAFTA) and in 2005 established the Central American Free Trade Agreement (CAFTA). Both Republican and Democratic presidents, however, have pushed hard for a *global* free trade agenda. After the demise of the Soviet Union, U.S. advisers prescribed unfettered capitalism for Eastern and Central Europe, and ridiculed as unworkable any move toward a "third way." In low-income countries from Mexico to Malaysia, the prescription has been the same: open markets, deregulate business, don't restrict international investment, and let the free market flourish.

In the push for worldwide free trade, the World Trade Organization (WTO) has been the principal vehicle of change, establishing rules for commerce that assure markets are open and resources are available to those who can pay. And the International Monetary Fund (IMF) and World Bank, which provide loans to many governments, use their financial power to pressure countries around the world to accept the gospel and open their markets. In each of these international organizations, the United States—generally through the U.S. Treasury—plays a dominant role.

Of course, as with any gospel, the preachers often ignore their own sermons. While telling other countries to open their markets, the U.S. government continued, for instance, to limit imports of steel, cotton, sugar, textiles, and many other goods. But publicly at least, free-trade boosters insist that the path to true salvation—or economic expansion, which, in this day and age, seems to be the same thing—lies in opening our market to foreign goods. Get rid of trade barriers at home and abroad, allow business to go where it wants and do what it wants. We will all get rich.

Yet the history of the United States and other rich countries does not fit well with the free-trade gospel. Virtually all advanced capitalist countries found economic success through heavy government regulation of their international commerce, not in free trade. Likewise, a large role for government intervention has characterized those cases of rapid and sustained economic growth in recent decades—for example, Japan after World War II, South Korea in the 1970s through the 1990s, and China most recently.

Free trade does, however, have its uses. Highly developed nations can use free trade to extend their power and control of the world's wealth, and business can use it as a weapon against labor. Most important, free trade can limit efforts to redistribute income more equally, undermine social programs, and keep people from democratically controlling their economic lives.

## A Day in the Park

At the beginning of the 19th century, Lowell, Massachusetts, became the premier site of the U.S. textile industry. Today, thanks to the Lowell National Historical Park, you can tour the huge mills, ride through the canals that redirected the Merrimack River's power to those mills, and learn the story of the textile workers, from the Yankee "mill girls" of the 1820s through the various waves of immigrant laborers who poured into the city over the next century.

During a day in the park, visitors get a graphic picture of the importance of 19th-century industry to the economic growth and prosperity of the United States. Lowell and the other mill towns of the era were centers of growth. They not only created a demand for Southern cotton, they also created a demand for new machinery, maintenance of old machinery, parts, dyes, *skills*, construction materials, construction machinery, *more skills*, equipment to move the raw materials and products, parts maintenance for that equipment, *and still more skills*. The mill towns also created markets—concentrated groups of wage earners who needed to buy products to sustain themselves. As centers of economic activity, Lowell and similar mill towns contributed to U.S. economic growth far beyond the value of the textiles they produced.

The U.S. textile industry emerged decades after the industrial revolution had spawned Britain's powerful textile industry. Nonetheless, it survived and prospered. British linens inundated markets throughout the world in the early 19th century, as the British navy nurtured free trade and kept ports open for commerce. In the United States, however, hostilities leading up to the War of 1812 and then a substantial tariff made British textiles relatively expensive. These limitations on trade allowed the Lowell mills to prosper, acting as a catalyst for other industries and helping to create the skilled work force at the center of U.S. economic expansion.

Beyond textiles, however, tariffs did not play a great role in the United States during the early 19th century. Southern planters had considerable power, and while they were willing to make some compromises, they opposed protecting manufacturing in general because that protection forced up the prices of the goods they purchased with their cotton revenues. The Civil War wiped out the planters' power to oppose protectionism, and from the 1860s through World War I, U.S. industry prospered behind considerable tariff barriers.

## Different Countries, Similar Experiences

The story of the importance of protectionism in bringing economic growth has been repeated, with local variations, in other advanced capitalist countries. During the late 19th century, Germany entered the major league of international economic powers with substantial protection and government support for its industries. Likewise, in 19th-century France and Italy, national consolidation behind protectionist barriers was a key to economic development.

Britain—which entered the industrial era first—is often touted as the prime example of successful development without tariff protection. Yet, Britain embraced free trade only after its industrial base was well established; as in the U.S., the early and important textile industry was erected on a foundation of protectionism. In addition, Britain built its industry through the British navy and the expansion of empire, hardly prime ingredients in any recipe for free trade.

Japan provides an especially important case of successful government protection and support for industrial development. In the post-World War II era, when the Japanese established the foundations for their economic "miracle," the government rejected free trade and extensive foreign investment and instead promoted its national firms.

In the 1950s, for example, the government protected the country's fledgling auto firms from foreign competition. At first, quotas limited imports to $500,000 (in current dollars) each year; in the 1960s, prohibitively high tariffs replaced the quotas. Furthermore, the Japanese allowed foreign investment only insofar as it contributed to developing domestic industry. The government encouraged Japanese companies to import foreign technology, but required them to produce 90% of parts domestically within five years.

The Japanese also protected their computer industry. In the early 1970s, as the industry was developing, companies and individuals could only purchase a foreign machine if a suitable Japanese model was not available. IBM was allowed to produce within the country, but only when it licensed basic patents to Japanese firms. And IBM computers produced in Japan were treated as foreign-made machines.

In the 20th century, no other country matched Japan's economic success, as it moved in a few decades from a relative low-income country, through the devastation of war, to emerge as one of the world's economic leaders. Yet one looks back in vain to find a role for free trade in this success. The Japanese government provided an effective framework, support, and protection for the country's capitalist development.

Likewise, in many countries that have been late-comers to economic development, capitalism has generated high rates of economic growth where government involvement, and not free trade, played the central role. South Korea is a striking case. "Korea is an example of a country that grew very fast and yet violated the canons of conventional economic wisdom," writes Alice Amsden in *Asia's Next Giant: South Korea and Late Industrialization,* widely acclaimed as perhaps the most important analysis of the South Korean economic success. "In Korea, instead of the market mechanism allocating resources and guiding private entrepreneurship, the government made most of the pivotal investment decisions. Instead of firms operating in a competitive market structure, they each operated with an extraordinary degree of market control, protected from foreign competition."

Free trade, however, has had its impact in South Korea. In the 1990s, South Korea and other East Asian governments came under pressure from the U.S. government and the IMF to open their markets, including their financial markets. When they did so, the results were a veritable disaster. The East Asian financial crisis that began in 1997 was a major setback for the whole region, a major disruption of economic growth. After extremely rapid economic growth for three decades, with output expanding at 7% to 10% a year, South Korea's economy plummeted by 6.3% between 1997 and 1998.

## Mexico and Its NAFTA Experience

While free trade in goods and services has its problems, which can be very serious, it is the free movement of capital, the opening of financial markets that has sharp, sudden impacts, sometimes wrecking havoc on national economies. Thus, virtually as soon as Mexico, the United States and Canada formed NAFTA at the beginning of 1994, Mexico was hit with a severe financial crisis. As the economy turned downward at the beginning of that year, capital rapidly left the country, greatly reducing the value of the Mexican peso. With this diminished value of the peso, the cost of servicing international debts and the costs of imports skyrocketed—and the downturn worsened.

Still, during the 1990s, before and after the financial crisis, free-traders extolled short periods of moderate economic growth in Mexico —3% to 4% per year—as evidence of success. Yet, compared to earlier years, Mexico's growth under free trade has been poor. From 1940 to 1990 (including the no-growth decade of the 1980s), when Mexico's market was highly protected and the state actively regulated economic affairs, output grew at an average annual rate of 5%.

Most important, Mexico's experience discredits the notion that free-market policies will improve living conditions for the masses of people in low-income countries. The Mexican government paved the way for free trade policies by reducing or eliminating social welfare programs, and for many Mexican workers wages declined sharply during the free trade era. The number of households living in poverty rose dramatically, with some 75% of Mexico's population below the poverty line at the beginning of the 21st century.

## China and Its Impact

Part of Mexico's problem and its economy's relatively weak performance from the 1990s onward has been the full-scale entrance of China into the international economy. While the Mexican authorities thought they saw great possibilities in NAFTA with the full opening of the U.S. market to goods produced with low-wage Mexican labor, China (and other Asian countries) had even cheaper labor. As China also gained access to the U.S. market, Mexican expectations were dashed.

The Chinese economy has surely gained in terms of economic growth as it has engaged more and more with the world market, and the absolute levels of incomes of millions of people have risen a great deal. However, China's rapid economic growth has come with a high degree of income inequality. Before its era of rapid growth, China was viewed as a country with a relatively equal distribution of income. By the beginning of the new millennium, however, it was much more unequal than any of the other most populace Asian countries (India, Indonesia, Bangladesh, Pakistan), and more in line with the high-inequality countries of Latin America. Furthermore, with the inequality has come a great deal of social conflict. Tens of thousands of "incidents" of conflict involving violence are reported each year, and most recently there have been the major conflicts involving Tibetans and Ouigers.

In any case, the Chinese trade and growth success should not be confused with "free trade." Foundations for China's surge of economic growth were established through state-sponsored infrastructure development and the vast expansion of the country's educational system. Even today, while private business, including foreign business, appears to have been given free rein in China, the government still plays a controlling role—including a central role in affecting foreign economic relations.

A central aspect of the government's role in the county's foreign commerce has been in the realm of finance. As Chinese-produced goods have virtually flooded international markets, the government has controlled the uses of the earnings from these exports. Instead of simply allowing those earnings to be used by Chinese firms and citizens to buy imports, the government has to a large extent held those earnings as reserves. Using those reserves, China's central bank has been the largest purchaser of U.S. government bonds, in effect becoming a major financer of the U.S. government's budget deficit of recent years.

China's reserves have been one large element in creating a giant pool of financial assets in the world economy. This "pool" has also been built up as the doubling of oil prices following the U.S. invasion of Iraq put huge amounts of funds in the pockets of oil-exporting countries and firms and individuals connected to the oil industry. Yet slow growth of the U.S. economy and extremely low interest rates, resulting from the Federal Reserve Bank's efforts to encourage more growth, limited the returns that could be obtained on these funds. One of the consequences—through a complex set of connections—was the development of the U.S. housing bubble, as financial firms, searching for higher returns, pushed funds into more and more risky mortgage loans.

It was not simply free trade and the unrestricted flow of international finance that generated the housing bubble and subsequent crisis in the U.S. economy. However, the generally unstable global economy—both in terms of trade and finance—

that has emerged in the free trade era was certainly a factor bringing about the crisis. Moreover, as is widely recognized, it was not only the U.S. economy and U.S. financial institutions that were affected. The free international flow of finance has meant that banking has become more and more a global industry. So as the U.S. banks got in trouble in 2007 and 2008, their maladies spread to many other parts of the world.

## The Uses of Free Trade

While free trade is not the best economic growth or development policy and, especially through the free flow of finance, can precipitate financial crises, the largest and most powerful firms in many countries find it highly profitable. As Britain preached the loudest sermons for free trade in the early 19th century, when its own industry was already firmly established, so the United States—or at least many firms based in the United States—find it a profitable policy at the beginning of the 21st century. The Mexican experience provides an instructive illustration.

For U.S. firms, access to foreign markets is a high priority. Mexico may be relatively poor, but with a population of 105 million it provides a substantial market. Furthermore, Mexican labor is cheap relative to U.S. labor; and using modern production techniques, Mexican workers can be as productive as workers in the United States. For U.S. firms to obtain full access to the Mexican market, the United States has to open its borders to Mexican goods. Also, if U.S. firms are to take full advantage of cheap foreign labor and sell the goods produced abroad to U.S. consumers, the United States has to be open to imports.

On the other side of the border, wealthy Mexicans face a choice between advancing their interests through national development or advancing their interests through ties to U.S. firms and access to U.S. markets. For many years, they chose the former route. This led to some development of the Mexican economy but also—due to corruption and the massive power of the ruling party, the PRI—huge concentrations of wealth in the hands of a few small groups of firms and individuals. Eventually, these groups came into conflict with their own government over regulation and taxation. Having benefited from government largesse, they came to see their fortunes in greater freedom from government control and, particularly, in greater access to foreign markets and partnerships with large foreign companies. National development was a secondary concern when more involvement with international commerce would produce greater riches more quickly.

In addition, the old program of state-led development in Mexico ran into severe problems. These problems came to the surface in the 1980s with the international debt crisis. Owing huge amounts of money to foreign banks, the Mexican government was forced to respond to pressure from the IMF, the U.S. government, and large international banks which sought to deregulate Mexico's trade and investment. That pressure meshed with the pressure from Mexico's own richest elites, and the result was the move toward free trade and a greater opening of the Mexican economy to foreign investment.

Since the early 1990s, these changes for Mexico and the United States (as well as Canada) have been institutionalized in NAFTA. The U.S. government's agenda since then has been to spread free trade policies to all of the Americas through more regional agreements like CAFTA and ultimately through a Free Trade Area of the Americas. On a broader scale, the U.S. government works through the WTO, the IMF, and the World Bank to open markets and gain access to resources beyond the Western Hemisphere. In fact, while markets remain important everywhere, low-wage manufacturing is increasingly concentrated in Asia—especially China—instead of Mexico or Latin America.

The Chinese experience involves many of the same advantages for U.S. business as does the Mexican—a vast market, low wages, and an increasingly productive labor force. However, the Chinese government, although it has liberalized the economy a great deal compared to the pre-1985 era, has not abdicated its major role in the economy. For better (growth) and for worse (inequality and repression), the Chinese government has not embraced free trade.

## Who Gains, Who Loses?

Of course, in the United States, Mexico, China and elsewhere, advocates of free trade claim that their policies are in everyone's interest. Free trade, they point out, will mean cheaper products for all. Consumers in the United States, who are mostly workers, will be richer because their wages will buy more. In Mexico and China, on the one hand, and in the United States, on the other hand, they argue that rising trade will create more jobs. If some workers lose their jobs because cheaper imported goods are available, export industries will produce new jobs.

In recent years this argument has taken on a new dimension with the larger entrance of India into the world economy and with the burgeoning there of jobs based in information technology—programming and call centers, for example. This "outsourcing" of service jobs has received a great deal of attention and concern in the United States. Yet free-traders have defended this development as good for the U.S. economy as well as for the Indian economy.

Such arguments obscure many of the most important issues in the free trade debate. Stated, as they usually are, as universal truths, these arguments are just plain silly. No one, for example, touring the Lowell National Historical Park could seriously argue that people in the United States would have been better off had there been no tariff on textiles. Yes, in 1820, they could have purchased textile goods more cheaply, but in the long run the result would have been less industrial advancement and a less wealthy nation. One could make the same point with the Japanese auto and computer industries, or indeed with numerous other examples from the last two centuries of capitalist development.

In the modern era, even though the United States already has a relatively developed economy with highly skilled workers, a freely open international economy does not serve the interests of most U.S. workers, though it will benefit large firms. U.S. workers today are in competition with workers around the globe. Many different workers in many different places can produce the same goods and services. Thus, an international economy governed by the free trade agenda will tend to bring down wages for many U.S. workers. This phenomenon has certainly been one of the factors leading to the substantial rise of income inequality in the United States during recent decades.

The problem is not simply that of workers in a few industries—such as auto and steel, or call-centers and computer programming—where import competition is an obvious and immediate issue. A country's openness to the international economy affects the entire structure of earnings in that country. Free trade forces down the general level of wages across the board, even of those workers not directly affected by imports. The simple fact is that when companies can produce the same products in several different places, it is owners who gain because they can move their factories and funds around much more easily than workers can move themselves around. Capital is mobile; labor is much less mobile. Businesses, more than workers, gain from having a larger territory in which to roam.

## Control Over Our Economic Lives

But the difficulties with free trade do not end with wages. In both low-income and high-income parts of the world, free trade is a weapon in the hands of business when it opposes any progressive social programs. Efforts to place environmental restrictions on firms are met with the threat of moving production abroad. Higher taxes to improve the schools? Business threatens to go elsewhere. Better health and safety regulations? The same response.

Some might argue that the losses from free trade for people in the United States will be balanced by gains for most people in poor countries—lower wages in the United States, but higher wages in Mexico and China. Free trade, then, would bring about international equality. Not likely. In fact, as pointed out above, free trade reforms in Mexico have helped force down wages and reduce social welfare programs, processes rationalized by efforts to make Mexican goods competitive on international markets. China, while not embracing free trade, has seen its full-scale entrance into global commerce accompanied by increasing inequality.

Gains for Mexican or Chinese workers, like those for U.S. workers, depend on their power in relation to business. Free trade or simply the imperative of international "competitiveness" are just as much weapons in the hands of firms operating in Mexico and China as they are for firms operating in the United States. The great mobility of capital is business's best trump card in dealing with labor and popular demands for social change—in the United States, Mexico, China and elsewhere.

None of this means that people should demand that their economies operate as fortresses, protected from all foreign economic incursions. There are great gains that can be obtained from international economic relations—when a nation manages those relations in the interests of the great majority of the people. Protectionism often simply supports narrow vested interests, corrupt officials, and wealthy industrialists. In rejecting free trade, we should move beyond traditional protectionism.

Yet, at this time, rejecting free trade is an essential first step. Free trade places the cards in the hands of business. More than ever, free trade would subject us to the "bottom line," or at least the bottom line as calculated by those who own and run large companies. ❏

*Article 9.2*

# DOLLAR DOMINANCE

## BY ARTHUR MacEWAN
*January/February 2015*

> Dear Dr. Dollar:
> *What does it mean that the dollar is the "dominant" global currency? Why does this situation exist? And how does it matter?* —Anonymous

Suppose that, when you paid for things with checks, all the recipients of those checks believed that you were a very responsible person, that you would keep plenty of money in the bank to honor those checks. Moreover, not only did the check recipients believe in you, but people in general had this same opinion.

Under these circumstances, the people holding your checks wouldn't have to cash them in. Those checks could simply be used as money. The checks themselves would be acceptable in transactions among all those people who believed you were so responsible.

This situation would be nice for you because you could write plenty of checks and not worry about those checks being cashed in against your account. Extra buying power for you. At the same time, the people who used your checks as money would have an easier time with transactions, having your checks as a widely acceptable form of currency—i.e., they would have more "liquidity." Also, holding onto your checks—keeping them "in reserve"—would be a safe way for people to store money for when they needed it.

## Fiction and Reality

To a large extent, this fictional situation with your checks is analogous to the real situation of the U.S. dollar in global commerce. With people and banks around the world using dollars and holding dollars, not "cashing them in" for U.S. goods, the United States— primarily its government and businesses—is able to spend more abroad without giving up so much in goods and services produced in the United States. Governments, businesses, and people around the world have more liquidity than they would otherwise, and they have more confidence than they would otherwise in the value of the currency (dollars) they are using and holding in reserve

Like you in the fictional scenario, the U.S. government in the real scenario is viewed as "responsible." An important part of the U.S. government being viewed as "responsible" is that it would keep the value of the dollar relatively stable—i.e., not much inflation (at least compared to other currencies). This organization of the global finance system, with the dollar in this special, or dominant, position has an interesting history—and some powerful implications.

## Where Did This System Come From?

The crucial formal step in creating the dollar-dominated system came at the end of World War II, with the United States in an extremely strong economic position. Indeed, the high level of government spending on the war had brought the U.S. economy out of the Great Depression, while other high-income countries (and many low-income countries) had had their economies physically decimated by the war. Combined with this economic power, the United States had extreme military power. Thus, the era following World War II came to be called "The American Century" (Of course it was not really a full century, but let's not quibble.)

As the end of the war was coming into sight, in July 1944, representatives of the U.S. government and of 43 allied governments (over 700 delegates in all) met over three weeks at the Mt. Washington Hotel in Bretton Woods, N.H. The purpose of this conference was to set up the arrangements for the operation of the global economy in the postwar era. Although the Soviet Union and China were both represented at the Bretton Woods conference, in subsequent years they did not take part in the arrangements. (Today you can go to Bretton Woods and, at the entrance to the hotel's driveway, see the sign commemorating this conference, but you have to pay an entrance fee to actually get onto the hotel grounds.)

Unsurprisingly, given the relative economic and political power of the allied governments, the U.S. government basically dictated the conference outcomes, arrangements by which commerce among capitalist countries would be organized in the decades following World War II—the "Bretton Woods era." The central feature of these arrangements was that the dollar would be at the core of global commerce. Other countries' currencies would be "pegged" to the dollar, which meant that each government would set the value of its currency in terms of the dollar. For example, in 1949 the French franc was pegged at $0.37 and the British pound at $2.80. The dollar itself was set in relation to gold: $34 to the ounce. Other countries' banks could redeem their dollars for gold at this rate, but, as with your checks, they generally didn't do so. When the gold-redemption promise was terminated in 1971, it turned out not to make much difference—more on that in a moment.

Of course, economies change in relation to one another. In the postwar era, different rates of inflation and different rates of productivity growth meant that the values of the currencies in terms of the dollar had to be changed from time to time. For example, if France was running a trade deficit with the rest of the world (importing more than it was exporting), this meant that the value of its franc was too high in relation to the dollar—i.e., in terms of dollars, the cost of French goods was too high and France's exports would be low, while the cost for France of goods from elsewhere would be too low and France's imports would be high. Moreover, with French exports not paying for its imports, France would necessarily build up a foreign debt to pay for the excess imports.

One could look at this franc-dollar relationship another way: instead of the franc being too high, one could say that the dollar was too low. But the rules that were established at Bretton Woods excluded the dollar from having to adjust. In this example, it was the French who would have to adjust the value of their currency—i.e., France would have to devalue its currency. And, importantly, it would have to borrow to cover the foreign debt it had built up. The U.S. economy, on the other hand, was protected from the disruption that would have been caused by changing the value of the dollar.

The International Monetary Fund (IMF) was established at Bretton Woods to provide countries in this kind of situation with the loans they needed. The IMF provided these loans, but with various conditions—in particular that the county taking the loans would have to take steps to reorganize their economies, generally in ways that opened them to more foreign commerce, trade and investment.

While the IMF did play a role in European adjustments, its actions became especially important in lower-income countries, where it used its loan conditions to push countries towards a greater openness to international investment and trade—very much in the interests of multinational firms based in the richer countries. (The World Bank was also created at Bretton Woods, but its role is not a central part of the story here.)

## Change Without Change

The Bretton Woods rules of the game worked fairly well for twenty-five years. In fact, from the perspective of the United States one might say they worked too well. While the Bretton Woods system promoted U.S. commerce, opening up trade and investment opportunities around the (capitalist) world, it also provided a stability in global affairs in which firms based elsewhere—in Japan and Europe—were able to also expand and ultimately challenge the dominant position of U.S firms.

A critical juncture in global commercial arrangements then came in 1971: the Bretton Woods system fell apart. A combination of heavy spending abroad by the U.S. government (on the Vietnam War), the economic challenge from other rich countries, and inflation in the United States led the U.S. government to drop its promise of redeeming dollars for gold. Yet, while the system fell apart, there was surprisingly little change in international trade and investment. The relative economic and military power of the United States, though not as extreme as it had been in the immediate post-World War II era, continued. And the perceived threat of the Soviet Union served as a glue, binding the world's major capitalist powers in Europe and Asia to the United States, and leading them to accept continued U.S. economic, as well as military, dominance.

After 1971, various new arrangements were put in place—for example, a system of partially managed "pegs" was established. Yet the dollar remained the central currency of global commerce. Prices of internationally traded goods—most importantly oil—continued to be set in dollars, and countries continued to hold their reserves in dollars.

Although 1971 marked the beginning of a new era in international financial arrangements, the dollar retained its dominant position. Regardless of the various economic problems in the United States, the dollar has remained both relatively stable and in sufficient supply to grease the wheels of international commerce. Indeed, an ironic example of the continuing role of the dollar came in the Great Recession that began in 2008. Even while the U.S. economy was in the doldrums, businesses and governments elsewhere in the world were buying U.S. government bonds—a principal means of holding their reserves in dollars—since they still considered these the safest assets available.

## Power and a Symbol of Power

In years leading up to the Great Recession, China had entered the global for-profit economy and was exporting at a high rate, exceeding its imports. The Chinese government used the extra money that China was obtaining from its trade surplus to heavily invest in U.S. government bonds. That is, China built up extensive reserves in dollars. In effect, China was loaning money to the United States—loans which filled both the federal budget deficit and the U.S trade deficit. What many observers decried as a dangerous situation—We are becoming indebted to the Chinese! Horror!—in fact served both the U.S. and Chinese governments quite well.

The international role of the dollar is a symbol of U.S. power and is based on that power. At the same time, the dollar's role works to enhance that power, giving the U.S. government and U.S. business the liquidity needed for carrying out global operations—everything from wars to benign commerce.

There are problems with the system. The continued role of the dollar depends to a large extent on the avoidance of significant inflation in the United States. Yet restraints on inflation—e.g., the Federal Reserve raising interest rates—generally work against expanding employment. So maintaining the role of the dollar can come at the expense of most people in the country.

Also, there is always the risk of change. Just as the position of the dollar supports U.S. power in world affairs, if that position is undermined, U.S. power would suffer. In recent years, there has been some threat that other governments would challenge the dollar with their own currencies. China, in particular, has attempted to establish its own positon in world affairs, which, if successful, could ultimately undercut the dominance of the dollar. Indeed, the fear associated with China holding reserves in dollars (i.e., as U.S. government bonds) is to some extent based on concern about the potential implications of China shifting out of dollars (or threatening to do so). Yet, especially with the recent weakening of the Chinese economy, this particular challenge does not appear likely in the near future.

Over the last several decades, the role of the dollar in world affairs has become like the role of the English language. Both developed as a consequence of the extreme power of the United States. in the global economy, and both give advantages to the U.S. government, to U.S. firms, and to any individuals engaged in international activities. Most important, the roles of both the dollar and the English language have become thoroughly entrenched. Even as the power of the United States weakens, then, those roles are likely to continue for some time to come. ❏

*Article 9.3*

# NAFTA: IT LOWERED WAGES, AS IT WAS SUPPOSED TO DO

## BY DEAN BAKER
*November 2013,* New York Times

Given the trends in U.S. trade with Mexico over the last two decades, it is strange that there is much of a debate over NAFTA's impact on wages. At the time NAFTA was passed in 1993 the United States had a modest trade surplus with Mexico. In 2013 we are on a path to have a trade deficit of more than $50 billion. The $50 billion in lost output corresponds to roughly 0.3 percent of gross domestic product, assuming the same impact on employment, this would translate into more than 400,000 jobs. If each lost job would have led to half a job being created as a result of workers spending their wages, this would bring the total impact to 600,000 jobs.

Of course some of the shift from surplus to deficit might have occurred even without NAFTA, but it would be difficult to argue that NAFTA was not a major contributing factor. After all, one of the main purposes of the agreement was to make U.S. firms feel confident that they could locate operations in Mexico without having to fear that their factories could be nationalized or that Mexico would impose restrictions on repatriating profits. This encouraged firms to take advantage of lower cost labor in Mexico, and many did.

This can produce economic gains; they just don't go to ordinary workers. The lower cost of labor translates to some extent into lower prices and to some extent into higher corporate profits. The latter might be good news for shareholders and top management, but is not beneficial to most workers.

Lower prices are helpful to workers as consumers, but are not likely to offset the impact on wages. To see this point, imagine that NAFTA was about reducing the wages of doctors by eliminating the barriers that made it difficult for Mexican school children to train to U.S. standards and practice medicine in the United States.

If we got an additional 200,000 doctors from Mexico over the last 20 years then it would likely go far toward bringing the pay of doctors in the United States more in line with the pay of doctors in other wealthy countries. This would lead to tens of billions of years in savings in health care costs to patients and the government.

Even doctors would share in these savings, since they too would have to pay less for their health care. However no one would try to tell doctors that they were better off from this trade deal because of their reduced health care costs. The hit to their wages would have swamped the savings on their health care bill. This is the same story with ordinary workers and the impact of NAFTA.

NAFTA could have been structured to bring the pay of doctors and other highly paid professionals more in line with their pay in other wealthy countries by removing barriers. This would have produced substantial economic gains to the economy as a whole (it's the exact same model as economists use to show gains from the NAFTA we have), except these gains would be associated with a downward rather than an upward redistribution of income.

The doctors and their allies among the elite have been able to prevent such a deal from being considered by the politicians in Washington, American workers don't have that power. ❏

Article 9.4

# TRANS-PACIFIC PARTNERSHIP: CORPORATE POWER UNBOUND

## BY JOHN MILLER
*July/August 2015*

> The case [for opposing the Trans-Pacific Partnership] put forth by a show-boating Sen. Elizabeth Warren is almost worse than wrong. It is irrelevant.
>
> Less than 10 percent of the AFL-CIO's membership is now in manufacturing. It's undeniable that American manufacturing workers have suffered terrible job losses. We could never compete with pennies-an-hour wages. Those low-skilled jobs are not coming back.
>
> Some liberals oddly complain that American efforts to strengthen intellectual propertylaws in trade deals protect the profits of U.S. entertainment and tech companies. What's wrong with that?
>
> Then we have Warren stating with a straight face that handing negotiating authority to Obama would "give Republicans the very tool they need to dismantle Dodd-Frank."
>
> —Froma Harrop, "The Left Is Wrong on Fast-Track Trade Issue," *Spokesman Review*, May 16, 2015.

The Trans-Pacific Partnership (TPP) sounds more like an international consortium of corporate law firms than a trade deal. That's for good reason. TPP is less about trade than about corporate- dominated globalization.

But that's all a mystery to Froma Harrop, liberal columnist, business writer, and robotic Obama supporter. (Obama has pushed hard for the TPP.) Why should the AFL-CIO, with so few members in manufacturing, oppose this trade deal, Harrop asks? And what so wrong with protecting corporate profits by enforcing intellectual property rights, as the TPP would?

The answer is plenty. And that's especially true now that the Obama administration and both Republicans and corporate Democrats in Congress have engineered the passage of the "fast-track authority," guaranteeing an up or down vote for the TPP.

## The TPP Is Not About Trade

The TPP is surely marketed as a trade deal. And economist after economist supporting TPP has touted it as a giant step toward free trade that will bestow benefits on all nations in just the way every student learns it will in introductory economics.

But what economists have to say about the virtues of free trade, as flawed as that may be, has little to do with the TPP. The TPP is not about free trade or even principally about the gains from trade.

The TPP would be the largest regional "trade" agreement ever. It involves 12 countries: the United States, Australia, Brunei, Canada, Chile, Japan, Malaysia, Mexico, New Zealand, Peru, Singapore, and Vietnam. Those dozen countries collectively produce 40% of global output (GDP).

But if trade is the hype, it is not the substance of the deal. To begin with, the TPP would do little to reduce barriers to trade in these countries, which are already quite low. The average tariff level in each of the 12 countries is lower than the world average (6.8% in 2012) and far lower than global tariff rates two decades ago. In addition, Australia, Canada, Chile, Mexico, Peru, and Singapore are already members of other free trade agreements with the United States. In 2014, nearly three-quarters (74%) of U.S. goods traded with the TPP group was with those six nations. As tariff levels have dropped, so have potential gains from further lowering tariffs, as envisioned by those who have drunk the free trade Kool-Aid served up by economists.

For instance, the Peterson Institute for International Economics, a Washington-based pro-free trade thinktank, estimates that the TPP would add $77.5 billion of income to the U.S. economy by 2025, a figure the Obama administration uses to make the case for the TPP. That number might sound impressive, but those gains would add just 0.38% to U.S. GDP over the next ten years. And it is undoubtedly an overestimate, for it relies on the assumption that the U.S. economy and the economies of its trading partners will be at full employment during those years.

The Obama Administration claims that the TPP would create 650,000 new jobs in the next decade. They get that number by dividing the $77.5 billion income gain from the TPP in the Peterson report by the average cost to a company when it hires an additional worker. But nowhere in its report does the Peterson Institute project that the TTP would create jobs. Rather, the position of the Peterson Institute, according to Fred Bergsten, its founder, is that "a trade agreement does not on balance, create, or destroy jobs, it alters the composition of the workforce."

Nor would the meager income gains produced by the TPP be widely shared. In a Center for Economic and Policy Research (CEPR) report, economist David Rosnick estimates that just the top 10% of U.S. workers would see real wage gains, if the Trans-Pacific Partnership were enacted. Worse yet, the real wages of a broad swath of middle-income U.S. workers (from the 35th percentile to the 80th percentile) would fall, even under Rosnick's most conservative assumptions about the likely effect of the TPP on inequality.

Losses from trade agreements have been visited upon the same groups, especially manufacturing workers, time and time again. For instance, labor economists Avraham Ebenstein, Ann Harrison, Margot McMillan, and Shannon Phillips have found that, between 1983 and 2002, globalization forced U.S. workers out of manufacturing into lower-paying jobs, reducing their real wage by 12% to 17%.

## TPP is About Corporate Power

Why would the labor movement go all out to defeat the TPP with so few of its members in manufacturing, and with lost manufacturing jobs unlikely to return to the United States?

Economic journalist Robert Kuttner gave perhaps the best answer: "The labor movement is not motivated just by the loss of factory jobs but by the entire ideological assault on the security of ordinary wage earners and consumers." That's also what lies behind the complaints about how the TPP would protect corporate profits in what Nobel Prize winning economist Joseph Stiglitz calls a "secret corporate takeover."

At the heart of the TPP is an Investor-State Dispute Settlement (ISDS) process that would give corporations yet more power to make the economic rules that govern our lives. The settlement process would allow investors who think that a country's laws have reduced their profits to take their case before a "tribunal" of three private attorneys; that is, to sidestep the country's own legal system. Unlike national courts, which can order corporations to be compensated for losses of actual assets, ISDS tribunals would be empowered to order taxpayers to compensate corporation for losses of expected profits—even those projected decades into the future.

These are not just hypothetical concerns. In other free trade agreements, the ISDS process has enabled:

- Phillip Morris to sue Australia and Uruguay, arguing that warnings required on cigarette packages are cutting their profits.
- Nuclear power operator Vattenfall to sue Germany for $3.7 billion in lost future profits over the German government's decision to phase out nuclear power after the Fukushima nuclear disaster.
- The oil and gas company Lone Pine Resources Inc. to sue the Province of Quebec for $250 million (in Canadian dollars) after Quebec imposed a fracking moratorium.
- Veolia, French waste management company, to sue Egypt because the country raised the minimum wage, increasing Veolia's costs.
- A Dutch subsidiary of a Japanese bank to sue the Czech Republic, arguing that the country had violated its rights by extending its bailout program only to "too big to fail" banks.

Defenders of the ISDS process maintain that it will have little effect in the United States with its corporate friendly legal system that they call the "good rule of law." The U.S. government, they hasten to point out, has not lost an ISDS case. And President Obama, as Harrop emphasizes, has vehemently denied that he would ever sign an agreement that would threaten the Dodd-Frank financial reforms. But Obama's assurances are nearly meaningless. While he would have control over appointments to the ISDS tribunals, he would not be able to control what decisions his appointees reach, or who the Presidents who follows him appoint to the tribunals. And the "good rule of law" has not prevented Canada from having to pay out six ISDS claims brought by corporations. But whatever the ramifications for the United States, ISDS provisions shrink the "policy space" for other countries less inclined to have their governments constrained by what would pass muster with an ISDS tribunal.

Other TPP provisions would actually limit trade, not prompt it. Its provisions to enforce "intellectual property rights," which Harrop praises, would strengthen patents restricting the availability of prescription drugs. While a boon to big pharma, those provisions would drive up the cost of already expensive drugs to fight cancer and other diseases. Public health researchers Hazel Moir, Brigitte Tenni, Deborah Gleeson, and Ruth Lopert estimate that it would cut in half the share of Vietnam's AIDS patients who have access to life-saving antiretroviral drugs.

## Not For Industry Alone

Just before the passage of fast track in June, Senator Elizabeth Warren (D-Mass.) who led the fight against TPP in the Senate—warned against enacting more "trade agreements that offer gold-plated enforcement for giant corporations and meaningless promises for everyone else."

But TPP surely would do just that. Worse yet, it would exacerbate inequality and compromise democracy, as it exempts corporations from environmental and labor standards, or whatever laws interfere with their accumulation of profits.

Now that's not about the "good rule of law." It's about corporations using their power to evade the rule of law. ❏

***Sources:*** Elizabeth Warren, "Trade agreements should not benefit industry only," *Boston Globe*, June 23, 2015; Robert Kuttner, "The Real Meaning of Obama's Trade Deal," *Huffington Post*, June 16, 2015; Joseph Stiglitz, "The Secret Corporate Takeover," Project Syndicate, May 13, 2015; Kevin Gallagher, "Saving Obama from a Bad Trade Deal," *The American Prospect*, March 4, 2015; Peter Petri and Michael Plummer, "The Trans-Pacifc Parternship and Asia- Pacific Integration," Peterson Institute for International Economics, June 2012; David Rosnick, "Gains from Trade?" Center for Economic and Policy Research, September 2013; Glen Kessler, "The Obama administration's illusionary job gains from the Trans-Pacific Partnership," *Washington Post*, Jan. 30, 2015; Peter Evans, "Our Delegation Stood Up to Bad Trade Deal," *Santa Fe New Mexican*, June 26, 2015; Avraham Ebenstein, Ann Harrison, Margaret McMillan, and Shannon Phillips, "Estimating the Impact of Trade and Offshoring on American Workers using the Current Population Surveys," *The Review of Economics and Statistics*, October 2014; Hazel Moir, Brigitte Tenni, Deborah Gleeson, and Ruth Lopert, "Assessing the impact of alternative patent systems on the cost of health care: the TPPA and HIV treatment in Vietnam," Asia-Pacific Innovation Conference, University of Technology Sydney, 27-29 November 2014.

*Article 9.5*

# TRANSATLANTIC TRADE AND INVESTMENT PARTNERSHIP: IT'S NOT ABOUT TRADE

## BY DEAN BAKER
*February 2014; Atlantic-Community*

The most important fact to know about the Transatlantic Trade and Investment Partnership (TTIP) is that promoting trade is not really the purpose of the deal. With few exceptions, traditional trade barriers, in the form of tariffs or quotas, between the United States and European Union (EU) are already low. No one would devote a great deal of effort to bringing them down further; there is not much to be gained.

The pursuit of free trade is just a cover for the real agenda of the TTIP. The deal is about imposing a regulatory structure to be enforced through an international policing mechanism that likely would not be approved through the normal political processes in each country. The rules that will be put in place as a result of the deal are likely to be more friendly to corporations and less friendly to the environment and consumers than current rules. And, they will likely impede economic growth.

In a wide variety of areas, the EU has much stronger protections for consumers and the environment than in the United States. For example, the United States has a highly concentrated mobile phone industry that is allowed to charge consumers whatever it likes. The same is true for Internet access. As a result, people in the United States pay far more for these services.

Fracking for oil and natural gas has advanced much more in the United States than in Europe in part because it is largely unregulated. In fact, the industry got a special exemption from laws on clean drinking water, so that the companies don't even have to disclose the chemicals they are using in the fracking process. As a result, if they end up contaminating ground water and drinking water in areas near a fracking site, it will be almost impossible for the victims to prove their case.

These are the sorts of regulatory changes that industry will be seeking in the TTIP. It is unlikely the governments of individual European countries or the EU as a body would support the gutting of consumer and environmental regulations. Therefore the industry groups want to use a "free trade" agreement to circumvent the democratic process.

However, the worst part of the TTIP is likely to be in its rules on patents and copyright. The United States has a notoriously corrupt patent system. A major food manufacturer once patented a peanut butter sandwich and of course Amazon was able to get a patent on "one-click shopping." These frivolous patents, which are common in the United States, raise prices and impede competition. Europeans will likely see more of such patents as a result of the TTIP.

The deal is likely to have even more consequences for the cost and availability of prescription drugs. The United States pays roughly twice as much for its drugs as

Europe. This is due to the unchecked patent monopolies granted to our drug companies. A major goal of the pharmaceutical industry is to be able to get similar rules imposed in the EU so that companies can charge higher prices.

There is an enormous amount of money at stake in this battle. The United States spends close to $350 billion a year on drugs that would sell for around one-tenth this price in a free market. The difference is almost 2% of GDP, or more than 25% of after-tax corporate profits. This amounts to a huge transfer from the public at large to the pharmaceutical industry.

The enormous gap between the patent-protected price and production costs gives drug companies an incentive to mislead the public about the safety and effectiveness of their drugs, which they do with considerable regularity. In short, an outcome of the deal can be much higher drug prices and lower-quality health care.

None of the models used to project economic gains from the TTIP even try to estimate the economic losses that would result from higher drug prices or other negative consequences of stronger patent protection. For this reason these models do not provide a useful guide to the likely economic impact of the TTIP.

The notion that the TTIP will provide some quick boost to the economies of the EU and the United States is absurd on its face. The public should scrutinize whatever comes out of the negotiating process very carefully. If politicians demand a quick yes or no answer, then the obvious answer must be "no." ❏

*Article 9.6*

# A WAY OUT FOR GREECE AND EUROPE
*Keynes' Advice from the 1940s*

## BY MARIE CHRISTINE DUGGAN
*May/June 2015*

I s there a way for Greece to honor its debts without impoverishing its people? Most
people see only two ways out of the current crisis: Either Greece services its debts,
and the wealth gap between creditor and debtor nations in Europe rises; or Greece
defaults, and the European banking system is forced to write-down its assets by the
value of the Greek IOUs. However, there is a third way: creditors could promise to
spend the money they receive from Greece (in the form of debt service payments)
on Greek imports or on long-term for-profit investments in Greece. This third way
involves re-aligning institutional incentives so that the creditors only gain when the
debtors themselves grow.

Problems like those Greece faces are not new. And, in fact, the best solutions
are not new either. During the Second World War, Britain faced a similar situation
of trade deficits coupled with a cut-off of international credit. John Maynard Keynes
devised a solution which did not impose all the burdens on the debtors by reducing
wages. Instead, it would not be just debtor countries—but also creditor countries—
that would have to "adjust." The creditors would have to spend their surpluses (rather than building up reserves), allowing the debtors, in turn, to grow their economies
and pay back their debts. Dependence on the fickle whim of the foreign investor
is the story line that unites the post-war British context with that of Greece today.
In another similarity, the subtext for Greece, since it joined the eurozone in 2001,
has been the need to increase its productive capacity and infrastructure so that its
products—priced in euros—are produced efficiently enough to compete with those
from other eurozone countries. A solution like the one Keynes proposed for Britain
towards the end of the war would offer Greece the best way out today.

## The Trap of Short-Term Debt

The euro became Greece's sole currency in 2002. This opened the door to marketers
of credit from wealthier eurozone nations. The Greek government, firms, and households had previously been making payments in drachmas, which were considered
"funny money" by international investors because the currency could lose value in
a depreciation of its exchange rate relative to the euro. But after 2002, the Greeks
began making payments in euros on loans denominated in euros, so the creditors
faced no risk of exchange rate loss. No one had ever been so enthusiastic before
about lending to the Greeks. Between 2005 and 2008, foreigners opened bank accounts or moved into the country (capital account increases), or invested in Greek
stocks and government bonds (portfolio investment), as shown in the top half of
Figure 1. As these moneys flowed in, they permitted Greece to finance an excess of
imports over exports which resulted in the growing current account deficit shown in

## FIGURE 1. GREEK BALANCE OF PAYMENTS, 2005-2008

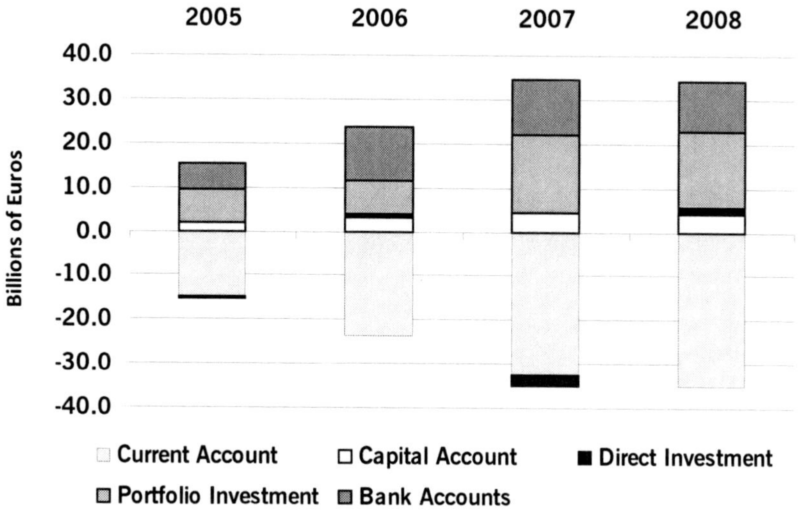

Source: IMF Balance of Payments (billions of euros); bank accounts also include "other."

Note: The figures are based on the IMF balance-of-payments data. In this accounting system, foreign portfolio investment (purchases/sales by private foreign sector or foreign governments of stocks and bonds) and foreign direct investment are included in the "financial account." The financial account "other" includes government-to-government loans, bank loans, loans to and from international organizations, and trade credits.

the bottom half of Figure 1. The fact that investors from other European countries were willing to lend to Greece was not the problem. Rather, the problem was the short-term nature of the loans. There are basically two types of foreign investment: short-term and long-term. Portfolio investment and foreign bank accounts are both short-term purchases of paper assets. Foreign direct investment, on the other hand, involves an institution in a creditor nation opening a physical business in Greece as a subsidiary, or engaging in a joint venture with a Greek business partner. Without the option of a quick and easy exit, the direct investor has more of a stake in ensuring the growth of the business activity undertaken in Greece.

In 2008, foreign lenders provided Greece with short-term funds to the tune of 16.4 billion euros, while foreign direct investment was barely one-tenth that amount, only 1.7 billion euros! Such a predominance of foreign portfolio investment and bank accounts is problematic because the flow can reverse in the time it takes to push a button on a computer, giving the portfolio investor incentive to flee at even the slightest hint of trouble. As Figure 2 shows, net portfolio investment demonstrated its short-term nature by turning negative—into a net outflow from Greece—in 2010. The outflow reached panic proportions by 2012.

When short-term investment dominates, foreign creditors hold the debtor nation hostage. If the creditors don't like the country's public policies, they can quickly sell off their holdings. Had the eurozone wanted each nation to preserve its political sovereignty, it should have put in rules to heavily discourage short-term speculative

### FIGURE 2. THE GREEK FINANCIAL ACCOUNT:
### CAPITAL FLIGHT FROM 2010 TO 2012

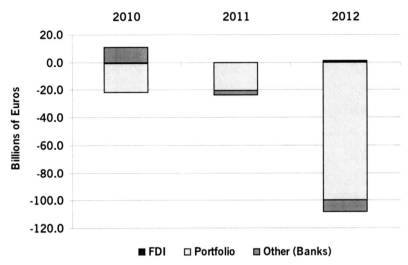

Source: Greek Article IV Report, IMF June 30, 2013 in billions of euros. "Other" refers mostly to bank accounts.

loans between eurozone partners. In fact, the opposite occurred. Greek entry into the eurozone was viewed as a marketing opportunity for short-term credit from financial institutions in wealthier nations.

When foreign holders of Greek government bonds decided to sell in 2010, Greece was running a fairly high trade deficit, on the order of 10% of GDP. It is possible for a nation to import more than it exports, but only so long as foreigners are willing to lend to or invest in the nation. In 2008, foreigners were interested in lending to Greece, but the global economic crisis in 2009 made them jittery. By 2010, they no longer wanted to lend to the Greek government, but rather to sell off their holdings of Greek government bonds (for 8.5 billion euros). Meanwhile, Greece planned to import more than it exported (23 billion euros), so the IMF came up with 31.5 billion euros to fill the gap. In the short term, it would have been very punitive to the economic base to cut off imports completely, since some are inputs to the economy (such as computers) and others are essential to subsistence (such as medicine).

Why did the international banking system step in with the first 31.5 billion euro bailout? The answer is that creditor institutions were unwilling to let Greece default. Between 1990 and 2010, many banks made loans around the world to borrowers who might never be able to pay those loans back. If the international banking system were to admit that some loans will never be repaid, then banks would have to write down their assets by the amounts of those loans. Greece is just the tip of the iceberg in that regard. The last thing that the international banking system wants is for Greece to repudiate the loans.

IMF loans are designed to rescue the international banking system, rather than to assist the debtor nation. That explains why the loans did not end Greece's problems. The IMF wanted Greece to let holders of Greek bonds sell them off—for the money that the IMF had newly lent. The IMF hoped that the ability to liquidate Greek bonds would deter the bondholders from actually selling. The IMF was playing a confidence game to prevent portfolio investors from hitting the "sell" button.

The long-term solution for Greece, however, is completely different. To reduce reliance upon foreign financing, Greece would like to export more than it imports. Winning over international buyers will require lowering Greek production costs. The way to lower costs significantly and sustainably is to invest in new technology and infrastructure that permits the same workers to produce more during any given period. However, the IMF insisted that Greece lower the cost of production while also reducing imports (read: no more new technology) and ceasing to borrow above emergency levels. Under those circumstances, the only way for Greek products to gain any market share would be for wages to drop—by a lot. Real wages did drop and unemployment rose to 27%. Many households had accumulated debt between 2002 and 2010, and as they lost jobs, debt burdens relative to incomes rose. At the same time, the Greek government could no longer borrow by issuing bonds (because Europeans, including Greeks, were no longer willing to buy them), so the government reduced benefits (as the IMF was also urging). By 2014, the Greek people had endured enough and voted the left-wing SYRIZA coalition in on a platform to end IMF control of government policy.

IMF loans are not meant to rebuild a country, but rather to tide it over through a panic until the private sector is willing to lend to the country again. If IMF loans fail to reverse a temporary panic, they wind up growing dangerously large (look at 2010 to 2012 in Figure 3). As the SYRIZA government's finance minister, Yanis Varoufakis, has pointed out, "We have resembled drug addicts craving the next dose. What [SYRIZA] is all about is ending the addiction." Greece is in a bind: IMF loans are emergency funds

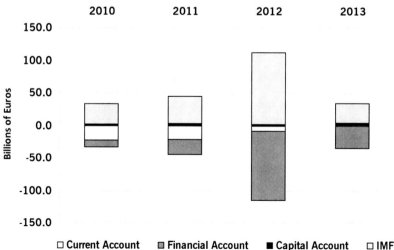

**FIGURE 3. IMF BAILOUTS PLUG EVER-LARGER HOLE IN GREEK BALANCE OF PAYMENTS, 2010-2012**

*Source:* Greece: Article IV Report, IMF on June 30, 2013 (in billions of euros).

that cannot be used to improve productive capacity, educate the people, or build infra-structure. Wages and employment are falling at the same time as social insurance, so the people are understandably bitter. If Greece leaves the eurozone now, the return to the drachma will put salaries back into drachma, which will not have the purchasing power of euros. All exits seem to lead to a lower standard of living for the people of Greece and greater income inequality between nations in Europe.

## Enter John Maynard Keynes

Let us now turn to Keynes' suggestion for Britain at the end of World War II. Like Greece today, Britain at the time had a damaged industrial base and poor infrastruc-ture (due to Hitler's bombs). Furthermore, wealthy foreigners who had lent Britain money in a short-term way were trying to liquidate their British holdings just when Britain needed long-term credit. In Britain's case, the short-term holdings of foreign money came in the form of the London bank accounts of imperialists in South Af-rica, Canada, Australia, India, and other nations of the collapsing British Empire. These wealthy families wanted to transfer their money to New York banks, and to import products from the United States as well. Britain was running a trade deficit, and the rest of the world was trying to remove funds all at the same time. In both respects, the situation was similar to Greece today.

Keynes gave considerable thought to the problem: How could Britain's banks honor the commitment to permit depositors to remove funds while also rebuilding its industrial base? And he came up with a logical solution: put pressure on credi-tors as well as debtors to "adjust." His logic was that debtors always feel the pressure to make payments—on pain of cut-off from future loans, threat of asset seizure, or other punitive measures (such as the threat today of pushing Greece out of the eu-rozone). However, creditor nations do not feel a similar pressure to spend what they get from exporting more than they import—i.e., running a trade surplus. They can hoard the surplus by building up reserves. The first rule for Keynes, then, was that creditor nations should have their surpluses confiscated if they did not spend it by the end of the year. He never anticipated any confiscation actually taking place—like any "use it or lose it" account, the point was to provide an institutional incentive for the creditor to spend the entire surplus by a certain time.

The second rule would have consisted in limiting the types of spending that creditors could make to long-term investments, imports, or donations. This brings us to the way out for the eurozone and Greece. It will be safe for Greece to repay its debts to the creditor nations of Europe, if the eurozone nations agree that the creditor nations will spend the money they receive from Greece on Greek imports or long-term loans or joint ventures in Greece. Since Greece is not exporting enough to pay for imports that will build up its infrastructure, then by definition the eurozone nations do not find it sufficiently enticing to buy imports from Greece. In this case, eurozone nations would make long-term investments in Greece so that Greece could generate the capacity to produce imports that were appealing to Europe.

Perhaps this scenario seems too draconian—forcing creditors to purchase from or make long-term investments in Greece on penalty of losing the income from an-nual Greek debt payments. Consider, then, that the eurozone nations could simply make a rule that every member nation would need to spend its trade surplus with other eurozone nations by end of year, and that such spending take the form of imports, long-term investment, or donations. (Portfolio investment would be highly discouraged.) Each nation could import, invest in, or donate to the individual country of its choice, but since any surplus would have to be spent by a certain time, the effect would be to make every eurozone economy balance its international payments. Imagine an inflatable rubber glove. As air goes into one finger, that finger inflates. Once that finger is filled, the air will naturally flow to another finger. In the end all five fingers of the rubber glove will be equally inflated. In just this way, if every creditor nation must spend its current account surplus by the end of the year in other eurozone nations, then the entire eurozone economy will expand.

## Postscript for Europe Then, Prescription for Europe Now

Keynes' plan did not pass at the Bretton Woods Conference in 1944, but his proposal did influence debate. The United States rejected the "use it or lose it" clause that would have required it to import from or physically invest in debtor countries until its huge post-war surplus was gone. However, the United States did donate via the Marshall Plan, and financed long-term loans through the International Bank for Reconstruction and Development. Britain obtained a long-term loan from the United States for reconstruction (see photo on p. 19), rather than the gift that Keynes sought, and it was several years before Britain permitted deposits to be freely converted out of London banks. Yet the negotiations did result in restrictions on portfolio investment, so that foreign direct investment became the dominant form of international investment between 1945 and 1973. During that period, global income inequality was reduced.

In 1944, Europe and the United States had been chastened by two world wars and the rise of Nazism and Fascism. All 44 nations sending representatives to Bretton Woods understood that economic forces had contributed to the horror in which so many had lost so much. Nobody wanted to live through it again. To prevent political extremism and its deadly consequences, governments were willing in that moment to put restrictions on how banks made money, and to commit to economic policies that would bring jobs and prosperity to the working class. For a similar scenario to come off today, policymakers must remember the fragile nature of global institutions and the importance of curtailing investments where creditors escape with profits while debtors lose ground. Europe is a family, and when the business owned by one family member is small and precarious, other members do not make short-term loans at high interest, or push the firm into bankruptcy and seize the assets. Family members buy from each other and invest for the long-term in each other's enterprises because such willing and profitable action fosters family strength and stability. ❑

*Sources:* Marie Duggan, "Taking Back Globalization: A China-United States Counterfactual Using Keynes's 1941 International Clearing Union," *Review of Radical Political Economics*, 2013; Eric Helleiner, States and the Reemergence of Global Finance (Cornell, 1994); Robert Skidelsky, Chapter 36: "Keynes 'New Order,'" *John Maynard Keynes 1883-1946* (Penguin, 2003).

*Article 9.7*

# MISSING WOMEN WORKERS

*Explaining the decline in women's labor-force participation in India.*

## BY SIRISHA C. NAIDU

*September/October 2015*

Between 2005 and 2012, nearly 25 million women—roughly the size of the population of Australia—withdrew from the Indian wage-labor market. Imagine the frenzied reaction of news media, researchers, and policymakers if the entire population of Australia pulled out of the labor market in less than a decade! This decline in Indian women's labor force participation rate—which counts women who are employed in regular or casual wage work, self-employed or working in family-owned businesses, plus those who are seeking work, as a percentage of all working-age women—is part of a longer-term trend. The labor force participation rate for rural women declined from 42.5% in 1988 to 18% in 2012, and for urban women from 24.5% to 13.4% over the same span.

Development scholars and policymakers often assume that economic growth is a panacea that will unshackle women from the confines of the domestic sphere, increase their social status, and allow them to participate in economic and political decision-making as equals. It is puzzling, then, that the decline in women's participation in the labor market has continued into the current period, during which India has experienced robust economic growth—the World Bank expects India to overtake China as the world's fastest-growing economy by 2017.

## No Cause for Alarm?

The most common understanding of women's labor force participation rate is as a "U-shaped" curve—high for countries with very low or very high levels of development, and low for countries at middling levels of development. At low levels of economic development, countries are more likely to be labor-intensive agrarian economies using low levels of technology and high inputs of female labor. Poverty compels women to contribute to household income. These factors lead to a high participation rate. As countries begin to develop and achieve moderate levels of development, they make the transition from agricultural to industrial production. Agriculture begins to employ more "advanced" technology, which reduces the demand for labor, particularly women's labor. Meanwhile, the increase in non-agricultural jobs increases household incomes and reduces the need for women to participate in the labor market. (Economists call this the "income effect.") The overall result of the demand and supply factors is a lower proportion of women in the labor force. Finally, as these countries continue to develop, there is increased demand for highly skilled labor which, as women secure higher levels of education, they are able to fulfill. The net result is an increase in women's participation in the labor force once again.

Applying this hypothesis to India, some researchers argue that the declining proportion of women in the Indian labor force is no cause for alarm. Rather, it is just a reflection of the downward portion of the U-shaped relationship. Women, according to this argument, can afford the luxury of not working for pay due to higher household income. Indeed, India has some of the trappings of a middle-development country. Per capita income has increased from about $1,100 in 1990 to over $5,000 in 2012. Meanwhile, the contribution of the agricultural sector to GDP has declined from 29% to 18%, as the economy transitions toward higher-value sectors.

## Demand Deficiency

To test the plausibility of the assertion that "there is no cause for alarm," let's explore some features associated with the demand and supply of women's labor in India. We start with the demand-side. Even though agriculture's contribution to GDP has declined, it still accounted for 47% of total employment in India by 2012. The rural female labor force, which is almost four times the size of the urban female labor force, derived 75% of its total employment from agriculture. Therefore, the sectors that create jobs for women are suffering from low growth in a period of overall high economic growth. Between 2005 and 2010, women workers suffered a net loss of 21.5 million agricultural and 3.1 million manufacturing jobs; meanwhile, more than 80% of the 22.3 million non-agricultural jobs created in this period went to male workers. The decline in agricultural employment, while perhaps desirable in the process of economic development, has not been sufficiently compensated by an increase in jobs in other sectors. The biggest losers of this phase of "jobless economic growth" in India have been women workers.

A second undesirable trend in the process of Indian economic development is that there is a far greater demand for contingent or informal workers than regular workers. Informal employment is contractual or insecure in nature and, according to a recent report from the Indian government, is characterized by lower wages, little or no benefits, lower job security, and higher instances of sexual harassment, compared to regular employment. Thus, along with jobless growth, women workers have to contend with poor quality, insecure jobs with a higher risk of harassment. These, along with some other factors, suggest that conditions on the demand side of the labor market are very undesirable for women workers.

Now let's look at the supply side. As stated earlier, according the "U-shaped" explanation, women reduce their labor market participation because of the income effect. While Indian per capita income has indeed increased, it has been accompanied by lower overall calorie consumption and poorer nutrition. It is thus possible, as research by economists Amit Basole and Deepankar Basu suggests, that despite higher incomes, many Indian households are suffering from increased expenditures on other essentials such as education and health, thus leading to a food-budget squeeze. Further, there is evidence of increased income inequality, which indicates that the benefits of economic development have not been widely shared. The latest data released by the Indian government's Socio Economic and Caste Census reveals that 75% of Indian households live on less than 5,000 rupees ($78.74) per month. Thus, it seems overly optimistic to claim that women, especially in the poorest households, are withdrawing from the labor market due to higher household incomes.

Women's reduced participation in the labor force coincides with an increase in working-age women's participation in "domestic and other allied activities." These consist of production for household consumption—such as processing one's own food or caring for animals that produce milk and meat for the household. It also includes cooking, cleaning, and caring for one's own family. These activities increase the consumption of total goods and services by the household, but do not show up in official GDP or labor-force statistics because they do not pass through the market. (See the interview with Nancy Folbre, "Household Labor, Caring Labor, Unpaid Labor," p. 33.) Under the current system, if the very same work performed for the family is offered in the market, it increases GDP without actually increasing the value of goods and services in the economy. At the household level, if a family member earns just enough to purchase goods and services that she was previously producing for household consumption, she would add to household income but not household consumption. As feminist economists have argued, the exclusion of domestic and other allied work from the calculation of labor force participation rate underestimates the economically active population.

Indian women's increased participation in household production—at a time of high poverty and inequality, and low demand for women's labor—fails to square with the argument that women's labor force participation has declined due to the income effect. Rather, it suggests that women and their households are scrambling to ensure a minimum level of consumption for survival. Withdrawal from the labor market does not allow women to engage in leisure activities; it has instead pushed them back into the undervalued and invisible domestic sphere. This condition is exacerbated by the Indian government's dismal role in providing essentials such as education, healthcare, and well-paying decent jobs.

## A Development Program

Thus, it is imperative that the Indian government take the following steps that dovetail with higher economic development:

- Include domestic and other allied activities in the calculation of women's labor force participation rate so that adequate policies can be formulated.

- Direct economic growth toward employment-generating sectors so that women workers can secure jobs.

- Regulate the labor market to ensure a living wage and better working conditions

- Provide basic services essential for survival and a healthy workforce, and free women from the drudgery of housework.

- Pass and enforce laws against gender discrimination in the workplace and enforce existing laws against sexual harassment.
  Such intervention is necessary for two reasons. First, countries in North America

and Western Europe that experienced an upturn in women's labor force participation, after an initial decline, often put in place deliberate policy measures—such as implementing anti-discrimination laws and investing in public education. Second, these countries faced different global economic conditions at the same stage of development as India presently. In today's economic environment, in which public sector jobs have declined, workers increasingly depend on employment in the private sector, which can relocate to almost any part of the world. This threatens workers' ability to negotiate higher wages, better working conditions, and a higher standard of living. It also reduces the promise of higher investment and jobs in the domestic economy by high-performing businesses. All of this negatively affects women's participation in the labor market. Rather than accepting the decline in women's participation rate as a necessary but temporary fallout of the development process, it is essential that the Indian government take corrective measures, so the Indian economy can fully employ its vast working age population, both male and female. ❏

*Sources*: Vinoj Abraham, "Missing labour or consistent 'de-feminisation'?" *Economic and Political Weekly*, Vol. 48, No. 31, 2013; Deepankar Basu and Amit Basole, "The calorie consumption puzzle in India: an empirical investigation," PERI Working Paper Series No. 285, University of Massachusetts-Amherst, 2013; Indrani Mazumdar and Neetha N., "Gender dimensions: employment trends in India, 1993-94 to 2009-10," Occasional Paper No. 56, Centre for Women's Development Studies, 2011; MRD, *Socio Economic and Caste Census 2011*, Ministry of Rural Development, Government of India, 2015; National Commission for Enterprises in the Unorganised Sector, *The Challenge of Employment in India: An Informal Economy Perspective, Volume I*, 2014; NSSO, Employment and Unemployment Situation in India, 68th Round July 2011-June 2012, Ministry of Statistics and Programme Implementation, Government of India, 2014; NSSO, Participation of Women in Specified Activities along with Domestic Duties, 68th Round, July 2011-June 2012, Ministry of Statistics and Programme Implementation, Government of India, 2014; Jayan Jose Thomas, "India's labour market during the 2000s: Surveying the Changes," *Economic and Political Weekly*, Vol. 48, No. 51, 2012; Jayan Jose Thomas, "The demographic challenge and employment growth in India," *Economic and Political Weekly*, Vol. 49, No. 6; The World Bank World Development Indicators (data.worldbank.org), 2014.

# Chapter 10

# RESISTANCE AND ALTERNATIVES

## INTRODUCTION

**M**any of the articles in this book are about problems in the U.S. and global economies. Both the dominant economic ideologies and the ruling institutions, many authors argue, favor the wealthy and powerful and are stacked against workers, poor people, developing countries, and other less-powerful actors in the domestic and intenational economies. That is not, however, the whole story. Those who are getting a raw deal under existing arrangements are not merely passive victims. Some are standing up and resisting poverty, inequality, and enforced powerlessness. Some are fighting for changes in policies and institutions that would help shift the existing balance of power, and improve conditions of life for those at the "bottom," for a change. This chapter describes both resistance and alternatives to the current "neoliberal" economic orthodoxy, on the domestic U.S. and international scenes.

The first five articles in this chapter focus on the U.S. economy and its institutions.

To start, Arthur MacEwan points out that the burning problems in the U.S. economy—how to achieve sustainable growth and good jobs for all who want them—are not economic, but political (Article 10.1). That is, we have the resources we need to solve our problems, but they are not deployed correctly because powerful interests stand in the way.

Next, economist Jeannette Wicks-Lim looks at the energy sector. She argues that a clean-energy program would produce more jobs, dollar for dollar, than fossil-fuel related activities. She adds that while a such a program would generate jobs for workers at all levels of education, many of those jobs would be accessible to workers without a college education, who were the hardest hit in the Great Recession (Article 10.2).

Gerald Friedman turns our attention to health care. He makes the case that a single-payer health-care system can not only solve the health-care mess in the United States but also reduce the strain on government budgets that comes from continuously rising health costs (Article 10.3).

Dean Baker calls for a return to the regulations separating basic banking functions from speculation—rules that were put in place in the wake of the Great Crash in 1929 but abandoned at the urging of banks in the 1990s (Article 10.4).

Economist Robert Pollin makes the case for transforming the Fed into a demo-cratically controlled investment bank that serves the interests of all of us (Article 10.5).

The next three articles address issues from around the world.

Robin Broad (Article 10.6) harkens back to the 1964 "Tokyo No." In 1964, 19 lower-income countries opposed a World Bank proposal to create a tribunal where investors could sue governments, sidestepping national courts. The issue of "investor/state dispute settlement" mechanisms—included in existing U.S. "trade" agreements, like the North American Free Trade Agreement (NAFTA), and proposed ones like the Trans Pacific Partnership (TPP)—is ever more press-ing, as the institutions governing them have grown in power.

Jawied Nawabi (Article 10.7) focuses on land reform and its importance to eco-nomic development. Part of the case for land reform, he notes, is "economic"—for example, small farms actually produce more output per acre than large landhold-ings. However, the crux of the case is not narrowly economic, but "socio-political." Land reform is so essential to economic development, Nawabi argues, because the power of large landlords stands in the way of needed development policies.

John Miller (Article 10.8) looks at the worker-safety accord put in place in Bangladesh in the wake of the 2013 Rana Plaza disaster, a factory collapse that killed over 1,100 workers. Miller argues that the legal liability of major clothing companies (who outsource clothing production to subcontractor companies) is a major positive step for worker safety. He also notes, however, that most major U.S. clothing companies have so far refused to sign onto the accord.

Rounding out the chapter, an interview with economist Juliet Schor (Article 10.9) explores the causes behind U.S. consumerism in international comparative perspec-tive. Schor looks beyond some of the "usual suspects"—like advertising—by linking the rise of consumerism to labor-market forces that have prevented the reduction of work time. She argues that future changes in U.S. consumption behavior, and there-fore long-term environmental sustainability, depend on reducing hours of work

## Discussion Questions

1. (Article 10.1) According to MacEwan, in what way are powerful vested interests standing in the way of needed reforms in the United States? How could this resistance ever be overcome?

2. (Article 10.2) What factors make government spending on clean energy an ef-fective economic stimulus and jobs program?

3. (Article 10.3) What are the different cost savings that Friedman argues a single-payer, universal health-care system would provide while improving heath-care results? In your estimation, how does the single-payer proposal Friedman dis-cusses measure up against our current health-care policies?

4. (Article 10.4) What was the Glass-Steagall Act and why does Dean Baker argue it should be revived?

5. (Article 10.5) What are the chief elements of Pollin's proposal to transform the Fed? How would the Fed's focus and decision-making change? Do you think the proposal would be effective?

6. (Article 10.6) Should private companies be able to sue governments in international tribunals, rather than the national courts of that country? Why does Broad argue that this is a bad feature of recent "trade" agreements? What do you think?

7. (Article 10.7) Nawabi argues that land reform is important mainly for "sociopolitical" reasons—that it is necessary to break landlords' stranglehold on political power in order to adopt needed economic development policies. What is the rationale of this argument? Are there analogous arguments to be made for societies that are mostly urban and industrial, rather than rural and agricultural?

8. (Article 10.8) Opponents of international labor standards argue that workers in very low-income countries just need jobs, and will only be hurt by well-intentioned efforts to raise wages or improve working conditions. How do such arguments hold up to the experience in Bangladesh since the Rana Plaza disaster?

9. (Article 10.9) Schor argues that, far from being the consequence of human beings' inherently insatiable wants, consumerism is the result of various social and institutional factors. What does she see as the key factors pushing people to consume more and more? What does Schor's view imply about the possibility of fundamental change in consumption, work, and environmental aspects of economic behavior?

*Article 10.1*

# WHAT WOULD FULL EMPLOYMENT COST?

## BY ARTHUR MacEWAN
*May/June 2015*

> Dear Dr. Dollar:
> What is the cost, the minimum budget the U.S. government could spend, to ensure everybody who wants a job can have one with decent pay and benefits? How could that be paid for?   —*Brett O'Sullivan, Denver, Colo.*

The barriers to change of this magnitude—creating good jobs for everyone—are not so much economic as political. We can imagine arrangements by which the economy could function well and would achieve full-employment, good jobs, and benefits. It is, however, hard in the present climate to think that steps in this direction would be politically possible (at least at the national level, though there are political possibilities in some states and localities).

There are things that could be done to move the economy in this direction without significant costs to society. Examples of steps that could improve pay and jobs without major government expenditures include raising the minimum wage and shortening the work week (e.g., requiring time-and-a-half pay for more than 30 hours of work per week). The former would improve workers' pay, and the latter would lead many employers to hire more workers to avoid the higher overtime rates. Also, the rules surrounding unionization could be improved; indeed, simple enforcement of existing rules (e.g., protecting workers trying to form a union) would be a significant step toward improving workers' opportunities.

Also, in terms of providing benefits, a major step forward would be the establishment of a single-payer ("Medicare for All") healthcare system, which would pay for itself by reducing the large overhead costs and profits of the private insurance companies while providing everyone with a prime benefit. Because a single-payer system would cost less than the current system, the payments (taxes) that the government would need would come from and be less than the current insurance premiums. The costs would go through the government, but there would be savings for society. Because this benefit would be for everyone, it would remove the problems that arise when health care is tied to employment.

Yet, full employment would also require government spending to stimulate job growth. While the economy operates as it has over the last several years, deficit spending is necessary to move us toward full employment. Especially in the current circumstances, with the economy far from full employment and with interest rates on U.S. government bonds extremely low, deficit spending would not impose large costs (i.e., the costs of paying the interest on the government borrowing to cover the deficit).

It is not hard to figure out what kinds of jobs should be created with government stimulus spending. Prime examples include environmental repair and preservation (including energy conservation), education and training, and infrastructure repair and extension (e.g., especially in public transportation).

Further, stimulus through deficit spending could be used be used for the government to directly create jobs. The quickest and most effective way to do this would be for the federal government to provide funds to the states to reverse the tens of thousands of layoffs of educational workers in the last few years. Also, there is an increasing need for workers in universal early childhood education, as has been instituted in New York City and a few states. Like expenditures on physical infrastructure, these expenditures on social infrastructure would have both short-run multiplier demand impacts and long-run impacts by raising productivity.

Such actions by the government would not require large tax increases, though higher taxes on people with very high incomes would help. Moreover, as the economy approached full employment, the bargaining power of workers would improve and unionization could be facilitated. As the economy moved back to full employment and incomes rose, taxes would increase without tax rate increases—thus preventing a continuing increase of the government debt.

There would certainly be objections to these sorts of changes. Defenders of the status quo would argue that stimulation of the economy would cause inflation and that raising the minimum wage and facilitating unionization would harm businesses' profits and lead them to cut back on investment (a "capital strike"). The inflation and cutbacks would, the argument goes, mean fewer jobs, and especially fewer good jobs.

With plenty of slack in the labor market, however, there is no reason to believe that government deficits would bring inflation, and as the economy approached full employment, deficit-based stimulus would no longer be needed. The real concerns of those opposed to stimulation of the economy are their opposition to the social programs that would probably grow with larger stimulation and their fear that the growth of those programs might ultimately lead to higher taxes on people with high incomes—prime defenders of the status quo.

As to the fear that business profits would suffer with the sorts of reforms proposed here, that would also be likely. Yet, weaker profits, while a real loss for those at the top, need not be bad for the rest of society. It is only necessary to look at the relatively recent period in our history when wages—including the minimum wage—were relatively higher, unions were stronger, and the distribution of income less unequal. Through the 1950s and into the early 1970s, these conditions were largely met, and the economy grew relatively strongly. There were many economic problems in those years (though not severe inflation) and many circumstances were different from today, but the experience of that period gives the lie to the claims that government stimulus, better working conditions, and greater economic equality would necessarily result in economic disaster.

These changes are blocked by the political power of business and the very wealthy—the infamous 1%—who employ specious arguments about inflation and the undermining of employment to protect their own interests. Changes that would move us toward more and better jobs would be good for most of us. But they would impose costs on those at the top, who raise the fearful specter of "drastic change of the economic system."

Yet, these changes that would meet the goal of more well-paying jobs with good benefits could be accomplished without some drastic system change or some large increase in the costs to society through greater government expenditures and taxation. Could we get more substantial improvements with greater change? Perhaps. But let's first recognize that, even within the profit system, things do not have to be as they are today. ❑

*Article 10.2*

# WE NEED A (GREEN) JOBS PROGRAM
*Clean-energy investment would promote job growth for a wide swath of the U.S. workforce.*

## BY JEANNETTE WICKS-LIM
*September/October 2010*

Fourteen months of an unemployment rate at or near 10% clearly calls for the federal government to take a lead role in job creation. The White House should push its clean-energy agenda as a jobs program but steer clear of all the hype about "green-collar" jobs. Green-collar jobs are widely perceived as job opportunities accessible only to an elite segment of the U.S. workforce—those with advanced degrees, such as environmental engineers, lab technicians, and research scientists. Such jobs are inaccessible to the 52% of unemployed workers with no college experience. The truth is, however, that clean-energy investments could serve as a powerful engine for job growth for a wide swath of the U.S. workforce.

My colleagues at the Political Economy Research Institute and I examined a clean-energy program that includes making buildings more energy efficient, expanding and improving mass transit, updating the national electric grid, and developing each of three types of renewable energy sources: wind, solar, and biomass fuels. Here's what we found.

First, clean-energy activities produce more jobs, dollar for dollar, than fossil fuel-related activities. This is because clean-energy activities tend to be more labor intensive (i.e., more investment dollars go to hiring workers than buying machines), have a higher domestic content (i.e., more dollars are spent on goods and services produced within the United States) and have lower average wages than fossil fuel-related activities. The figures in the table below show how a $1 million investment in clean-energy activities would create more than three times the number of jobs that would be created by investing the same amount in fossil fuels.

Second, many clean energy sector jobs would be accessible to workers with no college experience. The table also shows how the jobs created by a $1 million investment in clean energy would be spread across three levels of education: high school degree or less, some college, and B.A. or more. Nearly half of the clean energy jobs would be held by workers with a high school degree or less. These include jobs for construction laborers, carpenters, and bus drivers. Fewer than one-quarter of clean-energy jobs would require a B.A. or more. The figures for the fossil fuels sector (second column) show that they are more heavily weighted toward jobs requiring college degrees.

Does this mean green investments will just create lots of low-paying jobs? No. The figures in the table on the next page show that investing $1 million in green activities rather than fossil fuel-related activities would generate many more jobs for workers at *all three levels* of formal education credentials. Compared to the fossil fuels sector, the clean energy sector would produce nearly four times the number

## JOB CREATION: CLEAN ENERGY VS. FOSSIL FUELS

Number of jobs created by investing $1 million dollars in clean energy versus fossil-fuels activities, by education credentials

| Education Credentials | Clean Energy | Fossil Fuels |
|---|---|---|
| Total | 16.7 jobs (100%) | 5.3 jobs (100%) |
| High school diploma or less | 8.0 jobs (47.9%) | 2.2 jobs (41.5%) |
| Some college, no B.A. | 4.8 jobs (28.7%) | 1.6 jobs (30.2%) |
| B.A. or more | 3.9 jobs (23.3%) | 1.5 jobs (28.3%) |

of jobs that require a high school degree or less, three times the number of jobs that require some college experience, and 2.5 times the number of jobs that require a B.A. or more. Green investments would produce more jobs at all education and wage levels, even while generating proportionately *more* jobs that are accessible to workers with a high school degree or less.

Workers are right to worry about whether these high school degree jobs would offer family-supporting wages. Construction laborers, for example, average at $29,000 annually—awfully close to the $22,000 official poverty line. In addition, women and workers of color have historically faced discrimination in the construction industry, which would be the source of a lot of the lower-credentialed jobs in the clean energy sector. Workers will need to do some serious organizing to put in place labor protections such as living-wage laws, strong collective bargaining rights, and affirmative action policies to insure that these jobs pay decent wages and are equally accessible to all qualified workers. ❏

*Sources:* Robert Pollin, Jeannette Wicks-Lim, and Heidi Garrett-Peltier, *Green Prosperity: How Clean-Energy Policies Can Fight Poverty and Raise Living Standards in the United States*, Political Economy Research Institute, 2009, www.peri.umass.edu/green_prosperity.

*Article 10.3*

# UNIVERSAL HEALTH CARE:
# CAN WE AFFORD ANYTHING LESS?

*Why only a single-payer system can solve America's health-care mess.*

**BY GERALD FRIEDMAN**
*July/August 2011*

America's broken health-care system suffers from what appear to be two separate problems. From the right, a chorus warns of the dangers of rising costs; we on the left focus on the growing number of people going without health care because they lack adequate insurance. This division of labor allows the right to dismiss attempts to extend coverage while crying crocodile tears for the 40 million uninsured. But the division between problem of cost and the problem of coverage is misguided. It is founded on the assumption, common among neoclassical economists, that the current market system is efficient. Instead, however, the current system is inherently inefficient; it is the very source of the rising cost pressures. In fact, the only way we can control health-care costs and avoid fiscal and economic catastrophe is to establish a single-payer system with universal coverage.

The rising cost of health care threatens the U.S. economy. For decades, the cost of health insurance has been rising at over twice the general rate of inflation; the share of American income going to pay for health care has more than doubled since 1970 from 7% to 17%. By driving up costs for employees, retirees, the needy, the young, and the old, rising health-care costs have become a major problem for governments at every level. Health costs are squeezing public spending needed for education and infrastructure. Rising costs threaten all Americans by squeezing the income available for other activities. Indeed, if current trends continued, the entire economy would be absorbed by health care by the 2050s.

Conservatives argue that providing universal coverage would bring this fiscal Armageddon on even sooner by increasing the number of people receiving care. Following this logic, their policy has been to restrict access to health care by raising insurance deductibles, copayments, and cost sharing and by reducing access to insurance. Even before the Great Recession, growing numbers of American adults were uninsured or underinsured. Between 2003 and 2007, the share of non-elderly adults without adequate health insurance rose from 35% to 42%, reaching 75 million. This number has grown substantially since then, with the recession reducing employment and with the continued decline in employer-provided health insurance. Content to believe that our current health-care system is efficient, conservatives assume that costs would have risen more had these millions not lost access, and likewise believe that extending health-insurance coverage to tens of millions using a plan like the Affordable Care Act would drive up costs even further. Attacks on employee health insurance and on Medicare and Medicaid come from this same logic—the idea that the only way to control health-care costs is to reduce the number of people with access to health care. If we do not find a way to control costs by increasing access, there will be more proposals like that of Rep. Paul Ryan (R-Wisc.) and the Republicans in the House of Representatives to slash Medicaid and abolish Medicare.

## The Problem of Cost in a Private, For-Profit Health Insurance System

If health insurance were like other commodities, like shoes or bow ties, then reducing access might lower costs by reducing demands on suppliers for time and materials. But health care is different because so much of the cost of providing it is in the administration of the payment system rather than in the actual work of doctors, nurses, and other providers, and because coordination and cooperation among different providers is essential for effective and efficient health care. It is not cost pressures on providers that are driving up health-care costs; instead, costs are rising because of what economists call transaction costs, the rising cost of administering and coordinating a system that is designed to reduce access.

The health-insurance and health-care markets are different from most other markets because private companies selling insurance do not want to sell to everyone, but only to those unlikely to need care (and, therefore, most likely to drop coverage if prices rise). As much as 70% of the "losses" suffered by health-insurance providers—that is, the money they pay out in claims—goes to as few as 10% of their subscribers. This creates a powerful incentive for companies to screen subscribers, to identify those likely to submit claims, and to harass them so that they will drop their coverage and go elsewhere. The collection of insurance-related information has become a major source of waste in the American economy because it is not organized to improve patient care but to harass and to drive away needy subscribers and their health-care providers. Because driving away the sick is so profitable for health insurers, they are doing it more and more, creating the enormous bureaucratic waste that characterizes the process of billing and insurance handling. Rising by over 10% a year for the past 25 years, health insurers' administrative costs are among the fastest-growing in the U.S. health-care sector. Doctors in private practice now spend as much as 25% of their revenue on administration, nearly $70,000 per physician for billing and insurance costs.

For-profit health insurance also creates waste by discouraging people from receiving preventive care and by driving the sick into more expensive care settings. Almost a third of Americans with "adequate" health insurance go without care every year due to costs, and the proportion going without care rises to over half of those with "inadequate" insurance and over two-thirds for those without insurance. Nearly half of the uninsured have no regular source of care, and a third did not fill a prescription in the past year because of cost. All of this unutilized care might appear to save the system money. But it doesn't. Reducing access does not reduce health-care expenditures when it makes people sicker and pushes them into hospitals and emergency rooms, which are the most expensive settings for health care and are often the least efficient because care provided in these settings rarely has continuity or follow-up.

The great waste in our current private insurance system is an opportunity for policy because it makes it possible to economize on spending by replacing our current system with one providing universal access. I have estimated that in Massachusetts, a state with a relatively efficient health-insurance system, it would be possible to lower the cost of providing health care by nearly 16% even after providing coverage to everyone in the state currently without insurance (see Table 1). This could be done largely by reducing the cost of administering the private insurance system, with most of the savings coming within providers' offices by reducing the costs of billing and processing insurance claims. This is a conservative estimate made for a state with a relatively efficient health-insurance system. In a report prepared for the state of Vermont, William Hsiao of the Harvard School of Public Health and MIT economist Jonathan Gruber estimate that shifting to a single-payer system could lead to savings of around 25% through reduced administrative cost and improved delivery of care. (They have also noted that administrative savings would be even larger if the entire country shifted to a single-payer system because this would save the cost of billing people with private, out-of-state insurance plans.) In Massachusetts, my conservative estimates suggests that as much as $10 billion a year could be saved by shifting to a single-payer system.

## Single-Payer Systems Control Costs by Providing Better Care

Adoption of a single-payer health-insurance program with universal coverage could also save money and improve care by allowing better coordination of care among different providers and by providing a continuity of care that is not possible with competing insurance plans. A comparison of health care in the United States with

### TABLE 1: SOURCES OF SAVINGS AND ADDED COSTS FOR A HYPTHETICAL MASSACHUSETTS SINGLE-PAYER HEALTH SYSTEM

| Change in health-care expenditures | Size of change as share of total health-care expenditures |
|---|---|
| Savings from single-payer system | |
| Administration costs within health-insurance system | -2.0% |
| Administrative costs within providers' offices | -10.1% |
| Reduction in provider prices through reducing market leverage for privileged providers | -5.0% |
| Savings: | -17.1% |
| Increased costs from single-payer | |
| Expansion in coverage to the uninsured | +1.35% |
| Increased utilization because of elimination of copayments, balanced by improvements in preventive care | +/- 0.0% |
| Total increased costs: | +1.35% |
| Net change in health-care expenditures: | -15.75% |

Source: Calculations by the author from data in OECD Health Data 2010 (oecd.org).

health care in other countries shows how large these cost savings might be. When Canada first adopted its current health-care financing system in 1968, the health-care share of the national gross domestic product in the United States (7.1%) was nearly the same as in Canada (6.9%), and only a little higher than in other advanced economies. Since then, however, health care has become dramatically more expensive in the United States. In the United States, per capita health-care spending since 1971 has risen by over $6,900 compared with an increase of less than $3,600 in Canada and barely $3,200 elsewhere (see Table 2). Physician Steffie Woolhandler and others have shown how much of this discrepancy between the experience of the United States and Canada can be associated with the lower administrative costs of Canada's single-payer system; she has found that administrative costs are nearly twice as high in the United States as in Canada—31% of costs versus 17%.

The United States is unique among advanced economies both for its reliance on private health insurance and for rapid inflation in health-care costs. Health-care costs have risen faster in the United States than in any other advanced economy: twice as fast as in Canada, France, Germany, Sweden, or the United Kingdom. We might accept higher and rapidly rising costs had Americans experienced better health outcomes. But using life expectancy at birth as a measure of general health, we have gone from a relatively healthy country to a relatively unhealthy one. Our gain in life expectancy since 1971 (5.4 years for women) is impressive except when put beside other advanced economies (where the average increase is 7.3 years).

## TABLE 2: GREATER INCREASE IN COST FOR
## U.S. HEALTH-CARE SYSTEM, 1971-2007

| | U.S. vs. Canada | | U.S. vs. 5-country average | |
|---|---|---|---|---|
| | Dollars | Share of GDP | Dollars | Share of GDP |
| Extra increase 1971-2007 | $3,356 | 5.40% | $3,690 | 4.72% |
| Extra adjusted for smaller life expectancy gain | $4,006 | 5.98% | $4,480 | 5.73% |
| As share of national health expenditures | | | | |
| Extra increase 1971-2007 | 45% | | 49% | |
| Extra adjusted for smaller life expectancy gain | 53% | | 59% | |

*Note:* The first line shows how much faster health-care spending rose per person and as a share of gross domestic product in the United States compared with Canada and with the average of five countries (Canada, France, Germany, Sweden, and the United Kingdom). The second row adjusts this increase for the slower rate of growth in life expectancy in the United States than in these other countries. The third and fourth rows estimate the degree of waste in our health-care system as the proportion of total expenditures accounted for by the extra increases in health-care expenditures in the United States.

*Source:* Calculations by the author from data in OECD Health Data 2010 (oecd.org).

## FIGURE 1: INCREASE IN HEALTH-CARE EXPENDITURES PER CAPITA ASSOCIATED WITH AN INCREASE OF ONE YEAR IN FEMALE LIFE EXPECTANCY, 1971-2007

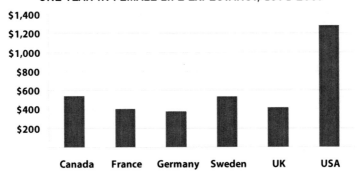

*Source:* Dataset—OECD Health Data 2010, Selected Data, data extracted on 23 Apr 2011 12:19 UTC (GMT) from OECD.Stat. Calculations by the author.

The relatively slow increase in life expectancy in the United States highlights the gross inefficiency of our private health-care system. Had the United States increased life expectancy at the same dollar cost as in other countries, we would have saved nearly $4,500 per person. Or, put another way, had we increased life expectancy at the same rate as other countries, our spending increase since 1971 would have bought an extra 15 years of life expectancy, 10 years more than we have. The failure of American life expectancy to rise as fast as life expectancy elsewhere can be directly tied to the inequitable provision of health care through our private, for-profit health-insurance system. Increases in life expectancy since 1990 have been largely restricted to relatively affluent Americans with better health insurance. Since 1990, men in the top 50% of the income distribution have had a six-year increase in life expectancy at age 65 compared with an increase of only one year for men earning below the median.

## FIGURE 2: DIFFERENCE IN FEMALE LIFE EXPECTANCY AT BIRTH (IN YEARS), U.S. COMPARED WITH OTHER COUNTRIES, 1971 AND 2007.

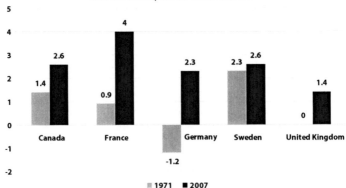

*Source:* Dataset—OECD Health Data 2010, Selected Data, data extracted on 23 Apr 2011 12:19 UTC (GMT) from OECD.Stat.

Rising health-care costs reflect in part the greater costs of caring for an aging population with more chronic conditions. As such, the United States looks especially bad because our population is aging less quickly than that of other countries because of high rates of immigration, relatively higher fertility, and the slower increase in life expectancy in the United States. Countries also buy higher life expectancy by spending on health care; rising health expenditures have funded improvements in treatment that have contributed to rising life expectancy throughout the world. Female life expectancy at birth has increased by nearly nine years in Germany since 1971, by over eight years in France, by seven years in Canada and the United Kingdom, and by six years in Sweden. By contrast, the United States, where female life expectancy increased by a little over five years, has done relatively poorly despite increasing health-care expenditures that dwarf those of other countries. In other countries, increasing expenditures by about $500 per person is associated with an extra year of life expectancy. With our privatized health-insurance system, we need spending increases over twice as large to gain an extra year of life (see Figure 1).

The international comparison also provides another perspective on any supposed trade-off between containing costs and expanding coverage. In countries other than the United States, almost all of the increase in health-care spending as a share of national income is due to better quality health care as measured by improvements in life expectancy (see Figure 2). The problem of rising health-care costs is almost unique to the United States, the only advanced industrialized country without universal coverage and without any effective national health plan.

In short, the question is not whether we can afford a single-payer health-insurance system that would provide adequate health care for all Americans. The real question is: can we afford anything else? ❏

*Sources:* Cathy Shoen, "How Many Are Underinsured? Trends Among U.S. Adults, 2003 and 2007," Health Affairs, June 10, 2008; "Insured but Poorly Protected: How Many Are Underinsured? U. S. Adults Trends, 2003 to 2007," Commonwealth Fund, June 10, 2008 (commonwealthfund.org); David Cutler and Dan Ly, "The (Paper) Work of Medicine: Understanding International Medical Costs," Journal of Economic Perspectives, Spring 2011; Stephen M. Davidson, Still Broken: Understanding the U.S. Health Care System, Stanford Business Books, 2010; P Franks and C M Clancy, "Health insurance and mortality. Evidence from a national cohort," The Journal of the American Medical Association, August 11, 1993; Allan Garber and Jonathan Skinner, "Is American Health Care Uniquely Inefficient?" Journal of Economic Perspectives, Fall 2008; Jonathan Gruber, "The Role of Consumer Co-payments for Health Care: Lessons from the RAND Health Insurance Experiment and Beyond," Kaiser Family Foundation, October 2006 (kff.org); David Himmelstein and Steffie Woolhandler, "Administrative Waste in the U.S. Health Care System in 2003," International Journal of Health Services, 2004; "The Uninsured: A Primer: Supplemental Data Tables," Kaiser Family Foundation, December 2010; Karen Davis and Cathy Shoen, "Slowing the Growth of U.S. Health Care Expenditures: What are the Options?" Commonwealth Fund, January 2007 (commonwealthfund.org); "Accounting for the Cost of Health Care in the United States," McKinsey Global Institute, January 2007 (mckinsey.com); "Investigation of Health Care Cost Trends and Cost Drivers," Office of Massachusetts Attorney General Martha Coakley, January 29, 2010 (mass.gov); Trends in Mortality Differentials and Life Expectancy for Male Social

Security-Covered Workers, by Average Relative Earnings by Hilary Waldron, Social Security Administration, October 2007; Richard G. Wilkinson, The Spirit Level, Bloomsbury Press, 2010; William Hsiao and Steven Kappel, "Act 128: Health System Reform Design. Achieving Affordable Universal Health Care in Vermont," January 21, 2011 (leg.state.vt.us); Steffie Woolhandler and Terry Campbell, "Cost of Health Care Administration in the United States and Canada," New England Journal of Medicine, 2003.

## Update

### (Why) Didn't Obamacare Take Care of All This? (January/February 2014

Under the Affordable Care Act (ACA), or "Obamacare," expansion of Medicaid and mandates for individuals to buy subsidized private insurance will expand health insurance to an additional 30 million people. Regulations establishing minimum standards for coverage and barring exclusions for pre-existing conditions will improve coverage for many. On the other hand, by maintaining the existing system of for-profit medicine and private insurance, the ACA does little to rein in out-of-control cost growth while leaving millions without coverage. We can hope that the ACA's strengths and its failures will soon pave the way for a rational universal system such as single payer health care.

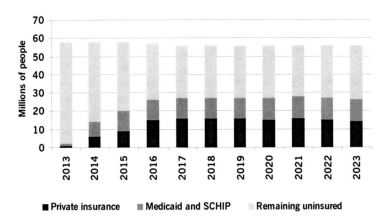

**PROJECTED EFFECTS OF ACA ON UNINSURED, 2013-2023**

Note: SCHIP is State Children's Health Insurance Program. All figures are projections.

While the ACA will provide health insurance to millions of Americans, millions of others will remain uninsured. Over 25 million will gain coverage either through the expansion of Medicaid or by buying subsidized private insurance, but somewhat more will remain without coverage. Some are not covered by the act (including undocumented immigrants); others will be excused from the requirement to have insurance because of cost; and others will not comply.

Because it builds on the existing private health-insurance system, the ACA does little to reduce access problems for people with health insurance. Those with insurance have dramatically fewer problems accessing health care (including seeing doctors, arranging follow-up visits, and filling prescriptions) than those without. But even insured Americans are twice as likely as citizens of countries with public insurance to have trouble getting care.

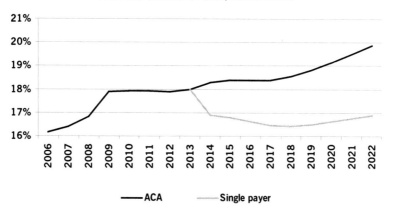

**PROJECTED HEALTH CARE SPENDING, PERCENTAGE OF GDP, ACA VS. SINGLE PAYER, 2006-2022**

*Note:* Figures from 2014 on for ACA are projections. Figures for single payer are estimates.

The ACA does not establish a sustainable health-care finance system in the United States. Under the ACA, health care spending will continue to increase significantly faster than the economy as a whole and the share of the economy going towards health care will rise in the next decade to nearly 20%. By controlling administrative costs and drug prices, a single-payer system can hold healthcare spending to less than 17% of the GDP. ❏

*Article 10.4*

# GLASS-STEAGALL NOW:
# BECAUSE THE BANKS OWN WASHINGTON

**BY DEAN BAKER**
*August 2013, Al Jazeera English*

A bipartisan group of senators recently put forward a proposal for new Glass-Steagall legislation that would restore a strict separation between commercial banks and speculative trading. Anyone familiar with the ways of Washington knows that such legislation is badly needed. It is the only way to prevent the Wall Street gang from continuing to rip off the public and subjecting the rest of us to the risks of their speculation.

The idea of the original Glass Steagall was to create two completely distinct types of banks. On the one hand there would be the standard commercial banks with which most of us are familiar. These are the banks where people have checking and savings accounts and where they might go to take out a mortgage or small business loan.

Because of the central role that commercial banks play in the day-to-day workings of the economy, the government established the Federal Deposit Insurance Corporation (FDIC) to guarantee the vast majority of accounts in full. The goal was to let people know that their money is safe in the bank.

Since the government guaranteed the money, people need never worry about racing to the bank to get their money before the bank vault is empty. As a result we have not seen the sort of old-fashioned bank-runs that were a mainstay of the pre-FDIC era.

The quid pro quo for having the government guarantee deposits was that commercial banks were supposed to restrict their loans to a limited number of relatively safe activities, such as mortgage loans, small business loans, car loans and other simple and standardized forms of credit. These restrictions are essential, because if customers know their money is guaranteed by the government, they won't care if their bank is taking enormous risks. The government must act to impose discipline on bank behavior that will not come from the market when deposits are insured.

By contrast, investment banks were set free to engage in whatever risky behavior they liked. Investment banks did not take deposits but rather raised money through issuing bonds or other forms of borrowing. In principle, their potential failure did not pose the same risk to the economy.

The ending of Glass-Steagall removed the separation between investment banks and commercial banks, raising the possibility that banks would make risky investments with government-guaranteed deposits. In principle, even after the ending of Glass Steagall banks were supposed to keep a strict separation between their commercial banking and the risky bets taken by their investment banking divisions, but this depends on the ability of regulators to enforce this restriction.

The Volcker Rule provision in Dodd-Frank was an effort to re-establish a Glass Steagall type separation but the industry is making Swiss cheese out of this regulation in the rule-writing process. Serious people cannot believe that this will keep the Wall Street banks from using their government-guaranteed deposits as a cushion to support their speculative game playing.

If anyone questions how this story is likely to play out in practice, we need only go back a few years to the financial crisis of 2008-2009. At that time, most of the major banks, Bank of America, Citigroup, Goldman Sachs and Morgan Stanley, almost surely would have failed without government support.

In fact, some of the top economic advisors in the Obama administration wanted to let them fail and have the government take them over, as the FDIC does all the time with insolvent banks. However Larry Summers managed to carry the day by arguing that such a move would be far too risky at a time when the financial markets were so unsettled. As a result, the big banks got their government money and were allowed to consolidate so that they are now bigger than ever.

This was primarily a problem of banks that are too big and too interconnected to fail, not just a problem of commercial banks merging with investment banks. But these mergers certainly help banks to reach too-big-to-fail status.

Some may argue that the crisis of 2008-2009 involved extraordinary circumstances. However when banks fail it is generally because the economy faces a crisis. They do not typically fail in good times. And it is a safe bet that there will always be a smart and belligerent Larry Summers on the scene aggressively arguing the case against anyone who wants to subject the banks to market discipline.

What is striking about the argument on re-instating Glass-Steagall is that there really is no downside. The banks argue that it will be inconvenient to separate their divisions, but companies sell off divisions all the time.

They also argue that foreign banks are not generally required to adhere to this sort of separation. This is in part true, but irrelevant.

Stronger regulations might lead us to do more business with foreign-owned banks since weaker regulations could give them some competitive edge. That should bother us as much as it does that we buy clothes and toys from Bangladesh and China.

If foreign governments want to subject themselves and their economies to greater risk as a result of bad financial regulation, that is not an argument for us to do the same. Are we anxious to be the next Iceland or Cyprus?

In short, the senators are on the right track pushing for a new Glass-Steagall. The public should hope that bankers' lobby doesn't derail their efforts. ❏

*Article 10.5*

# TRANSFORMING THE FED

## BY ROBERT POLLIN
*November 1992*

The U.S. financial system faces deep structural problems. Households, businesses, and the federal government are burdened by excessive debts. The economy favors short-term speculation over long-term investment. An unrepresentative and unresponsive elite has extensive control over the financial system. Moreover, the federal government is incapable of reversing these patterns through its existing tools, including fiscal, monetary, and financial regulatory policies.

I propose a dramatically different approach: transforming the Federal Reserve System (the "Fed") into a public investment bank. Such a bank would have substantial power to channel credit in ways that counter financial instability and support productive investment by private businesses. The Fed would use its powers to influence how and for what purposes banks, insurance companies, brokers, and other lenders loan money.

The U.S. government has used credit allocation policies, such as low-cost loans, loan guarantees, and home mortgage interest deductions, extensively and with success. Its primary accomplishment has been to create a home mortgage market that, for much of the period since World War II, provided non-wealthy households with unprecedented access to home ownership.

I propose increasing democratic control over the Federal Reserve's activities by decentralizing power to the 12 district Fed banks and instituting popular election of their boards of directors. This would create a mechanism for extending democracy throughout the financial system.

My proposal also offers a vehicle for progressives to address two separate but equally serious questions facing the U.S. economy:

- how to convert our industrial base out of military production and toward the development and adoption of environmentally benign production techniques; and
- how to increase opportunities for high wage, high productivity jobs in the United States. The U.S. needs such jobs to counteract the squeeze on wages from increasingly globalized labor and financial markets.

Transforming the Federal Reserve system into a public investment bank will help define an economic path toward democratic socialism in the United States.

My proposal has several strengths as a transitional program. It offers a mechanism for establishing democratic control over finance and investment—the area where capital's near-dictatorial power is most decisive. The program will also work within the United States' existing legal and institutional framework. We could implement parts of it immediately using existing federal agencies and with minimal demands on the federal budget.

At the same time, if an ascendant progressive movement put most of the program in place, this would represent a dramatic step toward creating a new economic system. Such a system would still give space to market interactions and the pursuit of greed, but would nevertheless strongly promote general well-being over business profits.

## How the Fed Fails

At present the Federal Reserve focuses its efforts on managing short-term fluctuations of the economy, primarily by influencing interest rates. When it reduces rates, it seeks to increase borrowing and spending, and thereby stimulate economic growth and job opportunities. When the Fed perceives that wages and prices are rising too fast (a view not necessarily shared by working people), it tries to slow down borrowing and spending by raising interest rates.

This approach has clearly failed to address the structural problems plaguing the financial system. The Fed did nothing, for example, to prevent the collapse of the savings and loan industry. It stood by while highly speculative mergers, buyouts, and takeovers overwhelmed financial markets in the 1980s. It has failed to address the unprecedented levels of indebtedness and credit defaults of private corporations and households.

## New Roles for the Fed

Under my proposal, the Federal Reserve would shift its focus from the short to the long term. It would provide more and cheaper credit to banks and other financiers who loan money to create productive assets and infrastructure—which promote high wage, high productivity jobs. The Fed would make credit more expensive for lenders that finance speculative activities such as the mergers, buyouts, and takeovers that dominated the 1980s.

The Fed would also give favorable credit terms to banks that finance decent affordable housing rather than luxury housing and speculative office buildings. It would make low-cost credit available for environmental research and development so the economy can begin the overdue transition to environmentally benign production. Cuts in military spending have idled many workers and productive resources, both of which could be put to work in such transformed industries.

Finally, the Fed would give preferential treatment to loans that finance investment in the United States rather than in foreign countries. This would help counter the trend of U.S. corporations to abandon the domestic economy in search of lower wages and taxes.

The first step in developing the Fed's new role would be for the public to determine which sectors of the economy should get preferential access to credit. One example, suggested above, is industrial conversion from military production to investment in renewable energy and conservation.

Once the public establishes its investment goals, the Fed will have to develop new policy tools and use its existing tools in new ways to accomplish them. I propose that a transformed Federal Reserve use two major methods:

- set variable cash ("asset reserve") requirements for all lenders, based on the social value of the activities the lenders are financing; and
- increase discretionary lending activity by the 12 district Federal Reserve banks.

## Varying Banks' Cash Requirements

The Fed currently requires that banks and other financial institutions keep a certain amount of their assets available in cash reserves. Banks, for example, must carry three cents in cash for every dollar they hold in checking accounts. A bank cannot make interest-bearing loans on such "reserves." I propose that the Fed make this percent significantly lower for loans that finance preferred activities than for less desirable investment areas. Let's say the public decides that banks should allocate 10% of all credit to research and development of new environmental technologies, such as non-polluting autos and organic farming. Then financial institutions that have made 10% of their loans in environmental technologies would not have to hold any cash reserves against these loans. But if a bank made no loans in the environmental area, then it would have to hold 10% of its total assets in reserve. The profit motive would force banks to support environmental technologies without any direct expenditure from the federal budget.

All profit-driven firms will naturally want to avoid this reserve requirement. The Fed must therefore apply it uniformly to all businesses that profit through accepting deposits and making loans. These include banks, savings and loans, insurance companies, and investment brokerage houses. If the rules applied only to banks, for example, then banks could circumvent the rules by redefining themselves as another type of lending institution.

## Loans to Banks That Do the Right Thing

The Federal Reserve has the authority now to favor some banks over others by making loans to them when they are short on cash. For the most part, however, the Fed has chosen not to exercise such discretionary power. Instead it aids all banks equally, through a complex mechanism known as open market operations, which increases total cash reserves in the banking system. The Fed could increase its discretionary lending to favored banks by changing its operating procedures without the federal government creating any new laws or institutions. Such discretionary lending would have several benefits.

First, to a much greater extent than at present, financial institutions would obtain reserves when they are lending for specific purposes. If a bank's priorities should move away from the established social priorities, the Fed could then either refuse to make more cash available to it, or charge a penalty interest rate, thereby discouraging the bank from making additional loans. The Fed, for example, could impose such obstacles on lenders that are financing mergers, takeovers, and buyouts.

In addition, the Fed could use this procedure to more effectively monitor and regulate financial institutions. Banks, in applying for loans, would have to submit to the Fed's scrutiny on a regular basis. The Fed could more closely link its regulation to banks' choices of which investments to finance.

Implementing this procedure will also increase the authority of the 12 district banks within the Federal Reserve system, since these banks approve the Fed's loans. Each district bank will have more authority to set lending rates and monitor bank compliance with regulations.

The district banks could then more effectively enforce measures such as the Community Reinvestment Act, which currently mandates that banks lend in their home communities. Banks that are committed to their communities and regions, such as the South Shore Bank in Chicago, could gain substantial support under this proposed procedure.

## Other Credit Allocation Tools

The Fed can use other tools to shift credit to preferred industries, such as loan guarantees, interest rate subsidies, and government loans. In the past the U.S. government has used these techniques with substantial success. They now primarily support credit for housing, agriculture, and education. Indeed, as of 1991, these programs subsidized roughly one-third of all loans in the United States.

Jesse Jackson's 1988 Presidential platform suggested an innovative way of extending such policies. He proposed that public pension funds channel a portion of their money into a loan guarantee program, with the funds used to finance investments in low cost housing, education, and infrastructure.

There are disadvantages, however, to the government using loan guarantee programs and similar approaches rather than the Fed's employing asset reserve requirements and discretionary lending. Most important is that the former are more expensive and more difficult to administer. Both loan guarantees and direct government loans require the government to pay off the loans when borrowers default. Direct loans also mean substantial administrative costs. Interest subsidies on loans are direct costs to government even when the loans are paid back.

In contrast, with variable asset reserve requirements and discretionary lending policies, the Fed lowers the cost of favored activities, and raises the cost of unfavored ones, without imposing any burden on the government's budget.

## Increasing Public Control

The Federal Reserve acts in relative isolation from the political process at present. The U.S. president appoints seven members of the Fed's Board of Governors for 14 year terms, and they are almost always closely tied to banking and big business. The boards of directors of the 12 district banks appoint their presidents, and these boards are also composed of influential bankers and business people within each of the districts.

The changes I propose will mean a major increase in the central bank's role as an economic planning agency for the nation. Unless we dramatically improve democratic control by the public over the Fed, voters will correctly interpret such efforts as an illegitimate grasp for more power by business interests.

Democratization should proceed through redistributing power downward to the 12 district banks. When the Federal Reserve System was formed in 1913, the principle behind creating district banks along with the headquarters in Washington was to disperse the central bank's authority. This remains a valuable idea, but the U.S. government has never seriously attempted it. Right now the district banks are highly undemocratic and have virtually no power.

One way to increase the district banks' power is to create additional seats for them on the Open Market Committee, which influences short-term interest rates by expanding or contracting the money supply.

A second method is to shift authority from the Washington headquarters to the districts. The Board of Governors would then be responsible for setting general guidelines, while the district banks would implement discretionary lending and enforcement of laws such as the Community Reinvestment Act.

The most direct way of democratizing the district banks would be to choose their boards in regular elections along with other local, regional, and state-wide officials. The boards would then choose the top levels of the banks' professional staffs and oversee the banks' activities.

## Historical Precedents

Since World War II other capitalist countries have extensively employed the types of credit allocation policies proposed here. Japan, France, and South Korea are the outstanding success stories, though since the early 1980s globalization and deregulation of financial markets have weakened each of their credit policies. When operating at full strength, the Japanese and South Korean programs primarily supported large-scale export industries, such as steel, automobiles, and consumer electronics. France targeted its policies more broadly to coordinate Marshall Plan aid for the development of modern industrial corporations.

We can learn useful lessons from these experiences, not least that credit allocation policies do work when they are implemented well. But substantial differences exist between experiences elsewhere and the need for a public investment bank in the United States.

In these countries a range of other institutions besides the central bank were involved in credit allocation policies. These included their treasury departments and explicit planning agencies, such as the powerful Ministry of International Trade and Industry (MITI) in Japan. In contrast, I propose to centralize the planning effort at the Federal Reserve.

We could create a new planning institution to complement the work of the central bank. But transforming the existing central banking system rather than creating a new institution minimizes both start-up problems and the growth of bureaucracies.

A second and more fundamental difference between my proposal and the experiences in Japan, France, and South Korea is that their public investment institutions were accountable only to a business-oriented elite. This essentially dictatorial approach is antithetical to the goal of increasing democratic control of the financial system.

The challenge, then, is for the United States to implement effective credit allocation policies while broadening, not narrowing, democracy. Our success ultimately will depend on a vigorous political movement that can fuse two equally urgent, but potentially conflicting goals: economic democracy, and equitable and sustainable growth. If we can meet this challenge, it will represent a historic victory toward the construction of a democratic socialist future. ❏

**Resources:** Robert Pollin, "Transforming the Federal Reserve into a Public Investment Bank: Why it is Necessary; How it Should Be Done," in G. Epstein, G. Dymski and R. Pollin, eds., *Transforming the U.S. Financial System,* M.E. Sharpe, 1993.

*Article 10.6*

# REMEMBERING THE "TOKYO NO" FIFTY YEARS LATER
*When 21 Countries Defied the World Bank*

**BY ROBIN BROAD**
*January/February 2015*

Fifty years ago last fall, at the 1964 World Bank annual meeting in Tokyo, 21 developing-country governments voted "no" on the convention to set up a new part of the World Bank Group where foreign corporations could sue governments and bypass domestic courts. It was to be called the International Centre for Settlement of Investment Disputes (ICSID). The 21 included all of the 19 Latin American countries attending, as well as the Philippines and Iraq.

The historic vote was dubbed "El No de Tokyo," or the "Tokyo No." It could well be the largest collective vote against a World Bank initiative ever. And perhaps the one time that all Latin American representatives voted "no."

So I write in part to toast that Tokyo No on its fiftieth anniversary. But I also write because it is time to recognize that the 1964 "no" vote has been vindicated by history.

What were the 21 voting against? Rather than paraphrase, let me turn to the then-representative of Chile, Félix Ruiz, speaking on behalf of the Latin American countries:

The legal and constitutional systems of all the Latin American countries that are members of the Bank offer the foreign investor at the present time the same rights and protection as their own nationals; they prohibit confiscation and discrimination and require that any expropriation on justifiable grounds of public interest shall be accompanied by fair compensation fixed, in the final resort, by the law courts.

The new system that has been suggested would give the foreign investor, by virtue of the fact that he is a foreigner, the right to sue a sovereign state outside its national territory, dispensing with the courts of law. This provision is contrary to the accepted legal principles of our countries and, de facto, would confer a privilege on the foreign investor, placing the nationals of the country concerned in a position of inferiority.

In short, the new investor/state dispute settlement system was both unnecessary and unfair.

The ICSID treaty went forward, despite the "no" votes. For the record, Brazil never joined, and in fact has never agreed to investor-state dispute settlement in any venue.

Those who follow the World Trade Organization (WTO) and its dispute resolution mechanism might note the irony: A fundamental rule of today's neoliberal push towards "ultra-globalization," as embedded in the WTO, is that a country's rules must treat foreign and domestic investors the same. As ICSID's existence shows, ultra-globalization proponents do not find it problematic to have foreign investors privileged over domestic investors.

The Tokyo No criticisms were prescient in terms of the track record of ICSID in the ensuing decades. ICSID moved center-stage in the wake of the neoliberal bilateral and multilateral trade and investment agreements that expanded starting in the 1980s. Forty years after ICSID's first case was filed in 1972, a record 48 new arbitration cases were added to ICSID's docket in 2012. To put this in perspective, the number of cases registered never reached five in any year between 1972 and 1996. Since 2003, the number has been over twenty every single year. The last three years for which data have been published, 2011-2013, have the three highest figures to date, with at least 37 cases registered each year. (See figure.)

As the number of cases being brought before ICSID has ballooned, so too have the criticisms—mainly by sovereign states but increasingly by trade lawyers. The arguments are that ICSID rulings are: 1) increasingly biased in favor of investors over the state (sound familiar?), and 2) too narrow in their focus on "commercial" rights (that is, the private foreign investor) over broader "non-commercial" issues. Shouldn't the government of El Salvador, for example, have the right to protect its key watershed from the environmental ravages of gold mining? Indeed, shouldn't El Salvador be rewarded rather than sued at ICSID? And, why should the investor—as a non-state actor—get to sue the government, while other presumably key non-state actors such as the affected communities are not even allowed to listen to ICSID's often secret hearings, never mind participate equally? (OK: communities can submit amicus briefs—if they find a lawyer willing to write one on their behalf. But there is not even any assurance that such briefs will be read by the World Bank-certified tribunal members who preside over any given case.)

Indeed, as ICSID's case-load has expanded, the verbal criticism has been matched with action. Bolivia, Ecuador, and Venezuela—all part of the original Tokyo No—have left ICSID. South Africa is establishing a new investment law that allows foreign corporations to bring such claims only to domestic courts. India is conducting a review of its treaties in the face of several corporate lawsuits, and In-

## TOTAL NUMBER OF ICSID CASES REGISTERED, BY CALENDAR YEAR

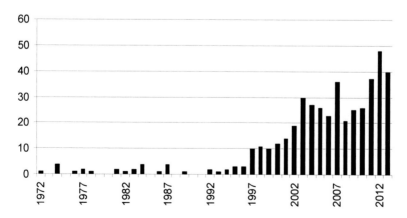

Note: Includes ICSID Convention Arbitration Cases, ICSID Additional Facility Arbitration Cases.

Source: The ICSID Caseload–Statistics (Issue 2014-2).

---

### The "Tokyo No" Roll Call

There were 21 votes against ratifying the ICSID convention, including the 19 Latin American World Bank member countries. The countries voting no were: Argentina, Bolivia, Brazil, Chile, Colombia, Costa Rica, Dominican Republic, Ecuador, El Salvador, Guatemala, Haiti, Honduras, Iraq, Mexico, Nicaragua, Panama, Paraguay, Peru, Philippines, Uruguay, and Venezuela.

Sources: Antonio R. Parra, *The History of ICSID* (Oxford University Press, 2012); ICSID, Database of ICSID Member States (icsid.worldbank.org).

---

donesia has announced its intention not to renew its bilateral investment treaties. Australia declined to include these corporate rights in the 2005 Australia-U.S. Free Trade Agreement. Recently leaked documents suggest that several of these governments are attempting to at least scale back investors' rights (and, thus, the power of ICSID) in the Trans-Pacific Partnership (TPP) trade deal. So, too, are countries in the European Union—notably France and Germany—voicing concerns about investor-state provisions.

But, wait: won't the global economy fall apart without such investor rights and its key venue ICSID? Won't foreign investment dry up? Well, actually, no. Case in point is Brazil, a leading host to foreign investment but, again, a country that has never accepted investor-state dispute settlement. To make a more general point: Foreign investors, if they believe they are making a risky investment, should simply rely on foreign risk insurance. And, like domestic investors, they have recourse to the relevant domestic courts in a given country.

There is increasing urgency to say "no" to ICSID. If the Trans Pacific Partnership (TPP) and the Transatlantic Trade and Investment Partnership (TTIP) are approved, as President Obama hopes, ICSID's case-load will mushroom further, thanks to the investor-state dispute settlement clauses currently in both drafts. And we can expect even more action in terms of investors' propensity to sue governments not just for "direct taking" via expropriation—the original purpose of ICSID— but also for "indirect taking" via environmental, social, and other regulations that might just impinge on a foreign investor's future ability to make profits by pillaging said resources.

So, a shout-out to those governments of the 21 countries who so rightly said "no" in Tokyo fifty years ago. Let's celebrate the 50th anniversary by urging current member governments to withdraw from this forum that undermines democracy, fairness, and the broader common good.

To borrow a slogan that seems apropos: Fifty years is enough. ❏

*Sources:* Antonio R. Parra, The History of ICSID (Oxford University Press, 2012); Andreas F. Lowenfeld "The ICSID Convention: Origins and Transformation," *Georgia Journal of International and Comparative Law* (2009) 38, pp.47-62; Silvia Fiezzoni, "The Challenge of UNASUR Member Countries to Replace ICSID Arbitration," I, (2011) 2, pp. 134-144.

*Article 10.7*

# LAND REFORM
*A Precondition for Sustainable Economic Development*

## BY JAWIED NAWABI
May/June 2015

> *It is in the agricultural sector that the battle for long-term economic development will be won or lost.* —Gunnar Myrdal, economist and Nobel laureate

The phrase "land reform" often conjures up memories, for those leaning right, of frightening extreme-left ideologies. On the progressive left, meanwhile, land reform is often treated as a passé topic.

With the advent of rising inequality, climate change, weak government institutions, failed states, terrorism, corruption, and a whole slew of other socio-economic problems—sown or exacerbated by three decades of neoliberal policies in the "developing world" (Global South)—it is high time we revisit the issue of land reform. We need to bring it back to the center of the discussion on sustainable economic development. Land reform is not political extremism; rather, it is a critical policy mechanism for the world to address issues of poverty, hunger, urban slums, and good governance.

What is "land reform"? It is usually defined as the redistribution of large landholdings to smaller ones. Land is transferred from large landlords to those who have been working the land as tenants (such as sharecroppers) or paid agricultural workers, as well as dispossessed underemployed or unemployed urban workers who migrated from rural areas looking for employment and wound up living in urban slums. That is one model of land reform. Another model is redistribution in the form of rural communes or cooperative or collective farms. A combination of the two models is also possible.

## Reemergence of Land Reform Movements

Despite the attempts by international institutions (like the IMF and World Bank) and oligarchic political elites in the global South to suppress land reform policies, there have been growing social movements pushing for land reform in the last two decades. Neoliberal "free trade" policies have exposed small farmers to devastating global competition (especially from giant mechanized industrial farms in the global North), leaving hundreds of millions of them dispossessed, and have forced them into the reserve army of impoverished unemployed or underemployed living in urban slums. From Brazil and Mexico to the Philippines and Zimbabwe, social movements for a more just and fair distribution of wealth—particularly land—are confronting these devastating consequences of neoliberalism.

Social protest has led even elite institutions such as the World Bank to acknowledge the issue. The Bank's *World Development Report 2008: Agriculture for Development*, at least rhetorically put agriculture and the productivity of small farmers "at the heart of a global agenda to reduce poverty."

# Agriculture as a Technical Problem?

The central tendency of mainstream economic development theory since the 1940s and 1950s has been to view agriculture as a mere stepping stone towards industrialization. Economist Arthur W. Lewis' "dualist" model was particularly influential in casting agricultural labor in developing countries as redundant—with a "surplus" of workers adding little or nothing to agricultural production. This surplus labor force, Lewis argued, should be moved out of the agricultural sector—this would supposedly not reduce output—and into the industrial, which he viewed as the key sector of the economy.

Besides moving inefficient peasants out of the rural sector, mainstream development economists proposed to boost agricultural yields by consolidating small farms into large ones—supposedly to take advantages of economies of scale. Thus, instead of reducing land concentration, this would increase it, essentially accomplishing a reverse land reform. Such an industrial model of agriculture would use expensive capital equipment (imported from the global North), petroleum-based fertilizers, herbicides, and pesticides. Today's version of the model increasingly pushes the adoption of genetically modified seeds controlled by corporations like Monsanto.

During the 1960s and 1970s, this frame of thought led many international institutions (such as the World Bank, Asian Development Bank, etc.) and governments in the global South to embrace the "Green Revolution." The Green Revolution was essentially a plan to use "science and technology" to increase crop production in developing countries. The use of fertilizers, pesticides, and high-yield crop varieties was supposed to boost agricultural productivity, reduce rural poverty, solve problems of hunger and malnutrition, and thus avoid peasant movements and rural political instability. This was, as economists James M. Cypher and James L. Dietz put it, a "strategy wherein it was hoped that seed technologies could be substituted for missing land reform and for more radical 'red revolutions' of the socialist variety threatening to sweep across the globe at the time."

Viewing agricultural productivity as a purely technical problem, advocates of the Green Revolution did not aim to transform the structure of land inequality and landlord power. To take the case of India, the Green Revolution boosted agricultural yields, making the country technically self-sufficient in food production. However, the changes primarily benefited medium and large-sized landowners who used capital-intensive technologies, high-yielding mono-crop seeds, and large inputs of fertilizers and pesticides. "Rural inequity worsened because of the growing prosperity of the large and medium farmers and the unchanged position of the landless and small farmers," concludes Indian scholar Siddharth Dube. "And because large farms use more capital and less labour per unit of produce than small farms, rural employ-

## Land Reform and Colonization

If we broaden the concept of land reform, the whole process of colonial settlement in North America, Central and South America, Australia, and New Zealand was one big land reform, appropriating the lands of indigenous peoples and distributing it to the European settlers. So land reform can be understood as a much more common experience of the "developed" world than it is usually thought of in the economic literature.

ment grew much less than it would have if land reform had taken place and the increase in production come from smaller farms."

## The Economic and Socio-Political Cases for Land Reform

There are two broad arguments for the importance of land reform. The first is based on the widely observed inverse relationship between farm size and output per unit of land area: smaller farms produce more per acre of land than larger farms. Smaller land holdings are more productive and ecologically sustainable for a number of reasons:

1) Higher labor intensity. Small farmers use more labor per unit of land, which helps generate more output and more employment per unit.

2) Higher multiple cropping. They grow more crops per year on a given piece of land.

3) Higher intensity of cultivation. Small farmers leave a lower proportion of land fallow or uncultivated. In addition, they cultivate crops that are higher value-added per unit of land.

4) Lower negative environmental impacts. Small farms use fertilizers, pesticides, and other agrochemicals more sparingly than large farms. This reduces negative impacts of harmful chemicals on workers and neighbors. Small farmers, overall, have a greater incentive to employ environmentally sustainable techniques than large industrial ones.

While the economic case for land reform can be construed as a narrow technical argument on how best to boost agricultural productivity—which land-reform opponents could argue is unnecessary due to the advent of the Green Revolution—the socio-political argument is aimed against this kind of narrow technical thinking. The importance of a land reform is in changing the hierarchical structure of agrarian class relations while increasing productivity. The idea is to break the power of landlords, who keep peasants as a captive labor force in rural areas and act as a conservative political force at the local and national levels of the state.

The central mechanism by which landlords wield their power is through patron-client networks that give them control over local and regional government institutions. Landlords keep the poor majority dependent on them for jobs and access to land, while also using them as a captive power base for local elections (in countries where there are elections, such as India and Brazil). This way, they can block the development of state programs providing public goods—like public roads,

---

### Good Governance

The "good-governance functions" of the state are policies beneficial to the large majority of the population. Good-governance states exercise control over a certain territory, depend on a broad part of their population for revenue, and in turn provide the population with a wide range of public goods: the rule of law, transportation infrastructure (paved roads, extensive and affordable public transportation, etc.), public utilities (electricity, clean water, sewage systems), human services (health, education systems), and job security or at least temporary unemployment insurance.

clinics, schools, water systems, etc.—for everyone. Instead, they perpetuate a more narrowly targeted development relying on private goods—fertilizer, pesticides, expensive high-yield seeds, privately controlled water wells, loans that put peasants in ever-deeper debt, etc. They provide, also, a form of private insurance system for those clients who exhibit proper loyalty, in contrast to social support systems available to all—which would reduce the peasants' vulnerability and the landlord's power. The consequence is that the state's good-governance capacities are distorted and corrupted, favoring the narrow interests of the landlords and the political elite that is connected to them (often by kinship).

Transformative socio-political land reform for developing countries is aimed at diminishing wealth inequalities in the initial stages of development and breaking the grip on power of the upper-class elite (including not only landlords but also big industrial, financial, and commercial capitalists generally allied with them). This democratization of society would make it possible to orient the state towards long-term national development policies which can create more conducive socioeconomic and sociopolitical conditions serving the population as a whole, and not just the elite.

The socioeconomic conditions would include a more egalitarian class structure in the rural sector, greater incentives for farmers to increase their productivity due to owning the land they work, greater farmer incomes allowing the farmers to send their children to school, better nutrition due to higher caloric intake, and greater small-farmer purchasing power leading to greater demand for the products of labor-intensive manufacturing. The sociopolitical democratization would mean the breaking of landlord power, political stabilization resulting from the inclusion of the peasant masses in the political system, and democratization of decision making now liberated from landlord capture of local and national state bureaucracies.

## Land Reform Is Not Enough

There have been many more failed land reforms than successful ones. Reforms have failed mainly because they have not been thorough enough in breaking the power of the landed elite, and in extending the role of the government in an inclusive development process. Across Latin America—in Mexico, Bolivia, Brazil, Chile, and Peru—land reforms have had partial success, but for the most part have not dislodged rural elites and their industrial counterparts from political dominance. This has contributed to an image of land reform, even among the progressive left, as a tried and failed policy. There are also examples of half-successful land reforms in South and East Asia—in India, the Philippines, Indonesia, and Thailand—where peasants did reap some benefits like reliable ownership titles, which allowed them to borrow on better terms, boosted crop yields, and reduced malnutrition, though without fundamentally altering the class structure.

On the other hand, successful land reforms were thorough, extensive, and swift. Key examples in the twentieth century include Japan, Taiwan, South Korea, and China. Land in the first three countries was distributed as family-sized farms. (China initially had a collectivized land reform.) Looking at the Japanese and South Korean cases: In Japan in 1945, 45% of the peasants were landless tenants. By 1955, only 9% were tenants and even they benefited from much-strengthened protective laws. In pre-reform South Korea in 1944, the top 3% of landholders owned about 64% of the land, with an average holding of 26 hectares. By 1956, the top 6% owned just 18% of the land, with an average of about 2.6 hectares. Meanwhile, 51% of family farmers owned about 65% of the land, with an average holding of 1.1 hectares.

Nowhere in Latin America or Africa, nor elsewhere in Asia (except Kerala, India), did land reforms come so close to such equalization and radical reshaping of traditional social structures. The East Asian land reforms succeeded in bringing about the long-term national development policies by creating more conducive socioeconomic and sociopolitical conditions—breaking the existing power structure, allowing for the emergence of developmentally oriented states (as opposed to neoliberal models that saw state promotion of economic development as anachronistic and "inefficient"). Successful land reforms require follow up—supportive policies investing in rural infrastructure development (irrigation, electricity, roads, health clinics, schools), plus providing services such as clear and legitimate land records, micro-credit at reasonable rates of interest, and training for farmers in the newest skills for sustainable farming. Japan, Taiwan, South Korea, and arguably even China's development paths serve as examples of transformative land reforms in the last fifty years. What these countries achieved was remarkable growth with equity. ❑

*Article 10.8*

# AFTER HORROR, CHANGE?
*Taking Stock of Conditions in Bangladesh's Garment Factories*

**BY JOHN MILLER**
September/October 2014

On April 24, 2013, the Rana Plaza factory building, just outside of Bangladesh's capital city of Dhaka, collapsed—killing 1,138 workers and inflicting serious long-term injuries on at least 1,000 others.

While the collapse of Rana Plaza was in one sense an accident, the policies that led to it surely were not. Bangladesh's garment industry grew to be the world's second largest exporter, behind only China's, by endangering and exploiting workers. Bangladesh's 5,000 garment factories paid rock-bottom wages, much lower than those in China, and just half of those in Vietnam. One foreign buyer told *The Economist* magazine, "There are no rules whatsoever that can not be bent." Cost-saving measures included the widespread use of retail buildings as factories—including at Rana Plaza—adding weight that sometimes exceeded the load-bearing capacity of the structures.

As Scott Nova, executive director of the Worker Rights Consortium, testified before Congress, "the danger to workers in Bangladesh has been apparent for many years." The first documented mass-fatality incident in the country's export garment sector occurred in December 1990. In addition to those killed at Rana Plaza, more than 600 garment workers have died in factory fires in Bangladesh since 2005. After Rana Plaza, however, Bangladesh finally reached a crossroads. The policies that had led to the stunning growth of its garment industry had so tarnished the "Made in Bangladesh" label that they were no longer sustainable.

But just how much change has taken place since Rana Plaza? That was the focus of an International Conference at Harvard this June, bringing together government officials from Bangladesh and the United States, representatives of the Bangladesh garment industry, the international brands, women's groups, trade unions, the International Labor Organization (ILO), and monitoring groups working in Bangladesh.

## How Much Change on the Ground?

Srinivas B. Reddy of the ILO spoke favorably of an "unprecedented level of ... practical action" toward workplace safety in Bangladesh.

The "practical action" on the ground, however, has been much more of a mixed bag than Reddy suggests. In the wake of massive protests and mounting international pressure, Bangladesh amended its labor laws to remove some obstacles to workers forming unions. Most importantly, the new law bars the country's labor ministry from giving factory owners lists of workers who want to organize.

But formidable obstacles to unionization still remain. At least 30% of the workers at an entire company are required to join a union before the government will grant recognition. This is a higher hurdle than workers face even in the not-so-union-friendly United States, where recognition is based at the level of the workplace, not the company. Workers in special export-processing zones (the source of about 16% of Bangladesh's exports), moreover, remain ineligible to form unions.

The Bangladesh government did register 160 new garment unions in 2013 and the first half of this year, compared to just two between 2010 and 2012. Nonetheless, collective bargaining happens in only 3% of garment plants. And employers have responded with firings and violence to workers registering for union recognition or making bargaining demands. Union organizers have been kidnapped, brutally beaten, and killed.

After protests that shut down over 400 factories last fall, the Bangladesh government raised the minimum wage for garment workers from the equivalent of $38 a month to $68. The higher minimum wage, however, fell short of the $103 demanded by workers.

The government and the garment brands have also set up the Rana Plaza Donor Trust Fund to compensate victims and their families for their losses and injuries. But according to the fund's website, it stood at just $17.9 million at the beginning of August, well below its $40 million target. Only about half of the 29 international brands that had their clothes sewn at Rana Plaza have made contributions. Ineke Zeldenrust of the Amsterdam-based labor-rights group Clean Clothes Campaign estimates that those 29 brands are being asked to contribute less than 0.2% of their $22 billion in total profits for 2013.

## The Accord and the Alliance

Following Rana Plaza, a group of mostly European retail chains turned away from the business-as-usual approach of company codes that had failed to ensure safe working conditions in the factories that made their clothes. Some 151 apparel brands and retailers doing business in Bangladesh, including 16 U.S.-based retailers, signed the Accord on Fire and Building Safety in Bangladesh. Together the signatories of this five-year agreement contracted with 1,639 of the 3,498 Bangladesh factories making garments for export.

The Accord broke important new ground. Unlike earlier efforts:

- It was negotiated with two global unions, UndustriALL and UNI (Global).
- It sets up a governing board with equal numbers of labor and retail representatives, and a chair chosen by the ILO.
- Independent inspectors will conduct audits of factory hazards and make their results public on the Accord website, including the name of the factory, detailed information about the hazard, and recommended repairs.
- The retailers will provide direct funding for repairs (up to a maximum of $2.5 million per company) and assume responsibility for ensuring that all needed renovations and repairs are paid for.
- Most importantly, the Accord is legally binding. Disputes between retailers and union representatives are subject to arbitration, with decisions enforceable by a court of law in the retailer's home country.

But most U.S. retailers doing business in Bangladesh—including giants like Wal-Mart, JCPenney, The Gap, and Sears—refused to sign. They objected to the Accord's open-ended financial commitment and to its legally binding provisions.

Those companies, along with 21 other North American retailers and brands, developed an alternative five-year agreement, called the Alliance For Bangladesh Worker Safety. Some 770 factories in Bangladesh produce garments for these 26 companies.

Unlike the Accord, the Alliance is not legally binding and lacks labor-organization representatives. Moreover, retailers contribute a maximum of $1 million per retailer (less than half the $2.5 million under the Accord) to implement their safety plan and needed repairs, and face no binding commitment to pay for needed improvements beyond that. The responsibility to comply with safety standards falls to factory owners, although the Alliance does offer up to $100 million in loans for these expenses.

Kalpona Akter, executive director of the Bangladesh Center for Worker Solidarity, told the U.S. Senate Foreign Relations Committee, "There is no meaningful difference between the Alliance and the corporate-controlled 'corporate social responsibility' programs that have failed Bangladeshi garment workers in the past, and have left behind thousands of dead and injured workers."

## Historic and Unprecedented?

Dan Mozena, U.S. Ambassador to Bangladesh, believes that, despite facing significant obstacles, "Bangladesh is making history as it creates new standards for the apparel industry globally."

While the Accord may be without contemporary precedent, joint liability agreements that make retailers responsible for the safety conditions of their subcontractor's factories do have historical antecedents. As political scientist Mark Anner has documented, beginning in the 1920s the International Ladies Garment Workers Union (ILGWU) began negotiating "jobber agreements" in the United States that held the buyer (or "jobber") for an apparel brand "jointly liable" for wages and working conditions in the contractor's factories. Jobber agreements played a central role in the near-eradication of sweatshops in the United States by the late 1950s. In today's global economy, however, international buyers are once again able to escape responsibility for conditions in the far-flung factories of their subcontractors.

Like jobber agreements, the Accord holds apparel manufacturers and retailers legally accountable for the safety conditions in the factories that make their clothes through agreements negotiated between workers or unions and buyers or brands. The next steps for the Accord model, as Anner has argued, are to address working conditions other than building safety (as jobber agreements had), to get more brands to sign on to the Accord, and to negotiate similar agreements in other countries.

That will be no easy task. But, according to Arnold Zack, who helped to negotiate the Better Factories program that brought ILO monitoring of Cambodian garment factories, "Bangladesh is the lynch pin that can bring an end to the bottom feeding shopping the brands practice." ❑

*Sources:* Arnold M. Zack, "In an Era of Accelerating Attention to Workplace Equity: What Place for Bangladesh," Boston Global Forum, July 8, 2014; Testimony of Kalpona Akter, Testimony of Scott Nova, Senate Committee on Foreign Relations, Feb. 11, 2014; Mark Anner, Jennifer Bair, and Jeremy Blasi, "Toward Joint Liability in Global Supply Chains," *Comparative Labor Law & Policy Journal*, Vol. 35:1, Fall 2013; Prepared Remarks for Rep. George Miller (D-Calif.), Keynote Remarks by U.S. Ambassador to Bangladesh Dan Mozena, Remarks by Country Director ILO Bangladesh Srinivas B. Reddy, International Conference on Globalization and Sustainability of the Bangladesh Garment Sector, June 14, 2014; "Rags in the ruins," *The Economist*, May 4, 2013; "Bangladesh: Amended Labor Law Falls Short," Human Rights Watch, July 18, 2013; Rana Plaza Donor Trust Fund (ranaplaza-arrangement.org/fund).

*Article 10.9*

# THE FUTURE OF WORK, LEISURE, AND CONSUMPTION

## AN INTERVIEW WITH JULIET SCHOR
*May/June 2014*

E conomist Juliet Schor is known worldwide for her research on the interrelated issues of work, leisure, and consumption. Her books on these themes include The Overworked American: The Unexpected Decline of Leisure, The Overspent American: Upscaling, Downshifting, and the New Consumer, *and* Plenitude: The New Economics of True Wealth (retitled True Wealth *for its paperback edition). She is also a professor of sociology at Boston College.* —Eds.

**DOLLARS & SENSE**: We wouldn't expect patterns of work, leisure, and consumption to change overnight, but we're now more than half a decade into a profound crisis. Obviously it's had a big impact on employment, incomes, and so forth, but do you see any lasting changes emerging?

**JULIET SCHOR**: Some of the trends that were pretty significant before the crash have abated. I'm thinking most particularly about what I've called the "fast fashion model" of consumption—cheap imports of manufactured goods that people were acquiring at accelerating rates, the acceleration of the fashion cycle, and the cycle of acquisition and discard. The trend was people buying things, holding them for shorter and shorter periods of time and then discarding them either into some kind of household storage, into a waste stream, or into secondary markets. You had an amazing period of acquisition of consumer goods. I first started looking at this in the realm of apparel, but it was also in consumer electronics, ordinary household appliances, and pretty much across the board in consumer goods.

Of course, a lot of it was financed by debt or longer working hours, but manufactured goods just became so cheap. The idea that you could buy a DVD player for $19—and yes, people were trampling each other in the stores on Black Friday to get them—but that's just an extraordinary period. So that has changed, because the economics of that have changed. Going forward, I don't think we're going to see that level of availability of cheap goods that we saw before. So I think that cycle has slowed down.

The other big thing has been the bifurcation of the consumer market. That's something that's been going on for a long time—the falling out of the middle as a result of the decline of the middle class, the growth of a really low-end in the consumer market with dollar stores and a retail sector where even Walmart is considered expensive. The other side was the expansion of the hyper-luxury market.

Trends in income and wealth are reflected in the consumer sphere. There's more reluctance to take on debt, so debt-fueled consumer buying is lessened. There's also less availability of consumer credit for households now. The other big thing that I've been looking at is the rise of "alternative cultures" of consumption; that is, people moving out of the branded, advertised goods and the mass-produced lifestyles that dominated in the last couple of decades into more ecologically aware lifestyles with more artisanal and self-production.

***D&S***: Stepping back and looking more broadly at the emergence of this mass consumer culture in the United States after the Second World War, what do you see that are the key factors that are at the root of consumer capitalism in the United States? It seems a little facile to focus too narrowly on just advertising. Some scholars point to mass media images and what kinds of lifestyles people aspire to. Galbraith pointed more generally to the relentless stream of new products fueling new desires—the so-called "dependence effect." How do you see those influences, as well as others, sorting out?

**JS**: I don't want to completely dismiss factors like the old monopoly capital idea or the advertising and marketing story, which is that shortfalls of demand led to a big effort to get people to buy things, but I don't buy that story, for the most part. If you think about the postwar period, you had a labor market in which firms were unwilling to use productivity growth to reduce hours of work, and I wrote a book about that, *The Overworked American*. Part of that was about firms and why they don't want to do that. So in the post-war period, you have, from the labor market side, a situation where all productivity growth is getting channeled into income—into expansion of output—so it goes to wages and profits.

Now, of course, workers aren't getting the benefits of productivity growth, but in the post-war era, they did. There were contracts that were explicitly tied—3% productivity, 3% real wage growth. So that creates consumer demand, because that income is getting into people's pockets. Now you can ask the question: Why don't they save it? I don't think it's advertising, primarily, that determines why people didn't save more. There, I think, you have to look at social competition, and the fact that you have an unequal society in which how you live, what you buy, and what you have are important determinants of social position. Rising income gives you a constantly rising norm, and people consume to keep up with that norm. I think it would have played out more or less similarly if there weren't any advertising. The products might have been different but this sort of "consumer escalator," the fact that you have growing levels of consumption, is really coming much more from the production side. So in that way, I'm much more Marxian than Keynesian, I would say.

***D&S***: Turning to the contrast between the United States and other high-income capitalist countries, especially in terms of the shape of the labor movement and the role of the state: How did working hours get reduced in other countries? In France or Germany, for example, the average employed person works about 300 hours less per year than in the United States. So that strikes me as quite central, in your analysis, in terms of understanding consumption patterns in different countries.

**JS**: In the United States in the post-war period, the state devoted a lot of energy to the promotion of consumption, whether it was the highway system or suburbanization. That was in part out of a fear of the "Keynesian problem" of inadequate demand after the Second World War. In Europe, I guess I would point to two things.

First, after the war, they had a supply-side problem, which was that they had to rebuild productive capacity rather than what we had, which was the demand-side problem. So our state was much more oriented to promoting consumption than European states, which were more oriented towards rebuilding their societies. In Europe, working hours continued to fall and they didn't in the United States.

That's the way you need to think about it—everybody was on a common trajectory of work-hours decline from about 1870. Of course, the United States was the leader in all of that. We had the shortest working hours and we were the first ones to put in reforms of working hours: The United States was the leader on no Sunday work, no Saturday work, etc. I think the factors are the role of trade unions—both that trade unions were much stronger in Europe and also that in the United States, trade unions turned against the reduction of working hours after the Second World War. That has to do mostly with the Cold War, and with the conservative nature of U.S. trade unions. So in the 1950s, the AFL-CIO became—"hostile" may be too strong a word—became extremely disinterested in the idea of shorter hours of work. That's something that did not happen in Europe.

The other thing is that the incentives facing firms in the United States were really different, in terms of U.S. employers having much higher per worker fixed costs, because of health insurance. There are some European countries where health insurance is provided at the firm level, but mostly not. In the United States that turns out to be a powerful disincentive to reduce working hours, and it becomes a powerful incentive for raising working hours. The growth in inequality, which is more pronounced in the United States, also raised working hours. I think those are the key factors which lead the United States and Europe to diverge quite rapidly on the issue of work time. That divergence turns out to have all sorts of very important consequences.

One of the things you have seen in the patterns of leisure time activities in the United States is you've got time-stressed households doing really money-intensive things like going to the Caribbean for three days, or spending a lot of money to "de-stress," or spending money to reward themselves for working so hard. So we definitely have quite a bit of that in the United States because work is so demanding and stressful and that shapes the leisure patterns. You get what economists call goods- or income-intensive leisure.

*D&S*: If we think of consumption behavior as social—as aiming to enhance a person's social status—can we think of any important social constraints on the amounts or patterns of consumption? If many people disapprove of polluting or wasteful forms of consumption, like the Hummer, can we observe a social constraint on that? Or, in what are very difficult economic times for a lot of people, is there any effect on people reining in unseemly levels of luxury consumption?

**JS**: Well, I'll start with the latter. I was reading about and experiencing people's reluctance to engage in ostentatious displays at the time of the crash, and in its early aftermath. I think, by now, that didn't last very long. One of the things about the most ostentatious stuff is that we're increasingly a gated society, so the wealthy are consuming lavishly outside of the view of the ordinary and the poor. There is certainly less celebration of it, and you see it less in the culture now than before the crash, for sure. The Hummers are a very interesting case. I have a friend who did research on the war between Hummer drivers and the Prius drivers, the Prius drivers being referred to as "pious" drivers by the Hummer folks. Now the Hummer vehicle has collapsed as a consumer product. Hummer drivers were subjected to a lot of social disapproval. It also became economically less-desirable when the price of gas went up.

There is definitely a rising ecological consciousness that is attempting to moralize consumption in ways that yield social approval or disapproval of low-carbon versus high-carbon lifestyles. It isn't mainstream yet. It's much more prevalent in highly educated groups, it tends to be more bicoastal, it's a kind of "forward trend" in the consumer culture. You do see more and more, as you move into the mainstream, people attempting to do more ecologically. I think there's widespread sentiment about that. Then, of course, you also have so many people who are just trying to make ends meet that they feel it is not possible for them to think about ecological impact. Of course, the irony is that the people who are just trying to make ends meet are the ones with the low carbon footprints, but the discourse of environmental impact is permeating through consumer culture.

*D&S*: Going back to something about advertising: It seems to have become more pervasive, both in terms of physical spaces that are filled with advertising and products advertised to users. In the last couple of decades, we've seen the advent of direct marketing of prescription pharmaceuticals, for example, directly to the people who will end up using them. There's a pushback, such as criticism of advertising to children, but it seems largely that there's widespread tolerance of this pervasiveness of advertising in daily life.

**JS**: This is a little counterintuitive, but part of why advertising has become so pervasive is that the core of advertising, which is television spots, have become so unimportant. People don't have to watch them anymore, and that's huge for advertisers. I think the 30- or 60-second TV spots are much more powerful than the kinds of things that advertisers have moved towards in terms of the spatial expansion of advertising. I think that advertising on the web is much less powerful. So, that's one of the paradoxes of advertising in the contemporary moment: the moment when advertising is much more pervasive in terms of space and place, is a moment when it's much less powerful. Advertisers have been able to move in a few directions that have been productive for them, like word of mouth advertising, and so forth, but those forms are also being delegitimized. People know the person sitting next to them in a bar telling them to drink this vodka might be paid by the company.

Prescription drugs are a big exception, because that came about as a regulatory change. Drug companies weren't allowed to advertise directly to consumers before. If it weren't for pharmaceuticals and ads directed at kids, the advertising industry would be in big trouble. Now the kid story is, I think, a little bit different than the adult story, in the sense that you have a much more powerful approach to children now than you did in the past. The approach to children, I think, is a lot more effective than the approach to adults, which I think is declining in effectiveness. So, you can see a theme in what I'm saying about advertising. Today, I would say I feel less worried about advertising than I did before I started studying it. I think people tune it out. I don't want to go too far on this, but to me it's not where the main action is in terms of what's driving consumer patterns.

**D&S**: We see some examples of people, in their purchasing decisions, transcending a kind of narrow consumer mentality: They're thinking about environmental impacts, say, in buying a hybrid or electric car. In terms of other products they may be thinking about labor conditions, such as buying fair trade goods or no sweatshop apparel or footwear. On the other hand, one might look at this as reinforcing a core aspect of consumerist capitalism: That whatever it is that you may want, it's for sale and you can buy it.

**JS**: There's a debate in sociology and the social sciences more generally—because there are other disciplines that have weighed in on this question—about the critique of ethical consumption, political consumption, green consumption. Some argue that it's actually detrimental because it leads people to think that this purchasing behavior can solve problems, and it leads them to be less likely to join in collective solutions to environmental problems, labor problems, poverty, and development in the global South.

I did a study of that, and I used two different data sets: One was a random sample survey of all Americans. The other was an intentional survey of people who are political or ethical consumers, or what we called "conscious consumers," with about 2,000 participants. What we found is that there are actually very high levels of correlation between people engaging in this kind of purchasing and being socially and politically involved in trying to solve these problems in collective ways. And we also looked at the time sequencing and found a group of people who are politically involved already and then you add on this "walk the talk" aspect—if you're going to be fighting sweatshops, then don't buy sweatshop clothing, and if you're concerned about environmental impacts then you don't want to be buying things that are at odds with your values.

So you have people who were political first, then extended to their purchasing behavior, and you have people who got into both at around the same time, and you have people who moved in the other direction—who first did the conscious consuming and then became politically active. Certainly the idea that becoming a "green consumer" undermines your likelihood of engaging in collective action around this is not at all supported by the data in the United States, and there have also been some studies in Europe that show the same thing.

I think the fact of the matter is that changing marketplace behavior in the kind of society we have today is an important component in a broad-based campaign, whether it's on the environment or labor conditions or whatever. We see a lot of the NGOs involved in campaigns that have a market-based dimension—and those have been some of the most successful campaigns in recent years—because it's so hard to get the state to act to do these things, because it is captured by business. People have turned to the market in part because it's an arena where it looks like you can have some results, at least in the short term.

Ultimately, can you stop climate change through consumer behavior and through just market behavior? Definitely not. Can you ensure good working conditions merely by market-oriented activity? Definitely not. To think that it's sufficient is the real mistake, but I don't think that most people who work in this field, who try to work on transforming consumer behavior, have such a naïve view.

*D&S*: We've already talked about ways in which consumption is connected to people's lives at work, and the availability of leisure time, as well as some changes in patterns of consumption related to broader social objectives. What kinds of changes in consumption—and in the forces shaping consumption—do you envision?

**JS**: Well, I have a hard time thinking about the future without orienting all of my thinking about climate, because I just don't see much of a positive future unless we can address climate change very significantly. And that means, for wealthy countries, pretty radical emissions cuts in a pretty short period of time. It actually means that for most countries. So, as I think about the future, I think about what we could do both to address climate change through radical emissions reductions and also increase social justice, reduce inequality, and start solving the enormous problems that we have in this country. My most recent book, *True Wealth*, is about how to do that. Obviously, we need to get onto a renewable energy system, there's no question about that. We need a carbon tax or carbon regulation, and that's stuff that is very well known. What is not understood, I don't think, is that we can't successfully address climate change with a model in which we continue to try to expand the size of the economy.

We're going to have to deal with working hours, because that's the only way to stop expanding the size of the economy in any sensible way. So the core of what we need to do is to get back on the trajectory of using productivity growth to reduce hours of work. And that then opens up incredible possibilities in terms of rebalancing the labor market, integrating the unemployed, and having a fairer distribution of hours. We're talking about the distribution of income, but not about the distribution of hours, which is one of the things that drives the distribution of income. So, fair access to the work that exists, giving people more time off from work, and doing much more as a society—and probably a lot on the local and community level—to ensure basic needs for people.

With declining work hours, people's incomes are pretty much stabilized, so you need to bring the incomes of the bottom up, and you need to bring the incomes of the top down. Part of that has to be a redistribution of work opportunity and creating community provisioning of basic needs, like publicly owned utilities which provide power and heat for people at reasonable prices, enhanced public transportation, more public provisioning of food. There are really interesting things going on in global-South countries bringing farmers and consumers together in local food economies that are not just about high-priced organic food, which is what we have here, but low-priced food that ensures food security for people. So, shorter hours, basic needs being met—including housing, education, healthcare—that's the direction I would like to see us go, and I think that really it all flows out from a kind of commitment to climate protection. It could all flow out from a commitment to basic needs, too. They really integrate.

Time use is central, and I think you get a totally different culture of consumption if people's incomes are on a basically stabilized trajectory and what they're getting is more and more free time. So, you have a new culture of consumption that is not about the acquisition of the new, it's not the "work and spend" pattern as I've called it, it's not "throw away" or media driven, it's more "true materialist," where you really pay attention to the things you have, and it's a kind of earthier consumption. ❑

# CONTRIBUTORS

**Dean Baker** is co-director of the Center for Economic and Policy Research.

**Peter Barnes**, co-founder of Working Assets, is a senior fellow at the Tomales Bay Institute.

**Robin Broad** is a profesor of International Development at the School of International Service, American University.

**Marie Christine Duggan** is a professor of economics at Keene State College in New Hampshire.

**Nina Eichacker** is an assistant professor of economics at Bentley University and a member of the *Dollars & Sense* collective.

**Gerald Epstein** is a professor of economics and co-director of the Political Economy Research Institute (PERI) at the University of Massachusetts-Amherst.

**Gerald Friedman** is a professor of economics at the University of Massachusetts-Amherst.

**Nancy Folbre** is emeritus professor of economics at the University of Massachusetts-Amherst. She contributes regularly to the *New York Times* Economix blog.

**Jayati Ghosh** is a professor of economics at the Centre for Economic Study and Planning at Jawaharlal Nehru University.

**Harry Konstantinidis** is an assistant professor of economics at the University of Massachusetts Boston.

**David M. Kotz i**s a professor of economics at the University of Massachusetts-Amherst and author of *The Rise and Fall of Neoliberal Capitalism*.

**Arthur MacEwan,** a *Dollars & Sense* Associate, is professor emeritus of economics at the University of Massachusetts-Boston.

**John Miller** is a *Dollars & Sense* collective member and a professor of economics at Wheaton College.

**Sirisha C. Naidu** is an associate professor of economics at Wright State University.

**Jawied Nawabi** is a professor of economics and sociology at CUNY Bronx Community College and a member of the *Dollars & Sense* collective.

**Evita Nolka** is a political theorist from Greece.

**Doug Orr** teaches economics at the City College of San Francisco.

**Robert Pollin** teaches economics and is co-director of the Political Economy Research Institute at the University of Massachusetts-Amherst.

**Steven Pressman** is a professor of economics and finance at Monmouth University and the author of *Fifty Major Economists*.

**Alejandro Reuss** (co-editor of this book) is a historian, economist, and co-editor of *Dollars & Sense*.

**Luis Rosero** (co-editor of this book) is an assistant profestor of economics at Framingham State University.

**Jonathan Rowe** was a fellow at the Tomales Bay Institute and a former contributing editor at the *Washington Monthly*. He died in March 2011.

**Juliet Schor** is a professor of sociology at Boston College and author of *The Overworked American*, *The Overspent American*, and *True Wealth*.

**Zoe Sherman** is an assistant professor of economics at Merrimack College and a member of the *Dollars & Sense* collective.

**Bryan Snyder** (co-editor of this book) is a senior lecturer in economics at Bentley University.

**Chris Sturr** (co-editor of this book) is co-editor of *Dollars & Sense*.

**Chris Tilly,** a *Dollars & Sense* Associate, is director of the Institute for Research on Labor and Employment and professor of urban planning, both at UCLA.

**Junji Tokunaga** is an associate professor in the Department of Economics, Dokkyo Univeristy, Saitama, Japan.

**Ramaa Vasudevan** is assistant professor of economics at Colorado State University and a former *Dollars & Sense* collective member.

**Jeannette Wicks-Lim** is an assistant research professor at the Political Economy Research Institute at the University of Massachusetts-Amherst.

**Rick Wolff** is a visiting professor in the Graduate Program of International Affairs at New School University.

**Marty Wolfson** teaches economics at the University of Notre Dame and is a former economist with the Federal Reserve Board in Washington, D.C.

CPSIA information can be obtained at www.ICGtesting.com
Printed in the USA
BVOW01s1151140816

458515BV00005B/11/P